WAR, PEACE,

AND

INTERNATIONAL

POLITICAL REALISM

The Review of Politics Series

A. James McAdams and Catherine H. Zuckert
Series Editors

War, Peace,

AND

International
Political Realism

Perspectives from *The Review of Politics*

edited by

Keir A. Lieber

University of Notre Dame Press
Notre Dame, Indiana

Copyright © 2009 by University of Notre Dame
Notre Dame, Indiana 46556
www.undpress.nd.edu

Manufactured in the United States of America

Library of Congress Cataloging-in-Publication Data

War, peace, and international political realism : perspectives from the Review
of politics / edited by Keir A. Lieber.
   p. cm. — (Review of politics series)
  ISBN-13: 978-0-268-03384-2 (pbk. : alk. paper)
  ISBN-10: 0-268-03384-6 (pbk. : alk. paper)
  1. International relations—Philosophy.   2. Realism.   I. Lieber, Keir A.
(Keir Alexander), 1970–   II. Review of politics.
  JZ1307.W37   2009
  327.101—dc22

                             2009022564

∞ *The paper in this book meets the guidelines for permanence and durability*
of the Committee on Production Guidelines for Book Longevity of
the Council on Library Resources.

Contents

Acknowledgments

I have been fortunate to draw upon the advice and assistance of many individuals while working on this book. Above all, I am grateful to A. James McAdams and Catherine H. Zuckert, co-editors of *The Review of Politics* series, for giving me the opportunity to organize this volume. It was an honor because it not only placed me in the company of a distinguished group of designated volume editors but also bestowed the responsibility of doing justice to the ideas and arguments of a diverse group of first-rate thinkers. Jim and Catherine provided unfailing encouragement and outstanding advice at every step, and simply trying to live up to their expectations has made this a better work than it otherwise would be.

For reading and commenting on the introductory essay, I thank David Edelstein, Robert Lieber, Sebastian Rosato, and Brian Schmidt. I am also grateful to Carol Hendrickson and Richard Maass for research assistance; Cheryl Reed for transcription and clerical help; and Peter J. Lysy for allowing me access to documents and correspondence from *The Review of Politics* at the Archives of the University of Notre Dame. I thank Dennis W. M. Moran for generously sharing his knowledge based on almost forty years of experience at the journal. In addition, I thank the staff at the University of Notre Dame Press for a terrific job in preparing this book for publication: Rebecca R. DeBoer, Margaret Gloster, Barbara Hanrahan, Katie Lehman, Wendy McMillen, and Kathryn Pitts. Finally, I thank my wife, Meredith Bowers, and my daughters, Sophie, Isabel, and Lucy, for helping me see the big picture.

Introduction

The Enduring Relevance of International Political Realism

KEIR A. LIEBER

Serious intellectuals in the 1940s and 1950s were compelled by international events to reexamine their understanding of the nature of man and his social institutions. Existing theories of the human condition—especially the dominant, optimistic liberal tradition in America—seemed woefully incapable of explaining World War I (which cost 20 million lives), the rise of German fascism and World War II (which killed roughly 70 million people), and the onset of the Cold War with the totalitarian Soviet Union (a conflict which, in the shadow of nuclear weapons, threatened to annihilate mankind).

It is not surprising that political realism, with its tragic view of man's drive for power and the inevitability of conflict among states, would blossom in this environment. Less obvious is why many scholars who were instrumental in developing the realist approach, including European secular Jewish émigrés such as Hans Morgenthau, would find a hospitable home for some of their seminal work in *The Review of Politics*, a new, Catholic opinion journal based at the University of Notre Dame in South Bend, Indiana. To be sure, the *Review* had emerged as a leading journal of politics and political theory soon after its first issue was published in 1939, and the founding editor, Waldemar Gurian, himself an émigré well known in European circles, had a brilliant mind, intellectual curiosity, and an exceptional personality, qualities that attracted innovative thinkers from extraordinarily diverse backgrounds and disciplines.[1] Moreover, the leadership at Notre Dame (notably under Father Theodore Hesburgh) genuinely encouraged free and open inquiry into both political and religious matters, welcoming contributions from Catholic, non-Catholic, and nonreligious authors alike.

But the main reason why the *Review* emerged as one of the most influential sources of commentary about the origins of international conflict and war was the shared intellectual orientation of the journal's contributors. Four core tenets united this diverse group of prominent thinkers: (1) an obligation to confront the big and difficult questions about international politics; (2) a recognition of the fundamentally tragic nature of relations among humans and states; (3) a rejection of historical optimism and its persistent belief in the perfectibility of man through religious purification, scientific progress, or any other rationalist project; and (4) a belief in practical morality—that is, a deep commitment to moral political action despite the inherent complexity and constraints of the world and the inevitable limitations of human knowledge and reason.

This set of core concerns, beliefs, and values stood in stark contrast to the prevailing approaches of the mid-twentieth century. Despite or because of the horrors of global war, political scientists were focusing on increasingly trivial matters, while American society remained mostly wedded to a liberal progressive vision that called for the eradication of selfishness, ignorance, and evil from domestic and international politics. Through the mechanism of right reasoning and carefully designed institutions, power politics would (once and for all) be replaced with a more benign, democratic, lawful, and pacific order. The *Review*'s writers offered a less comforting—but also more realistic—alternative, which recognized that the best one could do in navigating international affairs was to balance the morally desirable with the politically possible.

Half a century later, the arguments and advice contained in these essays seem just as relevant for current debates on international politics and American foreign policy. The decade of the 1990s—with its plethora of international and intra-state conflicts and general foreign policy confusion—undermined the idea, or at least the hope, that the end of the Cold War would be followed by a liberal millennium of democracy, capitalism, and peace. And, of course, the terrorist attacks of September 11, 2001, seemed to obliterate the universalistic beliefs and aspirations of the latest generation of liberal progressive cosmopolitans. Yet many of the same ideas and policies critiqued in the *Review* decades before are manifest in foreign policy discourse and behavior today. For example, it is difficult to think of a major contemporary international political issue where conflicting participants (states, leaders, groups) do not make political judgments in the name of absolute right and wrong, do not portray their own actions as wholly righteous and those of the other as utterly misguided, if not altogether evil, and do not hold out the prospect of total victory to attract greater support for their cause. In contrast, the *Review* authors understood that politics itself was defined by the never-ending struggle for power among self-interested actors—not by some kind of contest between the forces of pure good and evil that is resolved in favor of one or the other, depending on the circumstances.

Similarly, the *Review* authors in this volume would have found much to criticize in the way political leaders have responded to the rise of Islamic terrorism. The *Review* contributors likely would have recognized this force as a serious threat to Western civilization, and been skeptical of any approach that privileged diplomacy, negotiation, and dialogue as the primary means of directly dealing with such a threat. However, U.S. leaders' calls for total strategic and moral victory in a war on terrorism, as well as the use of religious imagery and the Christian faith to defend this central policy objective, would have been seen by these *Review* authors as counterproductive and even dangerous. Unlike radical Islamic fundamentalists, and contrary to the hyperbolic claims of some critics, the administration of George W. Bush did not back up its "you are with us or against us" rhetoric with a murderous crusade to convert the benighted. But the *Review* contributors would have rightly counseled the need for greater political humility, moderation, and understanding of the many conflicting interests involved in marshalling an international coalition to deal with this global threat.

The essays in this volume are drawn almost exclusively from the first two decades of *The Review of Politics*. Contributing authors include prominent theorists such as Morgenthau and Herbert Butterfield (each setting forth seminal ideas later found in *Politics among Nations* and *History and Human Relations*, respectively), commentators such as Waldemar Gurian and Kenneth Thompson, and policy practitioners such as George Kennan and Paul Nitze, as well as other like-minded and prominent European émigrés such as Hannah Arendt and Stefan Possony. Together, these works exemplify the core postwar roots of what we now know as the realist tradition and demonstrate the enduring relevance of realist insights for contemporary international relations scholarship and foreign affairs.

THE RESPONSIBILITY TO ASK BIG QUESTIONS

The *Review* contributors in this volume felt compelled by the events of their era to reconsider the timeless philosophical questions about the nature of man, society, and politics. Their approach did not represent a retreat from the brutality of international affairs to the safe confines of the ivory tower. In fact, as discussed below, Morgenthau and others relentlessly criticized both the theoretical abstractions of political theorists and the mathematical models of social scientists for having little relation to political reality. Rather, the motivation to ask big questions was based on the view that contemporary experiences could be understood only by probing beyond immediate historical facts to gain a deeper perspective on the perennial problems and truths of politics. And a deeper understanding of either domestic or international political phenomena required a clear picture of human nature. "It is a truism to say that events happen only once," as Kenneth Thompson writes (in chapter 9 in this volume). "But perhaps more important, those events are the manifestation of social forces which in turn are produced by the drives and tendencies inherent in human nature."

For the authors in this volume, what had emerged in international politics from beneath the surface of the legal and institutional arrangements of the interwar period was a struggle for power—"elemental, undisguised, and all-pervading," in Morgenthau's apt description. Totalitarianism threatened not only whatever justice and stability seemed to exist in political life, but also the dominant interpretations of the political world itself. In other words, the truly important questions raised by the problems observed in the real world were more philosophic than scientific in nature. For example, one could try to trace the historical rise of German fascism, but a valid understanding of that phenomenon would necessarily rest on philosophical reflections about the nature of power, political ideology, law, governance, public opinion, tyranny, democracy, and the relationships among these forces. In short, posing philosophical questions about the nature of man and society was essential to the task of understanding contemporary world politics.

The willingness to grapple with deeper truths—whether religious or secular—about the human condition as a way to explain international politics placed the *Review* authors in direct opposition to prevailing trends in political science and society at large. Neither existing approaches and methods in the field of international relations, nor the liberal intellectual tradition of modern times, could provide an acceptable understanding—much less a valid guide for dealing with—the forces of nationalism, imperialism, totalitarianism, and the struggle for power among states. In "Reflections on the State of Political Science" (chapter 12 in this volume), Morgenthau vigorously defends the necessity of political philosophy for political science and takes his colleagues to task for failing to grasp that fundamental point: "Contemporary political science, predominantly identified with a positivistic philosophy which is itself a denial of virtually all of the philosophic traditions of the West, has, as it were, mutilated itself by refusing itself access to the sources of insight available in the great philosophic systems of the past."

The particular content of the Western philosophic tradition that contributors to the *Review* wished to defend and preserve is discussed below, but it is worth noting here that the disparagement of political philosophy common in modern social science was only one of several reasons why many of the authors in this volume intensely disliked that enterprise. The dislike did not signify opposition to developing theories, drawing generalizations, or pursuing greater analytical rigor. In fact, the *Review* authors viewed themselves as "realists" because of their outspoken advocacy for sober, objective, and reasoned analysis and empirical research. In their discussions of the development of the field of international relations, Gurian, Thompson, and Morgenthau (chapters 5, 9, and 12 in this volume) commend the progression from pure description of current events to the study of recurring patterns and empirical testing of explanations. But they thought that the study of international relations was heading in the wrong direction both substantively and methodologically.

The *Review* writers repeatedly warned their academic colleagues about a looming cult of irrelevance in political science, whereby scholars seeking refuge from challenging and unpleasant truths about contemporary power politics were increasingly finding comfort in the analysis of trivial topics and reliance on barren quantitative methods. Writing at the dawn of the behavioral revolution, the authors in this volume were adamant that the study of international relations and the social sciences more broadly were being led astray by the natural science model. "Empirical science," as Morgenthau (chapter 12) describes the most vigorous branch of political science in his day, "tries to develop rigorous methods of quantitative verification which are expected in good time to attain the same precision in the discovery of uniformities and in prediction to which the natural sciences owe their theoretical and practical success." Similarly, in "On the Study of International Relations" (chapter 5), Gurian notes the modern tendency to seek to explain everything in international politics with mechanistic, one-dimensional explanations deriving from geography, economics, or the distribution of raw materials. The big problem with these approaches is that they fail to grasp the fundamental object of the social sciences: man. That object—man—should not be approached, as Morgenthau argues, "as a product of nature but as both the creature and the creator of history in and through which his individuality and freedom of choice manifest themselves. To make susceptibility to quantitative measurement the yardstick of the scientific character of the social sciences in general and of political science in particular is to deprive these sciences of that very orientation which is adequate to the understanding of their subject matter." The inadequacy of the quantitative method for understanding the essential topics of political science thus results in the study of lesser phenomena that do lend themselves to a certain measure of quantification, such as voting behavior. When applied to more crucial phenomena—power, freedom, tyranny, nationalism, conflict—the quantitative method can at best only confirm and refine knowledge which a theoretical approach has already discovered. Thus, in a conclusion as depressing for how long ago it was written (1955) as much as for its content, Morgenthau remarks that "much of quantitative political science has become a pretentious collection of trivialities."

These authors understood that when confronted with real-world political affairs, modern political science tended to retreat into a realm of self-sufficient abstractions. Foreshadowing the emergence of rational choice theory, Morgenthau describes the impact of a "new scholasticism" in political science, where a scholar "tends to think about how to think and to conceptualize about concepts, regressing ever further from empirical reality until he finds the logical consummation of his endeavors in mathematical symbols and other formal relations." Morgenthau then offers a revealing comparison between modern political science and modern art (which he suggests points to a "common root in the disorders of our culture"):

Both retreat from empirical reality into a world of formal relations and abstract symbols, which on closer examination either reveal themselves to be trivial or else are unintelligible but to the initiated. Both share in the indifference to the accumulated achievements of mankind in their respective fields; Plato and Phidias, St. Thomas and Giotto, Spinoza and Rembrandt have no message for them. That divorce from reality, contemporary and historic, deprives both of that wholesome discipline which prevents the mind from indulging its fancies without regard to some relevant objective standards.... Both abstract political science and abstract modern art tend to become esoteric, self-sufficient, and self-perpetuating cults, clustered around a "master," imitating his "style," and conversing in a lingo intelligible only to the members.

The retreat of modern social science into what they viewed as trivial substantive and methodological topics, with no relevance to the great political issues in which society has a stake, was especially galling for the realist authors and editors of the *Review* because it clashed with their basic understanding of the purpose of the intellectual. From their perspective, scholars have a social responsibility to confront contemporary problems of great public importance, grapple with the deep philosophical questions raised by these problems, and communicate their views to society so as to influence policy debates in positive ways. The experience of the first half of the twentieth century had refuted many of the dominant assumptions and expectations about international relations, be they radical, liberal, or conservative. Political science, armed with a healthy appreciation of the inherent limits of social science, was obligated to respond with newer and better understandings.

THE TRAGEDY OF MAN AND POLITICS

The realist view of human nature and international politics is a pessimistic and tragic one. Man is capable of great love, kindness, and sacrifice, of course, but realists recognize that all humans are also motivated in no small part by greed and a lust for power. All social relations are therefore marked to some degree by a clash of these selfish desires, regardless of our good intentions and aspirations. In fact, what defines the essence of politics as a social institution is the struggle for power. This intrinsic contest for influence and power is present within states and other domestic political communities, but it is often subdued by effective laws, government, or shared norms. The competition for power among groups of individuals (i.e., states) on the international scene, however, is particularly intense because those controlling factors are largely ineffective in the absence of a common authority. Thus, the unremitting struggle for power in international politics, which sadly but frequently manifests itself in violence and war, is an inevitable result of human nature.

Some contributors to the *Review* emphasized the religious sources of man's flawed nature, while others maintained a secular view. Whether because of original sin, nature and biology, or some other cause, the arena of politics is fundamentally tragic—we can imagine a better world, but our own actions necessarily render it impossible. Different philosophical bases exist for the tragic stance found in these essays, but the idea of a fundamental conflict between ethics and politics pervades all of them.

The *Review* authors believed that human nature was imperfect. These flaws would always prevent us from developing perfect institutions. For Morgenthau, the fundamental problem is that man is corrupted by his insatiable drive to dominate others. Like all animals, we have natural appetites and desires and are driven by the basic impulse of self-preservation. Beyond safeguarding the conditions necessary for existence, however, we also possesses an innate drive for self-assertion—a desire to assert ourselves as individuals against the world, thereby discovering our own power. This drive can manifest itself in many ways—for example, by overcoming physical barriers in the natural world, competing in sports, or writing books and articles. Whenever man, acting alone or in concert with others, seeks to control others he has entered the political sphere. Unfortunately, because man's natural urge to dominate others would be satisfied only if every other human became the object of his domination, the lust for power is effectively unquenchable. Thus, all politics is defined by the permanence and ubiquity of the struggle for power.[2]

The *animus dominandi* lies at the heart of the human predicament, but other contributors to the journal—who were no less persuaded than Morgenthau of man's flawed nature—emphasize how even the well-intentioned search for mere physical security (that is, the impulse of self-preservation) paradoxically generates anxiety, mutual fear, and conflict. International relations scholars today are familiar with this dynamic, as developed by Robert Jervis in his 1979 article, "Cooperation under the Security Dilemma," but all of the basic features are found nearly three decades earlier in the *Review* in Herbert Butterfield's article, "The Tragic Element in Modern International Conflict" (chapter 8 in this volume).[3] Butterfield argued that the great conflicts in world politics are too often mistakenly described in simplistic terms of good men fighting bad. In reality, at the heart of these conflicts one often finds a tragic human predicament that "would have led to a serious conflict of wills even if all men had been fairly intelligent and reasonably well-intentioned." To illustrate his argument, Butterfield poses a hypothetical scenario between the United States and the Soviet Union. He asks readers to suppose that both Russia and the United States fear the strategic consequences of a defeated Germany falling into the other side's camp. Assume also that both American and Russian leaders are moderately virtuous ("as men go in politics," Butterfield adds), comparatively reasonable, motivated solely by national self-interest, and uncertain about the intentions of the other side. According to Butterfield, this situation still presents "a grand dialectical jam" ("a terrible deadlock"; an "irreducible dilemma"), where the greatest war in history could be produced "without the intervention of any great criminals who might be out to do deliberate harm in the world. It could be produced between two powers both of which were desperately anxious to avoid a conflict of any sort." In other words, war could occur merely because the objective each side sought was vital for national security but also mutually exclusive. Butterfield argues that this kind of situation, which he felt typified the intractability in the human condition itself, is the basis for most tensions in the real world of international relations.

Butterfield further argues that the situation is potentially worse than that of two insecure states being drawn into a conflict that neither side desires. Any outbreak of violence is also likely to be "embittered by the heat of moral indignation" because neither side can recognize how its own fearful actions generate counter-fears in the other. "Neither party sees the nature of the predicament he is in, for he only imagines that the other party is being hostile and unreasonable." The resulting "shrieking morality of that particular kind which springs from self-righteousness" will make the conflict more intense than it would have been "if the contest had lain between two hard-headed eighteenth-century masters of *realpolitik.*"

Whether man seeks power over his fellow man because of a natural urge for self-assertion or simply in the cause of self-preservation, there is no escaping the evil inherent in politics. In "Reflections on the State of Political Science" (chapter 12), Morgenthau asks, "Why is it that the political act, in its concern with man's power over man and the concomitant denial of the other man's freedom, carries within itself an element of immorality and puts upon the actor the stigma of guilt?" Kenneth Thompson, in his discussion of the great realist contributions of Reinhold Niebuhr, Butterfield, Morgenthau, and E. H. Carr in "The Study of International Politics" (chapter 9), notes the "indisputable fact that ethics and politics are in conflict wherever man acts politically. That is the case because it is the essence of politics that man chooses goals and objectives which are limited and therefore equitable and just only for particular groups and nations." Only in the human imagination can policies and political acts be purely uncorrupted and undefiled by injustice. "As soon as we leave the realm of our thoughts and aspirations," Morgenthau writes elsewhere, "we are inevitably involved in sin and guilt. While our hand carries the good intent to what seems to be its consummation, the fruit of evil grows from the seed of noble thought. We want peace among nations and harmony among individuals, yet our actions end in conflict and war. We want to see all men free, but our actions put others in chains as others do to us. We believe in the equality of all men, and our very demands on society make others unequal."[4] In short, politics inevitably generates "dirty hands"—it necessarily entails some dose of evil.

The very act of acting destroys our moral integrity for two reasons. First, there is the problem of our natural limitations: we are unable to control all of the consequences of our actions (some of which will inevitably impinge on others) and we are unable to completely satisfy all competing moral ends through our actions (in order to satisfy one legitimate moral end we inevitably must neglect others). But the paramount reason politics entails doing evil is that its essence and aim is the struggle for power over men, "for it is to this degree that it degrades man to a means for other men."[5] Evil corrupts all politics, but especially international politics. For Niebuhr, a society "merely cumulates the egoism of individuals . . . into collective egoism so that the egoism of the group has a double force."[6] Similarly, as Thompson writes, "This universal aspect of the corruption of absolute justice in the realm of politics finds its out-standing expression in international morality. There my nation's justice means oftentimes your nation's injustice; my nation's security and the requirements assigned thereto may appear as the cause of your nation's insecurity."

Once one comprehends the tragedy of human nature, the problems and challenges of contemporary world politics can be seen in their true light. From Morgenthau's perspective in the year after World War II ended, the drop of evil which inevitably spoils the best of intentions had transformed "churches into political organizations . . . revolutions into dictatorships . . . [and] love of country into imperialism."[7] In analyzing the rise of fascism and communism in Europe, Kennan tried to disabuse Americans of the comforting belief that they were somehow different from the German and Russian people: "The fact of the matter is that there is a little bit of totalitarian buried somewhere, way down deep, in each and every one of us."[8] Arendt, Morgenthau, and Thompson all warn of a dangerous crusading nationalism, where nations see themselves as the repositories of values and ideas that are good for all mankind and hear a calling to extend the benefits of their system to peoples everywhere. The human desire for self-determination is thus transformed into a national mission aimed at, as Arendt describes it, "bringing its light to other, less fortunate peoples that, for whatever reasons, have miraculously been left by history without a national mission."

In summary, human nature being what it is, the *Review* authors had a deep distrust for solutions to real world problems that were based on a plan to fix men's souls. Thompson recounts how the evangelist preacher Billy Graham once proclaimed that if all men were Christians there would be no nuclear problem. Niebuhr responded, "Not if we fail to develop a viable nuclear policy." Realists were not silent on a strategy for developing viable foreign policies, but in comparison, their persistent condemnation of perfectionist illusions was deafening.

THE IMPERFECTIBILITY OF MAN

Many of the scholars, writers, and editors who contributed to *The Review of Politics* in the 1940s and 1950s shared a basic skepticism of the liberal, or "utopian," view of international politics. (The fact that many of these authors were not from the United States is no coincidence; European émigrés were struck by the pervasiveness of universalistic liberal aspirations in their new environment.) The liberal view was that because human beings were both essentially good and capable of reason, the scourge of war could be eradicated once and for all through a process of rational thought and discourse, public education, diplomatic dialogue and negotiation, and the construction of effective international legal institutions. If perpetual peace was admittedly a long way off, the legal, moral, and rational spirit of the liberal approach would at least gradually displace the evil and irrationality of power politics. In short, according to liberals, right reasoning was the antidote to aggression and the key to peace.

For realists and other critics, liberal "solutions" promulgated through two world wars and the onset of the Cold War were not only hopeless, but also counterproductive and dangerous. The rise and onslaught of German fascism and the dangers manifested in Soviet expansionism were not threats that could be ameliorated via a reasoned discovery of the natural harmony of national interests. Indeed, the liberal desire to assuage Hitler's grievances only emboldened Nazi aggression and helped cause the global conflagration that ensued. (Stefan Possony's essays in this volume—chapters 2 and 10—offer the strongest call to confront aggression with force rather than diplomacy.) But a naïve faith in the power of reason and institutions to bridge unbridgeable conflicts of interest was only one manifestation of the liberal folly. In addition to this Scylla was the Charybdis of portraying the world in terms of a struggle between the forces of absolute good versus absolute evil. Such misplaced faith in the righteousness of one's own cause ignored the complexity of human nature, limitations of human reason, and danger of unintended and unforeseen consequences likely to arise from crusading foreign policies. For realists, the "solution" to the problem of international politics was not to seek to transcend politics—as if traditional power politics were something abnormal or primitive to mankind—but to come to grips with the realities of political life and comprehend the ways in which political action could seek to navigate (if not calm) such treacherous waters.

Hannah Arendt's essay on Waldemar Gurian, written on the occasion of his death, noted that Gurian "had a deep contempt for all sorts of perfectionists and never tired of denouncing their lack of courage to face reality."[9] As a Christian and a realist, Gurian—like Niebuhr—was as deeply contemptuous of religious liberals who sought to eradicate sin from politics as he was of rationalist liberals who sought to eradicate religious sentiments from politics. The diverse set of authors in this volume believed that it was a dangerous fallacy— whether stemming from excessive faith or rationalism—to imagine that human nature and politics could be transformed or perfected. One problem is that perfectionism is an illusion; in Gurian's description, it is a "simplifying pseudo-ethical approach which believes that by some technical means or some external change all problems can be solved simply, and that only some villains and lack of education are responsible for the anguish which the world of the twentieth century has known, and I am afraid, will continue to know." In his article "Perpetual Peace?" (chapter 3), Gurian argues that the long-term optimism in this perfectionist stance serves only to absolve liberals of any real responsibility for what is going on in our actual imperfect world.

A bigger problem is that such perfectionism is very often the source of greater evil than that from which it seeks to purify politics and society in the first place. The essays here suggest at least three dimensions of the liberal perfectionist project that are counterproductive and dangerous: (1) the adoption of the logic of a dualistic or Manichean worldview; (2) the faith in international institutions, laws, and norms to ensure meaningful cooperation, establish world government, or achieve lasting peace; and (3) the belief that the consequences of foreign policies should be as predictable as cause and effect in the natural world.

First, the *Review* authors warn of the danger of a Manichean worldview which portrays the world in terms of a struggle between absolute good and evil. In its extreme form, this view entails the belief that one's own side is the repository for ideas, values, and goals that are good for all mankind and that should be exported to others. Again, the twofold problem with this worldview is that it is necessarily wrong and very often dangerous.

The Manichean view is wrong because it is based on the false premise that only certain individuals or groups are responsible for the immorality and conflict entailed in politics. One can believe in the existence of transcendental moral principles, and one can pursue what one thinks to be these moral values as best one can in a complex world, but political life is endlessly fraught with the tragedy of moral choice. International politics is especially marked by fragmented, interrelated, and often conflicting expressions of morality—for example, those based on national interest, self-determination, human rights, self-defense, and so forth. Thus, it is senseless to describe any conflict between states as a struggle of pure good versus pure evil, even if greater blame can be apportioned to one side. As Thompson writes in his 1952 article (chapter 9), "The unequivocal lesson of history is that conflicts which seem at the time to present to the parties a clear case of right and wrong, almost without exception have appeared to future historians, less blinded by passion and loyalty, as something infinitely more tragic than good men fighting bad ones. The real pattern of conflict and war is one of minor differences hardening into intractable political divisions, of men faced by terrible dilemmas and of nations eventually driven [to war] by the inner dialectic of events."

The Manichean view is also dangerous because it logically entails a mission to defeat and eliminate the evil enemy. If specific bad forces—certain races, classes, parties, nations, states, ideologies—corrupt politics, then those forces must be rooted out in the name of morality, justice, and world peace. As Thompson notes in his essay "The Ethical Dimensions of Diplomacy" (chapter 15), "The false logic of Manichaeism lies at the heart of every crusading ideology and of civilization's long record, ever since the wars of religion, of unspeakable brutalities of one people against another." The danger of crusading moralism—especially in its modern form of crusading nationalism—is also a central theme in the essays by Arendt (chapter 4) and Morgenthau (chapter 6). As Arendt argues, no nation can rightfully claim the mantle of divine origin or label another as a satanic evil; doing so automatically makes the members of one people superhuman and the members of another subhuman. For Morgenthau, "nationalistic universalism"—which "claims for one nation and one state the right to impose its own valuations and standards of action upon all the other nations"—was an altogether new and odious phenomenon of the twentieth century. The new nationalism "has supplied the aspirations for power of individual nations with a good conscience and a pseudoreligious fervor and has thus instilled them with a thirst and strength for universal dominion of which the nationalism of the nineteenth century knew nothing." Butterfield, Thompson, and Kennan warn of the danger in believing that power politics and war will disappear when the Soviet Union and international communism are defeated. Their main point is that the Cold War competition is based less on ideology than on a profound and underlying political struggle. This concept opens the possibility of some accommodation of conflicting political interests without denying that such accommodation may not be possible if truly mutually exclusive interests are at stake.

Second, realist contributors to the *Review* condemned excessive faith in international institutions, laws, and concepts of justice to solve conflicts, constrain aggressors, overcome sovereignty, generate meaningful cooperation, or ensure collective security. The *Review* authors recognized that international institutions could not transform international politics in such a way because these institutions were controlled by states with narrow ideas of national interest, were easily manipulated by the most powerful states, and were simply incapable of enforcing agreements if the stronger states chose to violate them. Great powers defined the "rules of the game" and would ignore or redefine those norms whenever abiding by them became too costly. For example, no amount of intelligent institutional design could make the United Nations in the post–World War II era any more inherently capable of moderating, let alone preventing, conflict than the League of Nations of the interwar period, if the interests of the great powers did not align with that goal.

The *Review* authors also took liberals to task for a naïve faith in the power of negotiation, diplomacy, and disarmament as a path to reconciliation with aggressors. Excessive confidence in reasoned discussion to solve serious international conflicts was not only foolhardy but counterproductive and even dangerous. Finally, the *Review* authors were quick to reject the possibility of a world state. Even if one could imagine a universal government not prone to tyranny over its subjects, the pursuit of such an objective was, again, hopeless and dangerous because it ignored the nature of international politics, which is a struggle for power among highly nationalistic groups bent on self-preservation and self-determination. No amount of liberal enlightenment would negate power politics.

The first four chapters of this volume exemplify the rejection of pernicious liberal abstractions about perpetual peace grounded in collective security, a world state, universal disarmament, or the like. Hans Rommen, in "Realism and Utopianism in World Affairs" (chapter 1), argues that the utopian goal of establishing a world state is impossible because it assumes that all international disputes are justiciable, ignores the power of nationalism, and would depend on an international police force possessing a monopoly on power to sanction law-breaking states. According to Rommen, the fundamental liberal error is to view the nature of disputes between states in legal, not political or moral, terms, which would imply that these disputes could be dealt with under the compulsory jurisdiction of a world court. For liberals, the rule of law, functioning unimpeded by narrow self-interest and the naked exercise of power, could produce just outcomes by which all rational and good states would abide. The problem is that "justice" in international politics is not simply a legalistic-rationalistic concept; rather, most disputes among states reflect competing political and moral claims over the distribution of power. No legal mechanism has the power to produce just outcomes for all states in these circumstances. Moreover, the assault on state sovereignty and the curbing of state power that would be required in order to create a world government—indeed, a world consciousness—would be repelled by the force of nationalism: "There exists a hierarchy of loyalties whereof loyalty to the state is the highest in the secular realm. . . . No people, . . . once it has found its political form of existence, will transfer the decision over its existence to an international authority. . . . The right of self-preservation is such a fundamental condition that all rights and duties are founded on it." Finally, misperception of the nature of international conflict and ignorance of nationalism render fantastic any notions of a global police force able to guarantee collective security and enforce the general will. The League of Nations failed not because of flaws in its legal structure, but because power politics lay behind the legal niceties of the institution.

Stefan Possony's "No Peace without Arms" (chapter 2) rejects the idea that arms control by itself offers a path to world peace. Writing in the spring of 1944, Possony accurately depicted the longing of many observers to make World War II the last war primarily by making it impossible for states to fight, or at least to fight with "offensive" weapons. The idea of qualitative disarmament—the abolishment of offensive weapons—remains the cornerstone of modern arms control theory and practice, yet Possony's essay noted many of the basic paradoxes and outright contradictions that continue to plague this alleged path to peace. First, it is impossible to differentiate offensive from defensive weapons; it all depends on which end of the barrel one is looking through. Second, assuming the international community could isolate and ban offensive weapons, this would likely be a boon only to aggressors because disarmed states would find it impossible to quickly come to the aid of one another. Third, in order to enforce disarmament agreements, at least some states must remain armed and be prepared to go to war for the sake of the disarmament agreement, which in turn would undermine the logic of the whole enterprise. For Possony, peace is a function of the will and vital interests of the great powers, and states that desire to keep the peace should focus on maintaining a military strength sufficient to deter would-be aggressors counting on quick and easy victories. This recognition of the importance of the balance of power and the application of military force as a means of keeping the peace was shared by many *Review* authors and remains a core theme in realism.

Gurian's "Pepetual Peace?" (chapter 3) and Arendt's "Imperialism, Nationalism, and Chauvinism" (chapter 4) offer additional critiques of the liberal faith in perfectionist solutions to the problems of international politics. For Gurian, the obstacles to achieving a world state and thus bringing about perpetual peace were not created by certain prejudices and an immaturity of thought. On the contrary, the kind of universal education advocated by liberals as a long-term cure for the social ignorance that makes war possible reflected "a perfectionism without responsibility for what is going on in our actual imperfect world"; "a looking for perfect solutions which are apparently deductions from self-evident definitions"; and "an intellectualism less interested in the complex and many-sided realities than in the imposition of its concepts." For Arendt, the liberal mission of spreading peace through education in practice serves only to justify imperialism because it entails the view that other peoples are both ignorant and deserving of enlightenment by those fortunate to possess superior knowledge.

Finally, the *Review* authors criticize liberals for failing to recognize that foreign policies, being as imperfect as their human creators, inevitably generate unintended and unforeseen consequences. Clearly, science and technology have brought about incredible advances in our ability to predict natural phenomena and human behavior, but the liberal confidence in the perfectibility of mankind ignores the fact that right reasoning and careful planning can anticipate only so much, and that humanity also pays a price for technological progress. Seemingly rational actions can produce suboptimal or even disastrous outcomes. Part of this critique is offered in John Nef's essay, "The Economic Road to War" (chapter 7). Industrialization and scientific progress made possible by the long period of European peace in the nineteenth century greatly improved man's standard of living, leading many observers at the dawn of the twentieth century to believe that better material conditions were in turn reinforcing international peace and solidarity. Nef, however, points to a crucial development missed by the optimists in modernity: scientific progress had also paved the way to total war and pushed mankind down the road to total destruction. As people increasingly became free to devote their attention and talents to revealing the secrets of matter, space, and time, science "was also preparing means for the almost complete annihilation of man" through steady and revolutionary advances in the weapons of war. But the moral and intellectual consequences of technological progress posed as much of a problem as the material consequences. As society shifted its attention from grappling with the philosophical dimensions of human nature toward the pursuit of greater material comforts, people lost sight of the higher values that helped counterbalance the inherent evil in human nature. In the realm of war, as scientific progress rendered battle more mechanized and impersonal, individuals faced fewer occasions to exercise basic human values such as courage, the willingness to sacrifice, or an abhorrence at killing others, whether soldiers or civilians. The consequences of this vast increase in destructive power combined with a great diminishment of human restraint were manifest in first one world war and then another: "Dismayed after 1914 by the evident recrudescence of evil and violence in a world they had thought of as civilized and humane, some [scientists and other proponents of modernity] supposed that the new evil and the new violence were a monopoly of certain groups, certain classes, certain countries. Many of the scientists belonged to a generation which had been taught that humanity and goodness were the normal products of industrial civilization. If only one got rid of the Jews, the Nazis, or the Fascists, and then of the Communists or the Capitalists, humanity and goodness would again prevail. The march towards a terrestrial paradise could be resumed."

Nef's deep ambivalence about twentieth-century progress is reflected in many of the essays in this volume. Convinced that science and technology had done great things for man, contributors to the *Review* (including Morgenthau) nonetheless repeatedly called for both moderation in our expectations of what science can do to ameliorate the problems of war and conflict that plague mankind and recognition that our good intentions are not enough to ensure that our actions will produce only benefits with no costs. As Pascal wrote, and liberals ignored, "Man is neither angel nor brute, and the unfortunate thing is that he who would act the angel acts the brute."

A Practical Morality

A final theme to emerge from these readings is the authors' expression of a deep morality and humanism—a *practical* morality, to be sure, but one totally at odds with the moral cynicism one might expect to accompany their fundamentally pessimistic worldview.[10] It would be mistaken to label the *Review* contributors, as well as many contemporary scholars or practitioners of realism in international politics, as immoral (or amoral) based on their belief that humanity is inherently flawed, politics is essentially a struggle for power, and international relations are doomed to a future of conflict and war. What guidance for peacemakers could these realists provide, however, once they had accepted the brutal reality of international politics, much less warned of the dangers in seeking to transform that world into anything better? Would not the only practical advice be to embrace the evil of international politics and learn to use it to one's advantage?

In fact, the perspectives in this volume not only allow but also call for moral considerations to loom large in the decisionmaking of political leaders. The *Review* authors believed that just as the problem of politics could not be solved by trying to reduce politics to moral principles (or legal, scientific, or religious ones), it made no sense to think that moral behavior was absent from politics. Both the moral perfectionism generated by the former approach and the moral cynicism produced by the latter approach—what Gurian called the "dangerous twin evils of our time"—stemmed from the same disastrous and irresponsible quest to escape from the tragic reality of the human condition. As a guide to foreign policy, all that was possible, according to the *Review* authors, was the continuous attempt to reconcile what is morally desirable with what is politically possible.

The existence of a practical, prudential morality is revealed in the authors' discussions of the actual role of morality in international relations; the disastrous consequences of modernity's rejection of the existence of objective moral principles; and the proper role and obligation of political scientists in society.

First, the *Review* contributors recognized the constant interplay of morality and power in international politics, while maintaining a healthy skepticism toward the ethical claims of political leaders when these claims were divorced from power considerations. Many have misunderstood the realist critique of the universalistic aspirations of liberalism as implying that international politics is devoid of moral purpose or ethical goals. But none of the *Review* authors believed that states are motivated by pure power calculations alone. Every period of history contains a set of norms that prescribe or proscribe state behavior; these norms frequently become codified in international law, are nearly always used by leaders to justify state actions and policies, and often conform to the national interests and actual behavior of states. However, the *Review* contributors went to great lengths to emphasize that moral principles can neither remain untarnished in the actual world of politics nor can they somehow transcend national interests.

As discussed above, politics involves injustice because politics entails the use of power to compel others. Clean hands in international politics are impossible: for example, collective military action to stop another state's naked aggression will inevitably hurt at least some innocents, yet inaction also will produce harm. There is no escaping the tragedy of politics, regardless of the justness of the cause. Moreover, it is unreasonable to assume that states pursue moral principles when these directly contradict their perceived national interest in self-protection. According to Niebuhr (as cited in chapter 11): "Nations are, on the whole, not generous. A wise self-interest is usually the limit of their moral achievements." Similarly, "Every nation is guided by self-interest and does not support values which transcend its life, if the defense of these values imperils its existence. A statesman who sought to follow such a course would be accused of treason." Of course, the just cause of opposing naked aggression can coincide with a state's self-interest—but, when it does not, one should expect that state to privilege its national interest over a common morality.

Second, despite the analytical pessimism with which the *Review* authors in this volume viewed the primacy of moral principles over the national interest in statecraft, they were clearly animated by a normative desire to improve the world by promoting foreign policies that would accord with universal moral standards. The source and content of those moral standards differed among authors: some derived their values from Christianity (e.g., love and service to one's fellow man), others from secular and classical philosophy (e.g., the pursuit of virtue and self-fulfillment), and still others provided no particular explanation. But it seems fair to say that most of the authors held some kind of belief in an objective moral order guiding human behavior, even as they emphasized that the full extent of such an order could never be understood or realized by man.

There is an obvious tension between a belief in objective moral principles and the recognition that no individual, nation, or civilization can lay claim to certain knowledge of those principles. Yet this tension explains two important normative themes that repeatedly arise in the *Review* authors' analyses of world politics and society. First, the skepticism about any claims of absolute certainty about what is good and evil or right and wrong in any real-world political conflict points to the need for humility, moderation, prudence, compromise, and restraint in foreign policy. These are classic traits of political realism. A second concern may be less familiar: that is, attempts to discern and follow certain transcendental ethical standards (despite the inability to ever fully grasp them) provide an important basis for peace and stability in international politics. Many prominent contributors to the *Review* in the immediate post–World War II period believed that modern society's abandonment of the search for moral truths was largely responsible for the catastrophic wars and troubling direction of international relations in the twentieth century.

As Thompson writes in "The Ethical Dimensions of Diplomacy" (chapter 15), true morality was the "endless quest for what is right amidst the complexity of competing and sometimes conflicting, sometimes compatible moral ends." Those searching for moral meaning in the largely Judeo-Christian tradition accepted the unavoidable clash between moral and political imperatives (that is, between the ethical norms that people feel bound to follow and the struggle for power in which they are necessarily forced to engage). This renders human existence tragic. But in the absence of any attempt to moderate the clash of morality and politics, Thompson argues, life tends to become wholly self-absorbed, meaningless, and even barbaric. In the realm of international politics, partial "solutions" to those contradicting ends—for example, in the general acceptance of the concept of national sovereignty and the mechanism of the balance of power—have provided a limited measure of stability in relations among states. However, when the classic tradition of moral reasoning was abandoned in the march of twentieth-century progress and modernity, there was little to prevent citizens and governments from turning to a host of other operative principles—such as relativism, nihilism, racism, chauvinism, nationalism, and totalitarianism—as a means of escaping the antinomies of the human condition. This, in turn, produced monstrous political consequences, most obviously in the rise of German National Socialism and Soviet Communism.

This critique of the modern rejection of the Western heritage is especially clear in Morgenthau's 1948 essay, "World Politics in the Mid-Twentieth Century" (chapter 6). As the common intellectual tradition of the Western world—along with its moral restraints on the struggle for power among states—was replaced by individual or national operating principles, "international morality . . . [gave] way to the ethics of individual nations which not only does not recognize any moral obligations above and apart from them, but even claims universal recognition from all the world." Of this "new moral force of nationalistic universalism," as Morgenthau labeled it, "not only has it fatally weakened, if not destroyed, the restraints which have come down to us from previous ages, it has also supplied the aspirations for power of individual nations with a good conscience and a pseudo-religious fervor and has thus instilled them with a thirst and strength for universal dominion of which the nationalism of the nineteenth century knew nothing." While the older version of nationalism "wants one nation in one state and nothing else, the nationalistic universalism of our age claims for one nation and one state the right to impose its own valuations and standards of action upon all the other nations. These rival claims to universal dominion on the part of different nations have dealt the final, fatal blow to that social system of international intercourse within which for almost three centuries nations were living together in constant rivalry, yet under the common roof of shared values and universal standards of action. The collapse of that roof has destroyed the common habitat of the nations of the world, and the most powerful of them assert the right to build it anew in their own image."

Despite this critique, many of the *Review* authors in this volume express a hope that the virtues of traditional political thought will be rediscovered, and the conviction that scholars have an obligation to council such virtues even when society remains unreceptive. As the specter of nuclear warfare between the United States and the Soviet Union—and hence the destruction of mankind—loomed as a real possibility, political scientists had a vital role to play in extolling moderation, humility, and prudence in foreign policy in light of the realities of international politics. Hot rhetoric might appeal to politicians and publics, but scholars faced a moral commitment to tell the truth about the complexity of the political world. Those truths—about the inescapable tragedy of politics, the inevitable grey lines between good and evil, the limitations of power—are not ones that society wants to hear when it faces off against an expansionist adversary. As Morgenthau writes (in chapter 12), "the truth of political science is the truth about power, its manifestations, its configurations, its limitations, its implications, its laws. Yet one of the main purposes of society is to conceal these truths from its members. That concealment, that elaborate and subtle and purposeful misunderstanding of the nature of political man and of political society, is one of the cornerstones upon which all societies are founded." A political science that speaks truth to society will inevitably be unpopular and subversive. It follows, Morgenthau continues, that "a political science which is respected is likely to have earned that respect because it performs useful functions for society. It helps to cover political relations with the veil of ideologies which mollify the conscience of society; by justifying the existing power relations, it reassures the powers-that-be in their possession of power." But Morgenthau and others were aware that the ultimate message political scientists are normatively obligated to teach depends on the circumstances of the times. When leaders place excessive faith in social, economic, moral, or legal constraints on the struggle for power among states in the international system—for example, in the run-up to World War II—then scholars must stress the realities of power politics. When leaders denigrate law and morality altogether in the name of a holy crusade against an implacable enemy—for example, as many did in the Red

Scare period of the late 1940s and 1950s—then scholars must emphasize the rightful place of those elements in guiding foreign policy.

There can be no doubt that the *Review* authors believed in the importance of moral principles in the functioning of international affairs, the danger in rejecting these principles in the course of statecraft, and the moral obligation of scholars to describe the realities of international politics even when doing so garnered social hostility and derision. In the mid-1980s (despite U.S. President Ronald Reagan's Manichean rhetoric), Kenneth Thompson could claim (in chapter 15) the "rediscovery" of realist truths about politics: "Prudence has once more become the master virtue in international politics at a moment in time when its absence becomes a threat to human existence. . . . From Aristotle and Augustine through Edmund Burke to Niebuhr and John Courtney Murray, prudence as an operative principle [is] not the rigid formulation or precise definition of what was right or wrong but a method of practical reason in the search for righteousness and justice under a given set of circumstances. Practical morality involves the reconciliation of what is morally desirable and politically possible. It offers few absolutes but many practical possibilities. . . . [It recognizes] the need for moral man in an immoral world to find his way through 'a maze of conflicting moral principles' no one of which reigns supreme. It undertakes to transform abstract reason into political reason. In a word, it aims to rediscover the ethical dimensions of diplomacy as philosophers and statesmen have searched for and discovered them throughout the ages."

CONCLUSION

An exceptional group of intellectuals were closely associated with *The Review of Politics* in the 1940s and 1950s. These thinkers were especially attracted to the journal's first editor, Waldemar Gurian, who was eccentric, charismatic, and adamantly opposed to dogmatic thought. The journal's embrace of dissenting views allowed a diverse group of writers to challenge many of the assumptions and arguments about the nature of international politics that dominated their era. The *Review* authors included in this volume recognized that the recent horrors of their time—World War II, the Holocaust, the crimes of Soviet totalitarianism—were perpetrated or facilitated by the most "enlightened" nations of the world. In the realm of international relations and foreign policy, the wishful thinking and dubious counsel of liberals had produced disastrous results. Political leaders had lost their bearings in a sea of universalist schemes for achieving progress, stability, and world peace, while the young discipline of international studies was turning away from the brutal realities of world politics to an increasingly specialized and quantitatively-oriented focus on trivial topics, without regard for the "old" lessons of political philosophy or the profession's larger societal obligations of their profession.

In the face of these disturbing trends, the *Review* authors tried to convey the classic insights and virtues of what we now call a realist view of politics. They sought to describe and deal with the world the way it really was, not the way one wished it to be. They demanded that scholars and policy analysts alike focus on the big questions—about human nature, society, and politics—because answers to those questions were crucial for understanding the major international problems and existential threats of their era. They accepted as tragic facts that humans were deeply flawed, that political choice inherently entailed the choice of lesser evils, and that international life was doomed to cycles of competition and conflict. The only thing worse than recognizing tragedy, in their view, was attempting to escape it through science, religion, or any other seemingly "progressive" scheme.

The perspectives collected in this volume contain much wisdom for contemporary international relations scholarship and foreign policy debates. The realist tradition remains the single most important approach for understanding international politics, yet its valuable lessons for practical policymaking and the process of political inquiry are routinely forgotten, ignored, or mischaracterized. The common themes to emerge from these essays are applicable today. For example, the *Review* authors demanded that scholars tackle the major political questions of the day, no matter how complex or unpleasant those questions might be and without regard for professional or societal hostility to possible answers. Yet a large and growing segment of the discipline of political science continues to concern itself with issues in which nobody has a stake and with methods that nobody outside a small coterie of "sophisticated" specialists can decipher. Too few contemporary political scientists need worry about the risk of social disapproval—from students or administrators, trustees or donors, politicians or professionals, friends or family—simply because their work has no relevance for the great and controversial issues in which society has a stake.

Similarly, the *Review* authors' warnings about the danger of imprudent and crusading foreign policies deserve renewed attention in light of the international events of the past decade. The rise of radical Islamic fundamentalism and the terrorist crusade against the United States and Western civilization launched by its adherents would clearly garner the focused enmity of the *Review* authors if they were writing today. In particular, there are clear parallels between the Nazi movement and radical Islamism—for example, in the teaching of hatred, incitement of global war, and the goal of world domination. It would be difficult to find better examples than Osama bin Laden and his al Qaeda associates and followers of those who reject the wisdom of ancient moral philosophy, relish the Manichean worldview and the vicious actions such a stance permits, and trample on human freedom and dignity in pursuit of their vision of human perfection. The *Review* authors would also find much to criticize in the classically liberal response of some of those targeted by Islamic radicalism: that is, the faith in international institutions such as the United Nations or some other manifestation of the international community to effectively confront this threat.

The essentially realist views in these essays also provide a useful contrast to the combination of neoconservative and liberal interventionist perspectives that informed the foreign policy doctrine of the Bush administration's first term and that continue to influence contemporary American foreign policy debates. The Bush administration's approach to international politics in the years immediately after the 2001 terrorist attacks has been described as "Wilsonianism with teeth,"[11] combining an idealist strand and a power strand. The idealist strand holds that democracy promotion is the remedy for much of what troubles international relations; the cause of both interstate conflict and substate extremism (e.g., terrorism) is an absence of democracy. The logical solution is to seek to transform aggressive and repressive dictatorial regimes into democracies. Neoconservatives and liberal interventionists also contend that military force provides a powerful tool for promoting foreign policy, sometimes including the goal of promoting democracy. Not only do adversaries respect big-stick diplomacy and respond to explicit threats of force, but also the nature of technology has progressed to the point where the most sophisticated states can inflict overwhelming damage on any recalcitrant state without suffering prohibitive costs. This dualistic worldview has deep roots in U.S. foreign policy traditions and continues to inform contemporary American debates, opinions, and policy positions. However, the combination of the terrorist attack on September 11, 2001, and unprecedented U.S. power at the dawn of the twenty-first century allowed the Bush administration to proclaim Wilsonianism-with-teeth in unusually forceful terms.

The faith in democracy, military threats, and technology to solve the enduring problems of international politics would have been anathema to the *Review* authors. It would be wrong to suggest that the *Review* contributors were not committed to promoting democratic traditions and individual freedoms at home and abroad—several of the authors probably would have perished in Nazi concentration camps had they not fled to the United States—but they believed that bold attempts to make the world over in America's image would not lead to a more peaceful or just international order. Moreover, they understood that ambitious military adventures tended to generate unintended consequences that could be far worse than any projected benefits. Again, most of the *Review* authors would probably agree that Islamic terrorism poses a major threat to the United States and its allies, and that this threat must be dealt with harshly, but would cringe at the Bush administration's Manichean depiction of an "axis of evil" and its insistence that the countries of the world must join the war on terrorism or else be consigned to the category of enemy.

The degree to which the Bush administration—despite its rhetoric—actually followed a policy of Wilsonianism-with-teeth is debatable. The invasion of Afghanistan in 2001 was followed by the promotion of democracy, but the invasion was driven by the strategic need to capture or kill Osama bin Laden, destroy al Qaeda, and remove the Taliban regime that sheltered al Qaeda. The occupation of Iraq beginning in 2003 demonstrated that military force is a blunt instrument with unpredictable effects and that superior military technology is no panacea for counter-insurgency warfare or nation-building. However, one could argue that the Iraq war was fought primarily for traditional strategic reasons—to overthrow a hostile regime thought to possess or be pursuing weapons of mass destruction—rather than as the first step in a revolutionary crusade to spread democracy in the Middle East. If the Iraq war is set aside, the recent record of American foreign policy behavior that can be reliably identified as neoconservative and interventionist is thin. Democracy promotion and military threats have been subordinated to strategic interests and diplomacy in U.S. dealings with other ostensibly "rogue" states, such as Libya, Iran (so far), and North Korea, as well as with powers such as Russia, China, and Pakistan. Nevertheless, the first decade of the twenty-first century may be seen in hindsight as the period in which the United States became reacquainted with the lessons that the *Review* contributors extolled half a century before: beware of nationalism, the claims of military power, bombastic rhetoric about good crusading against evil, false confidence in the consequences of political action, and, of course, grandiose plans to transform international relations. Battling radical Islamic terrorism and spreading democracy are worthy goals, and the United States and other countries with a stake in maintaining peace and stability must confront a range of serious and complicated foreign policy problems relating to nuclear proliferation, failed states, pandemic diseases, global warming, energy resources and other issues. Yet equally important is the wisdom of self-restraint in the exercise of power to meet these challenges. In short, a prudent and practical morality remains the best guide to statecraft in dealing with any era's challenges.

The essays in this volume accept the inevitability of international conflict, yet reflect a deep humanism based on prudence in identifying national interests and careful consideration of the possible consequences of political action so as to minimize morally offensive behavior and outcomes. By refusing to depict international conflict as a struggle between the forces of pure good and evil and by recognizing the stubborn discrepancy between means and ends, the *Review* contributors provide a useful guide for reconciling the morally desirable with the politically possible. This practical political morality, according to Morgenthau, "can disappoint only those who prefer to gloss over and to distort the tragic contradictions of human existence with the soothing logic of a specious concord." Such advice, which permeates the essays here, is as important and compelling today as it was half a century ago.

NOTES

1. See Hannah Arendt, "Waldemar Gurian, 1903–1954," in Arendt, *Men in Dark Times* (New York: Harcourt, 1968), 251–62; Kenneth W. Thompson, "The Religious Transformation of Politics and the Political Transformation of Religion," *The Review of Politics* 50, no. 4 (Autumn 1988): 545–60, at 545–47; and A. James McAdams, "Introduction: The Origins of *The Review of Politics*," in *The Crisis of Modern Times: Perspectives from* The Review of Politics, *1939–1962*, ed. A. James McAdams (Notre Dame, IN: University of Notre Dame Press, 2007), 1–28. Gurian's appointment as director of the new Committee on International Relations at Notre Dame in 1949 also helped him attract important articles for publication in the *Review*.

2. Morgenthau's analysis of the will to power was clearly influenced by Friedrich Nietzsche, although Morgenthau rejected Nietzsche's view that conflict and the struggle for power should be affirmed and embraced as an individual ethics. On this and Morgenthau's own normative ethics, see Christopher Frei, *Hans J. Morgenthau: An Intellectual Biography* (Baton Rouge: Louisiana State University Press, 2001).

3. Robert Jervis, "Cooperation under the Security Dilemma," *World Politics* 30 (January 1978): 167–214. Kenneth Thompson, in his 1955 article, "Beyond National Interest: A Critical Evaluation of Reinhold Niebuhr's Theory of International Politics" (chapter 11 in this volume), suggests the term "the security-power dilemma" to describe the situation, the same basic dynamic that Thucydides alluded to millennia ago in describing the history of the Peloponnesian War: "What made war inevitable was the growth of Athenian power and the fear which this caused in Sparta." John Herz, another important early realist, also clearly articulated the security dilemma concept in his work. See John H. Herz, "Idealist Internationalism and the Security Dilemma," *World Politics* 2 (January 1950): 157–80.

4. Hans J. Morgenthau, *Scientific Man vs. Power Politics* (Chicago: University of Chicago Press, 1946), 188. Morgenthau offers several apt illustrations of the point: "Oedipus tries to obviate the oracle's prophecy of future crimes and by doing so makes the fulfillment of the prophecy inevitable. Brutus' actions intend to preserve Roman liberty but bring about its destruction. Lincoln's purpose is to make all Americans free, yet his actions destroy the lives of many and make the freedom of others a legal fiction and an actual mockery. Hamlet, aware of this tragic tension between the ethics of our mind and the ethics of our actions, resolves to act only when he can act as ethically as his intention demands and thus despairs of acting at all, and, when he finally acts, his actions and fate are devoid of ethical meaning." Ibid., 188–89.

5. Ibid., 195.

6. Quoted in Thompson's "Beyond National Interest" (chapter 11 of this volume), from Niebuhr "Human Nature and Social Change," *Christian Century* 50 (1953): 363.

7. Morgenthau, as quoted in Keith Shimko's "Realism, Neorealism, and American Liberalism" (chapter 16 of this volume), from *Scientific Man*, 194–95.

8. George F. Kennan, as quoted by Keith Shimko (chapter 16), from *Memoirs 1925–1950* (Boston: Little, Brown and Co., 1967), 319.

9. Arendt, "Waldemar Gurian," 261. Hans Morgenthau, in an essay written on the occasion of Arendt's death in 1975, describes Arendt's essay on Gurian as "a masterpiece of literature, resurrecting in descriptive, probing, and living words the mind, soul, and body of an extraordinary man." Morgenthau adds, "I used to tell her that if all of her writings were lost and only this essay on Gurian remained, her place in English literature was secure." Hans J. Morgenthau, "Hannah Arendt, 1906–1975," *Political Theory* 14, no. 1 (February 1976): 5–8, at 8.

10. On the mistaken hostility toward realism on the subject of morality, see Michael C. Desch, "It Is Kind to Be Cruel: The Humanity of American Realism," *Review of International Studies* 29 (2003): 415–26.

11. John Mearsheimer, "Hans Morgenthau and the Iraq War: Realism Versus Neo-Conservatism," *OpenDemocracy* (October 2004), www.opendemocracy.net, pp. 1–7. On the relationship between neoconservatism and realism, see also Michael C. Williams, "Morgenthau Now: Neoconservatism, National Greatness, and Realism," in *Realism Reconsidered: The Legacy of Hans J. Morgenthau in International Relations*, ed. Michael C. Williams, 216–40 (New York: Oxford University Press, 2007); and Brian C. Schmidt and Michael C. Williams, "The Bush Doctrine and the Iraq War: Neoconservatism Versus Realists," *Security Studies* 17, no. 2 (April–June 2008): 191–220.

CHAPTER 1

Realism and Utopianism in World Affairs

HANS ROMMEN

I. FROM THE CONCERT OF EUROPE TO THE LEAGUE OF NATIONS

As a by-product of the Napoleonic wars the Concert of Europe emerged as the institution responsible for the order of the Continent and even for peaceful change. With the admission of France it was a system of equilibrium founded upon a balance of political power among the five Great Powers which acted in the name of Europe as a unity. The Concert of Europe contained elements that were clearly judicial. It was not at all a mere sociological or political fact. But its juridical elements were weak, obscured by the anti-nationalist and anti-liberal tendencies of the founders. Nevertheless, the Concert of Europe enjoyed more success in solving problems peacefully than did the League of Nations, because the former's responsibility as a *pouvoir minoritaire,* to use Hauriou's concept, was clear and distinct. It is of course self-evident that the existence and efficiency of the Concert depended upon a community of several interests. It is equally obvious, too, that the Concert grew weaker as more material for political conflict between the Great Powers piled up, and the more their general interest gave way to particular and opposing interests. By the close of the century the Concert of the Great Powers was being slowly rent asunder through the formation of the Triple Alliance and the emergence of the Triple Entente. So it was that Europe "stumbled," as Lloyd George has said, into the war of 1914–18.

World War I is significant because it was far more a *people's* war than were the wars of liberation from the Napoleonic yoke. Russia's czarism was abolished during the war. Prussian rule in Germany and the autocratic imperial regime were already considerably weakened by 1917, when the army, the Reichstag, and the labor unions, having achieved a very precarious equilibrium, had practically discarded the autocratic power of the Kaiser. In Austria-Hungary, too, the Emperor Charles had already acknowledged the right of the nationalities within the Monarchy to a considerable degree of self-determination and autonomy. On the other hand, the Allies were insisting that the war was being fought on behalf of democracy against autocracy and militarism. Thus the longings of all *peoples* were basically identical: democracy, national self-determination, and a lasting peace through an institutional set-up capable of guaranteeing united action against a disturber of the peace of the world.

Woodrow Wilson was looked upon as the hero of the peace by all peoples, victors and vanquished alike. Likewise, the demand of Pope Benedict XV that the moral power of justice should be substituted for the material force of arms found general acceptance. The international stage was accordingly set for a struggle between utopianism and realism. The new international structure itself, the League of Nations, combined utopian with realistic elements. The latter were chiefly the acknowledgement that the League was based upon the sovereignty of the member states and the recognition that since perfect equality is impossible the Great Powers should have a preponderance in the most important organ of the League, in the Council. This realism was further evident in the many notions that were intentionally left vague. The determination and application of these belonged to the political, not to the juridical, organs of the League. A genuine and effective system of collective coercive intervention, moreover, did not exist. The members had indeed a common duty of immediate action against an "aggressor," but only in their capacity as individual states: the member states were to decide severally what action they would take. They had also the right to secede. This right could be, and was, a fateful means of pressure upon the League's organs of collective action. The League did not outlaw war, therefore, nor did it do away with sovereignty. Decisions in the Assembly and Council required unanimity. The League was a "society," a permanent organization for deliberation, seldom for collective decisions. It was not a federation.

The utopian element in the League of Nations was the implicit assumption that merely through a legal organization—automatically, as it were, and because of an atmosphere—the *volonté de tous* would in some mysterious fashion be transformed into a *volonté générale,* infallible, able to guarantee collective security, and empowered to alter the status quo in the interest of justice. However, the concrete, ever-shifting interests of the still sovereign member states did not permit this transformation.

II. The Crisis of the League

The Council of the League should have been an improved form of the Concert of Europe. But since France and England could not agree upon a common policy, the Council proved to be an unworkable institution. The security which the League could provide was in the eyes of many nations so precarious that they began to fortify their position through ententes and military alliances, which weakened in fact though not in intention the confidence in and the authority of the League especially among the smaller states who began to look upon "neutrality"—in stark contradiction to the aim of the League—as a means of "security." Furthermore, the principle of national self-determination had not solved but multiplied the political problems of eastern and southeastern Europe. Most of the new states were multinational states, and their minority problems combined with their rising economic and military nationalism and mutual rivalries to produce a dangerous vacuum around Germany with its naturally high war potential. This vacuum created a lack of real power and left the peace of Europe at the mercy of a successful internal revolution in Germany because that revolution encountered no opposition from the outside world. The League thus saw itself splitting up into *status quo* powers, some of which like England had bad consciences, and revisionary powers. This external division was aggravated by the fact that almost all the revisionary powers changed to a dictatorial totalitarian regime. This voided one of the hidden presuppositions of the efficiency of the League: the formation of a democratic, i.e., free, public opinion so that the internal forces for peace—presumably always a majority in a democracy—could throw their full weight in the various countries for peaceful compromise and judicial arbitration of conflicts.

Thus the League began to lose much of its initial "good will" among the member states. In particular, the smaller nations felt that the League had become too much an instrument of the individual interests of the Great Powers, a pawn in the game of power politics, whereas the expectation had been that the Great Powers would be instruments of the League. Then, in proportion as important states themselves lost confidence in the authority of the League, the European nations again became armed camps. Without a Concert of Great Powers, the Europe of 1936 was more anarchic than that of 1914. Power politics, earlier concealed behind the legal niceties of the League of Nations, had now a field that was not only free but also enlarged by the perspectives of geo-politics. Feelings of resignation and fatigue prevailed in England. Indecision and internal strife shackled France. Suspicion was rife in Russia. Fear held the smaller states in its grip, while they jealously struggled for the favor of the powerful. The militarist and warrior ideology dominated the totalitarian states. An old order and a new order thus stood opposed to each other. A clash of very great dimensions was consequently unavoidable. Localization of the impending conflict was made impossible by the insatiable urge of the man who said that world peace could only be the effect of world conquest by a master race.

III. The Rise of Utopianism

The present military struggle is accordingly a war for a new international order. It is not surprising, then, that countless well-meaning people are busying themselves with devising, studying, and popularizing detailed plans for the new order. It is no less surprising, too, that utopianism has begun to shoot forth luxuriantly, nourished by the longings of mankind to make World War II the last war—at least for some generations to come, the more cautious add. One type of utopianism is especially rampant. It deals in grandiose plans for world government, for compulsory jurisdiction of a world court over all international disputes, for federations of a regional character within a world federation. The abstract perfection of these institutions is considered a sufficient guarantee that they will establish a concrete order of peace and justice. All this is accompanied, moreover, by violent attacks upon state sovereignty and power politics.

If we delve at all deeply into the matter we soon discover that such utopianism opposes law to power—though sometimes only to arbitrary power—and all too readily concludes that power, physical compulsion bearing upon life, limb or property, is, when used in political life, intrinsically evil. The dream of this type of utopianism is an organization of nations wherein the law or legal institutions are to take the place of power-force, wherein sovereignty is abolished and where the law alone reigns. Until now, so the argument runs, power has ruled in the community of nations. Political power and its attribute, state sovereignty, are responsible for the instability and "anarchy" characteristic of the international community as well as for the resultant wars. Sovereignty must therefore be abolished, and whatever power is left must be curbed under the rule of law. Two ways to achieve this objective seem to be open: (1) a world government possessing a monopoly of power to be exercised by an international police force; (2) a regional federation wherein the sovereignty of the member states is retained for internal purposes, while the federation itself has at least a certain sovereignty externally, which, however, may in turn be curbed or counter-balanced by a federation of the federations in the form of a world league with wide powers. It is assumed that such a harmony of interests exists, or at least that through education, propaganda, rational discussion, and public opinion conflicting interests can be so harmonized, that the individual member state will, by its own decision and out of utilitarian considerations, always prefer to sacrifice its interests for the sake of the world or federative whole than to withdraw and fight for its particular interests.

Aware of the necessity for some formal homogeneity, this thinking further requires that all member states have a democratic constitution. This latter leads to a government of law as well as to a strong public opinion which supposedly is not "managed," is therefore reasoning and reasonable, is also—probably—infallible, and finally is able to play the part of a pre-legal arbitrator that will always clearly see and promote the common interest. Furthermore, an international bill of rights of man and of the citizen is to be established so as to strengthen the individual against selfish group interests which, through abuse of democratic processes, may possibly get control of the government even under democratic rule. The enormously difficult problems of intervention when and if a people is subjected or subjects itself to undemocratic forms of government, and of the enforcement of the international bill of rights, are, however, usually not discussed, perhaps because they would unduly arouse the fears of small nations still so firmly attached to the principles of self-determination, liberty, and independence.

The suppositions implicit in all such plans may be briefly stated. First, all international and group disputes are justiciable, i.e., capable of being dealt with in a court of justice. Second, the intense national and traditional cohesion of present sovereign political groups can be superseded by the consciousness of federal or world citizenship. Third, the now generally accepted principles and values of modern civilization are and will remain undisputed as the basis of human existence. Fourthly, military sanctions against a law-breaking nation or territorial, socially homogeneous group of the rank of a great power can be applied by an international police force, and economic sanctions will succeed in the case of a naturally self-sufficient nation with a planned economy and a high war potential. The supremely important distinction, for instance, between nations that must export or perish and nations which enjoy a high degree of autarchy is scarcely perceived. Little attention, too, is given to the territorial, geographical, and strategic difficulties of military sanctions, although the dozens of reservations touching Article 16 of the Covenant of the League of Nations provide considerable food for thought.

In a legalistic and rationalistic spirit it is deemed possible to fit all inter-individual, inter-group, and international relations into a juridical framework and to deal fully with them in juridical terms. It thereby is expected to get rid of "power," which is conceived as something dangerous, irrational, and even intrinsically evil. The external power politics of sovereign states must be transformed into internal legal relations, into an internal and therefore peaceful policy. Then the sovereign world state will exercise a monopoly of power internally under the control of the governed, the united citizens. It will thus be a peaceful order of law with an internal police force under the law and with a supreme court to decide all conflicts which then will be internal conflicts of law, not international conflicts of power. The same must be said of the federation plan on a regional basis. In this way power—pre-legal, political power—is discarded, at least if we disregard the world government, the sole existing sovereign, and its merely instrumental police power. For such a world state no external enemy is possible. The federations will have of course external relations in a world so organized, but these external relations and the consequent potential conflicts will be handled by some legal institution like a world court. Until now, it is argued, conflicts have in fact been localized inside such regional but unorganized groups of sovereign states. Through world-federation the occasion for regional conflicts will actually be abolished.

IV. ERRORS OF UTOPIANISM

All these arguments—and the literary woods are full of others—are decidedly utopian. In the first place, they find no support in tradition and historical experience. Medieval Christendom, the *mundus christianus*, so often adduced as a model, was never *civitas maxima* with a monopoly of sovereign power, neither under the Pope nor under the Emperor. It is true that the papal curialists and the imperial legists contended with the help of various unsound arguments that the Pope or Emperor was sovereign of the world. Bartolus of Sassoferrato held such a view, and so did Henry of Ostia. Yet Innocent III, truly a dominating personality and jealously concerned with safeguarding all prerogatives of the papacy, admitted that the King of France had no superior *in temporalibus;* besides, the Popes constantly claimed that they did not sit in judgment on the political authority but on the moral evil, the sin, of the rulers. Medieval Christendom is not an instance in point for the further reason that even if we assume it to have been *civitas maxima,* it had a dual authority, spiritual and secular, which gave rise to a continuous jurisdictional struggle between the two powers. Who was to judge what in the concrete case might belong to the competency of the Pope or of the Emperor? To protect its competency the papacy had to exploit its political power, its ability to ally itself with powers which were also opposing the imperial pretensions.

The great masters of Scholasticism were not partial to a *civitas maxima.* St. Augustine preferred a multitude of smaller independent kingdoms to a world empire. Vitoria, Suarez, and Vasque did not favor the idea of a *civitas maxima* or world state. Suarez actually ridicules the ideas of Bartolus of Sassoferrato and Henry of Ostia. Bellarmine, after some favorable remarks concerning a universal empire, quickly drops the notion and holds instead that a multitude of sovereign states under the rule of natural law and subject to the strict demands of justice in the matter of war is preferable. This means something; for these writers were still living in intimate communion with the *mundus christianus.* Moreover, one would think that the idea of a universal Church ought to be a powerful stimulus to the conception of a world state. The fact remains, however, that in Catholic political philosophy the idea of a world state has not been of major importance.

It may be that this is connected with the fact the Catholic political philosophy has a clear, and compared with modern pluralism, very distinct concept of sovereignty. This sovereignty is not only a concept of internal policy but also one of external policy. The concrete order in which a people lives, individualized through a common tongue (as a rule), more or less "natural" frontiers, a traditional common way of living—in short, the people as an historical individuality—has to be protected against injury and destruction from the outside. What else can liberty or independence mean than precisely this ability of a people to be politically its own conscious self? The plurality of sovereign states is a necessary consequence of the pre-political national, geographical, and cultural factors which "individualize" the abstract "multitude" in the general concept of "state" into distinct "peoples" which form thus the "secondary matter" of the state as *forma populi.* Thus a people becomes even apart from the political form, an historic individuality. This does not exclude the multinational state. But it does imply that other unifying influences and forces making for homogeneity are both at work and intense enough to form a basis of the common will to live together, a basis that is more intense and powerful than mere human nature in the abstract.

Sovereignty is thus no new concept. It is a necessary property of the political authority which governs in accordance with distributive justice and is in charge of the common good of a community that is morally and legally self-sufficient. It means a *certain* "closedness" of the community, a certain legal impenetrability of the frontiers in relation to *equal* authorities. It means, moreover, even a qualified impenetrability in relation to the spiritual power.

The reason for this sovereignty is the traditional thesis that man finds his secular perfection in the citizenship of the perfect society. Consequently, modern pluralism is in final analysis wrong. There exists a hierarchy of loyalties whereof loyalty to the state is the highest in the secular realm. The trade union, the economic class, may determine much; but the trade union is a personal, not a territorial group. Members can withdraw from the trade union without falling into a socio-political vacuum, whereas the citizen today cannot secede from the state without becoming subject to another state. Indeed, even when a religious group migrates to unoccupied land, we find that before long it adopts all the essentials and forms of a body politic: a decisive supreme authority, a legal order embracing all external social activities, police, courts, etc. No people, therefore, once it has found its political form of existence, will transfer the decision over its existence to an international authority. A bill of inalienable rights of states is a necessary adjunct of any form of international life. Furthermore, there exists in international life no authority vested with vindictive justice that could, as a punishment, legally dissolve a people's political form against its will. Even *debellatio* and conquest become valid only through the passive consent and acquiescence on the part of the conquered. Clearly, pre-political individualization and sovereignty, however, narrowed down through international agreements, are integral and inevitable parts of the order of things. To these facts, together with the intrinsic necessity of nations and states to live together and with the undeniable truth that "mankind" also is a genuine "community" with the intrinsic duties of its members, correspond naturally international duties. And there is no doubt that these issue in the construction of international institutions able and fit to regulate a peaceful living together and a furtherance of the common interests and ideals. What is denied here is that these duties necessitate a full abandonment of sovereignty since they only demand such an abandonment as is reconcilable with the preservation of independence, liberty, and self-determination of the individual states.

The international limitations of sovereignty, present and future, have in this way an essential borderline. The right of self-preservation is such a fundamental condition that all rights and duties are founded on it. As the *forma populi,* the state's mode of existence depends on the identity of the people; nay more, the people achieves its full identity in the state as a self-sufficient, independent, self-determined, and self-governed internal order, in a word, in sovereignty. Accordingly, the conservation of itself and of its members is the *conditio sine qua non* of its willingness to accept any limitation of its sovereignty. The right of self-preservation is an essential pre-condition of all rights and duties. Just as the individual possesses this right and fears physical death, so a people requires this right as it fears political death. Individuals as rational substances, as persons, may continue to live under new rulers or in dispersal.

Yet with the final death of the state as the *forma populi* a people has lost its political identity. Various peoples may of course give up their individuality in
favor of a new form and may even be obliged to do so in order to reach a "more
perfect life." But they do so of their own will and they find thus a new but still
sovereign form of their political existence. The limits to the limitations upon
sovereignty are well known and obvious. Chamberlain could ask sacrifices of
Czechoslovakia, but not the sacrifice of its political existence. Even today the
German people is assured that its political identity and existence are not at
stake. The international community cannot sentence a state to "death" by dis-
memberment for crimes against international law, as all agree the state can
do in the case of individuals and even of associations of individuals (e.g., revolutionary parties).

The attempt to solve the difficulties about—limited—sovereignty and a
coercive international government by affirming that only external sovereignty
should be transferred to the world government while internal sovereignty
should continue to belong to the states gives rise to great doubts. For this distinction forgets that grave changes in the internal life of an individual state, especially of a great power, by acknowledged right of political self-determination
immediately and directly influence international life. Consequently to give up
external sovereignty to an international body would also require the grant of a
not easily defined power of intervention in the internal life, i.e., into the sphere
preserved for internal sovereignty. A genuine federation which acknowledges
internal sovereignty of the member-states guarantees to and demands from
them consequently a certain form of government as a basis of political homogeneity of the whole. To give up external sovereignty wholly means therefore
such a limitation of internal sovereignty as no great power and not even a small
power will grant to the world-government. As no right is unlimited, each state,
even when acting sovereignly in the field of internal sovereignty, has the duty
of considering the effects which this, its free act, has for its neighbor and the
common good of the international community.

Besides, an individual may be required to sacrifice his life for the whole
community, but to demand from a state, from a people or nation, the sacrifice of its political identity in the interest of the international common good
is preposterous. There consequently exists a genuine residue of sovereignty
that can be abolished only by a free and independent act of the people itself.

Such an act, too, would be, so to speak, the real argument for the inevitability of sovereignty so long as the *civitas Dei* and the *civitates terrenae* are not one. Sovereignty is thus much more a presupposition of, than a hindrance to, an international order. A bill of rights of states has been drawn up which justly "declares," but does not "create," the right of existence, independence, liberty, and self-determination; the right of cultural development, honor, and resistance to unprovoked intervention; the right of legal equality or rather of freedom from arbitrary discrimination; and the right to international trade, enlarged today to the right of free access to the raw materials of the world. We cannot simultaneously proclaim the right of states to liberty, independence, and self-determination and wholly reject sovereignty.

V. On the Distribution of Power

But even within the national state the law is a distribution of socio-economic power and, therefore, potentially of political power. If we exclude the totalitarian state, it is simply not true in the case of the national state that the government has a monopoly of power. Especially in the case of the liberal democratic state it is but partly true to say that the state has this monopoly. The famous minimizing of the state as a power center at the hands of classical liberalism served in reality a polemical purpose in the struggle against the absolutist state. Moreover, as soon as the third estate, through its cautious democratization of the state, had obtained control of the legislative and executive branches of government, it could easily afford such minimizing of the state as well as contemptuous derision of "irrational," discretionary, i.e., arbitrary political power. And it could do so all the more readily as it had possession of the commanding heights of socio-economic power. It minimized political power—which to a considerable degree is a necessary and wholesome bulwark of liberties of the individual—because it could accumulate so much private power behind the protecting screen of the socio-economic parts of the bill of rights: freedom of property and of contract, freedom of enterprise or, more exactly, entrepreneurial freedom.

It would be incorrect, however, to speak of the capitalistic market society as anarchical. There is an order in the market, but it is concealed under the trappings of legal formalism. It is in fact a power equilibrium that is supposed constantly to harmonize the conflicting interests of innumerable bargainers all of whom are approximately equal in bargaining power. It is plain that thinking such as this knows only commutative justice, the justice governing exchanges. Distributive justice, which interferes with the free play of societal forces in order to regulate and distribute socio-economic power in accordance with the importance and responsibility of social functions in an organic whole, simply goes unnoticed. The distribution of actual power has of course taken place in the market: industrial and financial power over the farm interests, producers' power over consumers, especially by means of protective tariffs. Instead then of social harmony arising out of the free play of diffused particles of bargaining power, the modern age has witnessed the rise of great associations of bargaining power, the accumulation of vast socio-economic power in the hands of a few. Domination and concentration of power have resulted from free competition. Yet, as Alexander Hamilton aptly said, the power over a man's support is power over his will.[1] Individuals and families have more and more been coming to exist upon the hazardous basis of short-term contracts that do not afford the degree of socio-economic security which after the venturesome lightheartedness of youth and bachelordom, man requires—a security which in earlier times either landed property ensured or guild membership guaranteed in the form of an assured and honest livelihood. The way from inequality of status to the equality of contractual freedom has led straight to modern insecurity and unequal bargaining power. The power over private contracts means private power over men's wills.

"Immense power and despotic economic domination," rightly asserted Pius XI, "is concentrated in the hands of a few."[2] The legal form of property has proved itself very weak. Property rights are rather widely diffused, nevertheless the economic power of property is exercised by a few. Now the thing that amazes is not that such a power exists but that, although it is essentially social and therefore potentially political power, it is actually private power; publicly irresponsible power, the 'invisible government' of which Woodrow Wilson was wont to speak. Students of power relations found the wild excitement over international cartels somewhat amusing. The public here learned to its astonishment that, by the use of legal devices in pursuit of their private interests yet responsible only to abstract private capital, private citizens could so use their economic power that it threatened to nullify in part the supposedly monopolized power of government which is, theoretically at least, responsible to the governed while today private economic power is in practice not even responsible to the legal owners of the corporate devices. It is small wonder, therefore, that the conquistador type of man, the man hungry for power, has gone into this field of private power and not into politics.

Thus the practical outcome of getting rid of political power has been anything but lasting harmony and true order. On the contrary, industrial and financial empires and monopolistic power concentrations have been built up that have led to a feudalizing of the modern state. The mass units of labor, of industrial and financial capital, of national trusts and international cartels represent even today such great concentrations of private but effectual power that the individual still needs more protection against these than against the government or the "politicians," since the latter are more often than not the servants of private power interests. The "invisible hand" of Adam Smith has become the invisible, irresponsible government of power groups.

The modern state is actually a field of embittered struggle for socio-economic but *private* power between interest groups. These social disputes are not always justiciable. They are not even always open to an accepted legislative decision, since the government and in particular the legislature are themselves drawn into the struggle. The private power groups, compelled to live together because they cannot secede, as they are not territorial units, begin to organize as status-quo powers and revisionary powers, with consequent danger to the unity of the state. The state finally intervenes in the name of distributive justice. The results are social legislation, conciliation agencies, efforts to remove inequality in bargaining power. A more just distribution of private social power is thus aimed at. Yet the real menace to unity and to individual freedom is overlooked or side-stepped. The groups may then engage in an all-out struggle for control of the executive and administrative apparatus of the state. Some may strive for socialization; others, for unhampered freedom of private power and for industrial and financial feudalism; the experts, for a state-controlled planned economy; the fascist-minded, for the taking over of the state by a political elite, a militant minority. There seem to be but two ways out of the dilemma: to make private power responsible publicly, as well as to the individuals concerned, by self-government of the groups under a strong executive; or totalitarianism through revolution accompanied by internal war, open or silent, with bloody sacrifices that are not visible because they are camouflaged by legalities and by control over the instruments of publicity.

The modern state thus provides a poor pattern for a world state. (1) Inside the state there exists power conflict, revolutionary danger. That it does not break out more frequently and more violently is owing to the strong homogeneity of the national state, to the fact that the struggling groups are personal and not territorial groups, and to the circumstance that these groups have a political interest in the preservation of the stage upon which they are fighting. (2) There exists even inside the state no absolute justiciability of the conflicts that touch the order of power distribution. (3) Although the legislative authority is formally competent to alter the distribution of power, this authority may itself, particularly in a democracy, be drawn into the power struggle. (4) The attempt of liberalism to substitute law for power has been unsuccessful. The banished political power returned as private power in the economic sphere. What makes the state a working order in spite of these internal conflicts is the fact that as the antagonists are not territorial but personal groups, they cannot secede *in montem sanctum.* The political will to live together, arising from a national culture, language, blood ties, and other uniting traditional and very concrete factors, usually restrains the antagonistic tendencies.

VI. ARE ALL DISPUTES JUSTICIABLE?

One other related utopian idea deserves to be stressed. This is the notion that all international disputes are justiciable and, therefore, can and should be laid before a world court. It is idle to deny that many more disputes are inherently justiciable than national pride and over-sensitiveness are willing to admit. But it is, I think, wrong to say that the distinction between legal disputes that are justiciable and non-justiciable or political disputes involving "vital interests" and "national honor," is unfounded and superfluous. The oft-favored comparison with the United States Supreme Court limps badly. It is possible for the Supreme Court to avoid political decisions by referring the parties to the legislative power. Moreover, as the history of the Court shows, it has not seldom acted precisely as a political chamber through its right to veto what it has been pleased to consider unconstitutional legislation, as in the Slavery, Anti-Trust and Social Security Legislation cases. Whenever it so acted, it did not face the relatively simple problems of legal subsumption, but it necessarily took into account the political power constellation. It was further aware that it could overrule itself and adapt its interpretation of the law to an alteration in group power relations appearing in a shift of public opinion. Yet whenever the vital interests of groups and parties within the community were involved in judicial issues, the quasi-political character of the Supreme Court appeared. In other words, the Supreme Court itself could not and did not remain in the sphere of mere formal legal austerity. It stepped down, or was compelled to step down, into the arena of internal power politics. Accordingly, this example, however opposite it may at first blush appear, is a rather faulty one.

An international court, on the other hand, as distinct from an arbitrational institution or from formalized procedures of conciliation, is in no such favorable situation as is the United States Supreme Court. In the first place, it cannot rely upon a rather exhaustive code of positive law, constitutional, statutory, and customary. Second, it cannot refer matters to an established legislative body. Third, it has at its disposal no independent enforcement agency, and it thus depends to a very great extent on the good will of the contending parties. What Montesquieu said of the judicial power, viz., that it is *quelque façon nul*, is eminently true of an international court.[3]

But cannot far-going disarmament on the one hand and an effective international police-power on the other serve as an enforcement agency just as the internal police-power and the army serve inside the state? Against this speaks first the undeniable fact that there exist great and small powers with very different degrees of economic self-sufficiency and of war potential. Thus the enforcement of the court's decision against a small power would be easy; but against a recalcitrant great power like Russia or the U.S., on account of their objective industrial power, economic self-sufficiency, and geographic situation, the outcome would in fact be war. Further, can we expect that the national contingent of a great power will overcome its national allegiance in favor of its international allegiance and actively participate in an action against its own nation? If not, enforcement seems at least improbable. The acceptance and execution of a decision against a great power would depend upon the prestige and authority of the court and the moral will of the great powers rather than upon the international police force.

The almost insoluble problem confronting an international court is that of the sources of international law. A court of this kind can function nicely, if the ascertainment of facts concerning an international treaty or the interpretation or application of the treaty in the case is solely in dispute. But what the court would have to do, in order to fulfill the task that the theory of the justiciability of all disputes calls for, is to establish or to find the rule of the case from general principles of law and morality. A court erected on Grotius's idea of a natural law emanating from the essence and nature of the community of nations might succeed. The crucial problem facing such a court, however, is that, in order to work, it must deal not only with legalities but with justice, that is, with the pre-legal, universal principles of right and morality.

The court would thus have to be a legislative authority in the international community. It would, for instance, have to decide whether the unilateral appeal of a state to the clause *rebus sic stantibus* were really justified. Legality and justice are here in question. Let us suppose that the state which thereby attacks the *status quo* is sincere. It would then seem that its vital interests are at stake. This problem is not the simple one of an adjustment of concrete rights and duties by reference to the principles of commutative justice, as, e.g., that the reparation costs or the debts should be scaled down because the legal debt is too high and may occasion a profound economic depression with resultant grave danger to the internal stability of the treaty-bound state and consequently to "world-economy." The critical problem in the case before us is that of the whole factual basis of the treaty by reason of eventualities for which the state cannot be made responsible (e.g., a considerable increase in the population or a newly demonstrated ability to maintain internal order and to provide for the full protection of foreigners, as in the case of China). Under such circumstances the state blames the entire treaty as a mere piece of legality, void of all morality and materially unjust. Here the problem is so little a legal one and so much a moral and political one, i.e., one of distributive justice and—perhaps—of charity, liberality, and political prudence, that any decision of the court becomes directly a sovereign legislative act.

In a case of this type, therefore, the court would become the genuine sovereign. It would be the supreme master over the police power of the states, a mastery which in the United States not even the Supreme Court has claimed, for the latter respects the sphere of "Acts of State," of "Acts of Sovereignty," of the discretionary power of political authority. It is worth observing that one of the main bones of contention between Church and State was always the appeal against the abuse of spiritual authority. The church realized clearly that to admit this claim of the State in the *recursus de abusu* theory to receive appeals would give to the State through its court control over itself and thereby do away with the sovereignty of the Church. We have to deal here, then, with a general principle of law itself which, since it is a pre-legal or even supra-legal principle, cannot be compressed into a positive-law form so as to make it available to the judicial process. It demands, in effect, political processes; conciliation, international political conferences, political pressure, approval or disapproval by the public opinion of the community itself, or finally compromise and arbitration which—not obliged like a court to apply legal rules—is led by careful balancing of the opposing interests of the "litigants" and the supreme interest of the community of nations and by the rules of political prudence.

International treaties, the Covenant of the League of Nations, the Locarno Pact, the various arbitration treaties after the model of the Bryan Treaties, can never play a truly political role. They are impotent as soon as a state objects that its vital interests are at stake. To hand down a decision in a political problem, that is to say, in a problem where the discretionary authority of the state is involved—and this authority is acknowledged and guaranteed by the very nature of international law—there exists no rule, no positive legal principle, that a court could apply. In such a case the only thing for a court to do is to declare itself incompetent. It is not denied that the nationalistic spirit will show a strong tendency to appeal on most occasions to this clause safeguarding vital interests. Nor is it denied that, between states which for a predictable future will have no conflict of interest, appeal will never be made to this clause. Yet we must maintain that no matter what the situation may be, so long as we adhere to the principle of the self-determination, liberty, and independence of states, a case can arise under this clause.

An example or two may serve to illustrate this point. Even though an international bill of rights should grant free migration and forbid discriminatory immigration laws, no politically organized people would allow an *unrestricted* migration into its territory on the part of other human beings whom it might deem unassimilable. And it would be justified in so doing, for without a minimum of assimilation the existence of the state as *forma populi* would be gravely endangered, since the basis of political existence, a minimum of homogeneity and an undivided—though not exclusive—loyalty, would be wanting. Again, it seems inconceivable that, should a concordat become inapplicable because of changed circumstances for which neither party can be held responsible (clause of good faith), Church or State would submit the matter to a judicial proceeding or even to arbitration *ex aequo et bono*. The question is purely "political," a fundamental problem arising from the pre-legal order of living together. In cases such as these a constitutional principle of the institutional order is involved. What a state here contests is not the law or the treaty as it is—on the contrary it acknowledges its "legality"; the state demands its abolition or modification. When in the nineteenth century the principle of national self-determination and unity clashed with the principle of Legitimacy no court, judiciary or arbitral, could have solved this problem. Only a political compromise or a coercive change in the international order could perform that task. Just as a sovereign people though it may entrust the judiciary with the protection of the constitution does not leave changes in the constitution of the state to the judicial power, which would then be the real sovereign, so too the international order and its basic pre-legal principles cannot be left to an international judicial body or even to arbitration *ex aequo et bono*. Legality is a matter for the judiciary; legitimacy is a moral and a political matter.

The political element cannot be wholly confined within a juridical framework; it cannot be totally reduced to legal terms and processes. No legal mechanism, be it abstractly as perfect as possible, has of itself the power to produce justice. The celebrated maxim embodied in the Massachusetts constitution of 1780, "a government of laws and not of men," has a polemic ring and significance. We must always distinguish justice *in* the concrete positive order, which is legality, and the justice *of* the concrete order as a whole, i.e., its legitimacy. The change from the status quo, frozen to legality and founding vested interests, to a new and more just order can indeed occur by means of a slow process. It can come about through a cautious new interpretation of the law, through tacit acknowledgement in customary law of the obsolescence of an inapplicable statute law or constitutional provision, or by legislation that proceeds step by step. In other terms, a silent revolution may take place, just as in social life generally quantity can alter quality. The other way to solve the contradiction between legality or the status quo and the irrepressible search for justice is that of revolution—in international life, by the threat or actual use of war power.

VIII. LEGALITY AND DISTRIBUTIVE JUSTICE

The real problem in foreign policy is therefore that of peaceful change in accordance with the demands of distributive justice. This is a moral and political problem, not a mere legalistico-rational thought operation. Sovereignty as *legibus solutus* means precisely this discretionary authority to change legality in the interest of natural and distributive justice. Persons holding authority must ever make this ultimate decision under their responsibility to their conscience, to the transcendental idea of justice, to the demands of the natural law, to the requirements of the common good, or whatever other phrase be used to signify that no legal mechanism provides an automatic solution in this problem. This personal element in an authoritative decision is the mark of the statesman; it belongs essentially to the political mind and to political formation. During the Spanish-American War President McKinley spoke of praying on his knees for light and strength to make the right decision. Hypocrisy this may have been, but hypocrisy in some particular case does not void the moral principle; the reproach of hypocrisy touches only the abuse of the latter. Besides, later events may prove the counsel of conscience mistaken. Yet once one in authority has made up his mind in conformity with his conscience the use of power to enforce the decision is unquestionably justified. The cynical view that a successful use of power, a victorious revolution or war is always right does not affect this problem of conscience. It touches merely the technical and artistic execution of the decision, not the decision itself which is essentially a moral judgment. And no legal mechanism can take the place of this personal decision.

There is a strong tendency to neglect this personal element in political life. We are too interested in historical causation and in impersonal trends which we like to call irresistible, thus substituting abstractions for concrete living individuals and their just or unjust decisions and actions. As a result, many authors profess to "explain" Hitlerism causally and then proceed to decry Hitler's crimes and to demand his punishment. It is wrong to minimize the great part that decisions of persons in authority have played and will forever play in the historical process.

There exists no "natural order," perfect and flawless, that could realize itself, were only prejudices, selfish and narrow interests, bias or bigotry eliminated. What leads us is only the "idea" of a natural order. But this idea must be realized, actualized, carried into effect by man. Thus every concrete order is afflicted with human imperfection and finiteness. All great minds are aware of this sobering fact, and Christianity has ascribed it to the fall of man.

IX. THE PAPAL PEACE PROGRAM

Legal institutions draw their very life not from the fear of their being enforced but far more from the underlying moral assent of the subjects to the "*telos*" of the legal institutions. It is not so much the certainty that enforcement will result if the law is broken which makes the law a formative force in social life. It is far more the moral obligation of which the law is an external expression that counts. Justice is the constant and perpetual will *suum cuique tribuere*. Without this innermost moral will, without this vivid consciousness that the moral purpose of the law binds the consciences, legal institutions would be utterly weak.

This is the reason why the Popes first and principally stress the universal moral law, the necessity of the virtues of justice, of liberty, of charity in international life as the *conditio sine qua non* of all attempts to compose peacefully all international disputes. The "political" processes of composing mediation, conciliation, arbitration along with the "juridical" settlement by decision of a world-court, are equally stressed. Also emphasized are—and more than world government and world-federation—disarmament, abolition of military conscription, declaration of war by referendum of the people or at least by a representative chamber, and finally sanctions by way of economic boycott and enforcement of the decisions of arbitration by military sanctions. Positive proposals are the freedom of the sea, the abolition of selfish hindrances to economic interchange, free access to raw materials, and coordinated efforts for social and economic progress in the individual states. These negative and positive means to preserve peace can be furthered by an "association" of nations and such institutions as may best serve the realization of these means. No world-government, no international police-force, no exclusive world court, no "Federation" is mentioned. Compared with so many "utopian" schemes all that the Popes have said looks rather sober and modest. But in contradistinction to such "schemes"—which to propose as to particulars one may say is not in the competency of the Pope—the natural law, the universal moral law, the virtues of justice, liberty and charity are emphasized, as are the responsibility and *duties* of the powerful nations and the rights of the small and economically more dependent nations. The Popes also rebuke the growth of internal sovereignty, i.e., the trend to political totalitarianism and the denial of the principle of subsidiarity, the spirit of a rather materialistic nationalism with the absence of a vivid sentiment of co-responsibility of the powerful nations for the international common good.

X. The Principles of International Life

Like national life, international life is built upon contrasting, opposing principles. Legality, security, peace, are its goals, *pacta sunt servanda* its first juridical principle. But changes in population, in economic power, in cohesion through class and religious strife; changes in internal power relations; technological, geographical changes in war potential: all these make for a change of external relations, legal and factual. What is just and legal today may be legal but unjust tomorrow. Hence the clause *rebus sic stantibus,* explicitly or tacitly expressed in all treaties, and the eternal quest for *justice.* Peace is not justice purely and simply. The object of international politics is peace *and* justice. The problem is not peace or war, law or power, but all of them together under the ideas of Justice and Charity.

Practical reason rarely enjoys absolute certainty. The positive law, the practical realization of the idea of justice cannot be absolutely just. Saints themselves have disputed over what is just in a concrete case. The ideal and the transcendental idea lose their timeless perfection by being realized in time and space. The real is not wholly the rational.

Coercive power is an existential necessity of human social life, since man's practical reason is all the more erring as the problems calling for action are the more concrete. Precisely because rational consideration shows that there are many ways of attaining some particular objective, and since no amount of discussion can overcome this plurality of ways, men stand in imperative need of an authority which decides after a discussion, or without one, which way is to be taken. Consent and compulsion are alike means to unity, and so is power that *enforces* obedience. In human life security and concrete order are never equivalent to justice for any great length of time. Life contains that irrational element which reason cannot wholly control. Man's passions tend blindly toward their specific object, toward their immediate and full satisfaction without regard for the fundamental harmony which reason must put and maintain in man's life, without regard for the place which the individual must take in the ordered social whole. In order, therefore, to make of the passions servants of the toilsomely constructed and ever endangered order of political life, power, and indeed coercive power, is needed wherever man has built up institutional forms.

It was and is the function of the natural law to afford a measure for the legitimate and reasonable use of power in changing legality so that in a new situation a new approximation of justice may be achieved.

There is no possibility of substituting law for power, legality for justice, self-working legal mechanisms or institutions for personal conscience and moral responsibility. In international life wealthy, powerful nations cannot discharge their direct responsibility for the peace of the world and for the realization of justice upon international mechanisms, upon such agencies as an international court. Are not many "plans" for a durable international peace motivated by a disinclination to assume these responsibilities? Do not many organizational schemes arise out of the longing to be free from the never-ceasing labor of adjusting international life to the ideas of justice and solidarity—from foreign policy—by transferring them to an automatically working institution? It is a tacit presupposition of many such plans that man is good and that the whole problem is therefore to have flawless institutions in order to have justice *and* peace at no price at all. The League of Nations could have functioned successfully if its organs, especially the Council, had been the legal cloak of the united will of the leading powers, of the honestly accepted moral hegemony of the great powers, and if these great powers had acted concertedly according to their proportionally higher responsibility for the international common good. But, instead, all too often they evaded this responsibility and "minded their own business" using the League all too much for their separate interests. The more clearly this basic fact common to all human social life is perceived by all, the easier it will be to discover and eliminate the utopian elements in foreign policy. The more actual power in all its modes a nation possesses, the more its moral responsibility grows, and for the most part without any increase of its legal responsibility. And no legal mechanism, whatever be its pretensions to produce justice in an automatic fashion, can take away this responsibility.

Notes

Reprinted from *The Review of Politics* 6, no. 2 (April 1944): 193–215.

This article was written before the publication of Mortimer J. Adler's *How to Think about Peace and War*, though it presents a criticism of the World State advocated in this book.—The Editors.

1. Alexander Hamilton, *The Federalist*, No. 73.
2. Pius XI, *Quadragesimo Anno*, No. 106.
3. Montesquieu, *Spirit of the Laws*, Book XI.

CHAPTER 2

No Peace without Arms

STEFAN T. POSSONY

The armed peace is expensive; but war is even more expensive.
—Note of the French government, April 17, 1934

Peace-planning is the attempt to invent institutions and to reformulate policies to prevent future wars. Among the numerous ideas on the future organization of the peace, the idea of disarmament has found particularly wide acceptance. In time of peace, there is no need of maintaining armies and armaments on their war time level. Far-reaching demobilization is an economic necessity. Consequently, no objections are being raised against the substantial reduction of armaments after the end of hostilities.

Many of those who speak of disarmament advocate considerably more than mere demobilization. They propose the virtual dissolution of the armed forces. Weapons, as Salvador de Madariaga told the Geneva Disarmament Conference, are the "raw materials of war." As one cannot see without eyes, one allegedly cannot wage war without arms, or to modify an old proverb: where there is no way, there is no will. A war between disarmed nations is assumed to be technically impossible. Hence general disarmament is praised as a means of securing lasting peace.

But what is the proof of this assertion? What is meant by general disarmament? Obviously, there are many arms which cannot be abolished, or which can be reinstituted in mass production within a very short time. Among these weapons are small fire arms, including machine-guns, trench mortars, rocket projectors, small caliber guns, and possibly field guns; high explosives and blank arms. Since all wars of history up to 1914 (and even many campaigns of the first World War) were fought with much less powerful equipment, it is hard to see why it should be impossible to fight a future war with such weapons. In a period of disarmament, they would not even be inadequate for invading a neighboring country. In such a period both belligerents would begin the war with similar and light equipment. As initiative, surprise and the concentration of force would provide a substantial military superiority, the attacker would have a good chance of winning the war. Otherwise, victory would go to the country with superior manpower and larger industrial capacity. The pattern of a "disarmed" war would thus not differ fundamentally from that of other wars fought between equal powers, except that in its initial phases it would be a war of light material.

The assumption that disarmament prevents war (and incidentally also the idea that federations make war impossible) has been clearly disproved by the American Civil War. This war occurred although both belligerents were almost completely disarmed, at any rate more radically disarmed than independent countries would be as a result even of a far-reaching disarmament agreement. The Civil War should also serve to prove that it is by no means certain that "disarmed" wars would be of short duration or cheap in human and material losses. In this connection, one might point also to the Spanish Civil War.

The concept of peace through general disarmament was, for all these reasons, never really taken seriously in any international discussion. The Geneva Disarmament Conference concerned itself chiefly with the problem of whether German rearmament could be organized in such a way that it would not upset the precarious balance of power painfully established at Versailles. At the same time, the attempt was made to make German rearmament compatible with the disarmament of other powers. Whenever the schedule of the Disarmament Conference was not being taken up with such problems of political alchemy, the idea of qualitative disarmament was being discussed. This idea had been conceived by Lord Robert Cecil who believed that by strengthening the power of the defensive at the expense of the offensive the danger of war could be lessened, or that, more specifically, peace could be secured through the abolition of "offensive weapons."

Lord Robert Cecil's thesis was accepted by Sir John Simon and Hugh Gibson, the British and American Delegate respectively. If the fear of invasion can be dispelled, they asserted, there will be no war. This fear is chiefly dependent upon the existence of certain offensive weapons. Consequently, if offensive arms are abolished and if, on the other hand, defensive armaments are strengthened, the feeling of insecurity must vanish.

When André Tardieu took the position that unfortunately the difference between offensive and defensive weapons is undefinable, Sir John Simon was compelled to admit that indeed he could offer no clear and scientific distinction between offensive and defensive armaments.

It is well known that despite hard and long labor the experts of the Disarmament Conference were not only unable to produce a scientific definition, but were unable even to posit a crude rule-of-thumb criterion for practical purposes. The experts came to the conclusion that there is only one distinction between offensive and defensive armaments, namely the "intentions" which guide their employment. Weapons are offensive if employed for offensive purposes and defensive if used in defensive operations.

To kill and to destroy is the purpose of any kind of weapon. The offensive—it was once said—is the fire that advances and the defensive the fire that stops. Thus, the only admissible differences between weapons are: stronger or weaker, more effective or less effective. The criterion of mobility in itself is inadmissible since even fortifications can be used offensively. Fortifications are an important means of providing for offensive troop concentrations. Their maintenance requires a steady production of "offensive" equipment and the continuous military training of large numbers of troops. Thus, even if reduced to fortifications, a potential aggressor could prepare aggression. Moreover, the strength of fortifications lies chiefly in their fire power. Heavy artillery is according to all possible definitions an "offensive" weapon. As there are no ways to prevent a potential aggressor from removing guns from fortifications and organizing an artillery assault force, the doctrine of qualitative disarmament is untenable.

Defensive strategy does not imply defensive tactics. A defensive war, if it is to be fought successfully, requires offensive armaments to undertake local counter-thrusts and full-fledged counter-offensives. A passive and static defensive has not once in history proved successful. Due to the advantage of initiative and surprise, at least initial successes of the aggressor can never be prevented. The integrity of the defender's territory and the survival of his defense forces can be secured only if his army is capable of maneuver, concentration, and offensive fighting.

"Defensive" and "offensive" are relative terms which have no meaning if used in an absolute sense. The same weapon can have offensive character if used against one opponent, and defensive value if used against another. In a war against Italy or Spain, the French army of 1939 would have had offensive character. The same army, however, in its war against the German army proved to be less than a defensive force. The German 10,000-ton "pocket battleship" had offensive potentiality in the Baltic, but little in the Atlantic. The bomber command of the Royal Air Force is an offensive organization. Yet in 1940 by attacking German "invasion ports" and invasion barges, it fulfilled an essential defensive mission. Also the Royal Navy, although an offensive force, acted during the critical years of the present war as Britain's main defensive, in fact as Britain's "Maginot Line."

A defensive army is unable to come to the assistance of allied countries or to intervene against the violators of international agreements. Defensive armaments, if it were possible to isolate such, would thus constitute a premium for aggression. They would make impossible any kind of mutual assistance and small countries would feel permanently insecure. Yet, oddly enough, the same people who advocate "qualitative disarmament" usually advocate also "military sanctions."

As unequal things cannot be compared in quantitative terms, no objective standards can be devised for measuring the military requirements of one country in relation to another. Consequently, only arbitrary disarmament agreements in the style of the 5:5:3 formula can be drawn up.

Nevertheless, from a purely military point of view, limitations of military expenditures and of the size of the armed forces and weapons are not without value, since a sound and financially strong economy is a military asset. Yet such limitations may easily interfere with military efficiency by making it impossible, say to provide the country with a sufficient number of cadre troops or to produce adequate weapons. For instance, the building of tanks would become pointless if tanks were limited to sizes below 10 tons.

It is important to notice also that no limitations can be placed on technical progress. Yet limitations on the size of weapons will in many cases prevent technical adjustments. Assume the penetrating power of artillery ammunition has been increased. This would require the strengthening of armor protection of ships and tanks, hence the increase of size and weight of both weapons.

If this cannot be done, the value of both weapons would be greatly diminished. For instance, the limitations of the Washington Naval Treaty made it very difficult to protect battleships appropriately against air attacks. If resistance of steel is being strengthened by the discovery of a new steel hardening process, it might become necessary to increase the caliber of naval and land artillery. Otherwise, the armored weapons might prove to be irresistible. It is also quite possible that by several new technical devices the performance of a weapon is greatly improved, although its size remains unchanged. And obviously no limitations can be put on the development of instruments regulating the aiming and speed of fire, not to mention "secret weapons" and novel tactical techniques. Even purely industrial inventions and preparations can be of extreme importance, such as installations permitting the sudden switch from the production of peace goods to military equipment, or the adaptation of civilian equipment for military use. Consequently, it should not be expected that armament limitations can provide any kind of military security. In the best case they will not impair military efficiency, but very often they will do just this. Besides, it is almost impossible to draft an armament limitation agreement without convenient loopholes for would-be aggressors.

The crux of the matter is whether an effective and mutual armament control can be set up. Obviously no country can be expected to remain disarmed unless there are adequate guarantees that no other country is taking advantage of the situation. Theoretically armament control appears to be feasible. It is just necessary, so it seems, to watch factories and all imports. In practice, however, things are much more complicated.

There must be a huge staff of technically and linguistically well-trained comptrollers to supervise hundreds of thousands of factories. Such a staff can hardly ever be gathered. At any rate, it will be so numerous that the selection standards must be lowered, hence there will be widespread fear of double-dealing, trickery, bribery, and inefficiency. In fact, it should not be difficult to deceive and trick such comptrollers, particularly those who have friendly feelings towards the country in which they work.

Second, in order to permit control of a country's industry, all its laws concerning commercial secrets, patents, and experimentation must be abolished. Every factory would be required to reveal the secrets upon which its very success depends. There is no doubt that all industries of all countries will fight such controls to the utmost. And they will be successful until and unless socialistic systems are introduced everywhere. If control is forced upon a reluctant industry and if at the same time, the individual industrial concern and entrepreneur are permitted to keep their secrets to themselves, disarmament control can only be perfunctory. It cannot be considered as reliable, and it will hardly reassure any country feeling itself menaced.

It is very often overlooked that disarmament control offers by itself excellent chances to an aggressor: it provides an outstanding opportunity for spying out the future victim's armaments, without necessarily preventing the aggressor from secretly equipping himself with superior weapons. Sometimes it is argued that secret armaments would reveal themselves through increased imports and production without an equivalent increase in consumption. This may be correct in the case of countries undertaking suddenly massive armaments within a short period of time. Yet even a country with huge imports of raw materials is capable of camouflaging its armaments if adequate preparations have been made over a number of years. The bigger the country, the larger its industrial capacity and the more plentiful its resources of raw materials, the easier even considerable armaments can be kept secret. Besides, if the victim country has conformed with its disarmament obligations, the amount of weapons necessary for aggression is not at all large.

Granting however that there are possibilities of a tight international armament control, it would be misleading indeed to discuss this problem merely on technical grounds. The essential question is: can armament control be effectively maintained under adverse political conditions? Aggression does not take place in a political vacuum. It is usually preceded by international dislocations and by the emergence of blocs, ententes, alliances between countries of similar interests. Appeasement might also spring up. In such a situation, the aggressor has a good chance that his violations of the disarmament agreement will be "overlooked," at least for some period of time. If they are finally openly admitted, it is by no means certain that action follows. The aggressor has by then acquired material superiority; those peaceful nations who want to penalize or disarm the aggressor will not have the means to implement their policy, unless they have also violated the disarmament agreement. There will also be a certain number of countries who sympathize with the aggressor or who are not adversely affected by his acts of aggression, and who therefore will discourage military sanctions. The course of international conflicts is hardly ever influenced by the network of legal obligations; policies with respect to war and peace are being shaped by the political interests of nations. Aggression will be countered if and when the vital interests of the Great Powers are involved. In all other cases, the Powers and their international organizations are more likely to have recourse to a not necessarily successful policy of "reconciliation," if only for the reason that in democratic countries public opinion might be opposed to a war by which their own country is neither directly nor indirectly affected.

And yet, one must by necessity resort to war even if one only wants to stop a country which is firmly resolved to arm itself. Thus, the paradox arises that in order to enforce a disarmament agreement, at least some countries must remain armed and be prepared to go to war for the sake of the disarmament agreement. It does not make any difference whether such a war is undertaken by the national armies of these countries or by a so-called international force. For after all, this international force must be stationed somewhere and get its supplies from someone. Assuming that an international force would intervene against Germany: would the main contingent of its armies not be recruited in Great Britain, the United States, and Russia? And where would its weapons and supplies come from if not from these same countries? The nature of war cannot be changed by rechristening an army "international police force."

Also the expedient of economic sanctions will often again be recommended. Sanctions can be effective against minor countries or against countries without adequate resources, like Italy. But an application of economic sanctions against the United States or Soviet Russia invites ridicule. Even against Germany their success will be indifferent, particularly if Germany can count upon imports from the Balkans. Sanctions against Great Britain are tantamount to a naval blockade of the British Isles prior to which undoubtedly the Royal Navy would have to be defeated and destroyed.

Although security cannot be achieved through disarmament, established security will automatically reduce armaments. First things come first. The international situation and the fundamental causes which sometimes lead to war cannot substantially be altered by interfering with some of the tools of war. A tool is nothing but a tool and nobody has as yet been able to prove that weapons cause war and to disprove that, on the contrary, it is war or the danger of war which produces the weapons.

But how can security be achieved? It is comparatively easy to find an answer which sounds impressive and convincing to large audiences, but it is difficult to answer this question correctly. One might seriously doubt the possibility of establishing any kind of international security in a period of fundamental changes, for the simple reason that these changes require adaptation and lead to the decline of old, and to the emergence of new, systems of order. These adaptations might be accomplished by "peaceful change," as long as they do not affect the vital interests of anyone. But once they do, they will destroy the feeling of security, and in most cases lead to war. Admittedly, no conflict must by necessity ever end in war. Theoretically, each conflict could be settled peacefully and each war could be avoided by timely preventive measures. But this presupposes excellent governing and the people's understanding of rather complicated international problems which usually become clear to the broad masses only when it is too late. The fact is that most wars break out not only because there are aggressors, but because the victims and the neutrals are badly governed and because the danger of war is not realized in time. The best international measures and organizations for the prevention of war will be inadequate so long as no system has been devised to ensure effective government at all times. The admonition of Baron Oxenstierna still holds today: "My son always remember with how little wisdom the world is governed."

Nevertheless, there are undoubtedly periods of comparative security even in times of fundamental changes. Disregarding the security caused by general war-weariness, one of the best peace guarantees seems to lie in the *unilateral* disarmament of the strongest potential aggressor. Of course, the only potential aggressor who can be disarmed is a recently defeated one.

Unilateral disarmament is basically different from general disarmament. Certainly, the potential aggressor cannot be stripped of all his weapons and he might be able to undertake secret armaments. Yet if his opponents possess well-equipped armies, he is obliged to arm on a huge scale and to produce superior weapons. Such armaments could not be kept secret long enough to ensure a substantial lead, while even the most skillful subterfuges would not be adequate for providing him with weapons equal to those produced by nations who maintained their right to arm themselves openly. The thesis set forth at the Disarmament Conference that unilateral disarmament by violating justice and right would *ipso facto* lead to aggression is, on the face of it, incorrect. Wars break out only if the would-be aggressor sees a chance to win decisively and speedily. No country is foolish enough to attack with inferior forces and weapons, unless its hopes for victory are kindled by non-military factors.

Nevertheless, the obvious dangers of unilateral disarmament should not be overlooked. The disarmed state is, of course, an easy prey if one of the armed countries should turn to aggression. Moreover, there is no law that a nation which was once aggressive will always remain so. After one or two generations, the formerly aggressive country might have become peaceful while another nation, formerly peaceful, hence well-armed, might consider expansion, possibly at the expense of the disarmed state. Unilateral disarmament is therefore only a short-term solution. As such, it is effective; yet if a status of unilateral disarmament is perpetuated, in spite of its *raison d'etre* having vanished, it might become the germ of a new war. It would be different if the new aggressor were disarmed prior to his attack (and the now peaceful former aggressor be permitted to re-arm in time), but this could be done only by a preventive war, or by war *tout court*.

Reviewing soberly the effects of past disarmament agreements one has to admit that, on the whole, disarmament conventions have done more harm than good, and to be more explicit: more harm to the cause of peace. During the Washington Conference a naval race between American and Great Britain was avoided, with the result that Japan became a first-class naval power and both America and Britain entered the present war with obsolete ships. Ironically enough, the Washington Naval Treaty is not only the origin of the German-Japanese alliance, but at the same time one of the most powerful psychological motives for Japan's aggression: Japan was not satisfied with her quota. To have a fleet one third weaker than the British or American navy was considered a national shame and Japanese school children were taught that "5:5:3" was the gravest injustice ever done to Japan. The treaty of Washington had for Japan the same psychological impact as the treaty of Versailles for Germany. As a matter of fact, considering that Japan is a one-ocean country, the Washington treaty actually made Japan the greatest of the individual sea powers!— In Europe, the disarmament ideology led the French to set up a defensive army.

Were it not for the Channel, Britain's disarmament would have ended with Hitler's world dominion.

Provided excessive armament races are avoided, it is perhaps better not to enter sweeping disarmament agreements. Under the present circumstances, due to the fundamental demographic, economic, and social changes of our time, war remains an ever-present danger. A country feels probably more secure if its armaments are adequate to repel invasion. True, it is desirable to abolish certain weapons and to reduce the size of the armed forces to the minimum compatible with military security. But the difficulty lies in clearly defining this minimum. In practice, no such scientific attempt will be made. The country which is most universally dreaded will set the pace of armaments. If that country can be induced to keep its armaments low, armaments can and probably will be reduced on an international scale. Yet the danger of war would be intensified if a far-going disarmament convention is imposed upon countries which are potential victims of aggression or potential enemies of the aggressor.

In conclusion, it appears that the old Roman principle, "*Si vis pacem, para bellum*" has as yet not been replaced by a more convincing and effective precept for the prevention of war. It has been said that this Roman principle was not more successful than modern schemes. It is argued that all their armaments have not protected the European nations from being repeatedly attacked. However, a closer scrutiny of the facts would reveal that in virtually all cases since Napoleon's times, the aggressor thought he had a chance not only to win, but to win speedily, although in some cases the opinion of the aggressor's general staff differed markedly from "world opinion," as for instance in the case of Japan's attack on Russia in 1904. The precept "*para bellum*" should however not be interpreted in terms of quantitative armaments alone. The quality of the belligerent armies, the time schedules for mobilization, the chances of surprise must be taken into consideration as well as, most important of all, the international situation. If an aggressor is convinced that he can localize the war and concentrate on one enemy, his risks may be insignificant. Yet if it is certain that the victim will be supported by the military might of other powerful states, aggression will very likely not take place. Germany would probably not have gone to war in 1914 if she would have known that Great Britain would come to the help of France, nor in 1939 if she had not persuaded herself that if the Western Powers entered the war at all it would be at best "symbolically." Nor would Japan have attacked in 1941, if she had been uncertain of Germany's victory in Europe.

The "*para bellum*" policy thus implies in the first place, the maintenance of military strength on a level that no would-be aggressor can count on easy, quick, and cheap victories. This implies not only weapons in adequate quantity, but also an overall, well-balanced military establishment of high tactical ability and immediate striking power. Secondly, foreign policy must be conducted in such a way that the would-be aggressor cannot isolate his acts of aggression. Upon attack he must be confronted by a superior coalition. One of the main causes of recent wars has been the tardy formation of coalitions against the aggressor. The replacement of the traditional post-aggression coalition by pre-aggression military and political understandings would be the most powerful deterrent against war. The aloofness, isolation, or neutrality of the strongest nations and their friends is the best encouragement to the aggressor. Or to quote George Washington: "To be prepared for war is one of the most effectual means of preserving peace."

Prolonged periods of peace are not impossible. But to achieve this goal, energy and initiative are required in military and foreign policy. The art of maintaining peace is the preventive extermination of the germs of aggression. It requires military power and the application of force. It rests upon the crucial question of whether the democracies will be ruled by foresight or by hindsight, by knowledge of facts or by wishful thinking. It rests finally on the realization that while the earth is not altogether a place of evil, it cannot be transformed into a paradise. Mankind must become much wiser before it will lose its oldest companion: war.

NOTES

Reprinted from *The Review of Politics* 6, no. 2 (April 1944): 216–27.

This article is not directed against disarmament as one of the means of maintaining peace but against an over-estimation of a purely technical disarmament which would overlook the importance of the fundamental will to keep peace and avoid war.—The Editors.

Perpetual Peace?

Critical Remarks on Mortimer J. Adler's Book

WALDEMAR GURIAN

I

Mortimer J. Adler's much quoted address in which he castigated American professors has been widely misunderstood. When he declared that their errors were more dangerous than the threat from Hitler, he did not intend to discount them. On the contrary, he was paying a most impressive compliment to the importance and effect of their writings and other activities. Adler is professor of the philosophy of law in the University of Chicago, and his yardstick must be applied to himself. It would be inappropriate to pass over his *How to Think about War and Peace*[1] in silence or to regard it as an unimportant and uninfluential work. This new book, praised as a product of hard thinking, will be read only by few, even though it will be bought by many in response to the intense propaganda of the publisher.

Adler claims that he describes the necessary approach to a most urgent problem. It is true that he modestly abstains from presenting any blueprints for the postwar world. He humbly abandons to Prime Minister Churchill and President Roosevelt a concern with such matters of immediate practical importance as relations with the Soviet Union or the fate of Germany. But on the other hand, he is more ambitious than those who are preoccupied with planning for our generation. He is trying not only to find principles of thought about peace and war but also to circumscribe the realm and the direction of practical, meaningful work in behalf of a truly lasting, and therefore universal and perpetual, peace.

His subject matter makes it necessary to take his analysis and proposals seriously. This must be the attitude, in any case, of those who regard Adler as a stimulating lecturer and challenging educator, as a man who dares to speak out and who can claim to have been for many their guide to philosophy. It would be unjust to Adler's intellectual honesty if his new book were viewed either as a skillful exercise of conceptual constructions or as a somewhat sensational display of the art of persuasion. Plato is a great friend, but truth is a greater one—this sentence must serve as a motto for the critical analysis of Adler's book. I am sure that Adler would resent mere non-committal praise, half-hearted recognition, polite evasion which would not face the real issue.

II

The fundamental thesis of Adler's book may be summarized in two sentences: "There will be wars as long as there are several sovereign states. Perpetual peace is only possible if there is one world state." Adler himself proposes to express his thesis by resolving a famous disagreement between Kant and Hegel.[2] Kant believed that a curtailment of national sovereignty by a perpetual pact excluding war would make lasting peace possible. Hegel rejected this belief, emphasizing that sovereignty of states cannot be bound and limited: "There is no praetor above states," he wrote. Adler accepts Kant's ideal of perpetual peace as well as Hegel's criticism. Hegel is right: so long as sovereignties are not replaced by one sovereignty, by one world state, there can be no peace. Kant also is right concerning his ideal of perpetual peace—but this peace can be achieved only if there is one world state. A league, a federation, an alliance system are completely insufficient. For Adler, perpetual peace is not, as for Kant, a regulative idea but a practicable objective. This world state will be realized, not at once, not after this war, but in a few hundred years, around, as Adler says, five hundred years. Therefore, Adler claims to be a pessimist in the short run—there will be another world war after World War II[3]—but an optimist in the long run. The one world state will come and with it real peace, universal and perpetual, not the pseudo-peace of peace treaties, which is in reality only a truce, an armistice between wars. This world state, first imperfectly organized in a federal way, will be perfected by becoming a world community under a government that is not federal in structure. "Our posterity will see other goals beyond perpetual peace, goals of which we cannot dream" (177).

Adler applies to humanity the same principle which has worked in the rise of the different political communities: No order and peace without governments. Therefore, no world order and no world peace without world government. He opposes "internationalism," for it does not face the decisive issue. As long as there are various sovereignties there is a continual threat of war. Self-determination of sovereignty is no help, because the sovereign himself decides about the limitation. International law is of no help, because it is a "law," a treaty between sovereign states which can discard and violate it. Therefore, "internationalism" does not abolish international anarchy, *the* cause of war, for it does not abolish sovereignties. It does not matter which approach we use, the result for Adler is always the same: One world state alone, one sovereign alone makes perpetual peace possible. This world state will be a constitutional and a democratic one. "The institution of world peace and the beginning of a world republic will come together or they will not come at all. The improvement of world peace and the democratization of that republic will follow parallel courses." "The 'people' must become coextensive with mankind" (187).

III

Adler's whole system is based upon his definition of peace. Peace for him is universal and perpetual. If there are sovereign states, universal and perpetual peace is impossible—the sovereign states may go to war.

But is perpetual peace secured if there is a world state? Adler apparently overlooks this question although in his lecture he mentions that a world state based upon conquest cannot have a perpetual character.[4] What gives the true world state its perpetual character? Adler identifies the function of world government—which according to him must be a world state that takes away external sovereignty from all states—with the function of governments in the various political communities. I think that this approach is erroneous: the fact that a government maintains peace in its community and enforces law does not guarantee its perpetual character. Frontiers change; states disappear. Why is it impossible that a world state, after having become a reality, should break up again?

This possibility is in no way refuted by Dr. Adler's discussion of civil war, in which he argues that "civil war is truly a breach of the peace . . . war between nations does not breach a peace, because none exists," and concludes that "civil war . . . may be the inevitable expedient by which a community . . . perfects its government, and so achieves a more nearly perfect peace" (125). Adler manifestly assumes that after a world state based upon a progression to democracy via constitutionalism has arisen, it will endure despite civil wars and will become perpetual. No proof is offered for this assumption, although this assumption is decisive in Adler's fundamental dilemma: either world state or no world peace. For if the world state does not make world peace perpetual, then the whole argumentation against systems based upon the existence of several states collapses. These systems cannot ensure "perpetual" peace, but they can ensure peace for some time, and in this would not be different from a world state whose peace also would not be a perpetual one.

The notion of perpetual peace—not as a regulative idea, but as a practicable objective—puts Adler in further trouble. By war he means whatever is not perpetual peace. It does not matter whether this war is an actual or a potential one. The sovereign states can transform potential tensions into actual wars. Only the world state cannot do that—for by definition it cannot wage war against itself. Its existence has ended the international anarchy, *the* cause of war, for, again by definition, anarchy presumes the existence of several independent sovereign states.

This "either-or" between perpetual peace and war is of no help for the understanding of history and of international relations. The term "potential war" covers situations much too varied to be of any use. It hides the necessary distinctions in the same way as the statement that wine, beer and water are liquids fails to settle a dispute about prohibition. Potential war can mean the fact that war remains a possibility—and that, unfortunately, would be true also after the rise of the world state. (I refrain, at this point, from expressing any doubt that this world state will ever come into being.) Potential war can mean many degrees of probability of actual war. But these differences of degrees are of the utmost importance. It is true that, abstractly speaking, all states as sovereign states are potentially at war—or potentially at peace with each other—but these statements are meaningless for the analysis of political situations. According to Adler's views there would be no essential difference between the relations of the United States and England, and the United States and Nazi Germany, before actual war was declared by Hitler in 1941. Adler's definitions are too abstract-static; they are not able to cover the concrete historical situations and their dynamics.

War to Adler is simply a social disease which can be cured, that is abolished, if the conditions of its definition change. War is the systematic use of violence between political groups. Manifestly it will disappear if there is only one organized political group, the world state. Even Kant, who regarded war as something irrational, as a proof of the imperfection of society, raised and tried to answer the question: What were the functions of war in human history? This question does not occur to Adler for whom war is a negative term, the absence of perpetual peace, the result of the non-existence of a world state.

This approach to history from abstract static definitions is not compensated for by remarks about the necessity of taking growth into consideration. These remarks do not remove the error of believing that history can be stopped, or at least, completely rearranged by setting up institutions which, by definition, have perfect effects. Federations, league of nations, etc., by definition do not abolish sovereignty. Therefore, they are rejected by Adler as insufficient though perhaps somewhat useful as transitory means. By definition the world state— a democratic world republic based upon justice—excludes war. Therefore it is proclaimed as a goal, as a practicable objective. Nor does Adler consider how it will maintain itself. Apparently its coming into existence and perpetual character are necessary because they are reasonable.

IV

The fundamental terms—"world peace," "potential war," "anarchy" as the cause of war—are insufficiently analyzed by Adler. But his defenders may object: "His theoretical analysis may be insufficient; perhaps he does not make enough distinctions. But why struggle about definitions? Is his book not full of most useful and wise considerations, on the trends of political and historical developments?" Unfortunately, the fundamental weakness of Dr. Adler's book reappears also in his discussions of probabilities.

After having proclaimed that without the world state no peace is possible, Adler announces that this world state will not rise before our eyes or even before the eyes of Adler's "sons and theirs" to whom the book is dedicated. The world state will come in about five hundred years. Of course, Adler does not mean exactly in 2444. Five hundred years are put down as a figure to express his belief that it will come at some specific, not too remote, time. (For instance, not in fifty thousand years.) The world state is not only a possibility, but a probability, dependent upon the maturation of historical and social trends, upon the advance of education, etc.

This prediction of Adler—a world state not now, but in five hundred years—calls for some remarks on the predictability of events in history. That something is fundamentally wrong in the attitude of Dr. Adler, who claims to know, some centuries ahead, the basic changes that will happen, is shown at once by the question: Was any man of the fifteenth century able to predict the events of the twentieth or even of the eighteenth or seventeenth centuries? According to Adler the knowledge of the past was in previous epochs less developed than in ours, and correspondingly also the capacity to anticipate the future was less developed; therefore I assume a range of predictability for the men of the fifteenth century which was shorter than Adler's five hundred years. Were the men living in the fifteenth century able to predict even in the most general way the rise of absolute monarchies, the Reformation and Counter-Reformation, the influence of the Discoveries, the consequences of the American and French Revolutions? Some general trends can be predicted, and the developments of certain movements, their interior logic, can be anticipated. Several famous examples are: Bossuet's prediction that Protestantism would produce more and more variations and not bring about more or a new religious unity; or Burke's realization—despite all his historical errors—that the abstract spirit of the French revolutionaries would result in a terroristic regime; certain views of Karl Marx—despite all his mistakes in detail and his wrong interpretation of human nature as well as of the aims of social life and history—on imminent contradictions in the Capitalist system and epoch. These predictions of the future can be based either on a knowledge of human nature and therefore the general spiritual and moral trends of human history, or if they are less general but on the other hand more limited, more short-termed, they can be based on the study of concrete historical and social trends, on an insight into the spirit of an epoch or a particular human activity.

But it is impossible to make meaningful predictions (or announcements of probabilities) about the rise of a political institution such as the world state more than fifteen generations ahead. There are so many contingent factors involved as to destroy the possibility of any reasonable forecast. The same may be said not only against Adler's predictions, but even against predictions more sophisticated than such as are based upon the immanent logic of the spirit working in history (Hegelian type) or on attempts to compare civilizations with each other and thereby to find out the degree of progress or decay of the various epochs (Spengler). The vagueness of the prediction about future history increases with the distance in time. It was, e.g., possible to assume that Mussolini's attempt to militarize the Italian nation would end in failure—though of course it was unpredictable that this attempt would be challenged by a serious test of war. But a prediction concerning Italy's status after five hundred years would have to be very general.

There are relations between the duration of human life and the predictability of political, social, and economic changes. Adler overlooks them in assuming that men can be interested in the world order which will exist in five hundred years—whereas he grants that fifty thousand years are too long a time. Insurance companies can build their business on an interest for children and perhaps grandchildren. But what would happen to an insurance company which would promise to pay the insurance in five hundred years? This company would not get many patrons, even if the premiums were extremely low. Everybody would ask: What will happen to the company during the five hundred years and why should I be interested in my heirs living after five hundred years (although, of course, I am interested in the continuation of my family)? Man can be interested in a future directly related to him, or in a future from which he is not separated by a specific number of years. But to suppose his interest for a very definite but at the same time very distant point in the future is an absurdity. Men may be interested in the continuation of their family; they are interested in their sons, their grandsons, but they are surely not interested in their heirs of the fifteenth or twentieth generation.

Adler's prediction of the world state's advent in five hundred years is therefore a purely intellectual construction, not the expression of a belief in a coming world, represented today in the enthusiasm of those who are united and inspired for action by this belief. Its justification—progress from despotism to constitutionalism and democracy, and quantitative increase of the size of states—is a product of a somewhat naïve philosophy of Enlightenment. What was impressive in the formula of Hegel who characterized the epochs of world history by the progress of liberty—first one is free, then some, finally all are free—appears in Adler's book as a glittering generality.

That is the consequence of Adler's mechanical concept of sovereignty. Despite verbal concessions the state for Adler is an exterior unification of individuals. Neither the importance of pre-political groups (though of course Adler quotes Aristotle's description of the various kinds of communities), nor the shaping forces of concrete traditions, historical experiences, and ideals are taken into account. The world state is simply a problem of quantity and education: it swallows up all states and is prepared as well as maintained by a universal education which will destroy all prejudices and sources of difficulties from racialism to economic social injustices. This education will make a citizenship possible which is directly related to the world state and therefore to humanity as such. The individual, subordinating all particular qualities to his pure human nature and liberated from all determination by a specific national or social background, becomes the citizen of the world state.

There is no discussion about how this world state will come into being. Conquest is of course rejected, the world state as a universalized *pax romana* is of course not Adler's world state. Will the world state rise by voluntary unions? But if some states resist? And what will happen if the abstract pure citizenship of the world state is regarded by some only as a masked expression of very concrete particular interests? These questions are not answered by remarks hinting that the world state must not be based upon a common religious belief. Dr. Adler grants that recognition of "the fatherhood of one God is necessary" . . . "for the deepest spiritual brotherhood . . . among all men," and he says: "For the peace of God nothing less than the theological virtue of charity will do" (237). "But," he continues, "justice—political and economic—is sufficient for civil peace." Can this justice be realized as pure abstract justice which disregards the factual conditions, e.g., traditions of communities, religious backgrounds? And why can this justice not be realized in several states? Why only by and in one world state? Can world government not work through different sovereign communities which act, not only for their common good, but at the same time for the common good of the whole world? Adler's demand for the one world state reveals itself as not based upon the requirements for justice, but on the belief that an ultimate decision by one sovereign is required in world affairs, although he tries to combine this attitude with a belief in the inevitable removal of political, economic, and social injustices. These imperfections and prejudices he regards as the only causes for the existence of several states.

V

Adler's book provides an insufficient analysis of its fundamental terms. It is inadequate in describing general trends and making predictions. But perhaps, the admirer of Adler will remark, it offers some help for practical work in behalf of peace in our time, and, after all, that is valuable enough.

Adler really gives some advice about what ought to be done now. Though he rejects internationalism, federations, systems of compulsory arbitrations—as proposed, e.g., by Kelsen—as insufficient because they do not abolish sovereignties, he advises men to do everything that makes new wars at least more remote and moves in the direction of the ultimate aim. On p. 290 ff, he enumerates the conditions required for maintaining peace in our time. They are so vague that most of them can be accepted by Marshall Stalin and the Polish Government in Exile without changing their policies and demands. Only conditions 5 and 6 are somewhat more concrete, for they stress the encouragement and institutions of international agencies such as the League of Nations, World Court, International Office of Education, etc. But condition 1 is typical of the character of the first four: "That they [powers] commit no political or economic injustice by way of inequitable distributions or unfair discriminations."

Not more precise are the actions which are proposed on p. 292. There he says: "Every citizen who has a voice in the matter (in any country where men are citizens) should support a settlement of this war which tends to facilitate, not merely the postponement of the next war, but the advent of peace. He should oppose any arrangements by treaty or alliance which, through their intrinsic injustice, impede the world's progress toward peace." I would not mention these general statements—which are as excellent as they are vague—if they did not contradict other fundamental theses of the book. On the one hand, Dr. Adler opposes all solutions which do not bring about the world state and therefore the possibility of world peace, and on the other hand he offers for today the same program as the "internationalists," as those who regard perpetual peace as a "regulative idea." How does he know that the new coming war period will result in a situation closer to world government, to his own world state? First he undermines the belief in the appropriate character of the proceedings which he then advocates. Kelsen is much more reasonable, for he too believes in the necessity of a world state, but realizing that this world state is not rising now, he centers his book, *Law and Peace,* around the recommendation of obligatory arbitration and judicial settlement of international disputes.

Adler's expectation of continual war in our time and a world peace possible in five hundred years makes his book really dangerous, at least for those who want to promote peace in our time. Adler's prognosis will, if taken seriously, provoke on the one hand despair and, on the other, indifference. Some will despair because war cannot be avoided except by the world state which can come only fifteen generations after us. Others will believe that everything is permitted today because the far distant future is bright anyhow and the present necessarily dark. Adler's long-term optimism and his short-term pessimism illustrate the connection between a perfectionism without responsibility for what is going on in our actual imperfect world and a cynicism which results from despair about the impossibility of being perfect now.

Adler's book is satisfactory neither for the philosopher nor for the man interested in the question: What can be done today? It is the result of a lack of patience, of a looking for perfect solutions which are apparently deductions from self-evident definitions, and of an intellectualism less interested in the complex and many-sided realities than in the imposition of its concepts. It is not the product of hard thinking, as some claim, but of a thinking which only appears as hard, of a thinking dominated by a will to power—by presenting bold constructions—but surely not by love of its objects. It is no accident that Dr. Adler claims calmly that for sixteen hundred years nobody has asked for perpetual peace and that the various peace proposals were all insufficient. He does not even suspect that his apparently bold originality may be the result of certain assumptions which he accepts without any attempt to analyze them. It is also not by chance that he is unable to understand positions which are not in agreement with his thesis. The papal peace program is rejected as insufficient because it is not based upon Adler's assumption that the world state is the necessary instrument for world peace. Adler does not ask the question: Why do the Popes not demand a world state? What is the difference between their concept of peace and the perpetual peace here on earth?

A book, written with such pretensions as *How to Think about War and Peace*, must be analyzed in the most direct way. Adler is an honest thinker, as he has proved in his public correction of the mistakes in his book on the *Problem of Species.* Also, in the preface of this new book he confesses his failure "as a teacher to give the fundamental insights which should be every one's possession" (xix).

If he agrees with these critical remarks—and they could be supplemented by much detailed discussion—he will, I am certain, correct his book which, in its present form, does not *really* help its readers to think about peace and war.

Notes

Reprinted from *The Review of Politics* 6, no. 2 (April 1944): 228–38.

1. Mortimer J. Adler, *How to Think about War and Peace* (New York: Simon and Schuster, 1944). Cf. also Adler's lecture "War and the Rule of Law" in *War and the Law,* ed. Ernst W. Puttkammer (University of Chicago Press, 1944).

2. About this discussion cf. *The Review of Politics* 1, no. 4 (October 1939), 371 ff.

3. He says in his lecture "peace will not be made at the end of this war. . . . That means another war at a not too distant future" (Adler, "War and the Rule of Law," 198).

4. Ibid., 196. He has also said, "It is true to say that military conquest does reduce the extent of anarchy in the world."

CHAPTER 4

Imperialism, Nationalism, Chauvinism

HANNAH ARENDT

I would annex the planets if I could!
—Cecil Rhodes

I. THE INNER CONTRADICTION BETWEEN THE NATIONAL AND THE IMPERIAL PRINCIPLES

"Expansion is everything," said Cecil Rhodes and fell into despair; for he saw every night overhead "vast worlds which we can never reach," part of the universe to which he could not expand.[1] He had discovered the moving principle of the new, the imperialist era; and yet, at the same moment, he recognized in a flash of wisdom its inherent insanity and contradiction of human conditions. Naturally, neither insight nor sadness prevented him from expanding. He had no use for his flash of wisdom that had led him far beyond his normal capacities which were those of an ambitious businessman with a marked tendency towards megalomania.

"World politics is for a nation what megalomania is for a single person," said Eugen Richter (leader of the German progressive party) at about the same historical moment.[2] But he gained a Pyrrhic victory when, through his opposition in the Reichstag, Bismarck's proposal to support private companies in the foundation of trading and maritime stations suffered defeat. It seemed as though national politicians and statesmen—like Eugen Richter in Germany, or Gladstone in England, or Clemenceau in France—had lost touch with reality and did not realize that trade and economics had already involved every nation in world politics. The national principle had led into provincial ignorance, and the battle fought by sanity was lost. Business men who never before had been much interested in politics, reasonably satisfied as they were with the police function of the National State which guaranteed them protection of their property, decided that their new, expanding affairs were no longer sufficiently safeguarded and that they had to go into politics for business' sake. They earnestly believed that "patriotism in overseas possession is best carried out through "money-making" (Huebbe-Schleiden), that the national flag is a "commercial asset" (Rhodes) and they did their best to win the national representatives as business-partners.

Even worse than corruption was the fact that the incorruptible became convinced that world politics was a working reality and not the megalomaniac product of imperialism. Since maritime stations and access to raw materials were a necessity for all nations, they ended by secretly believing that annexation and expansion as such had to be aimed at for the sake of the nation. They were the first not to understand the fundamental difference between the old foundation of trade and maritime stations for trade's sake and the new policy of annexation and domination.[3] They believed Cecil Rhodes when he told them to "wake up to the fact that you cannot live unless you have the trade of the world," "that your trade is the world, and your life is the world, and not England," and that this is why they "must deal with these questions of expansion and retention of the world."[4] Without willing it, sometimes even without knowing it, they became not only the accomplices of imperialist politics, but were the first to be blamed and exposed for their "imperialism." Such was the case of Clemenceau who, in his desperate worry about the future of the French nation, turned "imperialist" because he hoped that colonial manpower would protect French citizens against aggression. When, at the Peace table in 1918, during one of those short spells of anti-imperialist eruptions of public opinion, he insisted that he did not care about anything as long as he could draft in French colonies and mobilize the "force noire" for the protection of France,[5] he mobilized public opinion against the "imperialistic schemes" of the only great European people that did not have any. Compared to this blind nationalism in its last desperate stage, British imperialists, compromising on the Mandate system, looked like the guardians of the self-determination of peoples, even though they at once misused it through the concept of "indirect rule" by which the British administrator governed "the people . . . not directly but through the medium of their own tribal and local authorities."[6]

By adopting imperialist methods of domination Clemenceau has not saved, as we now fully realize, the French nation from German aggression, although his plan was followed up and carried out by the French General Staff. Poincaré's famous phrases of 1923, "France is not a country of forty millions; she is a country of one hundred millions," became the watchword of French nationalists and has been recently repeated by General De Gaulle. This imperialism for the sake of the nation has changed fundamentally the very foundations of French rule over conquered peoples and dealt, unknowingly, a deadly blow to what might have become a French Empire. For the French, in contrast to all other European nations, actually have tried in our times to build an Empire in the old Roman sense, to combine *ius* with *imperium.* They alone have attempted to develop the body politic of the nation itself into an imperial political structure. They did not leave the care of overseas possessions to the expanding affairs of businessmen, but conceived them as the result of "the French nation marching . . . to spread the benefits of French civilization;" they tried to incorporate the conquered peoples into the national body by treating them as "both . . . brothers and . . . subjects-brothers in the fraternity of a common French civilization, and subjects that they are disciples of French light and followers of French leading."[7] This was the reason for giving colored delegates seats in the French Parliament and of incorporating conquered Algeria into the mother country. That all these attempts were finally defeated and that France appears today as an imperialist power like others is partly due to the European population in the colonies, the so-called French colonials, who were not Empire-builders but a multinational clique of businessmen with imperialist ambitions, and partly to those nationalists in France herself who considered the colonies as lands of soldiers and their populations as "a really economical form of gunfodder, turned out by mass-production methods."[8]

Imperialism is not empire-building and expansion is not conquest. The imperial passion, old as history, time and again has spread culture and law to the four corners of the world. The conqueror either wanted nothing but spoils and would leave the country after the looting; or he wanted to stay permanently and would then incorporate the conquered territory into the body politic and gradually assimilate the conquered population to the standard of the mother country. This type of conquest has led to all kinds of political structures—to empires in the more distant and to nations in the more recent past. At any rate, conquest was but the first step toward preparing a more permanent political structure.

Conquest as well as empire-building, has fallen into disrepute during the last century for very good reasons. The new concept of the nation, born out of the French Revolution, was based upon the sovereignty of the people and its active consent to the government (*le plebiscite de tous les jours*) and it presupposed the existence of an indefinite number of equally sovereign national organizations. This meant in practical politics that wherever the nation appeared as conqueror, it aroused national consciousness as well as desire for sovereignty among the conquered peoples, thereby defeating all genuine attempts at empire-building. The British "empire-builders" never succeeded in including their nearest neighbor, the Irish people, in the far-flung structure of either the British Empire or the British Commonwealth of Nations. The "empire-builders" put their trust in conquest as a permanent method of rule—and failed miserably; but when after the last war Ireland was granted dominion-status and welcomed as a full-fledged member into the British Commonwealth, it ended with a new though less palpable failure. The oldest British "possession" and the newest British dominion unilaterally denounced its dominion status (in 1937), and severed all ties with the English nation by not participating in the war. The rule of permanent conquest since it "simply failed to destroy her"[9] had not so much aroused "the slumbering genius of imperialism"[10] of the English nation as it had awakened the national resistance of the Irish. The national structure of the United Kingdom had made impossible quick assimilation and incorporation of the conquered people; the British Commonwealth never was a "Commonwealth of Nations" but the heir of the United Kingdom and the political body of one nation dispersed throughout the world; it was not, as can be seen by the Irish example, an imperial structure in whose framework many and different peoples could live together and be contented.[11] This inner contradiction between the body politic of the nation and conquest as a political device has been obvious ever since the grandiose failure of the Napoleonic dream. It is due to this experience rather than to mere humanitarian considerations that conquest since that time has been officially condemned and has played but a minor role in the adjustment of borderline conflicts.

The British have tried to escape this dangerous inconsistency of modern attempts at imperial rule by leaving the conquered peoples to their own devices as far as culture, religion, and law were concerned, by staying aloof and by desisting from spreading British law and culture. This has hardly prevented the natives from developing national consciousness and clamoring for sovereignty and independence—though it might have retarded the process somewhat. It has, on the other side, tremendously strengthened the new imperialist consciousness of a fundamental, and not only temporary, superiority of man over man. This, in turn, has embittered the fight for freedom of the subject peoples and blinded them to the unquestionable benefits of British rule. From the very aloofness of their administrators who "despite their genuine respect for the natives as a people, and in some cases even their love for them, . . . almost to a man, do not believe that they are or ever will be capable of governing themselves without supervision,"[12] they cannot help concluding that they are to be excluded and separated from the rest of mankind forever. Although the British attempt at combining a national body at home with an empire abroad did not have the desired consequences of stabilizing the imperial structure, it had serious consequences for the political structure of the mother country. For empire's sake, they had to keep King and House of Lords, both of which are in contradiction to the free development of national sovereignty but desperately needed for the rule over subject peoples to whom one could not give the status of citizens. The result was that those who first of all were entitled to be British citizens had to remain British subjects. The final outcome of all these compromises and clever devices was imperialism.

Imperialism cannot even be granted the extenuating circumstances of being a mixture of conquest and empire-building, although it occasionally falls back to the old methods of the former and always boasts of the grandeur of the latter. The old "breakers of law in India" (Burke) were pirates and conquerors of the looting type whom the Indian peoples had reasonable hope to see leave some day. If they had changed into makers of law, they might have become empire-builders; but the English nation was not interested in this and would hardly have supported them. As it was, they were followed by an unending series of administrators all of whom wanted "the African to be left an African," although a few, who had not yet outgrown what Harold Nicholson once called their "boyhood-ideals,"[13] wanted to aid them to "become a better African"[14]—

whatever that may mean. In any case, they were not "disposed to apply the administrative and political system of their own country to the government of backward populations,"[15] and failed consequently to tie the far-flung possessions of the British Crown to the English nation. In contrast to true imperial structures where the institutions of the mother country are in various ways integrated into the empire as a whole, it is characteristic of imperialism that national institutions remain separated from the colonial administration although in its initial stages they are allowed to exercise some control over it. It is to the salutary restraining of these institutions that we owe those benefits which, after all and despite everything, the non-European peoples have been able to derive from Western domination. But the colonial services themselves have never ceased to protest against the interference of the "unexperienced majority," namely the nation, that tries to press "the experienced minority," namely the imperialists, "in the direction of imitation," governing in accordance with the general standards of justice and liberty at home.[16]

Here lies, incidentally, one of the many unhappy misunderstandings which still bar the way to adequate insight into the phenomenon of imperialism. The conscience of the nation, represented in parliament and free press, was equally represented by the colonial administrations of all European countries—be they England or France or Belgium or Germany. In England, however, in order to distinguish between the imperial government seated in London, and controlled by parliament, and local administrators or the white local population, this influence was called the "imperial factor," thereby crediting imperialism with those merits and remnants of justice which it eagerly tried to eliminate.[17] The political expression of the "imperial factor" in England was the concept that the natives are not only protected but in a way represented by the British, the Imperial Parliament.[18] Here, the English come very close to the French experiment of empire-building, although they never went as far as giving actual representation to subject peoples. Nevertheless, they obviously hoped that the nation as a whole could act as their trustee, and it is true that it invariably has tried its best to prevent the worst.

The imperial factor, therefore, should rightly be called the national factor in British imperialism; a factor which invariably came into conflict with the imperialists. The prayer which Cromer addressed to Lord Salisbury during his administration of Egypt in 1896: "Save me from the English Departments"[19] has been repeated over and over again until in the twenties of our century the nation and everything it stood for was openly blamed by the extreme imperialist party for the possible loss of India. The reason: the government of India that "knew well enough that it would have to justify its existence and its policy before public opinion in England" felt itself not free to proceed to those measures of "administrative massacre"[20] which had been tried out immediately after the close of the last war in the form of "punitive forces" as a radical means of pacification.[21] The same conflict between the national and the imperialist factor was characteristic of French rule. The Governor Generals appointed by the French Government in Paris were either subject to powerful pressure of French colonials as in Algeria, or they simply refused to carry out reforms in the treatment of natives, inspired as they were, by "the weak democratic principles of my Government," in the words of the former associate of Pétain, the Governor General of Madagascar, Leon Cayla. Everywhere, imperialist administrators felt that the control of the nation was an unbearable burden and an open threat to domination.[22]

And in this, the imperialists are perfectly right and know the conditions of modern rule over subject peoples better than those who, on the one side, protest against government by decree and arbitrary bureaucracy and, on the other, hope to retain their possessions forever for the greater glory of the nation. Paradoxically the imperialists know that the body politic of the nation is not capable of empire-building. They are perfectly aware of the fact that the march of the nation and its conquest of peoples, if it is allowed to follow its own inherent law, ends with these peoples rising to nationhood themselves and defeating the conqueror. The French methods, therefore, which always tried to combine national aspirations with empire-building have been much less successful than the English methods which, since the eighties of the last century, have been outright imperialistic, although restrained by the mother country that had retained its national democratic institutions.

II. IMPERIALISM AND THE DISINTEGRATION OF THE NATIONAL BODY

When imperialism entered the scene of politics during the scramble for Africa in the eighties of the last century, it was propagated by businessmen, opposed fiercely by those who were in power and welcomed by a surprisingly large section of the educated classes. To the latter it appeared as a God-sent life-saver, as a panacea for all evils, as an easy way out of all conflicts. And it is true that imperialism in a sense has not gone back on these promises; it has given a new lease of life to political and social structures which were even then quite obviously undermined by new social and political forces and which, under other circumstances, even without the interference of imperialist developments, it would hardly have needed two world wars to destroy. As it was, it conjured away all troubles and produced that deceptive feeling of security, so universal in pre-war Europe, from which only the most sensitive minds escaped, like Péguy in France or Chesterton in England, who knew by instinct that they lived in a world of hollow pretenses and that stability was the worst pretense of all, and who could only marvel at the miracle of longevity. The solution of the riddle was imperialism and the answer to the fateful question why the European comity of nations allowed this evil to spread until everything was destroyed, the good as well as the bad, is that all governments knew well enough that their countries were in a secret state of disintegration, that the body politic was being destroyed from within, and that they lived on borrowed time.

Innocently enough, expansion appeared first as the panacea for the evil of excess capital production and offered its remedy of capital export.[23] The tremendously increased wealth produced by capitalistic production under a social system based on maldistribution had resulted in "oversaving," that is, in the accumulation of capital that, within the framework of the existing national capacity for production and consumption, was condemned to idleness. This money actually was superfluous, needed by nobody though owned by a growing class of somebodies. In the decade which preceded imperialism, the owners of this superfluous wealth had first tried the way of foreign investments without expansion and without political control. This had brought about an unparalleled orgy of swindles, financial scandals, speculation, and gambling in the stock-markets. Big money resulting from oversaving showed the way and became the pioneer for little money, the result of the little fellow's hard work. Domestic enterprises, in order to keep pace with the high profits of foreign investments, turned likewise to fraudulent methods and attracted an ever-growing number of people who in the hope of miraculous returns threw their money out the window. The Panama scandal in France, the *Gruendungsschwindel* in Germany were classical examples. Tremendous losses resulted from the promises of tremendous profits. The owners of little money lost on such a scale and at such a tempo that the owners of superfluous big capital soon saw themselves left alone in the field which, in a sense, was a battlefield. After having failed to transform the whole of society into a community of gamblers, they were again superfluous, excluded from the normal process of production to which, after some turmoil, all other classes returned quietly though somewhat impoverished and embittered.[24]

Export of money, foreign investment as such is not imperialism and does not necessarily lead to expansion as a political device. As long as the owners of superfluous capital were content with staking "large portions of their property in foreign lands" and although this tendency already ran "counter to all past traditions of nationalism,"[25] they would only have confirmed their alienation from the national body in which they led the existence of parasites. Only when they appealed for government protection of their investments after the initial stage of gambling had opened their eyes to the possible use of politics, did they re-enter the political life of the nation. In this appeal, however, they followed the established tradition of bourgeois society that since its beginnings had wanted to use political institutions exclusively for the protection of property. It was the first class in history whose origin, as well as ultimate aim, was ownership as such and that so far had been satisfied with being the dominant class of society without aspiring to direct rule. Through the fortunate coincidence of the rise of this class of property-holders and the industrial revolution, the former had been transformed into producers and stimulators of production. As long as they fulfilled this basic function of modern society which essentially is a community of producers, their wealth had an eminently important function for the nation as a whole. The owners of superfluous capital were the first section of the class that no longer profiteered from some real social function—even though it be the function of an exploiting employer—and whom consequently no police in the long run would have been able to save from the wrath of the people. For this wrath rarely strikes those who derive their power from some necessary activity. It is not aroused by mere abuses, but it becomes violent and implacable as soon as profiteering fulfills no function at all, even though the profiteers may have lost all real power and exploit nobody.[26] Expansion then was not only escape for the superfluous capital itself, but still more for its owners from the menacing prospect of remaining entirely superfluous and parasitical. It saved the bourgeoisie from the consequences of maldistribution and gave a new lease of life to its ownership concept that only now, when wealth could no longer be used as a factor of production within the national framework, had come into conflict with the production ideal of the community as a whole.

Older than the superfluous wealth was another by-product of capitalist production. This was the human debris that every crisis, following invariably upon each period of industrial growth, would permanently eliminate from producing society, who would become permanently idle and as superfluous for the community as the owners of superfluous wealth. That they were an actual menace to society had been recognized for decades and their export had helped to populate the dominions of Canada and Australia as well as the United States. The new fact of the imperialist era is that these two superfluous groups, the owners of superfluous capital and the owners of superfluous working power, joined hands and left the country together. The concept of expansion, of exporting government power and of annexation of every territory in which nationals had invested either their wealth or their work seemed the only alternative to increasing losses of wealth and population. Imperialism with its idea of an unlimited expansion seemed to offer a never-ending remedy to an increasing and never-ending evil.[27]

Ironically enough, the first country where superfluous wealth and superfluous men were brought together was itself in a position in which only a miracle could save it. South Africa had been in British possession since the beginning of the century because it assured the maritime road to India. The opening of the Suez-canal, however, and the following administrative conquest of Egypt left the old trade station of the Cape without any greater importance. The British would, in all probability, have withdrawn from Africa as, before them, all European nations had withdrawn whenever their possessions and trade interests in India were liquidated. "As late as 1884 the British Government had still been willing to diminish its authority and influence in South Africa."[28] If any spot of the earth was threatened with becoming superfluous then, it was certainly South Africa.

The second ironical (and almost symbolical) fact about the unexpected development of South Africa into "the culture-bed of Imperialism"[29] lies in the very nature of its sudden attractiveness after it had lost all value for the Empire proper. In the seventies, diamond fields had been discovered and the eighties brought about the discovery of large gold mines. Gold became the god for the owners of superfluous wealth as well as for the superfluous men who came from the four corners of the earth;[30] preventing, with Government support, the development of all industries for the production of consumer goods,[31] they established the first paradise of parasites whose lifeblood is gold.[32] Imperialism, the result of superfluous money and superfluous men, began its startling career by producing the most superfluous and the most unreal goods.

It may still be doubtful whether the panacea of expansion would have been so great a temptation for national statesmen as it actually became, if it had offered its dangerous solutions only for those superfluous forces which, in any case, were already outside the pale of the body corporate of the nation. The curious weakness of national opposition to imperialism, the numerous inconsistencies and outright broken promises which were so characteristic of the behavior-patterns of modern national politics and which frequently have been ascribed to either opportunism or bribery[33] have another and deeper motive. They sprang from the conviction that the national body itself was so deeply split into classes, that class-struggle was so universal a symptom of modern political life, that the very cohesion of the nation was utterly jeopardized. Expansion again appeared as a lifesaver if and insofar as it could deliver a common stake to the nation as a whole, and it is mainly for this reason that imperialists were allowed to become "parasites upon patriotism."[34]

Partly, of course, such hopes belong to the old vicious devices which try to overcome domestic conflicts by foreign adventures and conquests. The difference, however, is marked. Adventures in politics are by their very nature limited in time and space; they may succeed in overcoming conflicts temporarily, although as a rule they would even fail in that and rather tend to sharpen them. The imperialist adventure of expansion appeared from the very beginning as an eternal solution, because expansion was conceived as unlimited. Furthermore, imperialism did not even appear as an adventure in the usual sense, because it based itself less on nationalist slogans than on the seemingly solid basis of economic interests. Within a society of clashing interests in which the common good had been identified with the common interest, expansion as such appeared to be a possible common interest of the nation as a whole. Since everybody had been convinced by the owning and dominant classes that economic interest and the passion for ownership are the sound basis for the body politic, national statesmen were only too easily persuaded to yield when a common economic interest appeared on the horizon of possibilities.

These then are the reasons why nationalism developed so clear a tendency towards imperialism, the inner contradiction of the two principles notwithstanding. From the very beginning of the new movement and in all countries alike, imperialists would preach (and boast) of their being "beyond the parties," and claim to be the only ones to speak for the nation as a whole. This language would attract and delude precisely those persons who still had some kind of political idealism left and some feeling for patriotism. The cry for unity resembled precisely the battlecries with which peoples always had been led to war; and yet, nobody detected in the universal and permanent instrument of unity the germ of universal and permanent war.[35]

The group which engaged most actively in the nationalist brand of imperialism and contributed most efficiently to the businessman's confusion of imperialism with nationalism, were the government officials. The national state has created, its functioning depending upon them, the civil services as a permanent body of officials who serve regardless of classes and regardless of government changes. Their professional honor and their self respect—especially in England and Germany—derived from their being servants of the nation as a whole. They constituted the only class that had a direct interest in supporting the fundamental claim of the State to independence from classes and factions. That the authority of the national state itself depends to a large degree on the economic independence and political neutrality of its civil servants has become obvious in recent times when the decline of nations invariably started with the corruption of its permanent servants and with the general conviction that these were in the pay—not of the state—but of the owning classes. At the close of the century, the owning classes had become dominant to a point where it was almost ridiculous for a state-employee to keep up the pretense of serving the nation. The disintegration into classes had left them somehow outside the social body and had forced them into forming a clique of their own. In the colonial services, they escaped the actual disintegration of the national body. In ruling foreign peoples in far-away countries, they could much better feel themselves to be heroic servants of the nation, as those "who by their services had glorified the British race,"[36] than if they had stayed at home. The colonies were no longer simply "a vast system of outdoor relief for the upper classes" as James Mill still could correctly describe them; they were to become the very backbone of British nationalism which found in the domination of far countries and the rule over strange peoples the only way to serve British and nothing but British interests. The services actually believed that "the peculiar genius of each nation shows itself nowhere more clearly than in their system of dealing with subject races."[37]

The point is that only far from England or Germany or France, a national of these countries could be nothing but an Englishman or German or Frenchman. Within his own country he was so entangled in economic interests or social loyalties that he felt actually closer to a member of his class in a foreign country than to a man of another class in his own. Expansion gave nationalism a new lease on life and therefore was accepted as an instrument of national politics. This shows in how desperate a state the European countries found themselves before the start of imperialism; how fragile their institutions had become; how outdated their social system proved in the face of the growing capacity of man to produce. The means for preservation were desperate too; and in the end, the remedy has proved worse than the evil which, incidentally, it did not cure.

III. CHAUVINISM AND THE BRIDGE BETWEEN NATIONALISM AND IMPERIALISM

Imperialism carries out the decline of the nation. The more ill-fitted nations are for the incorporation of foreign peoples (which contradicts the constitution of their own body politic), all the more are they tempted to oppress them. In theory, there is an abyss between nationalism and imperialism; in practice, it can and has been bridged. Ideologically speaking, the bridge between them is called chauvinism.

In contrast to imperialism, chauvinism is an almost natural product of the national concept insofar as it springs directly from the old idea of the "national mission." It has a logical affinity with expansion because a nation's mission might be interpreted precisely as bringing its light to other, less fortunate peoples that, for whatever reasons, have miraculously been left by history without a national mission. As long, however, as this concept did not develop into the ideology of chauvinism and remained in the rather vague realm of national or even nationalistic pride, it frequently resulted in a high sense of responsibility for the welfare of backward peoples. It produced that type of men whom one could find scattered in all the colonial services, particularly the British, who would take a fatherly interest in the peoples they were ordered to rule and who would easily assume the role of the dragonslayer, thereby fulfilling in a manly fashion the gallant ideals and dreams of their boyhood.[38]

The trouble with the "national mission" is that it implies a holy mission, that it presupposes a kind of divine origin of the people and that it claims "chosenness." Since, by its very definition, national divine election can be granted only to one people, this concept destroys the idea of the unity of mankind which, based on the divine origin of man, is inconsistent with any doctrine of the divine origin of peoples.[39] Whether the existence of peoples is explained through natural influences (Herder) or whether they are considered the product of political organization as in the best French tradition, under no circumstances should they be regarded as of divine origin. For only as long as peoples are recognized to be the product of Man, can man remain the creation of God. Any claim to divine mission—be it the German "*Wesen an dem die Welt genesen soll*," or the British "white man's burden," or "*la mission de la France éternelle*" or Polish Messianism—automatically makes the members of one people superhuman, and the members of all others subhuman.

Chauvinism has been latent in nationalism ever since its conscious beginnings at the end of the eighteenth century. For a long time, however, it was hardly allowed to influence practical politics and led a kind of innocent dream existence in the minds of romantic intellectuals, precisely because its trend towards expansion of the nation was in itself a hopeless affair. Up to the era of imperialism, chauvinist schemes would be judged and condemned for their lack of realism. When Eugen Richter denounced world politics as megalomania, he spoke up against this absence of common sense, of balance, of moderation which had so far been characteristic of chauvinist devices only.

Chauvinism, however, marked the nationalism of all imperialists from the beginning. This has much to do with the fact that the superfluous classes, which in one way or another were alienated from the normal destinies of their countrymen, would discover their national feelings far away from the motherland where the simple fact of being the citizen of a European country assumed an importance that it had held nowhere else. It was not only Cecil Rhodes who detected what a "rare and lovely virtue" it was to be born an Englishman,[40] and it was not only Carl Peters who left his country and went to Africa for the outspoken purpose of becoming a member of a "master-race."[41] Chauvinism was the result of experiences that had severed the national consciousness from the national soil, that had alienated nationalism from the country where the nation happened to live, that had shifted pride and loyalty of nationals from the visible achievements embodied in the whole of the national world and represented by its material as well as its spiritual aspects, to the qualities of the "soul" which every member through the accident of birth shared with every other member of the same people. This made possible the degrading identification of love for one's own self and love for one's nation. In the words of one of the last representatives of this chauvinist brand of imperialism, "Soul means race as seen from within, whereas race is the exterior of the soul."[42] In other words, not Germany, or France, or England was the center of their pride and loyalty, but rather they themselves. Cecil Rhodes, convinced that he came from "the first race in the world," saw himself as the incarnation of Saxondom and expected to be remembered at least four thousand years,[43] whereas the much less lucky Carl Peters, after being dismissed from the German colonial services for excessive cruelty, propagated among his countrymen the development of Germandom to a "national race" whose incarnation he felt himself to be.[44]

This inherent arrogance of all chauvinists who would think of themselves—not as Germans, or Englishmen, or Frenchmen—but as *the* German, *the* Englishman, *the* Frenchman, made them not only prone to criticize their countries and countrymen according to the single yardstick of what this country and these countrymen owe to them, but formed the psychological basis for that stress of the "personal element" in colonial administration which characterized imperialists from the beginning and has later been transformed into (or hidden by) the regime of experts.[45] Each of these administrators, once shipped abroad for domination purposes, condemned to the "artificial life (of a superior caste) removed from all the healthy restraint of ordinary European society,"[46] could feel himself so much the incarnation of all his country's possible virtues as in an emergency this country's might would be compelled to back anything he personally stood for—his best or his worst, his beneficence as well as his malfeasance.

Chauvinism in countries with overseas possessions would be essentially a severance of national sentiments from the national territory, but not from the state (in whose services more often than not the imperialists could be found). Chauvinism in those countries that aspired to continental empires and had no or only small overseas holdings was characterized by severance of national loyalty from the state. This was the case in the so-called pan-movements—in pan-Germanism as well as pan-Slavism—both of which originated in nationality-states where the State was not even supposed to represent the sovereignty of the people but appeared as a supra-national bureaucratic machinery whose authority was vested in the ruling houses. The oppressed peoples of Austria-Hungary became chauvinistic before they were given a chance to achieve nationhood, because the cautiously administered minimum of national freedom given to the nationalities amounted to nothing more and nothing better than the oppression of other nationalities. Over the exploitation of Czechs by Germans, of Slovaks by Hungarians, of Ruthenians by Poles rose the structure of the supra-national state—as the supra-social state of the homogeneous nations was supposed to rise over the fissures of class-struggle.

Since the dynasty put dynastic interests above all others, none of the numerous nationalities, not even the dominant ones, like the Germans and Hungarians, could feel represented by it. Furthermore, in this area of Europe where every spot is a place of mixed populations, the lack of political representation could not be compensated for through love of a homogeneously populated territory. Most of these peoples had never succeeded in striking such deep roots in their soil as those of Western Europe. Nationality, therefore, was already diverted from territory to a certain degree when it cut loose from the state absolutely and became a value in itself. The fact of being born a German, a Czech, or a Slovak took the place of all other loyalties normal in the development of national states. Used to living among other nationalities and in constant competitive struggle with them, their national consciousness itself would awake with the stressing of personal virtues rather than past or present common achievements which no body politic could adequately represent and for which no living community could give adequate testimony.[47]

This chauvinism, widespread among the nationalities in Austria-Hungary, took the most dangerous and aggressive forms in those two that had fellow-nationals beyond the borderlines of the country—the Germans and the Slavs.[48] They became adherents of expansion—not of their own countries but of the neighboring ones, Germany or Russia, that would bring them national re-demption as a gift.[49] Used to national oppression, they were as willing to rec-ognize the "mastership" of the big brother[50] and to bow under his superiority as they were prepared to achieve nationhood at the expense of others and to assume rule over weaker nationalities lacking the good fortune of a big brother beyond the borderline. Their nationalism, in other words, was chauvinistic from the very beginning and stimulated by dreams of oppression.[51] Living in territories where frontiers were not time-honored but had changed numer-ous times, their dreams of expansion were unlimited although clashing with one another.[52] These Slavs and these Germans were the first Europeans who *en masse* and not in small groups became chauvinistic.

The secret of the success of the pan-movements from which modern racial imperialism has inherited more than from any other form of imperialism or chauvinism,[53] lies in the solid mass-basis of people. Within the double monar-chy the people were already organized in a body corporate that as a rule could be realized only after the destruction of the national body. Chauvinism, cre-ated by the dissolution of the old trinity of people—territory—state was the natural though perverted form of their national feelings. Here were masses at hand who had not the slightest idea of the meaning of *patria,* not the vaguest notion of the responsibility of a common limited community and no experi-ence of political freedom. They indeed were ready for adventure and ripe for imperialist expansion. The chauvinist state of mind of the German minori-ties, scattered as they were all over Europe, was one of the main reasons that German imperialism chose the continental way of expansion rather than the way of colonial acquisitions.[54] The "Germans abroad" were not only easy stepping-stones for further expansion, they generated not only a comfortable smoke-screen of the right to national self-determination, but they also pro-vided the very models for organization at home.

Chauvinism may be the condition of continental or the result of overseas imperialism. It is, at any rate, the only ism that prepares the nation or the people for expansion, induces it into that great adventure which essentially is beyond the possibilities of a national body politic and lures it, under the pretext of empire-building, into the ruin of imperialism. For the only limit in space of permanent expansion is destruction and its only limit in time is death.

NOTES

Reprinted from *The Review of Politics* 7, no. 4 (October 1945): 441–63.

1. S. Gertrude Millin, *Rhodes* (London, 1933), 138. The whole quotation reads as follows: "These stars that you see overhead at night, these vast worlds which we can never reach! I would annex the planets if I could. I often think of that. It makes me sad to see them so clear and yet so far away."

2. Ernst Hasse, *Deutsche Weltpolitik*, Flugschriften des Alldeutschen Verbandes, no. 5 (1897), 1.

3. Within the British Empire, we have to distinguish between the Maritime and Military Stations such as the Cape of Good Hope during the nineteenth century, the Settlements or Plantations such as Australia and the other dominions and the colonial Empire proper such as it was acquired after 1884, when the era of expansion began. Not only were, during the following decades, vast stretches of new territories and many millions of people added to the older colonial possessions that had been acquired through "fits of absentmindedness" or through "incidents of trade"; but these possessions themselves, such as British India, received a new political significance and a new kind of government.

4. Millin, *Rhodes*, 175.

5. Cf. David Lloyd George, *Memoirs of the Peace Conference*, vol. 1 (Yale, 1939), 362 ff. "M. Clemenceau seemed in his speech to demand an unlimited right of levying black troops to assist in the defense of French territory in Europe if France were attacked in the future by Germany. . . . M. Clemenceau said that if he could raise troops, that was all he wanted."

6. Ernest Barker, *Ideas and Ideals of the British Empire* (Cambridge, 1941), 69.

7. Ibid., 4. Cf. also the very good introductory remarks on the foundations of the French Empire in *The French Colonial Empire*, Information Department Papers, no. 25 (London: Royal Institute of International Affairs, 1941), 9 ff: "The aim is to assimilate colonial peoples to the French people, or, where this is not possible in more primitive communities, to "associate" them, so that more and more the difference between la France metropole and la France d'outremer shall be a geographical difference and not a fundamental one."

8. See W. P. Crozier, "France and Her 'Black Empire,'" *New Republic*, January 23, 1924. A similar attempt at brutal exploitation of overseas possessions for the sake of the nation had been made by the Netherlands in the Dutch East Indies after the defeat of Napoleon had restored the Dutch colonies to the much impoverished mother country. By means of compulsory cultivation, the natives were reduced to slavery for the benefit of the Government in Holland. Multatuli's "Max Havelaar," first published in the sixties of the last century, was aimed at the Government at home and not at the services abroad. (See De Kat Angelino, *Colonial Policy*, vol. 2, *The Dutch East Indies* [Chicago, 1931].) This system was quickly abandoned and Netherland Indies, in a sense, has become "the admiration of all colonizing nations." (See Sir Hesketh Bell, *Foreign Colonial Administration in the Far East* [1928], pt. 1.) The Dutch system has many similarities with the French brand of imperialism: the grant of European status to deserving natives, introduction of a European school system, etc., and has achieved the same though less violent result: a strong national movement among the subject people.

In the present article we shall ignore both Dutch and Belgian imperialism. The first is a curious and changing mixture of French and English methods; in our context it is atypical because the Netherlands did not expand during the eighties, but only consolidated and modernized its old possessions. Belgium, on the other hand, would offer too unfair an example. Her expansion was first of all the expansion of her King personally, unchecked by any government or other control. The story of the Belgian Congo is sufficiently well known, but in its unequalled atrocity likewise atypical for the initial stages of imperialism.

9. See G. K. Chesterton, *The Crimes of England* (1915), 57 ff.

10. As Lord Salisbury put it, rejoicing over the defeat of Gladstone's first Home Rule Bill. During the following twenty years of Conservative—and that was at that time Imperialist—policy (1885–1905), the English-Irish conflict was not only not solved but became much more acute.

11. For the historian, it still is a riddle why in the initial stages of national development the Tudors did not succeed in incorporating Ireland into England as the Valois had succeeded in incorporating Brittany and Burgundy into France. It may be, however, that this process was brutally interrupted through the Cromwellian Government that treated the country as one great piece of booty to be divided among its servants. After the Cromwellian revolution, at any rate, which for the formation of the English nation was as crucial as the French Revolution became for the French, the United Kingdom had already lost the power of assimilation and integration which the body politic of the nation has only in its initial stages but loses gradually with its maturing. What then follows is, indeed, one long sad story of "coercion (that) was not imposed that the people might live quietly but that people might die quietly" (Chesterton, *Crimes of England*, 60). For a historical survey of the Irish question that includes the latest developments, compare the excellent unbiased study of Nicholas Mansergh, *Britain and Ireland*, Longman's Pamphlets on the British Commonwealth (London, 1942).

12. James Selwyn, *South of the Congo* (New York, 1943), 326.

13. These boyhood-ideals play a considerable role in the attitude of British administrators and officials when serving abroad. If they are taken seriously, they prepare for such tragedies as the life of Lawrence of Arabia. How they are developed and cultivated is very well described in Rudyard Kipling's *Stalky & Co.*

14. Barker, *Ideas and Ideals,* 150.

15. Lord Cromer, "The Government of Subject Races," *Edinburgh Review* (January 1908).

16. Ibid.

17. The origin of this misnomer is quite clear in the history of British rule in South Africa. It is well known how—to take the most famous instance—local administrators, Cecil Rhodes and Jameson, involved the Imperial Government in the war against the Boers, much against its intentions. The situation was that "the Imperial Government retained, indeed, nominal control. . . . In fact Rhodes, or rather Jameson, was absolute ruler of a territory three times the size of England, which could be administered 'without waiting for the grudging assent or polite censure of the High Commissioner'" (Reginald Ivan Lovell, *The Struggle for South Africa, 1875–1899: A Study in Economic Imperialism* [New York, 1934], 198). And what happens in territories in which the British Government has resigned its jurisdiction to the local European population that lacks all traditional and constitutional restraint of national States can best be seen in the tragic story of the South African Union since its independence, that is, since the time when the Imperial Parliament had no longer any right to interfere.

18. Cf. for instance the discussion in the House of Commons in May 1908, between Charles Dilke and the Colonial Secretary. Dilke warned against giving self-government to the Crown colonies because this would result in a rule of the white planter over the colored worker. Whereupon he is answered that the natives, too, had a representation which is the English House of Commons. See G. Zoepfl, "Kolonien und Kolonialpolitik," in *Handwoerterbuch der Staatswissenschaften,* 3. Auflage.

19. Lawrence J. Zetland, *Lord Cromer* (1932), 224.

20. A. Carthill, *The Lost Dominion* (1924), 41–42, 93.

21. Compare the great article on "France, Britain and the Arabs" which T. E. Lawrence wrote on this occasion in *The Observer* (August 8, 1920): "There is a preliminary Arab success, the British reinforcements go out as a punitive force. They fight their way . . . to their objective, which is meanwhile bombarded by artillery, aeroplanes, or gunboats. Finally perhaps a village is burnt and the district pacified. It is odd that we don't use poison gas on these occasions. Bombing the houses is a patchy way of getting the women and children. . . . By gas attacks the whole population of offending districts could be wiped out neatly; and as a method of government it would be no more immoral than the present system" (quoted in T. E. Lawrence, *Letters,* ed. David Garnett [New York, 1939], 311 ff).

22. The same conflict between national representatives and colonial administrators in Africa runs through the history of German imperialism. In 1897, Carl Peters was removed from his post and had to resign from the Government service because of atrocities

against the natives. The same thing happened to Governor Zimmerer. And in 1905, the tribal chiefs addressed their complaints for the first time to the Reichstag, with the result that the colonial administrators threw them into jail and the German Government intervened. See P. Leutwein (president of "Der Koloniale Volksbund"), *Kaempfe um Africa* (Luebeck, 1936).

23. For this and the following compare J. A. Hobson, *Imperialism,* who already in 1905 gave a masterly analysis of the driving economic motives and of many of its political implications. When, in 1938, his early study was republished, Hobson was perfectly right in stating in his introduction to an unchanged text that this book is a real proof "that the chief perils and disturbances . . . of today . . . were all latent and discernible in the world of a generation ago . . ." (v). Cf. Barker, *Ideas and Ideals,* who in 1941 still calls the colonial Empire proper—not the dominions—"an exportation of English money."

24. For France, compare George Lachapelle, *Les Finances de la Troisième République* (Paris, 1937) and D. W. Brogan, *The Development of Modern France* (New York, 1940). For Germany, compare the interesting contemporary testimonies, such as Max Wirth, *Geschichte der Handelskrisen* (1873), chap. 15, and A. Schaeffle, "Der 'grosse Boersenkrach' des Jahres 1873," in *Zeitschrift fuer die gesamte Staatswissenschaft* (1874), 30 Band.

25. J. A. Hobson. "Capitalism and Imperialism in South Africa," *Contemporary Review* 77 (January–June 1900): 1–17.

26. This has been conclusively demonstrated by Tocqueville with respect to the French aristocracy before the Revolution. The more the aristocracy lost its real power of government and administration, the more its privileges were hated by the people that no longer understood its very existence. See *L'Ançien Régime et la Révolution,* livre II, chapitre I.

27. These motives are especially prominent in German imperialism. Among the first activities of the "Alldeutsche Verband"—founded in 1891—were efforts to prevent German emigrants from changing their citizenship, and the first imperialist speech of Wilhelm II, on the occasion of the twenty-fifth anniversary of the foundation of the Reich, contained the following typical passage: "Aus dem Deutschen Reiche ist ein Weltreich geworden. Ueberall in fernen Teilen der Erde wohnen Tausende unserer Landsleute. . . . An Sie, meine Herren, tritt die ernste Pflicht heran, mir zu helfen, dieses groessere deutsche Reich auch fest an unser heimisches zu gliedern."

28. See the masterly study of C. W. De Kiewiet, *A History of South Africa: Social and Economic,* (Oxford, 1941), 113.

29. E. H. Damce, *The Victorian Illusion* (London, 1928), 164. "Africa, which had been included neither in the itinerary of Saxondom nor in the professional philosophers of imperial history, became the culture-bed of British imperialism."

30. See Lovell, *The Struggle for South Africa, 1875–1899,* on the Uitlanders, p. 403.

31. See Selwyn James, *South of the Congo,* (New York, 1943), 333 ff.

32. See De Kiewiet, *A History of South Africa,* chap. 7.

33. The instances are too numerous to be quoted. Interesting in our context, furthermore, are only those in which the honesty of the persons involved is beyond doubt.

Such for instance is the famous case of Gladstone who as the leader of the Liberal Party had promised to evacuate Egypt; when, however, his party came into power, the liberal government did not evacuate.

34. J. A. Hobson, "Capitalism and Imperialism in South Africa," 61.

35. The slogan "above the parties" has been repeated again and again in the course of the German imperialist movement. All Leagues, societies, and groups propagating overseas expansion pretended to direct their appeals to "men of all parties," to "stand far removed from the strife of parties and represent only a national purpose"—as the president of the Kolonialverein Hohenlohe-Langenburg put it in 1884. (See Mary E. Townsend, *Origin of Modern Colonialism.* [New York].) Likewise the official historian of the Pan-German League insists on its being "above the parties; this was and is a vital condition (for the League)." (See Otto Bonhard, *Geschichte des alldeutschen Verbandes* [1920].) The first party to claim to be "above the parties" as a "Reichspartei" was the national-liberal party under the leadership of Ernst Bassermann. (See Daniel Frymann [pseud. for Heinrich Class], *Wenn ich der Kaiser waer'—Politische Wahrheiten und Notwendigkeiten,* 1st ed. (1912).

The situation in England is far more complicated, although the disinterest of imperialist politicians in domestic politics is very marked and well known. (See for instance, Harold Nicolson, *Curzon: The Last Phase, 1919–1925* [Boston/New York, 1934], 7.) More important than this, more important even than such beyond-parties foundations as the Primrose League is the disturbing influence of imperialism upon the two-party system, which finally has led to the Front-Benches system. The "diminution of the power of opposition" in Parliament and the increasing "power of the Cabinet as against the House of Commons" as "chiefly attributable to Imperialism" have been noted already by Hobson ("Capitalism and Imperialism," 146 ff). The working of this system has been described by Hilaire Belloc and Cecil Chesterton, *The Party System* (London, 1911).

36. As Lord Curzon put it at the unveiling of Lord Cromer's memorial tablet. See Zetland, *Lord Cromer,* 362.

37. In the words of Sir Hesketh Bell, former governor of Uganda, Northern Nigeria etc. See *Foreign Colonial Administration in the Far East* (1928), pt. 1, p. 300.

The same sentiments prevailed in the Dutch colonial services. "The highest task, the task without precedent is that which awaits the East Indian Civil Service official. it should be considered as the highest honor to serve in its ranks ... the select body which fulfills the mission of Holland overseas." See De Kat Angelino, *Colonial Policy,* vol. 2 (Chicago, 1931), 129.

38. For a magnificent example of this attitude, see Rudyard Kipling's tale "The Tomb of His Ancestors," *The Day's Work* (New York, 1898).

39. Very typical are, in this respect, the recent remarks of Adolf Hitler on the subject: "God the Almighty has made our nation. By defending its very existence we are defending His work." Speech of January 30, 1945. Quoted from *New York Times,* January 31, 1945.

40. "If Rhodes did not realize the advantage of being English in blood and bone before he arrived in Kimberly, he learnt to appreciate it there ... it seemed a rare and lovely virtue." See Millin, *Rhodes,* 15.

41. "Ich hatte es satt unter die Parias gerechnet zu werden, und wollte einem Herrenvolk angehoeren." Quoted after Paul Ritter, *Kolonien im deutschen Schrifttum* (1936).

42. Alfred Rosenberg, *Der Mythos des zwanzigsten Jahrhunderts* (1930), 22.

43. Millin, *Rhodes*, 346.

44. Carl Peters, "Deutschtum als Rasse," in *Deutsche Monatsschrift*, ed. Lohmeyer, Bd. 7 (April 1905).

45. Up to the times of Nazi-imperialism, history has known only one clear-cut case of domination in which the "personal element" was allowed complete freedom from control. This was the well-known case of the King of Belgium's business enterprise in the Belgian Congo which reduced the native population from between 20 and 40 millions in 1890 to 8,500,000 in 1911. (Cf. James, *South of the Congo*, 305.)

An early insight into the importance of the personal element in imperialist politics can be found in Lord Cromer's letters with respect to the situation in Egypt: ". . . the working of the whole machine depends, not on any written instrument, or, indeed, on anything which is tangible, but on the personal influence which the English Consul General can exert on the Khedive . . ." (Letter to Lord Roseberry in 1886). One year earlier in a letter to Lord Granville (a Liberal) he was still dubious "whether it would be advisable to continue the present system of government in Egypt" precisely because "its working depends very greatly on the judgment and ability of a few individuals." Quoted from Zetland, *Lord Comer*, 134, 219.

46. Hobson, "Capitalism and Imperialism in South Africa," 150–51.

47. The Czechs are the exception that prove the rule. They were lucky to find and deserve praise to have listened to men who, like Masaryk, consciously stressed common history, common language and common spiritual achievements in order to achieve the transformation of their people into a nation in the genuine sense of the word.

48. It is a well-established fact that the pan-German aspirations of the German minority in Austria-Hungary were much more radical than those of the corresponding groups in Germany proper. The "*Alldeutsche Verband*" complains frequently about their aggressiveness, and the "exaggerations" of the Austrian movement. (Cf. Otto Bonhard, *Geschichte des alldeutschen Verbandes* [1920], 58 ff.) In 1913, the Alldeutsche Verein fuer die Ostmark published a program whose clear-cut aggressive aims at that time were almost unequaled; its main point was the "Aufrichtung eines . . . deutschen Mitteleuropa umfassenden einheitsstaates auf arischer Grundlage . . . der den Mittelpunkt des gesamten deutschen Lebens des Erdballs bildet und der mit allen Germanen-Staaten verbuendet ist." (Quoted from Eduard Pichl [alias Herwig], *Georg Schönerer* [1938], 6 Bde., Bd. 6, 375).

Russian pan-Slavists recognized very early in 1870 that the destruction of Austria-Hungary would be the best possible starting point of a pan-Slav federation or a pan-Slav Empire. (Cf. K. Staehlin, *Geschichte Russlands von den Anfaengen bis zur Gegenwart*, 5 Bde. [1923–1939], Bd. 4/1, 282.)

49. "Das deutsche Volk (in Oesterreich) sezt seine Hoffnung nur noch auf das deutsche Reich," said a delegate in Austria's Parliament in 1888. (See Pichl, *Georg*

Schönerer, Bd. 5, 60 ff.) It is in the same vein that quite recently the Bulgarian Metropolitan of Sofia called upon "the Russian people (to) remember their messianic mission" (from a radio broadcast on October 17, 1944, quoted from *Politics* [January 1945]).

50. Enthusiasm and admiration for Bismarck were unbounded among pan-German Austrians; and Slav peoples—they already, at the time of the Crimean war, had been called the only reliable allies of the Czar (see Staehlin, *Geschichte Russlands*, Bd. 5, 35)— were only too willing to help that "die Oberhoheit des grossrussischen Stammes ueber die ganze slawische Welt zur unanfechtbaren Tatsache werde" (as Dostoyevsky once put it; see ibid., 281).

51. This is especially true for the German brand. "Nicht gleichberechtigt," said Schönerer, "wollen wir werden mit jedem Juden, Bosniaker and Zigeuner. Wir wollen uns das Recht der Erstgeburt nicht rauben lassen." Pichl, *George Schönerer*, Bd. 6, 355–56.

52. It was upon this situation that during the last war French politicians based their hopes of defeating German domination in Europe. "Ce qu'il faut opposer à la Confédération germanique, c'est la Confédération slave, autrement dit le Panslavisme organisé." And: "Il nous faut une revanche absolue de la race slave contre le germanisme." See L. Léger, *Le Panslavisme et l'intérêt français* (1917). It is obvious that we today witness an attempted revival of this policy with, however, much better chances of success. Whether this actually is in support of French interests or whether France does not rather put herself between the devil and the deep sea—remains to be seen.

53. Adolf Hitler has frankly recognized his indebtedness to the Austrian Pan-Germans. There is little reason to doubt his words when he says: "Ich erhielt (in Wien) die Grundlage fuer meine Weltanschauung im Grossen und eine politische Betrachtungsweise im Kleinen, die ich spaeter nur noch im Einzelnen zu ergaenzen brauchte, die mich aber nie meter verliess." *Mein Kampf*, 137.

54. For the early conception of colonial possessions on the continent see Ernst Hasse, *Deutsche Politik*, especially Heft 3: Deutsche Grenzpolitik, 167 ff and Heft 4: Die Zukunft des deutschen Volkstums, 132 ff (1907). The same subject was even more systematically dealt with by Reismann-Grosse. *Ueberseepolitik oder Festlandspolitik?* Alldeutsche Flugschriften, no. 22 (1905).

CHAPTER 5

On the Study of International Relations

WALDEMAR GURIAN

Interest in the study of international relations has considerably increased
in American universities since the close of World War II. A School of World
Affairs has been established by Columbia University which is also planning
institutes for special areas, the first of which, the Russian Institute, will open
soon. To promote research and teaching, grants have been given to universities, such as that by the Rockefeller Foundation to Yale University. It is reported that in almost all educational institutions the students, particularly
veterans, show an especially great interest in international affairs. The Council on Foreign Relations, keenly aware of this situation, has organized conferences in various parts of the country to investigate problems of teaching and
research in international relations.

This development is not surprising. Everybody is aware that international
relations and foreign policies are of vital concern, not only for specialists, politicians, and diplomats, but also for the individual. These anxious and hopeful
questions are asked over and over again: Will the peace be won after the military victory? Is the UNO an instrument of lasting peace or will this new international organization be another failure, unable to prevent a new world war?
Is its creation only a preliminary and insufficient step which after a series of
wars may lead to the establishment of a world government? Crises are developing in various parts of the world, in the Far and the Near East, in Central and
Eastern Europe. There are tensions with the Soviet Union, difficulties in preparing even the drafts of peace treaties, disagreements with France on Germany,
on the loan to England, on the future of the British Empire. All these troubles,
emphasized daily by the headlines as well as by radio commentators, constantly

hammer in the importance of the relations between the various governments and nations. Returning home from service abroad, veterans are eager to understand what they have observed, what they have fought and suffered for. Many students anxious to find jobs believe that the study of international relations will open excellent opportunities for them. The Foreign Service of the United States is expanding; there are chances to serve in international organizations among which the UNO is the most important; there are also possibilities in the export and import business.

It would be fatal if the study of international relations were to be determined solely by professional and specialistic interests. I was very glad to hear that this danger is realized by those responsible for the recruiting of the Foreign Service personnel in the Department of State. One of the leading American students of world affairs has remarked that some of these men told him: "We prefer a general liberal education to a specialized training. This specialized training can be acquired later, in actual experiences in offices and in the preparation for particular jobs." It is obvious that professional training is very useful, and that those who will dedicate their lives to the study or to the handling of international relations must acquire special knowledge. Such professional and specialized training cannot replace a general, cultural approach— cannot be substituted for a liberal education.

But in this general, liberal education which aims finally at good citizenship, is there a place for a particular study of international relations? And if there is a place, how must this study be organized? That is our problem here. The examination of the fundamental approach should precede and determine the discussion of technical problems. Such questions as what department should supervise the study of international relations, the department of history, political science or a special committee, either completely independent of the departments or coordinating their work, are of secondary importance. I think, too, that it is necessary to clarify the nature of the study of international relations before the special requirements for graduate study can be stated. Here, of course, more specialization is obviously necessary. Even here specialization cannot be the first step—we must first know the kind of unity which will keep together the various specialized classes and seminars.

We have assumed as self-evident that there can be a study of international relations as a particular subject. But is such an assumption actually self evident? The question may be raised: Are general courses in international relations not a kind of mixture, concocted from various subjects, and determined in their composition by practical considerations and by the particular interest of the teacher? This study involves geography, economics, international law, history, anthropology, demography, social psychology (study of mass emotions, public opinion, propaganda), and comparative government. Therefore, a general course in international relations seems manifestly an unsystematic putting-together and presentation of material which the student can properly study only by taking separate courses in the component fields.

He should study economics, where he will hear about the importance of international trade, commercial competition, tariffs, about the influences of international financial organizations, etc. In a survey of geography, perhaps in an even more specialized class in political geography, he would discover how the environment influences political developments and at the same time raises challenges which have to be met, thereby becoming test cases and stimulants for the formation and development of peoples and nations. He would learn in a competent survey of world history or of American and European history how the modern state system came into existence, by what forces it was determined, how it developed, by what crises and conflicts it was threatened, how modern tendencies towards the creation of an international organization started to work. As a student of comparative government he would become aware of the various types and organizations of foreign policies. In a class on international law he would observe the rise and limitations of modern international law; he would realize that this international law must become the law of a truly international community, superseding old concepts connected with the acceptance of national parochial sovereignties. And he would listen, in a psychology course, to the analysis of the peculiar structure of the human mind, always influenced by the character of the society in which it exists, of the various forms of propaganda and of the causes for its appeal and success. This work in psychology could be supplemented by a course in anthropology, emphasizing the importance of the ethnic factors in human relations. It could also show that much has to be done to eliminate atavistic tendencies leading to war and conflict. Finally, in order to satisfy his need of finding norms for international relations, the student could attend courses in philosophy: ethics would teach him to understand that power politics are subordinated to higher aims, that conflicts and crises among nations derive from imperfections of human nature. In Catholic institutions, ethics would be studied in relation to the supernatural end of man, the consideration of which helps to evaluate human actions.

Therefore, it seems that there is no justification for a general course in international relations. The general course may be taken by attending other courses, and these courses may be supplemented by special classes, for example, on the techniques of diplomacy, particular international crises, peace conferences, and the international organizations which have become so important in our time. Influential teachers of international relations have characterized a general course in international relations as a "hodgepodge," whose existence can be justified only on the practical ground that many students have no opportunity of taking classes in geography, world economics, etc.

The situation would not be changed if international relations were limited to a study of international politics, destined to investigate and describe power, its application and forms. The concept of power is extremely broad and ambiguous, so broad and ambiguous that everything can be covered by it. How can power be studied as a pure abstraction without taking economic, geographic, historical and psychological factors, legal and diplomatic techniques and concepts into consideration? To replace the course on international relations by a course in international politics would simply be the old brew with a new label. In the well-known textbook of F. L. Schuman on *International Politics* we find that various disciplines are there used. It contains much historical material on state systems and the development of legal concepts, some observations and remarks on diplomacy, and even some theological concepts (surely used by the author involuntarily). Geography and economics are perhaps a little too much neglected. Had these studies been taken more into account, they would have increased the value of a very readable book.

However impressive this objection seems, I think that it must not be accepted at first sight. It is true that there is no specific subject matter in international relations which cannot be found in another special discipline; but international relations group and bring together these subject matters under a special point of view. They approach them from a particular focus. International relations are concerned with relations between nations, or, if this word has a too-specific modern meaning, relations between various groups organized in separate political units. Such a study would include not only relations among states, but also the influences of groups which are inside the state and at the same time often go beyond its frontiers, either in the form of visible organizations, like the Catholic Church, or without organization, simply in a bond of sympathies, common ideas and purposes, like some forms of the labor movement. Therefore, this study would not neglect the development away from the old state system of closed sovereignties to supranational empires like the USSR, which attempt to found their unity on social, economic elements and ideologies. It would also consider the trend in the direction of world government and federation. Obviously, various factors enter as basic elements and as determining forces in international relations. The geographic position of England, the poverty of Italy in iron and coal, Russia's drive toward the sea, the late unification of Germany, the peculiar historical traditions of Switzerland—to cite some examples—must be considered. Another important part of the study is an account of the changes in the whole atmosphere of periods and of the various traditions of countries and nations. Nationalistic and economic arguments today play the same role as theological differences formerly did, though sometimes even today some very important conflicts cannot be understood without a knowledge of differing religious traditions. In the United States, international loans are thought of in primarily economic terms, in Europe they are thought of more as political instruments. The study of international relations is a cultural one, and precisely for that reason it has a place in the curriculum devoted to general education. It contributes to the deeper understanding of other subjects. It exercises an integrating function. Of course, the danger of premature synthesis must be avoided.

Without a knowledge of history, comparative government, and geography, the student of international relations would be lost. It would be tragic if he would receive the impression that some mechanistic schemes of power relations could replace concrete factual knowledge and an understanding of the particular perspectives of historical situations. Formerly there was the danger of underestimating power and believing that an international organization for the guaranteeing of lasting peace would result simply from enlightenment about the intrigues of egoistic and shortsighted diplomats and from education in world affairs. Today, too much emphasis upon power may sometimes be observed. The various elements which make up for power are not analyzed. There is a prevalent inclination to think of power as a composite of material and geographical forces in the hands of skillful manipulators.

The course on international relations should be permeated by an understanding of history, and at the same time be free of a spirit of relativistic nihilism, in which all values are considered as expressions of unique situations and of the energy of particular peoples and great personalities. International relations must be described by analyzing the factors which are their material, for instance, the boundaries and the distribution of raw materials, so important in modern times. They must be interpreted by analyzing the differing characters of various foreign policies, the influence of national traditions and legal-diplomatic systems of procedure as well as of universal systems of ideas, to which in spite of its dialectic materialism the official doctrine of the USSR belongs. They must also be evaluated. In this evaluation, views on the nature of men become decisive. The Catholic student of international relations will claim that he has an insight which other students do not have, or, from their point of view, would be obliged to reject and regard as a subjective opinion. But the acceptance of a Christian philosophy of history which would be used as a yardstick for the study of international relations could not exclude differences among Catholic students who would emphasize different perspectives (German and French Catholics for instance interpret modern developments in quite different ways), and could not preclude the agreements of Catholics and non-Catholics in the analysis and interpretation of facts. An ethical metaphysical condemnation of the *principles* of atheistic communism, for example, could not be used as a substitute for the study of Russian foreign policy, of the development of the USSR, etc. On the other hand, even from a purely descriptive-analytical point of view, it is a defect of many modern textbooks on international relations that they underestimate the profound influence of religious forces and ideas (sometimes hidden in anti-religious guise or masked in a purely secular indifferentism) on international relations, and on the concepts of the future society and its order. In the most favorable cases, these religious influences are seen only in the form of visible effects of religious organizations, but such an approach is manifestly insufficient, because it expressly narrows the concept of religion.

What is the conclusion of these remarks? The author believes that a general course on international relations is very valuable. This class must be given and organized in such a way that it clearly shows the dependence of the study of international relations on other subject matters. It must be correlated with classes in history, economics, geography, and politics. For the students who have no opportunity of attending these other classes, it must be given in such a way that all members obtain at least some fundamental basic knowledge. On the other hand, it is obvious that it would be an error to label international relations as a study in which information about various subjects is conveyed in a vague, superficial form. The decisive feature is the endeavor to help the students understand the particular approach which brings the various subject matters together in the course. Then erroneous one-sided theories would be avoided, for instance, such theories which explain everything exclusively by geographical or economic determinism, by purely mechanistic power politics, by the distribution of raw materials, and by changes in the rate of population increase. Finally, this course must at least evoke in the student an understanding of the universal significance of the conflicts and general trends in international relations. It belongs to the studies dealing with a particular aspect of the nature of men and, therefore, is subordinated to theology and philosophy, which deal with the nature of men in the light of revelation or regarded from the point of view of reason, abstracting from concrete conditions as such.

Such a course would contribute to a better understanding of our present age. It would help the students to avoid quick judgments based upon superficial impressions. It would on the other hand make them immune to the despairing pessimism resulting from the observation that conflicts are likely not to be soon resolved and that more and more crises are likely to occur. It will also make it easier to grasp the particular role and situation of the United States.

Only a combination of the historical and philosophical approach can help the student avoid the misinterpretation to which an easy pseudo-moralism so often leads men. We condemn everybody because we have fortunately been kept away from real participation in fights and conflicts. This attitude was the result of particular conditions which today, when the USA is the leading power in the world, no longer exist.

I do not share the hopes of those who regard new courses as the solutions of all problems, overestimating the importance of institutional education and underestimating the decisive influence of factors outside the school, such as the family, the general atmosphere of life, etc. But I think that a well-organized class in international relations, accessible to all students, given with the right respect for other disciplines as well as for philosophy (and, I may add, theology) would help to bring about the unification of college and university threatened today by a combination of specialization and utilitarianism. Students and faculty would come to realize that in all temporal things something supratemporal appears. Therefore, they would be saved from the dangerous twin evils of our time—cynicism and perfectionism.

Two dangers which are a particular threat to the student of international relations must be avoided: the tendency to see only conflicts and crises, a tendency which would result in limiting oneself to the presentation of facts and trends and their relativistic interpretation; and the simplifying pseudo-ethical approach which believes that by some technical means or some external change all problems can be solved simply, and that only some villains and lack of education are responsible for the anguish which the world of the twentieth century has known, and I am afraid, will continue to know. Man is neither beast nor angel; rather he is a being faced by the task of making life as human as possible in the changing world of time and history, and, even though he belongs to some particular group, he must never forget that he participates always in the unity of mankind.

NOTE

Reprinted from *The Review of Politics* 8, no. 3 (July 1946): 275–82.

Chapter 6

World Politics in the Mid-Twentieth Century

Hans J. Morgenthau

From the end of the religious wars to the First World War, the modern state system was kept together by the intellectual and moral tradition of the Western world. That tradition imposed moral and legal limitations on the struggle for power on the international scene and provided in the balance of power an instrumentality which, in a certain measure, maintained order in the international community and secured the independence of its individual members. What is left of this heritage today? What kind of consensus unites the nations of the world in the period following the Second World War?

The answer can only be that the limitations upon the struggle for power on the international scene are weaker today than they have been at any time in the history of the modern state system. The one international society of the seventeenth and eighteenth centuries has been replaced by a number of national societies which provide for their members the highest principle of social integration. In consequence, the international morality which in past centuries kept the aspirations for power of the individual states within certain bounds has, except for certain fragmentary restraints, given way to the ethics of individual nations which not only does not recognize any moral obligation above and apart from them, but even claims universal recognition from all the world. World public opinion is but an ideological shadow without even that substance of common valuations and reactions in which in other times at least the international aristocracy shared. The main bulk of the rules of international law owes its existence to the sovereignty of the individual nations. Far from restraining the aspirations for power of individual nations, they see to it that the power position of individual nations is not adversely affected by whatever legal obligations they take upon themselves in their relations with other nations. What national morality is in the field of ethics, what national public opinion is in the domain of the mores, sovereignty is for international law, the manifestation of the nation as the recipient of the individual's ultimate earthly loyalties, as the mightiest social force, as the supreme authority giving and enforcing laws for the individual citizen.

I. The New Moral Force of Nationalistic Universalism

The supranational forces which bind individuals together across national boundaries are infinitely weaker today than the forces which unite peoples within a particular national boundary and separate them from the rest of humanity. This weakening of the supranational forces, which must be strong in order to impose effective restraints upon the international policies of nations, is but the negative byproduct of the great positive force which shapes the political face of our age: nationalism. Nationalism, identified as it is with the international policies of individual nations, cannot restrain these policies; it is indeed in need of restraint. Not only has it fatally weakened, if not destroyed, the restraints which have come down to us from previous ages, it has also supplied the aspirations for power of individual nations with a good conscience and a pseudo-religious fervor and has thus instilled them with a thirst and strength for universal dominion of which the nationalism of the nineteenth century knew nothing.

The nationalism of the mid-twentieth century is essentially different from what traditionally goes by that name and what culminated in the national movements and the national state of the nineteenth century. The latter pursued the goal of freeing the nation from alien domination and of giving it a state of its own, and this goal was considered to be a rightful one not for one, but for all nations. The national aspirations were satisfied, once a nation had united its members in one state, and there was room for as many nationalisms as there were nations which wanted to establish or preserve a state of their own. The international conflicts in which the nationalism of the nineteenth century was involved were, therefore, essentially of two kinds: the conflicts between a nationality and an alien master, such as the ones between the Balkan nations and Turkey, the Slav nations of the Danube basin and the Austro-Hungarian monarchy, the Poles and Russia, and the conflicts between different nationalities over the delimitation of their respective spheres of dominion, such as the ones between the Germans, on the one hand, and the Poles and the French, on the other. What led to conflict was either differing interpretation of the national principle or else the refusal to accept it at all. It was hoped as late as three decades ago that, once the aspirations of all nations for national states within which to dwell were fulfilled, a society of satisfied nations would find in the legal and moral principles of national self-determination the means for its own preservation.

To give the same name of nationalism to what inspired the oppressed and competing nationalities of the nineteenth century and what drives the superpowers of the mid-twentieth century into deadly combat, is to obscure the fundamental change which separates our age from the preceding one. The nationalism of today, which is truly a nationalistic universalism, has only one thing in common with the nationalism of the nineteenth century, that is, the nation as the ultimate point of reference for political loyalties and actions. Here, however, the similarity ends. For the nationalism of the nineteenth century the nation is the ultimate goal of political action, the endpoint of the political development beyond which there are other nationalisms with similar goals and similar justifications. For the nationalistic universalism of the mid-twentieth century the nation is but the starting-point of a universal mission whose ultimate goal reaches to the confines of the political world. While nationalism wants one nation in one state and nothing else, the nationalistic universalism of our age claims for one nation and one state the right to impose its own valuations and standards of action upon all the other nations. These rival claims to universal dominion on the part of different nations have dealt the final, fatal blow to that social system of international intercourse within which for almost three centuries nations were living together in constant rivalry, yet under the common roof of shared values and universal standards of action. The collapse of that roof has destroyed the common habitat of the nations of the world, and the most powerful of them assert the right to build it anew in their own image. Beneath the ruins of that roof lies buried the mechanism which kept the walls of that house of nations standing: the balance of power.

II. THE NEW BALANCE OF POWER

With the destruction of that intellectual and moral consensus which for almost three centuries confined the struggle for power on the international scene within its framework, the balance of power has lost the vital energy which transformed it from a metaphor into a living principle of international politics. Concomitant with the destruction of that vital energy, the system of the balance of power has undergone three structural changes which considerably impair its operations.

The Inflexibility of the New Balance of Power

The most obvious of these changes is to be found in the drastic numerical reduction of the players in the game. At the end of the Thirty Years War, for instance, the German Empire was composed of 900 sovereign states which the Treaty of Westphalia in 1648 reduced to 355. The Napoleonic interventions, of which the most notable one is the dictated reforms of the Reichstag of Ratisbon of 1803, eliminated more than 200 of the sovereign German states, and when the Germanic Confederation was founded in 1815, only 36 sovereign states were left to join it. The unification of Italy in 1859 eliminated seven, the unification of Germany in 1871, 24 sovereign states. In 1815, at the end of the Napoleonic Wars, eight nations, that is, Austria, France, Great Britain, Portugal, Russia, Prussia, Spain, and Sweden, had the diplomatic rank of great powers. With Portugal, Spain, and Sweden receiving such consideration only out of traditional courtesy and soon losing that undeserved status altogether, the number of actually great powers was really reduced to five. In the sixties, Italy and the United States joined their rank, followed towards the end of the century by Japan. At the outbreak of the First World War, there were then again eight great powers, of which for the first time two were located totally outside Europe: Austria, France, Germany, Great Britain, Italy, Japan, Russia, and the United States. The end of the First World War found Austria definitely, Germany and Russia temporarily, removed from that list. Two decades later one could count seven great powers, Germany and the Soviet Union having again become first-rate powers and the others having retained their status. The end of the Second World War saw this number reduced to three, namely,

Great Britain, the Soviet Union, and the United States, while China and France, in view of their past or their potentialities, are treated in negotiations and organizations as though they were great powers. In the aftermath of the Second World War British power has declined to such an extent as to be distinctly inferior to the power of the United States and of the Soviet Union, which are then the only two great powers left at present.

This reduction in the number of states which are able to play a major role in international politics has an important effect upon the operation of the balance of power. This effect gains added importance from the reduction in the absolute number of states through the consolidations of 1648 and 1803 and the national unifications of the nineteenth century, a reduction which was only temporarily offset in 1919 by the creation of new states in eastern and central Europe; for these states have in the meantime disappeared either as states, for example, the Baltic states, or, in any case, as independent factors on the international scene. This development has deprived the balance of power of much of its flexibility and uncertainty and, in consequence, of its restraining effect upon the nations actively engaged in the struggle for power on the international scene.

In former times the balance of power operated in the main by way of coalitions among a number of nations, the principal of which, while differing in power, were still of the same order of magnitude. In the eighteenth century, for instance, Austria, France, Great Britain, Prussia, Russia, and Sweden belonged in the same class, insofar as their relative power was concerned. Fluctuations in their power would affect their respective position in the hierarchy of power, but did not affect their position as great powers. Similarly, in the period from 1870 to 1914, the game of power politics was played by eight players of the first rank of which six, the European ones, were always playing. Under such circumstances no player could go very far in his aspirations for power without being sure of the support of at least one or the other of his co-players, and of that support nobody could generally be too sure. There was virtually no nation in the eighteenth and nineteenth centuries which was not compelled to retreat from an advanced position and retrace its steps because it did not receive the diplomatic or military support from other nations upon which it had counted. This was especially true of Russia in the nineteenth century. On the other hand, if Germany, in violation of the rule of the game, had not in 1914 given Austria a free hand in her dealings with Serbia, there is little doubt that the latter would not have dared to go as far as she did, and that the First World War might have been avoided.

The greater the number of active players, the greater is the number of possible combinations. Thus uncertainty increases as to the combinations which will actually oppose each other and as to the role which the individual players will actually perform in them. Both William II in 1914 and Hitler in 1939 refused to believe that Great Britain, and ultimately the United States, too, would join the rank of their enemies, and both discounted the effect of American intervention. It is obvious that these miscalculations as to who would fight against whom meant for Germany the difference between victory and defeat. Whenever coalitions of nations comparable in power confront each other, calculations of this kind will of necessity be close, since the defection of one prospective member or the addition of an unexpected one cannot fail to affect the balance of power considerably, if not decisively. Thus in the eighteenth century when princes used to change their alignments with the greatest of ease, such calculations were frequently almost indistinguishable from wild guesses. In consequence, the extreme flexibility of the balance of power resulting from the utter impermanence of alliances made it imperative for all players to be cautious in their moves on the chessboard of international politics and, since risks were hard to calculate, to take as few risks as possible. In the First World War it was still of very great importance, for the ultimate outcome of the conflict, whether Italy would remain neutral or enter the war on the side of the Allies. It was in recognition of that importance that both sides made great efforts, by competing in promises of territorial aggrandizement, to influence Italy's decision; the same situation then prevailed, to a lesser degree, even with respect to so relatively weak a power as Greece.

This aspect of the balance of power has undergone a radical transformation in recent years. In the Second World War the decision of countries, such as Italy, Spain, or Turkey, or even of France, to join or not to join one or the other side were mere episodes, welcomed or feared, to be sure, by the belligerents, but in no way even remotely capable of transforming victory into defeat, or vice versa. The disparity in the power of nations of the first rank, such as the United States, the Soviet Union, Great Britain, Japan, and Germany, on the one hand, and all the remaining nations, on the other, was then already so great that the defection of one, or the addition of another, ally could no longer overturn the balance of power and thus materially affect the ultimate outcome of the struggle. Under the influence of such changes in alignments one scale might rise somewhat and the other sink still more under a heavier weight, yet these changes could not reverse the relation of the scales which were determined by the preponderant weights of the first-rate powers. It was only the position of countries, such as the United States, the Soviet Union, and Great Britain on the one hand, Germany and Japan, on the other, that really mattered. This situation, first noticeable in the Second World War, is now accentuated in the polarity between the United States and the Soviet Union and has become a paramount feature of international politics. The power of the United States and of the Soviet Union in comparison with the power of their actual or prospective allies has become so overwhelming that they, through their own preponderant weight, determine the balance of power between them, which cannot be decisively affected by changes in the alignments of their allies, at least for the foreseeable future.

As a result, the flexibility of the balance of power and, with it, its restraining influence upon the power aspirations of the main protagonists on the international scene have disappeared. Two great powers, each incomparably stronger than any other power or possible combination of other powers, oppose each other. Neither of them need fear anything unexpected from actual or prospective allies. The disparity of power between the former and the latter, as we have seen, is such that changes in the allegiance of one or the other of the minor powers by themselves can have no decisive influence upon the balance of power. As a further result of that disparity of power most, if not all, of the nations ranking below the two big ones have lost that freedom of movement which in former times enabled them to play an important and often decisive role in the balance of power. What was formerly true only of a relatively small number of nations, like certain Latin American countries in their relations with the United States or Portugal in her relations to Great Britain, is true now of most, if not all, of them: they are in the orbit of one or the other of the two giants who can hold them there even against their will by making use of their own political, military, and economic preponderance.

This is the exact opposite of the era of ever-shifting alliances and new combinations demanding vigilance, and caution. Of that era the eighteenth century is the classic example. Its characteristics prevailed in the nineteenth and the first three decades of the twentieth century, and even during the Second World War played an important role at least with regard to the anticipated actions of the major belligerents. Today neither the United States nor the Soviet Union needs to be wary lest the defection of one ally or the addition of another upset the balance of power. Neither is any longer constrained to accommodate its policies to the wishes of doubtful allies and exacting neutrals. No such fears and considerations need restrain ambitions and actions. Each is, in a unique way, master of its own policy and of its own fate. The line between the two camps is clearly drawn, and the weight of those few still straddling the fence is so small as to be virtually negligible or is, as in the case of China and India, a matter of future development rather than of the present. There are no longer neutrals which, as "honest brokers," can mitigate international conflicts and contribute to their peaceful settlement or else, by maneuvering between the two camps and threatening to join the one or the other as occasion might require, can erect effective barriers to limitless aspirations for power.

The Disappearance of the Balancer

The second change in the structure of the balance of power, which we are witnessing today, is the inevitable result of the change just discussed, namely, the disappearance of the balancer, the "holder" of the balance. It was both her naval supremacy and her virtual immunity from foreign attack which for more than three centuries enabled Great Britain to perform this function for the balance of power. Today Great Britain is no longer capable of performing it; for, on the one hand, the United States has far surpassed her in naval strength and, on the other, the modern technology of war has deprived navies of the uncontested mastery of the seas, has put an end to the invulnerability of the British Isles, and has transformed from an advantage into a liability the concentration of a population and industries on a relatively small piece of territory in close proximity to a continent.

In the great contest between France and the Hapsburgs around which the modern state system revolved, at least till the "diplomatic revolution" of 1756 when France allied herself with the Hapsburgs against Prussia, Great Britain was able to play the controlling and restraining role of the balancer because she was strong enough in comparison with the two contenders and their allies to make likely the victory of the side which she joined. This was again true in the Napoleonic Wars and throughout the nineteenth and the beginning of the twentieth century. Today her friendship is no longer of decisive importance and, hence, her role as the "holder" of the balance has come to an end, leaving the modern state system without the benefits of restraint and pacification which she bestowed upon it in former times. While even as late as the Second World War the neutrality of Great Britain or her alignment with Germany and Japan instead of with the United Nations might easily have meant for the latter the difference between victory and defeat, it may well be that, in view of the probable trends in the technology of warfare and the distribution of power between the United States and the Soviet Union, the attitude of Great Britain in an armed conflict between these two powers would not decisively affect the ultimate outcome. In the metaphorical language of the balance of power one might say, rather crudely but not without truth, that, while in the Russian scale there is a weight of seventy, the weight of the American scale amounts to a hundred of which seventy is on account of the United States' own strength, ten on account of Great Britain, and the remainder on account of the other actual or prospective allies. Thus even if the British weight were removed from the American scale and placed in the Russian, the heavier weight would still be in the American scale.

It follows from what has been said that the decline of the relative power of Great Britain and her resultant inability to keep her key position in the balance of power is not an isolated occurrence solely attributable to Great Britain, but the consequence of a structural change which affects the functioning of the balance of power in all its manifestations. It is, therefore, impossible that the privileged and dominating place which Great Britain has held for so long could be inherited by another nation. It is not so much that the power of the traditional holder of the place has declined, incapacitating her for her traditional role, as that the place itself no longer exists. Alongside giants strong enough to determine with their own weight alone the position of the scales, there can be no chance for a third power to exert a decisive influence upon that determination. It is, therefore, futile at the present moment to hope for another nation or group of nations to take the place vacated by Great Britain. France has entertained such hopes for a time through the eloquent voice of General de Gaulle. He has advocated in a number of speeches that either France alone or a United Europe under French leadership should perform the pacifying and restraining task of the "holder" of the balance between the colossus of the east and the colossus of the west. He made this point with particular emphasis in his speech at Bar-le-Duc of July 28, 1946, which he started with a brilliant analysis of the transformation of the balance of power by saying:

> It is certain indeed that, with respect to what it was before this thirty-year war the face of the world has altered in every way. A third of a century ago we were living in a universe where six or eight great nations, apparently equal in strength, each by differing and subtle accords associating others with it, managed to establish a balance everywhere in which the less powerful found themselves relatively guaranteed and where international law was recognized, since a violator would have faced a coalition of moral or material interests, and where, in the last analysis, strategy conceived and prepared with a view to future conflicts involved only rapid and limited destruction.
>
> But a cyclone has passed. An inventory can be made. When we take into account the collapse of Germany and Japan and the weakening of Europe, Soviet Russia and the United States are now alone in holding the first rank. It seems as if the destiny of the world, which in modern times has in turn smiled on the Holy Roman Empire, Spain, France, Britain and the German Reich, conferring on each in turn a kind of preeminence, has now decided to divide its favor in two. From this decision arises a factor of division that has been substituted for the balance of yore.

After referring to the anxieties caused by the expansionist tendencies of the United States and the Soviet Union, De Gaulle raised the question of restoring a stable balance of power.

> Who then can reestablish the equilibrium, if not the old world, between the two new ones? Old Europe, which, during so many centuries was the

guide of the universe, is in a position to constitute in the heart of a world that tends to divide itself into two, the necessary element of compensation and understanding.

The nations of the ancient west have for their vital arteries the North Sea, the Mediterranean, the Rhine; they are geographically situated between the two new masses. Resolved to conserve an independence that would be gravely exposed in the event of a conflagration, they are physically and morally drawn together by the massive effort of the Russians as well as by the liberal advance of the Americans. Of global strength because of their own resources and those of the vast territories that are linked to them by destiny, spreading afar their influences and their activities, what will be their weight if they manage to combine their policies in spite of the difficulties among them from age to age![1]

But the weakness of France in comparison with the United States and the Soviet Union incapacitates her even more than Great Britain. Above all, General de Gaulle's argument leaves out of account the decisive fact that Great Britain was capable of making her beneficial contributions to peace and stability only because she was geographically remote from the centers of friction and conflict, because she had no vital interests in the stakes of these conflicts as such, and because she had the opportunity of satisfying her aspirations for power in areas beyond the seas which generally were beyond the reach of the main contenders for power.

It was that threefold aloofness, together with her resources of power, which enabled Great Britain to play her role as "holder" of the balance. In none of these three respects are France or a United Europe aloof from the centers of conflict; they are, quite to the contrary, deeply implicated in them in all three respects. For they are at once the battlefield and the prize of victory in an armed conflict between the United States and the Soviet Union; they are permanently and vitally interested in the victory of one or the other side; and they are unable to seek satisfaction for their aspirations for power anywhere but on the European continent itself. It is for these reasons that neither France nor Europe as a whole could enjoy that freedom of maneuver which the "holder" of the balance must have in order to fulfill his function.

The Disappearance of the Colonial Frontier

The balance of power owed the moderating and restraining influence which it exerted in its classical period not only to the moral climate within which it operated and to its own mechanics, but also in good measure to the circumstance that the nations participating in it rarely needed to put all their national energies into the political and military struggles in which they were engaged with each other. Since the possession of territory was considered the symbol and substance of national power, nations in that period had an opportunity, much less risky, of gaining power through the acquisition of land rather than trying to take it away from their powerful neighbors. The wide expanses of three continents offered that opportunity: Africa, the Americas, and the part of Asia bordering on the Eastern oceans.

Throughout the history of the balance of power Great Britain found in this opportunity the main source of her power and of her detachment from the issues which involved the other nations in continuous conflict. Spain dissipated her strength in exploiting that opportunity and thus removed herself from the struggle for power as a force to be reckoned with. What for Great Britain and Spain was a constant and major concern attracted the energies of the other nations to a lesser degree or only sporadically. The policies of France in the eighteenth century present instructive examples of the reciprocal effect of colonial expansion and imperialistic attacks upon the existing balance of power; the more intense the latter were, the less attention was paid to the former, and vice versa. The United States and Russia were for long stages of their history totally absorbed by the task of pushing their frontiers forward into the politically empty spaces of their continents and during those periods took no active part in the balance of power. The Austrian monarchy was in the main concerned, especially during the nineteenth century, with maintaining her control over the non-German nationalities of Central and Southeastern Europe which made up the bulk of her empire. Thus she was incapable of more than limited excursions into power politics. Furthermore, until deep into the eighteenth century, the threat of Turkish aggression limited her freedom of movement on the chessboard of international politics. Prussia, finally, as the latecomer to the circle of the great powers, had to be satisfied with defending and securing her position as a great power and was too weak internally and in too unfavorable a geographical position to think of a program of unlimited expansion. Even after Bismarck had made Prussian power predominant in Germany and German power predominant in Europe, his polity was aimed at preserving, not at expanding, that power.

In the period between 1870 and 1914 the stability of the status quo in Europe is the direct result, on the one hand, of the risks implicit in even the smallest move at the frontiers of the great powers themselves and, on the other, of the opportunity of changing the status quo in outlying regions without incurring the danger of a general conflagration. "At the center [of the group of states forming the balance of power]," observes Professor Toynbee, "every move that any one state makes with a view to its own aggrandizement is jealously watched and adroitly countered by all its neighbors, and the sovereignty over a few square feet of territory and a few hundred 'souls' becomes a subject for the bitterest and stubbornest contention. . . . In the easy circumstances of the periphery, quite a mediocre political talent is often able to work wonders. . . . The domain of the United States can be expanded unobtrusively right across North America from Atlantic to Pacific, the domain of Russia right across Asia from Baltic to Pacific, in an age when the best statesmanship of France or Germany cannot avail to obtain unchallenged possession of an Alsace or a Posen."[2]

With the unification of Germany in 1870 the consolidation of the great nation states was consummated. Territorial gains in Europe could henceforth be made only at the expense of the great powers or their allies. Thus it was not accidental that for more than four decades the great issues of world politics were connected with African names, such as Egypt, Tunis, Morocco, the Congo, South Africa, and with the decrepit Asiatic empires of China and Persia. Local wars arose from these issues, such as the Boer War of 1899 between Great Britain and the Boer Republics, the Russo-Japanese War of 1904, and the Russo-Turkish and Italo-Turkish wars of 1877 and 1911–12 respectively. But in all these wars one of the great powers fought against what might be called a "peripheric" power, which was either the designated object of the former's expansion or, as in the exceptional case of Japan, an outside competitor. In no case, however, was it necessary for a great power to take up arms against another great power in order to expand into the politically empty spaces of Africa and Asia.

The policy of compensations could here operate with a maximum of success, for there was much political no-man's land from which one could compensate oneself and allow others to do the same. There was always a possibility of compromise, without compromising one's vital interests, of retreat while saving one's face, of side-stepping, and of postponement. The period from 1870 to 1914, then, was a period of diplomatic bargains and horse-trading for other people's lands, of postponed conflicts and side-stepped issues.

The most persistent and the most explosive of the great issues of that period (from which the conflagration of the First World War arose): how to distribute the inheritance of the European part of the Turkish Empire, also called the Eastern or the Balkan Question, is significant in this respect. Located at the periphery of the circle of the great powers, the issue was closer to it geographically and weighed more directly upon the distribution of political and military power within it than any other of the great issues of that epoch. Whereas the Balkan Question was more likely than any other issue of that period to lead to open conflict among the great powers—especially since the vital interests of one of them, Austria, were directly affected by the national aspirations of Serbia—it is, however, doubtful whether this outcome was inevitable. One might even plausibly maintain that if the other great powers, especially Germany, had dealt with the Balkan Question in 1914, as they had done successfully at the Congress of Berlin in 1878, that is, in recognition of its peripheral character, the First World War might well have been avoided.

When Bismarck declared in 1876 that, as far as the interests of Germany were concerned, the Balkans were not worth "the good bones of one single Pomeranian musketeer," he affirmed emphatically the peripheral character of the Balkan Question in view of the political and military interests of Germany. When the German government in July, 1914, promised to support whatever steps Austria would take against Serbia, it did the exact opposite, and for no good reason. Germany identified herself with the Austrian interest in the prostration of Serbia as though it were her own, while Russia identified herself with Serbia's defense of her independence. Thus a conflict at the periphery of the European state system transformed itself into one which threatened to affect the overall distribution of power within that system.

Bargaining had become impossible if it was not to be the bargaining away of one's own vital interests. Concessions at somebody else's expense could no longer be made. Because of the identification of one's own interests with the interests of the smaller nations involved, concessions at the apparent expense of others would have meant concessions at one's own expense. The conflict could not be postponed because of the overriding fear of most of the great powers that postponement would strengthen the other side for an armed conflict considered to be inevitable. For once the issues had been brought from the periphery into the center of the circle of the great powers, there was no way of sidestepping them; there was, as it were, no empty space into which to step in order to evade the issue. Russia had to face the Austro-German determination to settle the Serbian problem on Austria's terms; in consequence, France had to face the invocation of the Franco-Russian Alliance by Russia, and Germany had to face the activation of that alliance and Great Britain, the threat to Belgium. There was no side-stepping these issues except at the price of yielding what each nation regarded as its vital interests.

What blundering diplomacy brought about in July 1914, has today become the ineluctable result of structural changes in the balance of power. It was possible in the period preceding the First World War for the great powers to deflect their rivalries from their own mutual frontiers to the periphery and into politically empty spaces because virtually all the active participants in the balance of power were European nations and, furthermore, the main weights of the balance were located in Europe. To say that there were during that period a periphery and politically empty spaces is simply a negative way of saying that during that period the balance of power was quantitatively and qualitatively circumscribed by geographical limits. With the balance of power becoming worldwide and the main weights being placed in three different continents, the American and the Eurasian, the dichotomy between the circle of the great powers and its center, on the one hand, and its periphery and the empty spaces beyond, on the other, must of necessity disappear. The periphery of the balance of power now coincides with the confines of the earth. The formerly empty spaces lie east and west, north and south, on the poles and in the deserts, on land, on water, and in the air, athwart the routes over which the two superpowers must approach each other for friendly or hostile contacts. Thus into those spaces the two remaining great contenders on the international scene have poured their own power, political, military, and economic, transforming these spaces into the two great blocks which border on each other and oppose each other at the four corners of the earth.

The Potentialities of the Two-Block System

These two blocks face each other like two fighters in a short and narrow lane. They can advance and meet each other in what is likely to be combat, or they can retreat and allow the other side to advance into what is to them precious ground. Those manifold and variegated maneuvers through which the masters of the balance of power would try either to stave off armed conflicts altogether or at least to make them brief and decisive yet limited in scope, the alliances and counter-alliances, the shifting of alliances according to whence the greater threat or the better opportunity might come, the side-stepping and postponement of issues, the deflection of rivalries from the exposed front yard into the colonial back yard—these are things of the past. With them have gone into oblivion the peculiar finesse and subtlety of mind, the calculating and versatile intelligence and bold yet circumspect decisions which were required from the players in that game. With those modes of action and intellectual attitudes there has disappeared that self-regulating flexibility, that automatic tendency of disturbed power relations either to revert to their old, or to establish a new, equilibrium.

For the two giants which today determine the course of world affairs only one policy seems to be left, that is, to increase their own strength and that of their satellites. All the players that count have taken sides, and in the foreseeable future no switch from one side to the other is likely to take place. If it were to take place, it would not be likely to reverse the existing balance of power. Since the issues everywhere boil down to retreat from, or advance into, areas which both sides regard as of vital interest to themselves, positions must be held. So the give and take of compromise becomes a weakness which neither side can afford.

While formerly war was regarded, according to the classic definition of Clausewitz, as the continuation of diplomacy by other means, the art of diplomacy now transforms itself into a variety of the art of warfare. That is to say, we live in the period of "cold war" where the aims of warfare are being pursued, for the time being, with other than violent means. In such a situation the peculiar qualities of the diplomatic mind are useless, for they have nothing to operate with and are consequently superseded by the military type of thinking. The balance of power, once disturbed, can only be restored, if at all, by an increase in the weaker side's military strength. Yet since there are no important variables in the picture aside from the inherent strength of the two giants themselves, either side must fear that the temporarily stronger contestant will use its superiority to eliminate the threat from the other side either by shattering military and economic pressure or by a war of annihilation.

Thus, as we approach the mid-twentieth century, the international situation is reduced to the primitive spectacle of two giants eyeing each other with watchful suspicion. They bend every effort to increase their military potential to the utmost, since this is all they can count upon. Each prepares to strike the first decisive blow, for if one does not strike it the other side might. Thus contain or be contained, conquer or be conquered, destroy or be destroyed, become the watchwords of the new diplomacy.

This political state of the world does not of necessity result from the mechanics of the new balance of power. The changed structure of the balance of power has made the hostile opposition of two gigantic power blocks possible, but it has not made it inevitable. On the contrary, the new balance of power is a mechanism which contains in itself the potentialities for unheard-of good as well as for unprecedented evil. Which of these potentialities will be realized depends not upon the mechanics of the balance of power, but upon moral and material forces which use that mechanism for the realization of their ends.

The Influence of Total War

The French philosopher Fénelon, in his advice to the grandson of Louis XIV, gives an account of the different types of the balance of power and, while trying to assess their respective advantages and weaknesses, bestows the highest praise upon the opposition between two equally strong states as the perfect type of the balance of power. "The fourth system," he says, is that of a power which is about equal with another and which holds the latter in equilibrium for the sake of the public security. To be in such a situation and to have no ambition which would make you desirous to give it up, this is indeed the wisest and happiest situation for a state. You are the common arbiter; all your neighbors are your friends, and those that are not, make themselves by that very fact suspicious to all the others. You do nothing that does not appear to have been done for your neighbors as well as for your people. You get stronger every day; and if you succeed, as it is almost inevitable in the long run by virtue of wise policies, to have more inner strength and more alliances than the power jealous of you, you ought to adhere more and more to that wise moderation which has limited you to maintaining the equilibrium and the common security. One ought always to remember the evils with which the state has to pay within and without for its at conquests, the fact that these conquests bear no fruit, the risk which one runs in undertaking them, and, finally how vain, how useless, how short-lived great empires are and what ravage they cause in falling.

Yet since one cannot hope that a power which is superior to all others will not before long abuse that superiority, a wise and just prince should never wish to leave to his successors, who by all appearances are less moderate than he, the continuous and violent temptation of too pronounced a superiority. For the very good of his successors and his people, he should confine himself to a kind of equality.[3]

In other words, the distribution of power which Fénelon envisages resembles distinctly the distribution of power which exists, as we approach the mid-twentieth century, between the United States and the Soviet Union, that is to say, a potential equilibrium with the preponderance at present on the side of the United States. The beneficial results which the French philosopher contemplated have, however, failed to attend this potential equilibrium between the United States and the Soviet Union and do not seem to be likely to materialize in the foreseeable future. The reason is to be sought in the character of modern war which, under the impact of nationalistic universalism and modern technology, has become total. It is here that we find the fifth and last of the fundamental changes which distinguish the world politics of the mid-twentieth century from the international politics of previous ages.

War in our time has become total in four different respects: with respect to the fraction of the population completely identified in its emotions and convictions with the wars of its nation, the fraction of the population participating in war, the fraction of the population affected by war, and the objectives pursued by war. When Fénelon wrote, at the beginning of the eighteenth century, war was limited in all these respects, and had been so since the beginning of the modern state system.

It is the revolution in the productive processes of the modern age that has made total war and worldwide dominion possible. Before its advent war was bound to be limited in its technological aspects; for the productivity of a nation was not sufficient both to feed, clothe, and house its members and to keep large armies supplied with the implements of war for any length of time. More particularly, national economies operated on so narrow a margin above the mere subsistence level that it was impossible to increase the share of the armed forces in the national product to any appreciable extent without endangering the very existence of the nation. In the seventeenth and eighteenth centuries it was not at all unusual for a government to spend as much as, or more than, two-thirds of the national budget for military purposes, which a few times during that period consumed more than ninety percent of the total outlay of the government; for military expenditures had of course precedence over all others and the national product was too small to be taxed extensively for other purposes. Thus it was not by accident that before the nineteenth century all attempts at universal military service failed; for in the interest of keeping national production going, the productive classes of the population had to be exempt from military service and only the scum which was unable to engage in productive enterprises and the nobility which was unwilling to engage in them could safely be conscripted.

The Industrial Revolution and, more particularly, the mechanization of agricultural and industrial processes in the twentieth century have had a triple effect upon the character of war and of international politics. They have increased the total productivity of the great industrial nations enormously. They have, furthermore, reduced drastically the relative share of human labor in the productive processes. They have, finally, together with the new techniques in medicine and hygiene, brought about an unprecedented increase in the population of all nations. Since the increase in productivity thus achieved exceeds by far the increased demands upon the national product caused by the higher standard of living and the greater number of consumers, that excess in productivity is now available for new purposes and can be guided into the channels of total war. The new energy created by the machine and much of the human energy which a century and a half ago was still absorbed in the business of keeping alive can now be employed for military purposes, either directly by way of military service or indirectly through industrial production.

Nor is that human energy now available for war of a muscular nature alone. The machine age has lightened immensely the intellectual and moral burden of keeping oneself and one's dependents fed, clothed, and protected from the elements and from disease, which still a century and a half ago absorbed most of the vital energies of most men. Moreover, it has provided most men with an amount of leisure which only few men have ever had before. Yet paradoxically enough, by doing so, it has freed tremendous intellectual and moral energies which have gone into the building of a better world, but which have also gone into the preparation and the waging of total war. This concatenation of human and material forces, freed and created by the age of the machine, has given war its total character.

It has also given total war that terrifying, world-embracing impetus which seems to be satisfied with nothing short of world dominion. With his intellectual and moral energies no longer primarily concerned about this life nor any more able of being deflected toward concern with the life thereafter, modern man looks for conquests, conquests of nature and conquest of other men. The age of the machine, which has sprung from man's self-sufficient mind, has instilled in modern man the confidence that he can save himself by his own unaided efforts here and now. Thus the intellectual and moral lifeblood of modern man streams into the political religions which promise salvation through science, revolution, or the holy war of nationalism. The machine begets its own triumphs, each forward step calling forth two more on the road of technological progress. It also begets its own victories, military and political; for with the ability to conquer the world and keep it conquered, it creates the will to conquer it.

Yet it may also beget its own destruction. Total war waged by total populations for total stakes under the conditions of the contemporary balance of power may end in world dominion or in world destruction or in both. For either one of the two contenders for world dominion may conquer with relatively small losses to himself, or they may destroy each other, neither being able to conquer, or the least weakened may conquer, presiding over universal devastation. Such are the prospects which overshadow world politics as we approach the halfway mark of the twentieth century.

Thus we have gone full circle. We recognized the driving element of contemporary world politics in the new moral force of nationalistic universalism. We found a simplified balance of power, operating between two inflexible blocs, to be the harbinger of great good or great evil. We discovered the menace of evil in the potentialities of total war. Yet the element which makes total war possible, namely, the mechanization of modern life, makes possible also the moral force which, through the instrumentality of total war, aims at total dominion.[4]

Notes

Reprinted from *The Review of Politics* 10, no. 2 (April 1948): 154–73.

1. *New York Times,* July 29, 1946, 1; cf. for later speeches, *New York Times,* June 30, 1947, 1; July 10, 1947, 3.

2. *A Study of History,* vol. 3 (London, New York, Toronto: Oxford University Press, 1934), 302.

3. *Oeuvres,* vol. 3 (Paris, 1870), 349–50.

4. This paper, in a slightly altered version, forms part of a systematic treatise which, under the title "Politics among Nations: The Struggle for Power and Peace," will be published by Alfred A. Knopf.

CHAPTER 7

The Economic Road to War

JOHN U. NEF

Little more than four decades separated the Franco-Prussian War of 1870–1871 from the first World War of 1914–1918. In terms of material welfare, upon which the economists helped to fix attention, these were the most successful decades in history. In 1650 there were apparently something like half a billion inhabitants of this planet. During the forty-five years from 1870 to 1914 nearly half a billion were added.[1] Population increased by almost as large a number in a generation and a half as it had increased during untold generations separating Adam from Newton. In the wealthier countries of Western Europe (Great Britain, Sweden, Norway, Germany, and France) and in North America, the real income per person gainfully employed has been estimated to have improved seventy-five percent or more, while the hours of work were substantially reduced.[2] In the United States the *per capita* output of the manufacturing industries grew nearly four times over.[3] Professor Tawney has explained that, "during the greater part of history, the normal condition of the world has been one of scarcity. . . . But, as a result of the modernization of production and transport, first in Great Britain, then on the continent of Europe and in North America, then in parts of the Far East, mere scarcity ceased, after the middle of the nineteenth century, to be, except in the last, the haunting terror which till recently it had been."[4]

Important among the conditions which made possible this extraordinary change from scarcity to abundance, were the peaceful relations which prevailed in Europe and throughout most of the world since 1815. Never in the history of Western Civilization had so large a proportion of the Europeans, both in Europe and overseas, lived with so little fighting over long stretches of time, as from 1815 to 1854 and from 1871 to 1914.

After the general use of gunpowder in war had begun at the end of the fifteenth century, various restraints had prevented the relentless exploitation of the new weapons for the sake of conquest. Christian charity, the fear of sin and its consequences, the consciousness of moral responsibility, the love of beauty in the production of tangible objects, the geographical isolation of leading states, had all imposed limits upon war. All these restraints, except the last, had been also, in varying degrees, restraints upon the multiplication of the volume of manufactured goods, which became phenomenally rapid during the industrial revolution. The collapse of the restraints helped to increase production, but at the same time it helped to create the conditions for total war.

A civilization so extensive, so sophisticated, and by comparison with most earlier civilizations, so gentle in its manners as that of Western Europe and North America had become by about 1900, required for war between large nations overwhelmingly greater and more refined means of destruction than any hitherto available to man. Behind new possibilities for destruction were the achievements of the inventor, the engineer, and every variety of technical expert. Behind their achievements was the genius of the natural scientist. Industrial civilization proved capable of harnessing for the purposes of more colossal welfare all the practical advances made by the human mind, even those devoted to the improvement of men's material lot, even those intended to maintain his health and postpone his death.

There are many reasons why science and technology made gigantic strides towards better production and better destruction during the nineteenth century and at the beginning of the twentieth. The key to the astonishing results obtained is not to be found, as people frequently suppose, especially in the United States, in the evolution of a new and higher type of intelligence. Actually the minds of men and women, like their innate characters, remain much the same as they have always been in their potentialities. But, since the late eighteenth century, and even more since the mid-nineteenth, the possibilities for directing the mind to the conquest of matter have been fostered as never before. Historical development combined with the new positive philosophy, expounded by Comte and in a different form by Spencer, to bring the human intelligence to bear undeviatingly on kinds of work which reach new sources of material power; and which exploit all material resources more effectively than in the past in the service of increased output and sale. Again and again, the ingenious application of machinery to processes hitherto confided to human labor, has reduced the human energy required to produce a given quantity of steel, of glass, of cloth, and to transmute these materials into commodities and instruments for quick and handy use in building, living, moving, and destroying. Machine methods took command not only in mining, manufacturing and transport, but in agriculture, finance and communications.[5] Montesquieu had supposed that sugar could never be produced economically from cane except by slave labor. Now machines have taken over much of the work of preparing the ground, cutting and loading the cane on large plantations. Mechanization threatens to leave the great majority of people without any economic need for the exercise of thought, at the very time when the concentration of the intellect on material improvement had resulted also in so remarkable a conquest of disease by surgery, drugs, sanitation, and new comforts, that the years of our sojourn on earth can be doubled.

During the first half of the nineteenth century the opportunities finally dried up for hiring foreign soldiers to fight, the chief means of filling the ranks during the sixteenth and early seventeenth centuries. Even in Switzerland, the traditional source of mercenaries, recruiting by foreign powers was finally forbidden by Swiss federal law in 1859, at the conclusion of the short war fought by France and Piedmont to drive the Austrians from Italy.[6] Meanwhile, with the increasing reservoirs of manpower it became easy to make up for this deficiency. The supply of able-bodied young men available for national service grew rapidly in every country, and after the decade of wars which ended with the German triumph over France in 1871, compulsory military training was decreed by all the principal powers of continental Europe on the plan which originated in early eighteenth-century Prussia. During the last half of the nineteenth century large national armies, capable of tremendous expansion in the event of war, came into being for the first time in history.

In spite of the large armies, educated men were persuaded that the diagnosis repeatedly made of modern civilization as industrial and non-military was correct. Scientists were fond of drawing reassuring inferences from the example of Switzerland. The Swiss had for centuries furnished fighting men for all the European powers, yet now that they had universal military service and a considerable standing army, they never fought. I can also remember a chemist of distinction, who lived from 1862 to 1915, remarking that the wars of Napoleon had lowered the physical stature of the French people by about an inch, and that in consequence such extensive wars were unlikely to be tolerated by civilized mankind. I am not suggesting that his facts about the height of the French were scientifically accurate, but the outlook which the remarks reflected, indicative of great confidence that men and women generally shared his common sense and could make it count in international relations, was prevalent during the times in which he lived.

Scientists and engineers especially held the opinion that the more men and women were provided with better material conditions, the less likely they would be to embark on military adventures. Partly for that reason the interest of the scientific mind in tangible results increased. It sought more than ever before to serve the practical, as measured in terms of increased productivity, better health, longer life. Any invention, any improvement in a technical process, was welcomed with enthusiasm regardless of its implications for the production of more powerful and effective weapons, because it was widely taken for granted that if the standard of living were raised, if life-expectancy were prolonged, nations, together with the peoples they represented, would be ever more disposed to let each other alone and to feel solidarity, if not actual affection, for one another.

As long ago as 1830 an eminent English mathematician, Charles Babbage, had suggested that the "English practice of leaving reward to private enterprise puts a premium on practical achievement as over against abstract truth, which is never rewarded under the system."[7] What in the beginning had been an English practice, during the nineteenth century became to an increasing extent the practice of all the principal countries of Europe and America. For a time the spread of private enterprise strengthened men's desire to improve the human lot. Men with scientific and technical knowledge were encouraged to pour all of it into channels leading to practical results. Still other younger men of talent, hesitating over what career to choose, turned to science, engineering, surgery and medicine. The appeal of these professions became almost irresistible. Were not the men and women who entered them paid for doing good to others? For centuries Christians had believed that virtue is rewarded in heaven; from the time of Spinoza until the late nineteenth century the view gained ground that virtue is its own reward; but during the nineteenth century it began to appear that virtue could obtain a reward here and now.

Another development working towards the application of the intelligence to tangible practical results was the growing departmentalization of knowledge. Great specialization in thought was a novel feature of scholarship in the new world of abundance which industrialism produced. Comte had already expressed concern over it in *La Philosophie positive*, which he finished in 1842. But the splitting of knowledge before that time was followed during the next hundred years by a splitting and resplitting of the divisions which make the scope of individual research and writing in Comte's time seem very wide. Scholars were encouraged to concentrate upon their specialty, oblivious of the general implications of their work, on the assumption that the labor of other specialists, combined with the law of progress, which was thought of as more continuous and inevitable than it had seemed to Turgot when he stated it two centuries ago, would lead automatically in directions which would benefit man.

A young man of thirty in 1850, Herbert Spencer had written that "progress . . . is not an accident, but a necessity. . . . The modifications mankind have undergone, and are still undergoing, result from a law underlying the whole organic creation, and provided the human race continues, and the constitutions of things remains the same, those modifications must end in completeness."[8] It was widely assumed that men were demonstrating this law when each specialist cultivated his own garden. The economist, for example, had a duty to show how goods could be produced and exchanged in larger quantities, and distributed in the manner best suited to further increases in output. Which peoples were to produce the goods, whether it was desirable in the interest of general human happiness to produce some of them at all, were construed questions for statesmen or philosophers. It was no part of the economist's responsibility to inquire whether statesmen or philosophers felt the mission or had the knowledge to settle these questions for the benefit of humanity. Economics itself was dividing into a number of specialties—theory, money and banking, public finance, labor relations, statistics, accounting, economic history, history of economic doctrines—and in the twentieth century each of these was developed independently of the others.

With the increasing respectability of agnosticism, most of the direct concern of scientists with religious faith vanished. Some of them were called religious men. But as words multiplied, they lost their older generally accepted content and changed their meaning. In dealing with the inspiration of the

French Revolution during the early nineteenth century, Michelet (1798–1874) was perfectly clear that it is not enough to be Christian merely to acknowledge, as the Mohammedans do, that Jesus is a great prophet. But the reception accorded a learned man like Spencer by the generation that followed Michelet, the generation of George Eliot (1819–1880), who became an agnostic partly under the influence of Spencer and Comte,[9] shows how confused people were becoming concerning the meaning of "Christian." Spencer concluded the passage in which he reaffirmed the law of progress with these words: "As surely as there is any efficacy in educational culture, or any meaning in such terms as habit, custom, practice, . . . so surely must the things we call evil and immorality disappear; so surely must man become perfect."[10] Some years afterwards, during the eighteen-seventies, a writer in *The Christian Spectator* said of Spencer's doctrine, it "is so profoundly, so intensely, so overwhelmingly religious, nay, so utterly and entirely Christian, that its true meaning could not be seen for very glory. . . . This is Science that has been conversing with God, and brings in her hand His law written on tables of stone."[11]

Among scientists in the twentieth century there was some recrudescence of interest in theological questions. Those who reflected upon these questions were disposed to make the subject of theology into a branch of the natural sciences. Thereby they reversed what had been for many human societies the natural order of knowledge, with theology as the "queen" of the sciences. If any of these "religious" scientists were shown the deep religious faith of their ancestors, it had for them the charm of complete novelty. A place for worship was the last provision that was thought of in creating the town of Los Alamos, where the first atomic bomb was hatched, while hundreds of scientists and technicians set up housekeeping with their families.

When scientists made excursions into philosophy or theology, it was frequently on the assumption that their special scientific knowledge had provided them with the credentials for judging all knowledge. Hesitant about their own powers in dealing with their special subjects, a few of them felt free to forget the caution of Socrates in the most universal of human inquiries, and to assume that they had found wisdom. After the mid-nineteenth century, specialists in the multiplying non-scientific disciplines had less and less with which to dispute the credentials of famous scientists. Many aped what they took to be approved scientific methods, applying them to economic, sociological, psychological, and even philosophical problems.

For two principal reasons the natural sciences were almost certain to carry the field in competition of this kind. The methods which the natural scientists depended upon for proofs were actually much better suited to the work they were doing than to that of their colleagues in other specialties. Further and still more decisive as time went on, the natural scientists could show that their discoveries had produced tangible results in mechanics, engineering, medicine, surgery. Achievements whose value was demonstrable became more and more the only works of the mind which the public and the political leaders alike were willing to accept without question as authentic. As a result of their increasing prestige, the physical and the biological sciences attracted an ever larger proportion of the intelligent at a time when, with the extraordinary growth in population and the equally extraordinary growth in the opportunities for leisure, there were in fact more potentially good minds available than ever before. Less and less hampered, as time went on, by serious concern over the evil in human nature, which had troubled Napier, Boyle and Newton; emancipated from the distracting concern with art, which had divided the attention of Leonardo and other great men of the Renaissance; the more and more numerous scientists were free to devote their undivided talent, attention, industry, and genius to revealing the secrets of matter, space, and time. They might enjoy music, the theater, books; they might even play instruments, paint, or write poetry. But they did these things for recreation. Such activities formed no integral part of their science and so were unrelated to their main business, however much the initial inspiration for their most remarkable discoveries originated in the intuitive insight which is fundamental to the achievements of the artist.

Along with the public appreciation of science went an unstinted public enthusiasm, that had begun early in the seventeenth century in Great Britain and had spread in the late eighteenth century to all Europe and North America, for engineers and inventors of every kind, for physicians and surgeons, and for administrators capable of organizing technical work efficiently. Technicians gained popular applause denied to many an original scientific mind. The applause might be deafening for those who had a flair for publicity. Such applause was not lost on children playing with toys and on young people seeking a career. By processes similar to those which drew into the natural sciences many of the most intelligent, decent, and humanely-inclined men and women of the age, gifted and conscientious persons, with extraordinary energy, were drawn as experts and administrators into those professions where the discoveries of science were practically applied.

The consequence of this exaltation of both science and technology was to orient an entire civilization in the direction of still more population, a still greater volume of production and equally greater powers of destruction. Progress was becoming cumulative in a variety of ways. As people's minds were directed more than ever before towards scientific knowledge and practical improvement, and toward pecuniary success, the habit of thinking in these terms spread in the schools and colleges, in the press, in the law courts, even in the churches. As scientific, technological, medical, and surgical knowledge increased, the foundation was continually broadened for further advances. Fresh increments of improvement were much easier to achieve than when, as in the sixteenth and seventeenth centuries, these realms of intellectual exploration had been largely unknown and almost entirely uncharted. Maps and equipment were made available which the early explorers had lacked.

Babbage had suggested that the growing interest in the tangible results of knowledge would cause a decline in "the more difficult and abstract sciences." He rightly pointed out that "those intellectual qualifications which give birth to new principles or to new methods, are of quite a different order from those which are necessary for their practical application."[12] But his assumption that interest in the practical would crowd out interest in the fundamental proved premature. The tremendous material success of the late nineteenth century made room for both. Until the era of world wars, scientific speculations retained a position of dignity, they commanded a quiet respect, which they had acquired during the seventeenth century especially in Great Britain, before engineers and technocrats were exalted.

During the nineteenth century an idea arose, which had not been current in the England of Newton, that men of genius were likely to be unrecognized by their contemporaries. Stendhal, for example, reconciled himself to writing for the "happy few," because the many were not inclined to read him. With the growing vulgarity of the popular press, the speculative mind often found advantages in withdrawing from the rewards of the market place, so long as its possessor was assured a modest income and abundant leisure. The absence of the publicity accorded to prominent engineers and other inventors, left the scientist with time for serious thought, and with a small audience of peers who could discuss his work. Men whose contributions to *science* were mediocre or non-existent, but who had spectacular popular success, like Edison with the use of electricity, or Marconi, with the wireless telegraph, took the public acclaim, accorded the interviews or went the rounds of dinners and festivities. They left to scientific geniuses, such as Rutherford and Einstein in his early years, the quiet indispensable to the development of great ideas, like Einstein's modification of what had been thought of hitherto as Newton's universal law of gravity, or Rutherford's discovery that the atom could be split and that matter is not composed of final particles.

"The more difficult and abstract sciences" came into their own on the eve of the first World War. The purity, the elegance and, above all, the originality of the new scientific work resembled that of Newton, his contemporaries and immediate predecessors, except that the modern scientists had a less cosmic view of knowledge and of man and that few of them devoted any serious thought to magic or astrology, as Newton had. The result was the quantum theory, the theory of relativity and other revolutionary discoveries, which have changed men's conceptions of the nature of the physical world.

This work, like the earlier work of Galileo, Kepler, and Newton, or that of Harvey and Boyle, had tremendous practical implications. Unlike the earlier work, it came when the training of the young and the outlook of society had created conditions under which practical implications were likely to be quickly and thoroughly exploited. Results in terms of production and destruction, which before the nineteenth century would have required decades and even generations to achieve, could now be obtained in months. With the economic, medical, and military progress already made, it became possible to extend man's dominion over matter with a frenzied speed such as would have baffled the comparatively modest mid-nineteenth-century prophets of progress. When in 1872 Jules Verne (1828–1905), author of some widely-read mechanical romances of the Victorian age, predicted that the tour of the world would be made in eighty days, few of his readers believed him. Yet some, then in their childhood, lived until men began to be shot around the globe in forty-eight hours.

Science was now able almost to annihilate space and time. But it was also preparing means for the almost complete annihilation of man. Still strong in the age of Newton, the restraints upon the use of knowledge for purposes of destruction had now largely disappeared. After the era of limited wars, and the "great peace" which filled much of the nineteenth century, the leading scientists themselves were less wary about the dangers which might be involved in discreetly telling all they knew. Few intelligent men felt, or, if they felt, dared profess a serious interest in mystery. With the relegation of mystery to the storyteller, the conjurer, and the charlatan, educated men felt they had no right to make a mystery of any of their discoveries. The circumstances of private life might still be properly allowed to die, but not the circumstances of scientific discoveries. It became almost a dogma among scientists that these were public property, that the only obligation of a scientist before publishing was to make sure that his discovery within the limits of his special subject was sound.

The advent of total wars dealt blows to this confidence, but failed to make many scientists more reticent. Dismayed after 1914 by the evident recrudescence of evil and violence in a world they had thought of as civilized and humane, some of them supposed that the new evil and the new violence were a monopoly of certain groups, certain classes, certain countries. Many of the scientists belonged to a generation which had been taught that humanity and goodness were the normal products of industrial civilization. If only one got rid of the Jews, the Nazis, or the Fascists, and then of the Communists or the Capitalists, humanity and goodness would again prevail. The march towards a terrestrial paradise could be resumed.

The construction of any weapon was justified in the eyes of scientists, no matter how total its powers of destruction, because of the excellence of the cause they believed they served. Some held back nevertheless, distrusting the purity of the cause, refusing to put their knowledge unreservedly at the service of destruction. Professor Frederick Soddy, an English inorganic and physical chemist, refrained from assisting in the first World War. Earlier than most recent scientists, he saw the danger of extinction to which scientific knowledge might condemn Western civilization, and in the nineteen-twenties he turned from science to economics. Beating his wings against the sides of the cage in which the learned were now imprisoned, he labored at his new specialty in hope against hope that his work might help save mankind from "the principle of death," which another scientifically-trained Englishman, W. Trotter, had suggested might be embodied in the very structure and substance of all constructive human effort.[13]

The conditions of technological advance had changed since the age of Newton. The abstention of one individual, the doubts of another, had lost almost all influence, now that so many were engaged in scientific research, and that astounding technical results could come from minds chained together.

Until almost the end of the first World War, the military administrators and the generals put their reliance mainly on guns—on the astonishing increase that was obtained after 1850 and especially after 1870 in speed, accuracy and quantity of fire, with new artillery and new rifled firearms of many kinds. In 1911, Colonel F. N. Maude, who edited an English edition of Clausewitz' treatise *On War,* estimated that in the eighty years since the time of Clausewitz the fire of infantry had increased from three to sixteen rounds a minute, while the range of accuracy from cannon fire had increased from one thousand to five or six thousand yards.[14] The machine gun was introduced into the French army in 1866. A French historian, Camille Rousset, pointed out that it could have a magic effect on the morale of the defender.[15]

So it proved in the war of 1914–1918. The avalanche of metal, especially steel, which came from newly invented furnaces and mills in Europe was more than a hundred times the quantity available a century earlier to Napoleon and his enemies. The new and more efficient artillery, when massed for an attack, tore up the earth by its fire and hurled into the air fragments of the bodies of thousands of enemy soldiers hiding in trenches—this before the first advancing waves of the attacking infantry went over the top with bayonets fixed, to destroy such life as remained. An English military commander, General J. F. C. Fuller, writing ten years after the war, affirmed that in the third battle of Ypres, in 1917 "the gunner personnel numbered no less than 120,000; we dumped at Ypres 321 four-hundred-ton loads of ammunition, and fired this off in a preliminary bombardment which lasted for nineteen days. In this bombardment were fired 4,283,000 shells weighing 107,000 tons."

No matter how efficient the artillery preparation, there were almost invariably surviving machine gunners buried in nests of earth. Their guns spit out a hail of fire at the advancing infantry, often more deadly than the shells of the artillery, because the human targets were now exposed and at nearer range. Mass murder became the order of the day; the reward for the attackers was seldom more than a few miles of trenches, captured while the defenders were perfecting another prepared network behind what had been the front. Indecisiveness was long the most striking tactical feature of the war, whether on sea or land. General Fuller's account of the third battle of Ypres proceeds: "The ground gained was approximately forty-five square miles, and each square mile cost us 8,222 casualties."[16]

This new indecisive warfare had none of the limiting features of the warfare which had been characteristic of Newton's age. Europe could now afford large standing armies, to replenish and supply them again and again under the exigencies of war. "More money" was needed to kill than ever before, but the money required turned out to be small in comparison with the money that could be raised (with the help of refined advances in the use and manipulation of credit), and in relation to the quantity of munitions which money and credit could buy. So the war cost "more blood" than any war ever fought before—lakes of blood and hills of dead bodies. The exact figure for the dead is unknown, but it could hardly have been less than eight million young men in four years.[17]

Though nominally a victor, France was harder hit than any other country. The French nation lost nearly a million and four hundred thousand soldiers. An additional four million and more were wounded. Three out of every four of the eight million men mobilized by France were casualties. Few Frenchmen of an entire generation were unmarked by wounds which plagued them to their dying day. The number of lives required to defend the Ile de France had multiplied at least a hundredfold between the battle of Valmy and the first battle of the Marne, although the French population had not doubled.

The only way to bring about quick decisive results in war was to devise means of producing havoc at longer distances, and at the same time to find ways of encasing spearheads of men in armor. The fulfillment of the early ideas of the airplane and the tank transferred the advantages overwhelmingly from the defense to the attack. The conception of the infinitely destructive bomb exploding on an ever more extensive target and wiping out all life in an area of many square miles, a notion which Napier, the inventor of logarithms in the early seventeenth century, had in a vague embryonic form, was finally made into a reality, with the very consequences which the scientific minds of early modern times had dreaded.

Almost the same number of men died in combat during the six years of the second World War as during the four years of the first. Several millions more were done away with in concentration camps or by mass electrocution in specially constructed railway carriages. The destruction of buildings and noncombatants in air raids, and the dislocation of orderly economic life were incomparably greater than in the first World War. Most of the large German cities, many of the Japanese cities, were mainly reduced to rubble. In Poland, European Russia, China, northern France, Italy, Greece, Austria, Hungary and Czechoslovakia, Holland, Belgium, and Norway large tracts in some towns were bombed to bits from the air; other tracts were smashed from the land with rapidly-moving artillery which was no longer stopped by trench defenses. Parts of some English towns went the way of the German. In the civil war of 1936–1938 Spain had had its taste of what was coming.

In the eighteenth century, when hopes ran high for the happiness of humanity, many intelligent men were shocked out of their optimism by a frightful earthquake, in 1755, which brought down large sections of the picturesque Portuguese town of Lisbon, killing many thousands of the inhabitants. No one was more affected by the reports of destruction than Voltaire. Professor Paul Hazard tells us that this was the decisive episode leading to the composition in 1759 of his *Candide,* a short satirical novel on optimism. Voltaire is among the masters of satire. His book made the system of optimism appear ridiculous. Lisbon in fire and ruins, the groans and shrieks of the injured and the dying, the pieces of dead bodies scattered about the streets, made a mockery of the influential philosophical doctrine of Leibnitz, that everything that happens is for the best.[18]

During the war of 1939–1945 the tragedy of Lisbon became almost a weekly occurrence. It was brought about not by nature but by man.

Material progress made this possible. Material progress makes much more possible in the future. Nearly every day we have impressed upon us over the radio, on the screen, in the newspapers and magazines how much science,

technology, medicine, surgery, engineering, and efficient business administration have done for man. They have done as much for war.

Since the time of Columbus' voyages, when the widespread use of gunpowder began, the oceans had provided broad moats, more efficacious as barriers to decisive fighting than the narrow trenches which surrounded strong
places in the twelfth and thirteenth centuries. Where the medieval moat had
protected only a castle, the channels, seas, and oceans protected large nations.
Sparsely settled islands and even continents provided territory beyond range
of the guns where the disgruntled and the persecuted could find a refuge, and
where adventurous men could go in search of enterprise. Many of le Blas' fellow Calvinists in Tournai sailed as refugees to the safety of England. Madame
de la Tour du Pin, the French noblewoman, who later got on well with Napoleon, escaped the guillotine in the French Revolution. With her husband and
children she stole aboard a small vessel at Bordeaux, the very night when
agents of the Terror were abroad to capture them, to settle and farm in the
lovely Hudson River country near Albany.

All that is ended. In the eighteen-eighties the last frontier was crossed in
the United States, with a destruction of the pioneer spirit and a change in the
American outlook that Tocqueville had predicted and that Professor F. J.
Turner was to describe. Since then one frontier after another has gone the way
of the American frontier. Between 1650 and 1850 the population of the world
is said to have doubled. There are now more than two billion inhabitants;
everywhere people are crowded together; they no longer have any place to go,
unless it be to the moon.

The conquest of the air, combined with the new transport facilities by
land and sea, made possible the rapid movement of hundreds of thousands
of marines and soldiers to places hardly accessible to tens of thousands a generation ago. All the countries of the earth were brought as closely face to face
as were the great powers of Western Europe before the first World War. During this very period of forty years from 1910 to 1950, when the most diverse
races, countries, and civilizations have been catapulted into a single entity,
when the speck on the map represented by Western Europe was replaced as
a potential battlefield by the globe, the proud civilization of whose essential
unity Gibbon wrote with such confidence nearly two hundred years ago found
itself less united. The Europeans no longer recognized a common Father in

heaven or a common culture on earth. The principle of nationality, which had been counted on to give divided peoples, such as the Italians and the Germans, a new hope and satisfaction which would make for peace, had provided a basis for a conflict such as the Europeans had not had since the Wars of Religion. Far from completing the Western community, the principle of nationality, and the fiery patriotism which it generated, had divided, first the Europeans and then the world, into vast armed camps. In each of them was to be found the kindling in men and munitions for a holocaust more vast than any the world had faced since Biblical times. Whatever justification can be made for the "contests" of 1914–1918 and 1939–1945, it cannot be said that they have been "temperate," as Gibbon had assumed all struggles between nations of the European "republic" were bound to be.

More than a hundred years before Gibbon wrote his *Decline and Fall,* another famous Englishman, Thomas Hobbes, foresaw the possible consequences of material progress on a world scale. Filled as he and many of his generation were with a consciousness of original sin and of the prevalence of evil, Hobbes looked to such a concentration of population and such a unified planet as science and invention have now achieved, not with confident hope but with fearful awe. "And when all the world is overcharged with Inhabitants," he wrote, "then the last remedy of all is Warre; which provideth for every man, by Victory, or Death."[19]

Everywhere on the sidewalks of enormous cities and in the suburbs that stretch beyond them, man is face to face with his neighbor. In a few hours he can be hurled in a fast plane through space to the most distant island; but he will still find his neighbor close at hand. He may reach the moon; others like him will reach it too. As Hobbes' words indicate, it is open to him to kill his neighbor. It is also open to him to recognize his neighbor.

During the period when industrialism has drawn the whole world into a unit, it has given all economic life military purposes. Gone are the old distinctions between peace and war industries. Every industry, every profession, every invention, however humane its intent, is of potential military value.[20] In the nineteenth century railways and telegraphs were seen to be hardly less important for war than guns. All the railway systems of continental Europe were laid out with military purposes in mind, at a time when the United States and even Great Britain were sufficiently isolated to build their railways almost exclusively for purposes of trade. Contrary to the views of Montesquieu, Kant, Constant, and Comte, commerce and industry did not continue to subdue war; war invaded the two leading commercial and industrial nations in their geographical isolation, and forced them back into the orbit of deadly struggle from which they had escaped after the Reformation. These views of Montesquieu and Kant had been formed when conditions of scarcity still prevailed. They were derived from a recognition that the economic resources available were inadequate to carry on both extensive war and extensive commerce at the same time. It was necessary to choose one or the other. This principle remained true even after the triumph of industrialism. But the great new opportunities for expansion made the principle less obvious. That was one reason why it became doubtful whether commerce would continue to work for peace after conditions of scarcity were replaced by conditions of abundance. By the twentieth century the very technical advances which make possible the production and distribution of food, clothing, and less indispensable comforts to the needy in distant places, were easily diverted to supply, on a scale without precedent, gigantic armed forces, whose mission was the destruction of both the needy and the well off in nations bulging with tens of millions of people.

During the Napoleonic Wars by far the greatest number of the deaths among the troops resulted from illness. When Napoleon hurried soldiers to Belgium to provide a defense against a threatened English invasion, fever swept among them, taking a heavy toll.[21] Such episodes had recurred in armies since the beginning of military history. Every leader had to take them into account in his strategy. In the Crimean War of 1854–1855, nineteen percent of all the British soldiers sent to the Near East died of disease, and twenty-seven percent of all the French. Among the remainder, few escaped a serious siege of illness; a larger proportion of the British than of the French were reported as gravely ill. By comparison casualties in battle were small. More than eight French soldiers died of disease for one killed in action.[22]

Since the Crimean War discoveries in medicine and surgery have made it possible to prevent some diseases and cure others. Economic abundance has provided the population generally with comforts, foods, and hygienic appliances which have diminished the ravages of deadly disease. Among the most advanced Western nations the annual death rate has been reduced from about forty per thousand a century and a half ago to about ten today. The death rate from illness in the armed forces has fallen even more, because it is those diseases which formerly destroyed the young and healthy which can now be eliminated or successfully treated.

In earlier wars, more died of wounds than were killed in action. Between the Franco-Prussian War of 1870–1871 and the World War of 1914–1918, a notable reduction was made in the number of the wounded who died.[23] Now the great majority are saved by the same advances in medicine and surgery that are available to repair the bodies broken in automobile accidents. Wounded soldiers and sailors can be flown home thousands of miles in large numbers to be patched together and put back into battle after a few days. Wars can now be fought with the help of drugs and surgical instruments as well as with guns and explosives. The humane scientist is faced with a dilemma that is largely novel. Shall he prepare the populations to live that they may destroy each other better? Before the recent advances in science, the choices confronting scientific minds were simpler. It was clear to Napier which of his inventions could kill if he divulged a knowledge of them. The discoverers of penicillin were faced with an issue far less clear.

The kinds of material progress which have accompanied the industrial revolution have led to total war, not only because of their material, but also because of their moral and intellectual consequences, and because of the new problems which abundance has raised for the national economics. The new weapons and the new means of employing them have made it more difficult to distinguish between aggression and defense. They have reduced overwhelmingly the trouble and the anguish involved in the act of killing. Their manufacture and use have provided an immense outlet for the products of the multiplying new engines and furnaces, whose operators have been hard put to find markets.

It is now more than a century since the German general, Karl von Clausewitz (1780–1831), became famous by publishing a book in which he considered war as a philosophical problem. With the rise of romanticism in thought and letters, writers were becoming less prone than they had been to follow the embarrassing practice of calling human qualities and vices by their names.

It had been a generally accepted principle in Western European thought, which was reaffirmed by Grotius, that "it is not the party who repels by force of arms, but the power who first makes the attack, that violates a peace." But in his book Clausewitz advanced the somewhat surprising doctrine that in a war the real aggressor is the defender. "The *offensive*," he wrote, ". . . has for its absolute object not so much *combat* as the *taking possession of something*." What leads to fighting, what causes a war, is overt acts by the soldiers of the invaded country.[24] It was a thesis put to continual use during the period of world wars. It encouraged the military enthusiasm of Clausewitz' countrymen, when no one had actually aimed a blow at their nation. Many Germans will tell one solemnly that in August 1914, Belgium attacked Germany, and in September 1939, Poland.

With the advances in industrial technology it became increasingly difficult to construct any preparations for war as defensive, when more and more the only means of defending was to attack. Even before the first World War had ended that ingenious American thinker, Thorstein Veblen, pointed out that "any well designed offensive can effectually reach any given community, in spite of distance or of other natural obstacles. The era of defensive armaments and diplomatic equilibration, as a substitute for peace, has been definitively closed by the modern state of the industrial arts."[25] Material abundance completely altered the stakes of diplomacy; the stakes were now all or nothing, total war or total peace. One consequence of the unparalleled material progress was to make it easier to inflame the passions of entire peoples on behalf of defense. In earlier times countries or groups had fought on behalf of some religious conviction, to gain trade advantages, or simply to conquer. Now the proclaimed object of every nation which fights is only to defend itself.

The spirit of defense, of resistance, is potent. We have seen to what lengths it carried the remarkably intelligent John Napier in the late sixteenth century. But then it was less difficult, especially for countries protected by water, to distinguish between defense and attack. Since Napoleon's time the instinct to defend which is universal, has come to operate with more equal force on both sides in war. The instinct requires no sophistication. Primitive, even animal, the instinct of fear can arouse the most stupid. In societies, like those of Europe, America, and Asia, which were losing all positive convictions at the beginning of the twentieth century, apart from the desire to become richer, defense alone was capable of mobilizing the general will to fight.

No army commander in the second World War made a more dramatic use of the new defense[26] on land than General Patton. His American armies swept across most of northern France in a few days. Months later they swept through southwestern Germany and across Czecho-Slovakia with equal rapidity. Shortly before his death in an automobile accident, General Patton is reported to have given a newspaper man his opinion of a gun which was incapable of effective execution at more than sixty yards. "To do much good at that distance," the general is said to have observed, "requires real human courage behind the weapon. And, let me tell you, human courage is spread mighty thin."

Thanks to the progress of the past fifty years, the amount of courage required to kill hosts of the enemy, including non-combatants, or to obliterate his naval forces, has been greatly reduced. In the second World War the final destruction of the Japanese fleet, built at enormous expense during a generation of time, occurred in the battle of Leyte Gulf "by any standard the greatest sea fight of all time." In five days the Japanese lost four aircraft carriers, three battleships, six heavy cruisers, and eleven destroyers. Some of the large ships were sent to the bottom in a matter of minutes. Most of the mischief was inflicted by torpedoes directed from distant submarines or by equally impersonal bombs dropped from the air at a great height; there was no major encounter between surface vessels.[27]

Warships costing tens of millions of dollars and carrying thousands of sailors can now be sunk, cities inhabited by a hundred thousand people can be wiped out from a distance of miles, by a mere touch of an executioner who moves his fingers in accordance with prescribed regulations. He has no picture of the persons or the property he is destroying, and at the time of execution, he runs comparatively little risk of bodily injury. A further refinement was achieved by robot planes and rockets. The human executioner was for practical purposes eliminated. Without men, machines did the work.

The military advantages of getting back from the target were described by Clausewitz when civilized Europeans had outgrown the sixteenth-century prejudice that, when a state of war exists or is created, there is anything cowardly about killing persons who are too far off to see their murderers. "Weapons with which the enemy can be attacked while he is at a distance, . . ." Clausewitz wrote, "allow the feelings, the 'instinct for fighting' properly called, to remain almost at rest, and this so much the more according as the range of their effects is greater. With a sling we can imagine to ourselves a certain degree of anger accompanying the throw, there is less of this feeling in discharging a musket, and still less in firing a cannon shot."[28] How little is left in releasing a blockbuster or in detonating an atomic bomb? Progress has purged actual warfare of much of the emotional anger which accompanied the struggles of olden times. Except among the infantry, killing has become so impersonal that the killer resembles a boy with a toy pistol, or a man in a bathroom stepping on cockroaches. The private soldier or petty officer is hardly more important in any skill or training he has to make use of, or any intellectual choice he is permitted, than the factory worker in the assembly line. Both have been mechanized, and with mechanization their opportunities for the exercise of human faults and human virtues alike, have largely disappeared.

Two conditions which had impeded the development of efficient weapons largely disappeared during the nineteenth century. One was the chase, especially as a sport for gentlemen. With the growth and migration of population, the number of regions abundantly populated with wild life diminished. Hunting had longer and longer closed seasons. With the decline of the aristocracy, the hunters were thinned out, especially those who could afford elegant fowling pieces, elaborately decorated. In earlier times a considerable proportion of all weapons had been for private use, and as long as the desire for artistic workmanship persisted, the makers loitered over problems of design and embellishment.[29] With the concentration of the manufacture of weapons for military purposes in large factories, operated by assembly-line methods, the only considerations of the producers have been the effectiveness and abundance of the weapons, and the mechanical ease with which they can be operated.

The result has been a revolution which forms a striking part of the industrial revolution itself. While experts on military tactics and strategy are prone to say that the object of making war always remains the same—the annihilation of the enemy—it is certain that the nature of the enemy to be annihilated and the means of annihilation have been changed. Whole nations are becoming targets. Mechanical power has now replaced courage as the decisive factor in war. Even in the first World War, only a negligible proportion of the casualties were from bayonet wounds. The principal use made of this long dagger was for holding sausages in a fire while they cooked, or for opening cans of food manufactured hundreds of miles from the front, and brought to the soldiers by an increasingly effective commissariat. Hand-to-hand fighting, which became less frequent with the general use of gunpowder during the sixteenth century, now seldom plays any serious part in deciding a battle; it plays still less part in deciding a war.

Herodotus, the father of history, calls the attention of his readers to the advantages possessed in war by a state comparatively poor but full of courageous citizens. He attributed the strength of the Persians, in their early period of conquest, more to their poverty than to their wealth. Later, when the Persians set out to conquer the Greeks, they were no longer "a poor people with a proud spirit." Herodotus attributed the successful resistance of the Greeks in the Persian War partly to their indifference to wealth. He depicted the consternation of a Persian leader of the invading armies, who, in the presence of the famous Xerxes, learned that the Greeks spent years training and preparing their bodies for games in which the reward was only an olive wreath. "Good heavens!" the leader exclaimed, ". . . what manner of men are these against whom thou has brought us to fight?—men who contend with one another, not for money, but for honor."[30]

With the rise of mechanized warfare, the extent to which victory is determined by courage and a willingness to sacrifice has diminished. There has been an immense increase in the extent to which victory is determined by the mere power to organize industrial production, deliver weapons and missiles in profusion, and guide by technical rules the hands of the fighters. As long ago as 1928 General Fuller took the position that machines would be the decisive factor in any future war.[31] The history of the second World War, its conclusion and its sequel suggest that they are no less decisive than he thought they would be. The fanatical willingness of the best Japanese troops to give their lives in battle was of little avail against combined mechanized operations of air, sea and land. It requires tremendous courage to dive with one's plane to certain death on the deck of an enemy airplane carrier, but how meager are the results from such exploits compared to those achieved by guiding mechanically from a distance unaccompanied torpedoes or rockets. These can be turned out by mass production. It is more difficult to manufacture courage.

Nearly a hundred years ago, the leading English advocate of free trade among the nations, Richard Cobden (1804–1865), laid down the maxim that war is the greatest of all consumers.[32] With the growing mechanization of industry, and the change noted by Tawney from conditions of scarcity to abundance, finding consumers became a major economic problem. Political leaders in the richest industrial countries were confronted periodically with unprecedented unemployment. Their task was not the more ancient one of providing food and other necessities, it was rather that of providing jobs, so that more persons would have money to buy. One way of accomplishing this was to keep up prices, especially in the case of farm products, so as to hold families on the land. While few producers could afford the small waste involved in fashioning beautiful objects, such as figureheads for the bows and arcades for the sterns of warships, waste on a national scale became for the first time almost a political virtue. In order to keep up prices it was felt necessary often to create an artificial scarcity, sometimes by using government credit to buy and destroy grain and other farm produce, including animals.

Organized war has always been the most effective means of destruction known to man. During the last hundred and fifty years its destructive powers have multiplied manyfold. With the coming of world wars, the openings for employment in connection with war expanded with unprecedented rapidity. In time of peace, the chief powers of Europe maintained at the beginning of the twentieth century some four million men under arms. This was almost eight times the number maintained in the early eighteenth century. In the meantime the European population had grown at least four times over. The really striking change was in the capacity for enlarging the forces when war came. The numbers under arms were then increased to thirty or forty millions and upwards. Women were conscripted for auxiliary war services. While casualties were very high among combat troops, statistics were brought forward to show that, by and large, more persons were injured in accidents under conditions of peace than were wounded in military service. It was hoped that young people would appreciate the advantages thrust upon them by their removal from the dangers of civilian life.

All the millions and tens of millions now mobilized had to be fed, clothed, and provided with increasingly expensive mechanical weapons and conveyances. The introduction of a mechanized air force was followed by the mechanization of the navy and then of the army. Each step enormously increased the consuming power of war. While the expenditure of all the belligerents in the first World War hardly exceeded two hundred billion dollars,[33] the United States alone spent more than this sum in the second World War.[34]

War was an unequalled means of creating an artificial scarcity. Tawney pointed out that, "labor, consumption goods and capital all became deficient"[35] in wartime, and so war recreated the conditions of scarcity which had been the common lot of civilized peoples until the last hundred years. If new wars were to be won, governments had to deal with shortages, such as had been normal before the triumph of industrialism. Once a nation engaged in war, its unemployment problems disappeared. Jobs were available for all who wanted them and for many who did not.

There was nothing to rival war as a frightful and temporary solution for the new problems of abundance. In the late seventeenth and early eighteenth century economic conditions had imposed restraints upon the waging of relentless warfare; the inefficiency of industry in terms of its productive power had helped bring about the era of limited war. At the beginning of the twentieth century, contrary to the wishes of many political leaders, economic conditions provided nations with a temptation to make war; or at least, if war had once begun and had fanned national passions, hatreds and fears, the nations had now the means to carry the war through to a material conclusion.

As total war with explosives became economically feasible for the first time, a novel notion arose, that war itself was economically a constructive force. The advantage of gaining territory and riches by conquest is, of course, one of the oldest justifications for war. But the new idea, brought forward by Sombart on the eve of the first World War, was different. He held that the economic experiences of modern war had actually served to raise the level of industrial efficiency and productivity within the participating nations. Is there anything about the triumph of industrial civilization and the revolution in the weapons and conditions of war, that has made this thesis more tenable for the twentieth century, than for the sixteenth, the seventeenth, or the eighteenth centuries?

In its essentials, the industrial revolution had been carried through before 1914. Among the conditions behind the remarkable technical progress that

made the industrial revolution possible the "great peace," as it has been sometimes called, that prevailed in Europe from 1815 to 1914, was of much importance. During that period peaceful requirements were of far greater importance than military ones in eliciting the ingenuity of inventors. We may doubt
whether the use of power-driven machinery and the level of technical efficiency
would have been appreciably lower in 1914, if Kant's "perpetual peace" had
been established by the Congress of Vienna and all military preparations had
been abandoned during the nineteenth century. For example, we do not owe
the invention of the explosives nitroglycerin and dynamite to war. They were
intended for mining.[36] Without the effective peace which prevailed in Western
Europe for a century, except during the twelve years from 1859 to 1871, there
would have been no such demand as occurred for peaceful inventions. In all
probability technological improvement would have been very much slower.
The industrial revolution might never have been completed.

To a greater degree than any preceding wars, the world wars of the past
thirty-five years have canalized technical ingenuity in the service of war. The
preceding hundred years of comparatively peaceful international relations
had presented the world with far more practical technical skill than was ever
available before, and with a far larger number of expert technicians. Just as
vastly more material things were manufactured, so there was also vastly more
technical skill to waste if mankind chose to waste it. What have been the consequences of the era of world wars for technical and scientific progress which
helped to make the world wars possible?

As the first World War drew to a close, a German scholar, Dr. C. F. Nicolai,
who occupied the chair of physiology in the University of Berlin, addressed
himself to this very question. "Of course if a war lasts as long as this one," he
wrote, "and absorbs all the intellectual and material forces of the nations, it is
not surprising that there should be a few inventions while it is going on. There
can be not the slightest doubt, however, that future statistics will prove that the
annual number of inventions in Europe during the war was smaller—much
smaller in comparison—than in any correspondingly long period we may select in the last few decades."[37]

The position of the United States from 1914 to 1945 resembled that of Great
Britain during the Revolutionary and Napoleonic Wars from 1792 to 1815.
Great Britain was then the only major European power not invaded. In the

enormously larger struggles of the past four decades, the United States was the only major world power that escaped both invasion and destruction. Technical progress in the direction of efficient machine production has gone on unabated since 1914. Such progress has been possible because the United States obtained most of the constructive advantages of military preparations without receiving at home any of the direct destructive consequences of warfare. The favorable conditions for mechanical progress which prevailed in Great Britain during the "early industrial revolution" of the Elizabethan Age, and during the early stages of the industrial revolution proper from 1785 to 1815, when Great Britain carried on war from a base out of range of the enemy, were repeated in the United States from 1914 to 1945, with the help of the enormous accumulation of scientific and technical knowledge and on the basis of the general mechanization of industry, transportation, agriculture, and finance, which occurred from 1815 to 1914. Before and during the second World War the United States provided an asylum for many of the leading scientific men of Europe and for some of the leading engineers. Aided by the knowledge and the skill which these foreign refugees put at our disposal with enthusiasm, the Americans built upon scientific knowledge and technical achievements which were already historically unique before the era of world wars began. The idea of exploiting the revolutionary scientific discoveries of the age of Rutherford and Einstein to release atomic energy for peaceful industry existed before the war of 1939–1945. It may be plausibly claimed that the actual release of this energy came sooner because of the vast sums assembled by the United States government as a consequence of the war to carry through the necessary research. But it cannot be claimed that war made the general use of this force for the material *benefit* of humanity more imminent.

The recent history of war and industry provides confirmation of the conclusions to which their earlier history have led. The role of war in promoting industrial progress had been small compared with the role of industrial progress in bringing on war. Warfare is less a cause for industrialism than its shadow and its nemesis. Even when soldiers no longer live mainly off the country they invade, as they came to do in the Napoleonic Wars, war is more devastating for economic life than ever before, for a number of reasons. Destruction has become enormously greater, because of the general and often indiscriminate attacks on civilian life in cities and towns. It has also become far greater in the country when there is serious resistance to an invading army. If, by rare luck, a nation escapes destructive attacks, as the United States almost completely escaped them during two world wars, the dislocation of orderly economic development offsets any temporary advantages derived from fuller employment. The very totality of modern wars has made the transitions from peace to war and then from war to peace much more difficult than those of the era of limited warfare. These transitions prevent the discovery of even a partial solution for the problem of abundance, such as a rebirth of faith and a renewed love of art might provide. The more total the wars, the more they comprehend all the nations of the earth, the more they have interfered with sound industrial progress. War now threatens to put an end to it.

Behind most of the progress has been the speculative genius of the experimental scientists. For generations they were doubtful about the desirability of revealing all their knowledge of the physical universe, hesitant about putting it to practical use, and reluctant about disclosing it for destructive purposes. Now pure science has lost virtually all control over the consequences of its own development.[38] With conditions as they are in the modern world—with the new kinds of explosives and the mechanized warfare made possible by science—war, or even the intellectual collapse which has helped to provoke two world wars, may destroy science itself. There may be an actual case of killing the goose that laid the golden eggs. Already in 1930, before the second World War, Ortega y Gasset suggested that there was evidence of the first retrogression in pure scientific research since its inception at the time of the Renaissance. "It is becoming difficult," he wrote, "to attract students to the laboratories of pure science."[39] The prestige suddenly directed towards the laboratories because of their demonstrated powers of destruction, may for a time lead larger numbers into the practical sides of scientific research. This is no substitute for the love of truth. And upon the love of truth the future of even material welfare depends.

Against the maintenance of a high standard of living during the past thirty-five years in the United States, and in other countries which have managed to stay out of destruction, has to be put the fall in the standard of living in Europe and a great part of Asia, where the wars have been fought. All our historical knowledge suggests that the most striking thing about recent military development is the increasingly destructive nature of war.

The material progress, which the industrial revolution brought with it, has helped to make total war feasible. But this progress has not made warfare constructive. Fathers and mothers have always been reluctant to entrust their children with knives or guns. But men have now entrusted themselves with powers of destruction which would be safe only in the hands of God the Father.

Notes

Reprinted from *The Review of Politics* 11, no. 3 (July 1949): 310–37.

1. Albert Demangéon, *Problèmes de géographie humaine,* 2nd ed. (Paris, 1943), 36; A. M. Carr-Saunders, *World Population* (Oxford, 1936), passim.
2. Colin Clark, *The Conditions of Economic Progress* (London, 1940), 79, 83, 87, 91, 144, and charts facing pp. 147–48.
3. Chester W. Wright, *Economic History of the United States* (New York, 1941), 551, 707.
4. R. H. Tawney, "The Abolition of Economic Controls, 1918–1921," *Economic History Review* 8 (1943): 24.
5. Sigfried Giedion, *Mechanization Takes Command* (New York, 1948).
6. J. Christopher Herold, *The Swiss without Halos* (New York, 1949), 62–63.
7. Charles Babbage, *Reflections on the Decline of Science in England* (London, 1830), 14–15.
8. Herbert Spencer, *Social Statics; or the Conditions of Human Happiness* (New York, 1886), 80.
9. Joan Bennett, *George Eliot: Her Mind and Art* (Cambridge, 1948), 24–25, 60–61, et passim.
10. Spencer, *Social Statics,* 80.
11. Spencer, *First Principles of a New System of Philosophy* (New York, 1879), 563.
12. Babbage, *Reflections on the Decline of Science,* 1, 17.
13. Frederick Soddy, *Wealth, Virtual Wealth and Debt,* 2nd ed. (London, 1933), 303–4 et passim. Cf. W. Trotter, *Instincts of the Herd in Peace and War,* 2nd ed. (1919), 242.
14. Karl von Clausewitz, *On War,* ed. F. N. Maude, trans. J. J. Graham, 3 vols. (London, 1911), 2: 21n. Colonel Maude's note is confusing. He speaks of "thirty rounds a minute," but this is "without aiming." Apparently the "normal rate" was "eight rounds in half a minute," therefore presumably sixteen rounds a minute.
15. Hans Delbrück, *Geschichte der Kriegskunst,* 7 vols. (Berlin, 1920–36) (as continued by Emil Daniels and Otto Haintz), 6:22.
16. J. F. C. Fuller, *On Fuller Warfare* (London, 1928), 62.
17. J. Holland Rose, *The Indecisiveness of Modern War* (London, 1927), 1.
18. Paul Hazard, *La Pensée européenne au XVIII siècle,* vol. 2 (Paris, 1946), 60–64.
19. Hobbes, *Leviathan,* pt. 2, chap. 30.

20. Cf. Delbruck, *Geschichte der Kriegskunst*, 4:530.

21. Cf. Madame de la Tour du Pin, *Journal d'une femme de cinquante ans*, 25th ed., vol. 2 (Paris, 1925), 299.

22. Delbrück, *Geschichte der Kriegskunst*, 5:80–82.

23. Ibid., 6:201n.

24. Grotius, *The Rights of War and Peace*, trans. A. C. Campbell (New York, 1901), 393; Clausewitz, *On War*, trans. O. J. M. Jolles (New York, 1943), 339.

25. Thorstein Veblen, *An Inquiry into the Nature of Peace and the Terms of Its Perpetuation* (New York, 1917), 203.

26. Clausewitz might have called it an "attack," since it would be possible to trace it back to the Japanese "invasion" of the Hawaiian Islands, though the American "attack" on Japan at that moment proved weak!

27. James A. Field, Jr., *The Japanese at Leyte Gulf* (Princeton, 1947), vii, 50, 87, 134 et passim.

28. Clausewitz, *On War*, trans. Graham, 3:250.

29. Cf. H. B. C. Pollard, *A History of Firearms* (London, 1928), 23, 25–26; Charles H. Firth, *Cromwell's Army* (London, 1902), 85.

30. *The History of Herodotus*, trans. Rawlinson, bk. 1, paras. 89, 153; bk. 8, para. 26.

31. Fuller, *On Fuller Warfare*, 155.

32. *Cambridge Modern History*, vol. 6 (Cambridge, 1934), 724.

33. *The World Almanac and Encyclopedia* (1920), 684.

34. Edward A. Shils, *The Atomic Bomb in World Politics* (National Peace Council Pamphlet) (London, 1948), 79.

35. Tawney, "The Abolition of Economic Controls, 1918–1921," 24.

36. C.-F. Nicolai, *The Biology of War*, trans. C. and J. Grande (New York, 1918), 200–201.

37. Ibid., 197. After perusing an earlier printed version of part II of my book, my colleague, Professor Theodore W. Schultz, has kindly given me the benefit of some conversations he had recently with an eminent American engineer concerning this matter of modern war and invention. This engineer's opinion was based on recent American experience. He suggested that the armed services have been completely stagnant between wars, that little technological progress is possible during a war, except of the "hothouse" variety, which is forced and superficial, and that whatever gains have been made in military technology have come as a consequence of more scientific and industrial advances.

38. Cf. Rose, *Indecisiveness of Modern War*, 5.

39. J. Ortega y Gasset, *The Revolt of the Masses* (New York, 1932), 88–98, 91, 94, 119, 126.

CHAPTER 8

The Tragic Element in
Modern International Conflict

HERBERT BUTTERFIELD

In the nineteenth century,[1] when many people were optimistic in their views of human nature, and confident that the course of progress was going to be continued into an indefinite future, there were one or two prophets who feared and foretold that the twentieth century would see great wars of peoples, popular military dictatorships, and the harnessing of the machines of industry to the science of warfare. It is interesting to note that, without knowing whether one country or another was going to emerge as the chief offender, and without basing his prediction upon any view that Germany was likely to present a special problem to the European continent, a writer could still feel assured, a generation beforehand, that this age of terrible warfare was coming. He could see, in other words, that, apart from the emergence of a special criminal, the developments in the situation itself were driving mankind into an era of conflict. In the midst of battle, while we are all of us in fighting mood, we see only the sins of the enemy and fail to reflect on those predicaments and dilemmas which so often develop and which underlie the great conflicts between masses of human beings. And though these conflicts could hardly have taken place if all men were perfect saints, we often forget that many of the inhuman struggles that have divided the human race would hardly have occurred if the situation had been one of completely righteous men confronted by undiluted and unmitigated crime. Given the ordinary amount of cupidity and willfulness in human beings, unmanageable situations are likely to develop and some of them may almost be guaranteed to end in terrible conflict. While there is battle and hatred men have eyes for nothing save the fact that

157

the enemy is the cause of all the troubles; but long, long afterwards, when all passion has been spent, the historian often sees that it was a conflict between one half-right that was perhaps too willful, and another half-right that was perhaps too proud; and behind even this he discerns that it was a terrible predicament, which had the effect of putting men so at cross-purposes with one another. This predicament is the thing which it is the purpose of this paper to examine; and first of all I propose to try to show how the historian comes to discover its existence.

If we consider the history of the historical writing that has been issued, generation after generation, on a given body of events, we shall generally find that in the early stages of this process of reconstruction the narrative which is produced has a primitive and simple shape. As one generation of students succeeds another, however, each developing the historiography of this particular subject, the narrative passes through certain typical stages until it is brought to a high and subtle form of organization. It would be difficult to give names to these successive stages in the development of the historiography of a given theme, but there is an early period in the writing-up of a subject, particularly when the subject itself is one form or another of human conflict, which seems to me to belong to the class of literature sometimes described as "Heroic." It does not matter whether the topic which the historian is writing about is the victory of Christianity in the Roman Empire, or the struggles of the modern scientists in the seventeenth century, or the case of either the French or the Russian Revolutions. There is a recognizable phase in the historical reconstruction or the chronicle writing which has distinctive features and shows a certain characteristic form of organization; and on more than one occasion in my life I have found myself saying that this kind of historiography bears the marks of the Heroic age. It represents the early period when the victors write their own chronicles, gloat over the defeated, count their trophies, commemorate their achievements, and show how righteousness has triumphed. And it may be true that the narrative has a primitive sort of structure that we can recognize, but it is a structure that requires little thought on the part of the writers of the history; for it was ready-made for them all the time—it is nothing more than the sort of organization that a narrative acquires from the mere fact that the author is taking sides in the conflict. We who come long afterwards generally find that this kind of history has overdramatized the struggle in its aspect as a battle of right versus wrong; and to us it seems that these writers refused to exercise imaginative sympathy over the defeated enemy, so that they lack the perspective which might have been achieved if they had allowed themselves to be driven to a deeper analysis of the whole affair. In England our own whig interpretation of history is only a development from the "Heroic" way of formulating the issues of human conflict—as though the parliamentarians of the seventeenth century were provoked to war by mere personal wickednesses and deliberate aggressions on the part of Charles I and his supporters.

Though I have no doubt that the progress of historiography to a higher level than this is really to be regarded as a collaborative achievement, I have always understood that the name of S. R. Gardiner is particularly associated with the developments which led to a drastic refocusing of these English constitutional conflicts of the seventeenth century. It seems to have been the case furthermore that with him as with other people the refocusing resulted from what in the last resort might be described as the method of taking compassion on the defeated. Gardiner's mode of procedure led him to be careful with the defeated party, and he tried by internal sympathetic infiltration really to find out what was in their minds. And this is a process to which there ought to be no limits, for historical imagination comes to its sublimest achievements when it can succeed in comprehending the people not like-minded with oneself. Once such a process is embarked upon, the truth soon emerges that it is an easy thing to produce a whig history of a constitutional conflict or alternatively a royalist version of the affair; but it is no easy matter to compromise the two in a single survey, since clearly they cannot be just joined or added to one another. In reality you find that at every inch in your attempt to collate the outlooks of the two belligerent parties you are driven to a higher altitude—you have to find a kind of historical truth that lies on a higher plane before you can make the evidence square with itself or secure a story that comprehends all the factors and embraces the purely partial visions of the two opposing sides. Then, after much labor, you may achieve something more like a stereoscopic vision of the whole drama. Similarly, if an English foreign secretary and an Austrian ambassador give curiously divergent reports of a conversation that they have had with one another, the historian would not be content merely to add the two reports together. Collating them inch by inch he would use one document to enable him to see new folds of implication in the other. So he would be carried to a higher version of the whole affair—one which embraces the contradictions in the original accounts and even enables us to understand how the discrepancies should have occurred. In the long run the historian will not limit himself to seeing things with the eyes of the royalist or with the eyes of the roundhead; but, taking a loftier perspective which puts him in a position to embrace both, he will reach new truths to which both sides were blind—truths which will even enable him to see how they came to differ so much from one another.

When the historiography of the English seventeenth-century constitutional struggles has developed through the work of Gardiner and his successors, and has been brought to a higher state of organization by virtue of processes somewhat on the pattern that I have described, what emerges is a new and drastically different formulation of the whole conflict. And this new way of presenting the entire issue has a peculiar characteristic which I wish to examine, because it shows us what the revised perspective really amounts to—it provides us with almost a definition of what is implied in the progress of historiography as it moves further away from the events that are being narrated, further away from the state of being contemporary history. The progress of historiography takes us away from that first simple picture of good men fighting bad; and not merely in the case of seventeenth-century England but in one field of history after another we find that it contributes a new and most uncomfortable revelation—it gradually disengages the structural features of a conflict which was inherent in the dialectic of events. It shows us situations hardening, events tying themselves into knots, human beings faced by terrible dilemmas, and one party and another being driven into a corner. In other words, as the historiography of a given episode develops and comes to be further removed from the passions of those who were active in the drama, it uncovers at the basis of the story a fundamental human predicament—one which we can see would have led to a serious conflict of wills even if all men had been fairly intelligent and reasonably well-intentioned. Perhaps it was this reformulation of the conflict which Lord Acton had in mind when he suggested that it needs the historian to come on the scene at a later time to say what it was that these poor seventeenth-century royalists and roundheads were really fighting about.

In the new organization of the narrative the personal goodness or badness of Charles I may still appear to be operative but it ceases to be the central issue, ceases to be the basis for the mounting of the whole story. We see the English monarchy coming into a serious predicament in this period in any case; and something of a parallel kind is seen to take place as we study the conflicts of the reign of George III. The central fact—the one that gives the new structure to the whole narrative—is a certain predicament, a certain situation that contains the elements of conflict irrespective of any special wickedness in any of the parties concerned; and the personal goodness or badness of Charles I or George III operates only, so to speak, on the margin of this, and becomes rather a fringing issue. So, while contemporary ways of formulating the human conflict have the structure of melodrama, the white hero fighting the black villain of the piece in a straight war of right versus wrong, historiography in the course of time leads us to transpose the lines of the picture and redraft the whole issue, especially as we come to comprehend more deeply the men who were not like-minded with ourselves. The higher historiography moves away from melodrama and brings out the tragic element in human conflict.

If all this is true, then we who are so deeply engaged in an age of conflict, are under an obligation not to be too blindly secure, too willfully confident, in the contemporary ways of formulating that conflict; and it is incumbent upon us not quite to forget how future historiography may expose the limitations of our vision. If all this is true, then an issue is drawn between the view which the contemporary historian so often tends to possess and the view associated with a higher and riper stage of historiography—the view of what I hope I may be allowed to call "academic history." The issue is drawn because the two kinds of history differ in the actual structure of the narrative and formulation of the theme, unless the contemporary history has been written after great prayer and fasting, which seldom happens to be the case. If what I have said is true, then the examination of the actual structure of a piece of historical narrative can be at any rate one of the tests of the intellectual quality of the work and the genuineness of its historical perspective. Furthermore, if any people should desire to envisage the events of their own day with a certain historical-mindedness, then we have at least a clue to the kind of direction in which they should move in their attempt to achieve the object. For if we realize the way in which historical science develops in the course of time—if we know even only one of the laws which govern its development as it proceeds further away from the merely contemporary point of view—then we have at any rate a hint of the kind of thing which historical perspective requires of us; and we can be to that degree more hopeful in our attempt to hasten or anticipate the future verdict of historical science. Behind the great conflicts of mankind is a terrible human predicament which lies at the heart of the story; and sooner or later the historian will base the very structure of his narrative upon it. Contemporaries fail to see the predicament or refuse to recognize its genuineness, so that our knowledge of it comes from later analysis—it is only with the progress of historical science on a particular subject that men come really to recognize that there was a terrible knot almost beyond the ingenuity of man to untie. It represents therefore a contribution that historical science itself has added to our interpretation of life—one which leads us to place a different construction on the whole human drama, since it uncovers the tragic element in human conflict. In historical perspective we learn to be a little more sorry for both parties than they knew how to be for one another.

The international situation of the present day is so difficult, and we are so greatly in need of a deeper vision that we ought to be ready to clutch at anything which might have a chance of leading us to fresh thoughts or new truths. We might ask, therefore, whether in the modern world there is any hint of the kind of human predicament that we have been considering and whether the idea can be of any use to us when we are seeking light on our contemporary problem. For the purpose of illustrating an argument I should like to describe and examine an imaginary specimen case in diplomacy—one which will enable me to isolate and to put under the microscope that very factor in human conflict which so often emerges at a later time, when historians have long been reflecting on the issue, but which is so often concealed from contemporaries in the heat of action and in all the bustle of life. For the purpose of assuring that the issue shall confront us more vividly I should like to present this imaginary instance in the guise of something real, something which will come to us as an actual problem of the present day.

Let us suppose then, that the Western powers on the one hand and Russia on the other hand have just defeated Germany and have reduced that country to total surrender. And let it be granted that the Western powers, confronted by the Russian colossus, feel that they cannot afford to allow the defeated Germany to be drawn into the orbit of the communist system; while Russia, for her part, faced by what to her is the no less formidable West, is ridden by the mathematically equal and opposite fear that the balance will be turned against her for all the future if Germany is enlisted in the non-communist group. Here then is a case in which the objects of the two parties are mutually exclusive, since if the one side is satisfied the other feels the situation to be utterly desperate; and it is a case not difficult to imagine, since it might be argued (though we need not commit ourselves to the fact) that it has actually existed in our world since 1945. If we can take this situation for granted for the purpose of argument, and then persuade our minds to perform a piece of abstraction, we may arrive at a result upon which we can do some mathematics. What is required is that we should stretch our imagination to the point of envisaging this particular international predicament in a purer form than either it or anything else ever exists in history. Let us assume that the Soviet group of states on the one hand and the western group on the other are absolutely level in point of virtue and in the moral qualities of the statesmen who conduct their affairs. Further, we will postulate that the level shall be a reasonably high one, that the statesmen on both sides are not saints, of course, competing with one another only in self-renunciation—a situation which would defeat our mathematics—but are moderately virtuous men, as men go in politics, anxious that their countries shall come to no harm, and moved by national self-interest to a degree that we must regard as comparatively reasonable. We will postulate that they have just those faults which men can have who feel themselves to be righteous and well-disposed—both sides anxious to avoid a war, but each desperately unsure about the intentions of the other party; each beset by the devils of fear and suspicion, therefore; and each side locked in its own system of self-righteousness.

Allowing for all this—which means that the problem before us is presented in what I should call its optimum setting—then I should assert that here is a grand dialectical jam of a kind that exasperates men—a terrible deadlock that makes ordinary human beings even a little more willful than they ordinarily are. Here is the absolute predicament and the irreducible dilemma—for I shall have something to say later to those who assert that it is no genuine predicament at all, and that every schoolboy knows the solution to the problem. Even granting throughout the whole of human nature no more than the ordinary amount of human willfulness such as we ourselves may be said to possess, here are the ingredients for a grand catastrophe. The greatest war in history could be produced without the intervention of any great criminals who might be out to do deliberate harm in the world. It could be produced between two powers both of which were desperately anxious to avoid a conflict of any sort.

Though the example that I have given is a purely hypothetical one, as I have said—for in the complicated realm of history so clear a pattern will never be found in its absolute purity—still there is a sense in which it typifies an essential human predicament; it illustrates a certain recalcitrancy that may lie in events as such, an intractability that can exist in the human situation itself. Here, in other words, is the mathematical formula—or perhaps one of the formulas—for a state of things which produces what I should call the tragic element in human conflict. As regards the real world of international relations I should put forward the thesis (which, if it is true, would seem to me to be not an unimportant one), that this condition of absolute predicament or irreducible dilemma lies in the very geometry of human conflict. It is at the basis of the structure of any given episode in that conflict. It is at the basis of all the tensions of the present day, representing even now the residual problem that the world has not solved, the hard nut that we still have to crack. So far as the historian is concerned, here is the basic pattern for all narratives of human conflict, whatever other patterns may be superimposed upon it later. Indeed, as I have said, when the historical reconstruction of a given episode has been carried on for generation upon generation, this is the structure the story tends to acquire as it becomes revised and corrected and reshaped with the passage of time. This tragedy of the absolute human predicament enters into the very fabric of historical narrative in proportion as we move further away from being mere contemporary historians.

Turning again to the hypothetical case which we have been using as our pattern, we may note that not only could the greatest war in history be produced between two powers both of which were moderately virtuous and desperately anxious to prevent a conflict, but such a struggle, far from being a nice, quiet, and reasonable affair, would be embittered by the heat of moral indignation on both sides, just because each was so conscious of its own rectitude, so enraged with the other for leaving it without any alternative to war. It is the peculiar characteristic of the situation I am describing—the situation of what I should call Hobbesian fear—that you yourself may vividly feel the terrible fear that you have of the other party, but you cannot enter into the other man's counter-fear, or even understand why he should be particularly nervous. For you know that you yourself mean him no harm, and that you want nothing from him save guarantees for your own safety; and it is never possible for you to realize or remember properly that since he cannot see the inside of your mind, he can never have the same assurance of your intentions that you have. As this operates on both sides the Chinese puzzle is complete in all its interlockings—and neither party sees the nature of the predicament he is in, for he only imagines that the other party is being hostile and unreasonable. It is even possible for each to feel that the other is willfully withholding the guarantees that would have enabled him to have a sense of security. The resulting conflict is more likely to be hot with moral indignation—one self-righteousness encountering another—than it would have been if the contest had lain between two hard-headed eighteenth-century masters of *realpolitik.* In such circumstances the contemporary historians on each side will tend to follow suit, each locked in the combative views of his own nation, and shrieking morality of that particular kind which springs from self-righteousness. That is one of the reasons why contemporary history differs so greatly from what I have called academic history. In all that I am saying I am really asserting, moreover, that the self-righteous are not the true moralists either in history or in life. Those who are less self-righteous may face the world's problems more squarely, even when they are less clever, than other people.

Pandit Nehru, when he was speaking at Columbia University, made a somewhat moving criticism of both East and West, because in his view they were intent upon what he called a race in armaments. Some people even say that a race in armaments is a cause of war—but nobody actually wills a "race"; and I personally would rather pity both sides than blame them, for I think that the race in armaments, and even the war that seems to result from it, are caused rather by that tragic human predicament, that situation of Hobbesian fear. All that we can say is that the predicament would not exist, of course, if all the world were like St. Francis of Assisi, and if human nature in general were not streaked with cupidities. The predicament, the race in armaments and the war itself are explained in the last resort, therefore, as the result of man's universal sin. Similarly, suppose two great groups of alliances have been at virtual deadlock for some years, so that even neutral states have begun to assert that war is inevitable—meaning that war is inevitable, human nature being what it is. Suppose you have such a situation, and then one party to the predicament becomes over-exasperated and makes too willful a decision; suppose in particular that he does it because he thinks that somebody must take a strong line at last; and we will say that he even intends to bluff, but the bluff does not come off and so a great war is brought about. Then, though this man has done wrong I could not personally agree that he should be charged as the sole author of the war and loaded with all the misery of it as though he were the only villain in a melodrama. I could not agree that he should be regarded as guilty in just the way he would have been if he had fallen unprovoked on a flock of innocent lambs. Ultimately the true origin of the war lies in that predicament; and on this basis the melodrama reshapes itself, assuming more of the character of tragedy—the kind of tragedy in which it is so to speak the situation that gives one a heartache, and sometimes, as in the case of *King Lear,* what seem to be little sins may have colossally disproportionate consequences.

The truth is that when faced by this human predicament—this final unsolved problem of human relations—the mind winces and turns to look elsewhere, and statesmen, for their case, pile all the blame on the handiest scapegoat. Men fix their attention upon what in reality are fringing issues, and they remove these from their proper place on the fringe to the center of the picture— you can evade all problems by saying that everything is due to the wickedness of King Charles I. The point can be illustrated best perhaps by the process of looking for a moment at its converse. Let us make it clear to ourselves: if in our present-day crises Stalin and his colleagues could be imagined to be as virtuous and well-intentioned as the statesmen of the Western world, still our predicament would exist, and there would be the same dilemma concerning the future of Germany—especially as we, because we look at him from the outside, could never be sure that Stalin's intentions were as good as ours. In any case we could never be sure that if we put our trust in him we should not really be placing weapons into the hands of some villain who might succeed to his power next year, supposing he passed off the stage. Of course, if we are in this same international predicament and the Russians happen to be thieves or adventurers or aggressors or drunkards or sexual perverts to boot, then that is an extra boon which Providence throws into the lap, so to speak of the Western powers—the kind of boon which, to judge from our assertions over a number of centuries, Providence has generally vouchsafed to the British in their wars. Even in such circumstances, however, we are evading an essential problem if we lose sight of the basic predicament—a predicament so exasperating sometimes that it can be responsible for making people more wicked and desperate than they otherwise would have been. It is like the case of the person who owed his neighbor £5 and refused to pay it on the ground that the neighbor was an immoral man and would make a bad use of the money. The moralizing might not be without its justice but in this case it would be introduced as a screen to cover a delinquency of one's own. Or it is like the case of those people who so often, as in 1792, would judge a revolution entirely by its atrocities—evading the structural problem and pouncing upon an incidental issue. I have no doubt it would be a boon to me, supposing I were challenged in debate on a point of history, if I could say: "Take no notice of this man; he has just come out of prison after serving sentence for forging a check." I should be picking up a fringing issue and turning it into the central issue; and in this way I might use the other person's immorality most unfairly for the purpose of evading a challenge that happened to be inconvenient to myself.

Not only may the problem of war present itself in the acutest possible form irrespective of any difference in morality between the contending parties, but the whole problem and the whole predicament that we are discussing exists absolutely irrespective of any differences in ideology. All the evidence that we have—and it seems to me that we have had very much in the last one hundred years for this particular case—shows that the basic problem would not be fundamentally altered, and would certainly not be avoided, supposing what we were confronted with at the moment were all the power of modern Russia in the hands of the Tsars, instead of the regime of the Soviet. The predicament would not be removed even if there were no communism in the world at all, or supposing that every state involved in the problem were a Christian state in the sense that so many countries were Christian throughout most of the centuries of modern times. Even supposing Russia were liberal and democratic—supposing the great powers on either side were so situated that their populations could put pressure on the government in the very matter of foreign policy—still the populations would be just as fearful or suspicious or exasperated or angry as the foreign offices themselves. Indeed it seems to be generally the case that they are more so, unless the knowledge of the predicament is withheld from them.

Insofar as international conflicts are concerned, therefore, I am suggesting that after many of the more incidental features of the case have been peeled away, we shall find at the heart of everything a kernel of difficulty which is essentially a problem of diplomacy as such. In fact I personally think that in the international crises of our time, we are muddying the waters and darkening our own minds and playing the very game the Russians want us to play, when we mix our drinks and indulge in a so-called "ideological" foreign policy, forgetting that the fundamental problems exist, as I have said, independent of the differences in ideology. The truth is that we could very well say to the Russians: "We would not have allowed you to steal this particular march on us, or to encroach in this particular direction or to dominate defeated Germany even if you had been a Christian empire as in the time of the Tsars." And, given the distribution of power which existed in Europe in 1945, the old Tsardom would have dominated Poland, Czechoslovakia, Hungary, and the Balkans, just as the Soviets do now, though it would have used something different from the Marxian ideology to facilitate the execution of its purpose. All this carries with it the further corollary that we ought to attach very great importance to a study which in England at least has gravely declined and is woefully out of fashion, namely, pure diplomatic history regarded as a technique in itself; for it was just the characteristic of this technical diplomatic history to lay bare the essential geometry of the problem and isolate for examination the fundamental predicament that required a solution. Indeed what I am doing in this paper is to elicit the moral implications of that whole system of thought which is invoked in diplomatic history—and I am asserting that the new diplomacy of our time, as well as its dependent forms of historiography, though they are more self-righteous than the old, are in reality less moral, at any rate in certain respects.

We have already noted, however, that in the complicated realm of historical events, no pattern ever appears in a pure and unadulterated form—and certainly, when a diplomatic issue is presented to us for resolution, we can never say that both sides are exactly balanced in point of morality, exactly equal in the virtues of their leading statesmen. The original issue may be aggravated and greatly intensified by the aggressiveness of a politician in one country or the barbarism of a regime in another country; and our fear of the expansion of Russia is considerably increased if Russia implies either a Tsarist despotism or the communist system. All the same, it is wrong to overlook that original diplomatic predicament which forms the kernel of the problem requiring to be solved; and it is a mistake to allow the incidental matters or the attendant circumstances to drive that essential issue out of our minds. I could express the point, for example—or I could illustrate its implications—by noting that we should not like to be conquered by Russia even if Russia were not a communist state. Alternatively I might say that supposing it could be made out that there were general reasons for conceding that Spain had a right to Gibraltar, it is not clear that the British would be justified in withholding that possession merely because they disliked the present regime in Spain and disapproved of General Franco. It was perhaps one of the virtues of the older type of diplomacy that in time of war it did not allow itself to be entirely obsessed by the question of the responsibility for the resort to violence—did not merely hark back continually to the actual occasion of the outbreak—but recognized that the war itself was partly tragedy, that is to say, partly due to a predicament. Attention was concentrated rather on the kind of world which would be produced once the victory had been achieved, and the aim was not so much to punish the culprits, but rather to make sure that there was a tolerable balance of forces at the finish. Even after the battle of Waterloo, the enemies of Napoleon did not allow themselves to be moved by the desire of giving due punishment to France, though that country had kept the world at war for over twenty years and had given itself over to Napoleon for a second time, after his return from Elba. France in 1815 lost practically none of the territory she had held before the outbreak of war, and in a remarkably short time she was readmitted to the comity of nations; and yet now we know that even the creators of the peace of 1815 made a mistake in fearing still that France would always be the aggressor; in consequence of which they insisted upon installing a strong Prussia in the Rhineland to defend Germany against France, and so helped the coming giant to be stronger than ever, because they had been too rigidly obsessed with the danger that had troubled them in the past. The essential thing is to guard against the kind of war which, if you win it absolutely, will produce another "predicament" worse than the one you started with.

We of the twentieth century have not been as wise as the men of over a hundred years ago. The great diplomatic issue that emerged—or rather reemerged—in Europe in the early years of this present century concerned the question whether Russia on the one hand, should dominate those countries of central and eastern Europe which run from Poland, through Czechoslovakia and Hungary to what we now call Yugoslavia and the Balkans. This is how it came about that the occasion for the war of 1914 was an episode involving Bosnia and Serbia, while the occasion for the war of 1939 occurred in regions concerning which Lloyd George had long before expressed his apprehensions— namely in Czechoslovakia and in Poland. Those two wars were embarrassing in certain respects for Great Britain, for though we claimed that we were fighting for democracy we were allied in the former case with Tsarist Russia, where the Jews had been oppressed, and the Poles were held in subjection, and the Baltic nations were prevented from achieving statehood; while in the case of the second World War we were the allies of the Soviet System. So far as I can interpret European history in general, the line of central European states which were in question—Poland, Czechoslovakia, Yugoslavia, etc.—can flourish beautifully when both Germany and Russia are reduced to impotence, as they were in the fifteenth century, and as they came to be again for a period after 1919. The same states may preserve their independence provided both Germany and Russia are strong, so that when the giant on the one side seeks to oppress them they can look for help to the giant on the other side. It is bound to be sad, however, for Poland, Czechoslovakia, etc., if only one of these giants is left standing and there is no other great power in the vicinity to challenge or check this monster. Indeed, we have seen how even in the last few years America, England, and the nations of Western Europe have been unable to prevent this whole line of states from coming quite into the power of the Russian bear. Supposing wars to be necessary and unavoidable—as indeed they seem to be sometimes—it might still be a question whether we have conducted ours with a right mentality or with a proper grasp of the essential issues. In respect of the great diplomatic problem of the twentieth century, we may wonder sometimes whether Russia was so much more virtuous than Germany as to make it worth the lives of tens of millions of people in two wars to insure that she (as a communist system—or even as a tsarist empire) should gain such an unchallenged and exclusive hold over that line of central European states as Germany never had in all her history, and never could have had unless Russia had first been wiped out as a great state. For it is just that kind of question—the question of the redistribution of territorial power—which war decides. We cannot spread democracy by war, which barbarizes peoples and tends rather to make democracy more impracticable over a greater area of the European continent.

The supporters of the new diplomacy, which has emerged since the opening of the epoch of world wars, like to tell us that the whole problem we have been discussing does not exist, because it ought not to exist. In any case, there is no Chinese puzzle at all, they say, for, whatever the issue might be, we could easily dispose of it by referring it to a conference or sending it to the United Nations. Against these specialists in wishful thinking it must be asserted that the kind of human predicament which we have been discussing is not merely so far without a solution, but the whole condition is a standing feature of mankind in world history. If the whole of Russia and the entire body of its satellites were to be buried under the deepest oceans from this very night, the predicament would still be with us tomorrow, though the terms of it would be transposed by a regrouping of the remaining powers. Supposing there were no Russian power in existence, supposing Germany herself were lying prostrate as a beaten and ineffective nation, and supposing the help of America were not essential to everybody concerned—all that fine show of unanimity between the countries of Western Europe, all that cooperation induced by the threat of an immediate danger, would break down into bitterness and anarchy. And if the issue which divides the world at a given moment were referred to a conference-table, then, though many good things might be achieved, we should not have eliminated the predicament which was most crucial—we should merely find it transplanted into the bosom of the conference itself. Even the organization of the United Nations has not proved essentially different in this respect from the case of the former League which had its headquarters in Geneva; and though the problem is transposed somewhat, so that different nations and different problems now produce the stumbling block, the new international order has not in fact prevented powers from remaining armed as never before, and racing one another in the development of the atomic bomb.

It was once my feeling that if, in a European crisis, Great Britain pressed for the assembly of a conference, while Germany rejected that procedure, then Germany was clearly in the wrong and my own country was plainly on the side of the angels. Unfortunately it comes to be borne in upon one's mind as one studies these matters that conferences themselves are only too liable to be the arena for a kind of power politics; and the greater states, in the very nature of things, hold a predominance in them which bears some proportion to their might. It even became evident to me that sometimes it was calculable in advance how the votes would be distributed if a conference met, since these would be affected by the alliances and affiliations of the various governments concerned, and might even be decided by sympathies in ideology. Supposing it became clear that if a conference were assembled the result was a foregone conclusion and Germany was so to speak outvoted in advance. I began to wonder whether in such a case she was necessarily more selfish than anybody else when she refused to put her head in the noose—I began to wonder also whether the virtues of Britain were quite so much to boast about when they coincided so nicely with her interests. This argument might be projected onto a wider canvas altogether; for without doubting the good intentions of the men who have ruled England in the last few decades, one must note that if a Machiavellian imperialist statesman had happened to be governing us with purely egotistical purposes in view, he would have found the conference method the best way of promoting our national interests, indeed the only way in view of the decline of actual British power and in view of the general distribution of forces in the world. In other words Great Britain in our time has been in a position which we must regard as fortunate in a certain respect, in that the policy which altruism would have dictated to her happened to be the same as the one which self-interest would demand—so that, though the conference method has been promoted so often by Englishmen who were only conscious of it as a noble aspiration, it has also been described as the only method of *realpolitik* left to us. The conference method is more advantageous to us than any decision to measure forces with a rival, even if the voting should go against us on occasion in a matter of some moment to us.

But when I take this crucial case and imagine a real predicament—when I think of the kind of issue which decides whether a state or an empire goes up or down in the world—then I find myself in a position of some doubt even in regard to Great Britain. Supposing it to be the case that the loss of our overseas possessions would bring about a serious reduction in the standard of living of the British people, and supposing a motion were to be proposed that all forms of colony or of subjection or of dependency were to be abolished through the wide world—I, in a situation of this kind, should like to know what the attitude of the government of my country would be. In particular I should like to know what its attitude would be to the idea of submitting such an issue to a conference or assembly in which the communists were known in advance to have the majority of votes. I should like to know what my country would do on the assumption that we still had enough power to make a valid and independent choice. Where the conflict is really a cut-throat one it seems to me that the conference method does not put an end to the predicament but merely changes the locality and the setting of it. The whole method is liable to break down if either the communists or the non-communists can be fairly sure in advance that on critical issues the other party is going to have the majority. And in any case I am not clear that anybody has ever devised a form of political machinery that could not somehow or other be manipulated by ill-intentioned people in the possession of power.

Like the Germans, we sometimes allow the academic and professorial mind to have too much sway among us; and with us this has helped to give currency to the heresy that everything can be settled if men will only sit together at a table—a view which may be justified on many occasions but which does not prove to be correct when the conflicting parties are in the extreme kind of predicament we have been discussing. Where the predicament really exists and the question is one of those which decide whether states are to go up or down in the world, those who do have the power will not allow themselves to be talked or voted out of their strategic positions, any more than empires will go under without putting up a fight, supposing a fight to be possible at all. Europeans have had hundreds of years in which to discuss theological problems, but mere discussion round a table has not brought them into agreement on the disputed points. This was the kind of issue upon which men can at worst agree to disagree, though I note that ecclesiastical systems were slow to come to this arrangement and they went on fighting one another, using weapons that kill, as long as it was feasible to fight at all. But if two different countries are claiming Gibraltar it is not so easy to settle the matter by saying that the parties can agree to disagree. The conference method does not get rid of the difficulty—it merely transplants the whole predicament into another place.

While we are at war, and the conflict is a matter of life or death for us, we may hardly have any part of our minds free for devoting to a general survey of the whole predicament in which the human race is standing. When the war is over, however, a time of healing ought to come, and it is our duty to carry all our problems to further analysis. Politicians, in the hurry of affairs, and in the stress of conflict, may hardly have an opportunity to cover the problem in an all-embracing survey, for we must regard them as generally acting under great pressures. We in universities, however—and especially those of us who study history—have a duty to think in longer terms and seize upon the problem precisely where the difficulties are most challenging. We ought to be straining our minds to think of new things and to enlarge the bounds of understanding; for though our enlarged understanding of the problem will not necessarily prevent war, it may remove some of the unwisdom which has made victory itself so much more disappointing in its results than it otherwise might have been.

NOTES

Reprinted from *The Review of Politics* 12, no. 2 (April 1950): 147–64.

1. This article was originally presented as a lecture at the University of Notre Dame under the auspices of the University's Committee on International Relations.

CHAPTER 9

The Study of International Politics
A Survey of Trends and Developments

KENNETH W. THOMPSON

I. GENERAL ORIENTATION

The question was raised at the end of World War II as to whether or not international relations could stand as a separate field of study.[1] Views were expressed by scholars and teachers in history and political science to the effect
that in substance there was nothing peculiar to the subject matter of international relations which did not fall under other separate fields of social studies.
At some universities and colleges there were dissenters to this prevailing viewpoint. Their particular philosophy manifested itself in attempts to create and
establish integrated curricula under academic committees or departments
dedicated to the broad generalized study of the sub-matter of the field. It is
still too early to pass judgment with any finality on the merits of these two
points of view, the one viewing international relations as a mere duplication
of the subject matter of many fields; the other insisting that there must be
an ordering and integrative approach to the field. No serious student would
presume to claim that the study of international relations had arrived at the
stage of an independent academic discipline. However, there have been three
significant developments within no more than a single generation which illuminate certain aspects of this problem. First we have witnessed the evolution
and development of a point of focus or core in the field. Second, there have
been the first faint and feeble beginnings of attempts to create a methodology
appropriate for the field, or at least to determine those related methodologies
in the social sciences whose methods and techniques could most usefully be

appropriated for the study of persistent international issues. Third, inventories have been drawn up by individual scholars, universities and institutes, of topics and concrete projects which would best serve in the development of general principles in the field and the validation of them through systematic inquiry.

The Core Subject of International Relations

The movement in the direction of a focus or point of reference has its origin in time primarily in the years immediately preceding and following World War II. To understand this development it is necessary to consider the four general stages through which the study of international relations has passed. While sometimes paralleling and supporting one another in time, these phases can be separated because of their particular implications. The first phase was the period in which the study of diplomatic history was prevalent. At this point the significant treatises and monographs, especially in England, dealt with concrete diplomatic events which had taken place over the past several centuries. For example, the studies of the conduct of British foreign policy by noted statesmen and diplomatists covering limited historical periods as, for example, the foreign policies of Palmerston, Castlereagh, and Canning, represent the best and most fruitful studies in this period. Perhaps what most distinguishes this period is the high level of historical accuracy and the faithful attention to the canons of historiography and historical method by which it was characterized. Indeed, it is plain from the words and deeds of historians that they conceived their first duty to have been the foreswearing of every temptation to generalize about their observations. We have current examples of this approach in present-day studies in history and political science. These include the studies by outstanding diplomatic historians like Professor Richard W. Leopold on the causes and conditions of World War I and similar studies by Professor Edward Meade Earle.[2] Professor Leopold, for example, sets himself the task of reporting and illuminating arguments that can be advanced in support of three or four major hypotheses regarding the outbreak of World War I. He deals in turn with the arguments that war was the outcome of our naval strategy, of the machinations of the munition makers, or of objective political necessity. But he leaves the issues essentially where he found them by avoiding any more than the most tentative speculation or generalization about the truth of any particular hypothesis. In a word, therefore, the approach of the diplomatic historian has been one of striving for the fullest and most extensive explanation of a given historical event. Professor Samuel Eliot Morison in his address as retiring president of the American Historical Association in 1950 declared that the sole aim of any objective and scientific historian ought to be the full and complete reconstructing of a selected incident in history. The historian should avoid every temptation to generalize or dabble in universal principles in recording a story which it was his duty to portray in all its essential simplicity. Every effort to connect an event with what had gone before or to draw up lofty and ambitious principles could only weaken this first paramount undertaking. Indeed, we are given in capsule form in Professor Morison's address the prevailing philosophy which influenced most early studies in diplomatic history. In all fairness, the participants in this approach must be praised for their faithful adherence to principles of historical research and documentation.

The price which was paid for this rigorous, objective, and non-generalized approach to the field was the absence of anything corresponding to a theory of international relations. Because of the poverty of available documentary material on recent events, historians have shown themselves reluctant to face instant problems or to offer propositions about others in the recent past. Moreover, the criticism was voiced that this approach left public opinion and the general citizenry without leadership and without guides for understanding and action. As a consequence there grew up during the truce between the two wars an overriding concern for some means of exploring and studying the immediate present. In place of the detached and highly specialized techniques of history in general and diplomatic history in particular there developed an approach that we may designate the current events point of view. The "bible" for the study of international relations became *The New York Times,* and the role and function of the teacher of international affairs became one of interpreting and explaining the immediate significance of current events. This occasioned a flurry of popular interest in the field which, however, proved premature in that it rested on weak and unstable foundations. For this version of teaching and scholarship in international affairs, requiring as it did qualities on the part of the individual for performing the dual functions of pundit and advocate, made of specialists in the field little more than "special pleaders." In this

sense, the areas which might have been exploited from the earlier study of diplomatic history were left essentially untouched. Since the study of the present
was pursued without any reference to history, there were no ordering principles drawn from past experience. Instead each scholar became a spokesman
for his own brand of international legislation or reform. Some discussed off
the cuff freed trade *versus* protectionism, others international monetary reforms, and others new ways and means of transforming international organization. But none attempted to relate the postwar political problems with comparable problems that might have existed at particular times in the past. To do
so would have been antiquarian and proved that the scholar was at odds with
his times.

President Wilson inveighed against the use of studies on the Congress of
Vienna which the British proposed at the time of the Paris Peace Conference.
From him any lesson or enlightenment which the methods of Talleyrand
and Metternich might have thrown on the methods of Clemenceau or Lloyd
George was ruled out of order. Therefore, the viewpoint of current events became a day-by-day exercise in proposing and disposing of each minor world
problem as it presented itself. Furthermore, the absence of any firm methodological foundation for the study of the events led to a grand and extravagant
conception of what international studies should encompass. It was said that
all experiences and events which involved peoples of many lands should constitute the core of the field. Everything from the anthropology of the most
primitive and pre-modern tribes to xenophobia was considered equally important. In these terms an informed discussion of the Olympic Games was as
appropriate as an analysis of the latest move in German diplomacy. However
engaging this appeared in theory and however appropriate for group discussion, it scarcely led to any carefully conceived approach to the most relevant
international problems upon which war and peace might hinge. Someone has
said, facetiously to be sure, that this was an era of letters to Congressmen, to
editors, and to the public without more than a line or two of scholarly political or diplomatic monographs.

A third phase was inaugurated immediately following World War I. Coming
at this time, it paralleled and strengthened and indeed gave its own emphasis
and meaning to the current events that students were discussing. The dominant viewpoint in international relations between the two wars was the view-

point of international law and organization. Here again, the conception of scholarship which underlay this method of study was twofold in nature. The mission of students in the field had been to discover the goals and objectives toward which international society ought to be tending. Once this step had been taken and the goal of an ideal world commonwealth accepted, the first explicit task of those engaged in this field of study was to bring about the necessary transformation of institutions and societies whereby these goals could be attained. In this way, the scholar became a crusader and reformer so that it was said by critics of this mode of thinking that in no other field had scholars become to such a degree captive of their own emotions and visions of the future.

The first chair at the University of Wales dedicated to the study of international politics is symbolic of this phase of international studies and of conditions which surround it. It was natural that the first two occupants of the chair should be diplomatic historians, Professors Sir Alfred Zimmern and C. K. Webster. It was no less surprising that the aims and purposes of international relations should be described as the stimulation and advancement of a spirit of international cooperation and good will among the world's peoples. In other words, through indoctrination and the propagating of ideas and information regarding the new international organization, the League of Nations, it was imagined that international studies could perform both an educational and transforming function. The purpose of the studies in this field was to inspire an appreciation for other cultures and peoples and prepare unruly and recalcitrant peoples everywhere, and not least in the United States, for the approval and acceptance of the institutions of international government. What inspired most of the thinking and a great deal of the writing in this period was a single belief. It was widely imagined that once an international organization had been established, all of the baffling and perplexing issues of international politics would disappear. International relations was defined as "the study of those related problems of law and . . . of ethics which were raised by the project of a League of Nations." Hence, the moral obligation of the scholar required that he preach and teach the urgent need for those actions by which an international organization could be established and made acceptable to all the world's peoples.

There are three characteristics of this period in international studies which are essential for considering its successes and failures. First, it was dominated by a spirit of unbounded optimism. Second, the research and academic interests, as well as the special competence and qualifications of men in the field, was concentrated primarily in the sphere of international law and organizations. Third, a tendency to draw moral judgments in favor of all international ventures and developments at the expense of any national experience or action which might have its own peculiar international implication was always apparent. The spirit of optimism which characterized this era derived, undoubtedly, from the philosophy of the enlightenment and from its stepchild, the peace movement of the nineteenth century. Prominent and powerful industrial figures like Ginn, the publisher, and Andrew Carnegie, the steel magnate, approached the solution of international problems with the same confidence and dispatch they had developed in their respective fields of enterprise.[3] Indeed, there was little doubt in the minds of these leaders that the expending of greater energy and zeal on the problem of war would before long bring about its eradication in much the same way that difficulties in industry had been "rationalized" and done away with. The Carnegie Foundation in its prescription for abolishing "the foulest blot on our civilization" hinted that the problem of war was only one in a series of problems which American ingenuity would soon efface. Carnegie himself instructed the trustees of the Carnegie Endowment for International Peace that: "When . . . war is discarded as disgraceful to civilized man, the trustees will please then consider what is the next most degrading evil or evils whose banishment . . . would most advance the progress, elevation, and happiness of man. . . ." The prevailing optimism and the conception of progress which had guided Western society received concrete expression in the thinking of such men and foundations.

Second, the research of specialists in the field indicates the degree to which the study of international law and organization prevailed.[4] The scholarship of individuals like Professors Berdahl, Colegrove, Fenwick, Garner, Hershey, Hyde, Potter, Shotwell, Wilson, and Wright was characterized in a positive way by great technical competence and a remarkable absence of parochialism and chauvinism. It is notable, however, that of the twenty-four scholars in the field who held the rank of professor by 1930, eighteen had devoted themselves exclusively to the study of international law and organization. Moreover a tendency persisted throughout these years of equating peace with government on the one hand, and war with power politics, and the balance of power on the other. When international politics and its enduring practices and techniques was studied at all, it was studied by the diplomatic historian, but within the limits of his orientation. The experiences of the nineteenth century in the easing of international tensions were considered irrelevant as subjects deserving serious inquiry. Instead, technical and procedural problems and organizational reforms and improvements of international government preoccupied almost every scholar.

Third, there was an implicit if unstated assumption which underlay the selection of almost every subject of inquiry. It was widely believed that everything international was good, and everything national was bad. Hence, those forms of international practice selected for study included such good and constructive international experiments as the League of Nations, and such questionable and dubious national issues and problems as imperialism and nationalism. The so-called bad or morally ambiguous international activities involved in the operations of the Third International were not discussed nor were examples of good national activities, such as the quest for national security by this country. Indeed, one of the illnesses from which the study of international relations still suffers is the cult of internationalism which places its own moral evaluations on the field of study in terms of the dichotomy of good internationalism and bad nationalism.

Following World War II, however, a tendency which has its inception in a period antedating World War II came to the forefront. The study of international politics replaced the study of international organization as the guiding concern and fundamental point of reference in international relations.[5] An approach was made to recurrent world issues not with a view to praise or condemn but to understand them. Professor Grayson Kirk, now Provost and Vice-President of Columbia University, in a survey of courses and students in the field immediately following the war found that international politics had become the basic introductory field of study almost everywhere throughout the country. In place of the examination of structure and organization in international society, students had turned to the study of underlying forces and trends which shape and mold the behavior of all nation-states. It became the objective of international politics to study the field in much the same terms that domestic politics had been studied for almost a generation. In the same way that American government has proceeded from the study of the American

Constitution and the basic law to the examination of practical politics and pressure groups, so international studies became concerned with the study of trends in the foreign policies of separate nation-states and the forms and techniques through which the various national policies of states could be compromised and adjusted on the international plane. Instead of beginning with the *international* structure and society, the new line of inquiry has emphasized the urgency of examining *national* goals and objectives as a logical point of departure. Just as no one would imagine for a moment that national policy on the domestic scene is a quantity that is given at the outset but instead would expect that national policy derived from compromise and adjustment among the major political parties and pressure groups, so it has been argued that international policy, say, within the United Nations, must be studied as the resultant policy of the pressures and claims of many nations on the international scene. The practices and policies of international organization are from this viewpoint no longer comprehended as abstract considerations.[6] Instead they are conceived in the framework of national aims and aspirations, the points of conflict of these aspirations and their areas of compatibility and incompatibility. In this way, the historic policies of England, the United States, or the Soviet Union become subjects of more vital interest than isolated studies of international government divorced from international politics as such. The international organization finds its proper and appropriate place if conceived of as a forum within which national rivalries are compromised and adjusted through novel political processes.

What this has done in practice has been to tie the study of international relations to political science as a primary unifying and integrating core. Without this core international relations had tended to ride off in all directions. With it the chances of discovering some relevant and general principles by which statesmen and citizens might be guided have become for the first time a reality. For political science assumes that the rivalry among groups and individuals for political power and the ways in which power and authority are exercised can be made a proper subject of inquiry and study. In the same way, international politics assumes that the struggle for power and influence on the international scene can be tested and examined on its own terms. More far-reaching than this, however, has been the development of the beginnings of a separate methodology for international politics as reflected in the studies presented in the journal *World Politics.* We shall consider the questions and problems which arise in connection with this development in our second section on methodology.

In summary, then, the development of the study of international affairs has progressed through four relatively distinct stages or phases. Prior to and including World War I, diplomatic historians enjoyed what amounted to a virtual monopoly over this area. However, the imprint they made on the field by techniques of historical research still left crucial areas of inquiry outside of the range of international studies. Specifically, the analysis of recent events was hardly amenable to scientific history with its twofold requirement of abundant documentation and the perspective of time. So the period between World War I and II found two distinct viewpoints vying for influence among teachers and scholars. There emerged, on the one hand, an energetic movement which aspired to examine the areas from which diplomatic history had excluded itself. Popularizers of international studies leaped boldly into the breach and a high-falutin' approach to everyday garden-variety current events grew up. The skills and techniques of the social sciences were used indifferently or not at all in this enterprise. Since the standard for embarking on research was the contribution a project would make to universal understanding and cooperation or to the encouragement of the aims and purposes of the League of Nations, it was hardly to be expected that any system for analysis could emerge at this time. Nor did the second viewpoint which prevailed during much of the inter-war period mitigate these problems. Alongside the modish conception of international studies as the equivalent of current events, the prevailing point of reference was international law and organization. International relations were construed as moving along two different planes. One plane was the legal sphere in which nations were told how to act. The other was the sphere of actual conduct among states which had to be judged and evaluated in terms of conformity or divergence from the rules of international law. So exclusive an emphasis on law and organization had three consequences in practice. It led to research that was generally devoid of social and political analysis insofar as it stressed the form instead of the functions of international affairs. It invited the acceptance of a line of least resistance in the choice of areas of research. That is to say, official reports and publications in the field of law and organization poured across the desks of teachers in the field in streams that overpowered even those whose natural bent might have guided their studies along other lines of inquiry. It insured that the model for analysis would be a universal world state characterized by perpetual peace. The present tragic order of power politics among states was studied and assessed not by attempting to understand the underlying conditions which were responsible for its persistence among nation-states but through establishing the sharp deviation of this situation from the model of one world commonwealth.

The failure of this point of view to conform even accidentally with the facts of the inter-war period ushered in the final stage in contemporary international studies. International politics has become the focal point of present-day research and teaching partly because of the march of events in the 1930s. For the crises which have followed one another in rapid succession from Mukden Bridge in 1931 to the present have found both teachers and students emotionally and intellectually unprepared for meeting each new challenge. The widespread belief which was engendered by claims that the new formal institutions would soon modify international behavior bore little resemblance to the events which followed. The relations of civilized nations which were to be modified by the operations of the League of Nations progressively deteriorated as the European balance of power was threatened by Germany and Italy. No minor constitutional defect of the League of Nations but the political conditions under which it operated was the primary factor which led to its breakdown. Yet only a realistic assessment of international phenomena could have anticipated and accounted for its decline and fall. The troublesome problem of assessing circumstances and conditions under which national interests could have been harmonized was subordinated to the study of form and structure of the novel international organization. The clue to the basic point of departure of international politics as distinguished from international organization may be found in the way that the current United Nations is evaluated. Formerly, the League had been at the center of the majority of recognized studies; now world politics is the milieu or setting in which every other subject is studied including the functions of the United Nations.[7] International organization, law, trade, and finance are studied in a political instead of a constitutional context. And political scientists are accorded the task of asking questions covering problems which continue to vex our society. Inasmuch as the rivalries which occasion international tensions are now generally assumed to be political in character, this movement of the political scientist to the center of international studies is rooted in the facts of the situation. Today the three-fold concern of international politics is with the forces and influences which bear on the conduct of foreign policy everywhere, the techniques, and machinery by which foreign policy is executed, and both the novel institutions and traditional practices whereby the conflicts among nations are adjusted and accommodated. The fundamental and persistent forces of world politics such as nationalism, imperialism, and the balance of power, however, have only belatedly become an appropriate subject for inquiry. The basic drives which determine the foreign policies of states, their desire for security and power, are the elemental facts with which international politics is fundamentally concerned.[8] International politics is the study of rivalry among nations and the conditions and institutions which ameliorate or exacerbate these relationships.

Three Theories of International Political Behavior

It is frequently said that one test of the independent character of a discipline or field of study is the presence in the field of theories contending for recognition by those engaged in thinking and writing. It may be significant that underlying the study of contemporary international politics are two general theories of human nature and politics. Moreover, there are already the first signs of the origin of a third way of conceiving the nature of international affairs. At this time, however, political idealism and political realism are the major competitors for recognition as the theory of international behavior.[9] In the past there has been no coherent political theory evolved from the ancients which deliberately sets forth to explain politics within a system that is not ordered and controlled by an all-powerful central authority.[10] Indeed idealism and realism as conceived and defined in political theory from Greek times to the present have little in common with the assumptions and premises of the two philosophies of contemporary international politics. Each in its sphere has its own tacit or explicit assumptions. In world politics, the philosophy of idealism or utopianism so-called includes most of the thinking which was done in the intervening years between the two World Wars. The philosophy of realism which had prevailed throughout most of the eighteenth and nineteenth centuries has been revived both in theory and practice especially in the years following World War II. The currently most useful and original literature has been contributed primarily by those concerned with testing the assumptions of realism. Yet it is fashionable especially in circles of older scholars to proclaim that the distinctions between realism and idealism are unreal and exaggerated. Moreover, there are many who contend that both terms are fraught with emotions and value judgments and thereby are disqualified from use in social studies. In contrast, great diplomats in the West including the most distinguished representatives in 1952 have rarely been seized by such fears and doubts. Our wisest diplomats and statesmen have taken idealism and realism for granted. For example, the most learned and perceptive of American diplomats and the present Ambassador to Moscow, George F. Kennan, has declared: "I see the most serious fault of our past policy formulations to lie in something that I might call the legalistic-moralistic approach to international problems. This approach runs like a red skein through our foreign policy of the last fifty years. . . . It is the belief that it should be possible to suppress the chaotic and dangerous aspirations of governments in the international field by the acceptance of some system of legal rules and restraints. . . . It is the essence of this belief that instead of taking the awkward conflicts of national interest and dealing with them on their merits with the view to finding the solutions least unsettling to the stability of international life, it would be better to find some formal criteria of a juridical nature by which the permissible behavior of states could be defined."[11] Kennan concludes his estimate of the philosophy of utopianism by pointing to the beliefs and attitudes in the United States which have made this viewpoint meaningful and creditable. "Behind all of this, of course, lies the American assumption that the things for which other peoples in this world are apt to contend are for the most part neither creditable nor important and might justly be expected to take second place behind the desirability of an orderly world, untroubled by international violence. To the American mind, it is unplausible that people should have positive aspirations, and ones that they regard as legitimate, more important to them than the peacefulness and orderliness of international life."[12]

Another wise statesman, a young Conservative Member of Parliament, Captain Peter Thorneycroft, who in 1951 was to become the youngest member of Prime Minister Churchill's Cabinet, voiced on February 28, 1945, essentially the same beliefs that Kennan was to express in 1951. In a debate in the House of Commons on the issues arising from the Polish settlement agreed to by Prime Minister Churchill, President Roosevelt, and Premier Stalin at the Crimean Conference, Captain Thorneycroft chose the occasion to cast his specific comments in the mold of general principles of international politics.

> I believe the real difficulty in which my hon. Friends find themselves is not so much Poland at all. I believe it is in the apparent conflict between documents like the Atlantic Charter and the facts of the European situation. We talk to two different people in two different languages. In the East we are talking to the Russians. The Russians are nothing if not realists. . . . I believe that the Russian Foreign Office is perhaps more in tune with the advice which would be given to the Tsars than to the potentates of the twentieth century. In such circumstances we talk in language not far removed from power politics. In the West we are faced by the Americans. They are nothing if not idealists. To them we talk in the polite language of the Atlantic Charter. Somehow or other we have to marry those two schools of thought. If I could persuade the Americans, particularly in the Middle West, to have something of the Russian realism in inter-national relations, and persuade the Russians to have the idealism that exists on the East coast of America, we might get somewhere, but let us face the fact that the process will be a long and painful one. You do not move suddenly from a world in which there are international rivalries into a world where there is international cooperation. It is the world that we are in that the Prime Minister has to deal with. We could not come back from Yalta with a blueprint for a new Utopia. . . . The rights of small nations are safeguarded by a mixture of diplomacy and military power. . . .[13]

These two expressions of an American and British conception of the nature of international politics are significant because of the strong clear light they throw on the two opposing theories. They indicate that professional diplomats and statesmen are unable to indulge themselves the luxury of shying away from the facts of international life. The assumptions underlying the two points of view may be enumerated in relatively simple terms. For the political realist, rivalry and some form of strife among nation-states is the rule and not a mere accident of backwardness in the past. There are harmonies as well as disharmonies to be sure but the failure of every scheme for world peace in the past must be sought in the conditions which have created the disharmonies and not through comparisons with a blueprint of a commonwealth of absolute world harmonies. In all social groups, whether in states or in smaller more intimate communities, a contest for influence and power goes on unceasingly. On the international scene, however, rivalries among states are uncontrolled by effective law or government. The business of statesmanship and diplomacy under the conditions of present-day international society is to limit the struggles and restrict their extent and scope. The means available in the absence of government are the unceasing pursuit of new balances of power and rough equilibriums among contending parties. The aims include adjustment and accommodation on the basis of mutual recognition that an equilibrium does exist. The realist strives to mitigate the rivalries among nations, through checks and balances and by compromise and bargaining. Abstract moral principles may be the ultimate object and purpose of the bargain or agreement but an abstract principle is not an essential part of the bargain itself. Realism would prepare the student of international politics for the tragic and stubborn discrepancy of means and ends in international politics. It accepts for the guide and premise of its thought the permanence and ubiquity of the struggle for power. But it strives unceasingly through every means at its disposal to contain and limit concentrations of power and to compose and relieve tensions which could lead to a situation of war.

The utopian philosophy has little in common with political realism nor has it shown much patience or understanding for this brand of thinking. It chooses to abjure the toils of power politics since at most they are considered an abnormal and passing historic phase. In fact, with the creation of one universal society, so primitive and barbaric a form of international politics, if not indeed politics itself, will be eliminated. Political realism, it is claimed, is a distortion and cynical corruption of the true meaning of history. It is claimed by the spokesmen of political idealism that if there have been group controversies throughout history, these struggles have centered not in political rivalries for influence and power but in the clash between incompatible ideals and principles. A concrete example which is offered is the aggression of fascism against democracy. At such time, therefore, as fascism and the other philosophies whose aims have made conflict inevitable have been permanently smashed and destroyed, power politics and war will disappear. Historically, utopianism has offered three alternatives for moral nations confronting the practical problems of survival in a world of archaic power politics. Ultimately, power politics must be eliminated through instituting a universal world government. Practically, power politics will be abolished when their main exemplars, the totalitarian states, have been erased from the face of the earth. Provisionally, their evil influence will be progressively and decisively undermined by the example of moral and upright nations foreswearing relations with corrupted, power-seeking nations, pursuing neutrality policies and abstaining from all forms of traditional power politics.

In practice, moreover, the nations of good will who have accepted the philosophy of utopianism have pursued foreign policies reflecting precisely these three alternatives. It is not by accident that the United States as the nation over recent decades that has yielded most readily to utopianism has pursued a foreign policy that has vacillated between these three possibilities. For in these terms we can account for the neutrality policy of the United States before both World Wars. In each pre-war period, we tried to abstain and withdrew from the impure and corrupted power politics of the European continent. Any concession in terms of territorial guaranties against German expansion would have been unworthy of the philosophy we espoused. Any intervention in the affairs of Europe for the purpose of bolstering and strengthening the Weimar Republic would have weakened our moral position. When at length we were driven by the inherent logic of utopianism to justify our role in World War II, we turned from neutrality to a holy crusade against the evil incarnate in fascism. When through no fault of our own war became unavoidable—for had we not meticulously avoided any political action that could have invited the conflict—we gave unstintingly of our resources and our principles. We engaged in the world struggle not selfishly or for political advantage but in order to end conflict in the west and destroy and eliminate those evil men and ideals who had been responsible. These wars were not ordinary struggles for more territorial adjustments, new balances of power or specified political gains but were crusades for advancing the spread of democracy. They were holy wars of "unconditional surrender" against solitary infidels and troublemakers. For these men and ideas had caused the catastrophes; therefore, with their elimination, aggrandizement and rivalry would disappear.

The third stage in the utopian journey, however, has been for us the most basic, fateful and far-reaching. After the war, it was clearly essential that what had been undertaken and achieved in war be sealed and perfected in peace. The agents of power politics lay mortally wounded; now the climate in which their nefarious policies had thrived must be cleansed and transformed and international organization substituted for politics. In this new common-wealth, the problem of power would disappear. What this meant in concrete terms was that the *status quo* with its prevailing lawfulness based on the rela-tive satisfaction of the victorious powers must be made permanent through the regularized procedures of new international organizations. Thus through our policies of neutrality, moralistic crusades, and the substitution of orga-nization for anarchic world politics, we have consistently pursued in recent times the aims of political idealism.

Hence the crucial difference and the real point at which political idealism and political realism diverge is with respect to the positions they take regard-ing the problem of power. Power is an attribute of an archaic and transitory international situation for idealists who have chosen not to recognize it as en-during. Power for the realist is the single most stubborn social psychological factor by which international behavior is influenced. Only through under-standing this phenomenon can man hope to improve the melancholy status of his present situation. There is a third general approach or theory, however, which departs explicitly from both of these theories of politics. A viewpoint which is perhaps best designated *eclectic* has been asserted to represent a new synthesis. Thus in the second revised edition of Georg Schwarzenberger's vo-luminous *Power Politics,* the author rejects both idealism and realism as un-scientific.[14] Neither, he claims, has seen fit to state its major premise which he finds on the one hand in the case of realism to be that of pessimism and on the other hand with idealism that of optimism. Schwarzenberger concludes: "What is actually required is a primarily empirical approach to international affairs."[15] Eclecticism in these terms asks the student to start without any *a priori* assumptions in making his inquiries in the field. The eclectic point of view has shown a preference for a sociological approach to the problems of world politics. There would appear to be three reasons alleged for this practicality. First, only present-day sociology with its separation of facts and values and its resistance to *a priori* judgments is equipped with a tradition of having pursued truly empirical studies. Also, the sole catholic and inclusive approach to the study of international politics is that of sociology. For example, in the case of tariff legislation, the international lawyer can discuss the legal and normative implications of treaties and treaty observance; the economist can assess the purely economic aspects of the problem; and the political scientist will contribute to an understanding of the political conflicts going on within a certain nation. Yet the only discipline which will cover all these separate facets under the enveloping umbrella of a single conceptual framework is sociology. Third, sociology alone is capable of providing tests or clues by which to separate subject matter that is clearly international in character from what is essentially domestic in nature. It finds this test in the general principle of whether or not a given issue or episode affects the growth or the disintegration of international society. A new unity called the international society which by definition falls short of a true community but in effect exceeds a condition of anarchy is the guidepost by which we must measure whether a thing is international or not. At the present stage of development international society is an emerging embryonic movement that is measurable. Any event must be examined and assessed in light of its effect on the degree of integration and disintegration in international society. In American foreign policy, for example, the scientific way in which to think about the Truman Doctrine or the Marshall Plan would be to estimate their effects on the integration or disintegration of international society.

Of the three approaches or theories of international politics, eclecticism has come on to the scene most recently. Its claim that it foreswears the espousal of one viewpoint or another regarding human nature and politics is hardly substantiated in concrete studies by scholars like Professor Schwarzenberger. For that author, after disclaiming the assumption of realism that man is competitive and possesses a lust for power as well as the belief of idealism that he is rational and good, actually proceeds throughout most of his analysis to employ the working concepts of political realism. Indeed the illusion of much of contemporary social science that the student can in fact approach his inquiry with a *tabula rasa* is hardly supported by the undertakings of Schwarzenberger or any of his colleagues. Yet this view is central to eclecticism as a theory of international politics. If this assumption is false, then much of the work of this approach will in all likelihood be seriously undermined. At this stage, however, the presence of three separate theories each avowing qualitatively distinct assumptions tends to give to the study of world politics the character of something approaching a discipline.

The Normative Aspects of International Politics

Probably the area of international studies which has evolved most painfully and slowly are studies in the relationship of morality and norms to international practice. Only in comparatively recent times has there been any evidence of a serious and deliberate attempt to approach this question objectively and systematically. The literature of the inter-war period is barren of conscious attempts to deal "scientifically" with the problem. Following World War II, a handful of philosophers and scholars turned their attention to this problem. Among them the most noteworthy have been the theologian Reinhold Niebuhr, the Cambridge historian Herbert Butterfield, and the political scientists Hans J. Morgenthau and E. H. Carr.[16] Their contributions can be understood most fully in the perspective of the fundamental problem of ethics and politics as it exists at all levels of politics but especially at the level of international politics. It is an indisputable fact that ethics and politics are in conflict wherever man acts politically. This is the case because it is the essence of politics that man chooses goals and objectives which are limited and therefore equitable and just only for particular groups and nations. For example, in practice those things which are done in the interest of labor will frequently work an injustice upon management. Indeed only in pure thought and reflection can policies and acts remain uncorrupted and undefiled by some margin of injustice. This universal aspect of the corruption of absolute justice in the realm of politics finds its outstanding expression in international morality. There my nation's justice means oftentimes your nation's injustice; my nation's security and the requirements assigned thereto may appear as the cause of your nation's insecurity. For the allies, armaments and spheres of influence essential to safety as viewed through my eyes may represent a threat to security when seen through your eyes. So the tendency everywhere present for ethics to be separated from politics, reaches its culmination in international affairs.

Three answers to this dilemma have been provided in modern thought. They are the answers of *moralism, cynicism,* and *political wisdom.* It will be our purpose now to review their main characteristic: first, it is tempting to seek to bridge the gulf and resolve the discrepancy between ethics and politics in simple moralistic terms. Moralism as a political philosophy maintains that at present men pursue a double standard of conduct in their private and public lives. Privately, man is honest and ethical; publicly he covers his acts with a tissue of lies and deception. His virtue in private affairs is seen as the conquest of culture over barbarism, of a moral age over an immoral one. At an earlier stage in man's evolution, his conduct in private affairs had been corrupted by violence. And in the same way in international affairs the cultural lag from which nations now suffer is being quickly erased. The forward march of history is carrying nations from a retarded condition into a new and enlightened era when private standards will become public rules. The same conception of ethics which determines the conduct of individuals will influence hereafter the behavior of nations in one universal society of nations. This was the faith of President Woodrow Wilson and more recently of Secretary of State Cordell Hull.[17]

The sanguine hopes and expectations of this moralistic outlook bear little resemblance to the conduct of nations. The melancholy unfolding of the past four decades has left the most ardent of the believers in this faith shaken and uncertain of its assumptions. Therefore in practice simple moralistic viewpoints have tended to induce the emergence of their opposite, namely, cynicism. Herein it is argued that when politics and ethics diverge it is only because they are unlike quantities. Politics are means and ethics are ends; means may be evil, but good ends, to which means are subordinated, can endow acts which are morally ambiguous with their own ethical content. The dictum which claims that the end justifies the means seems particularly in the realm of politics to furnish a simple clue to our problem. Yet for men and for nations, it is universally the practice to justify every evil measure by claiming it serves an ethical goal. For Stalin the brutality of liquidating the kulaks found its justification in communist eschatology; for Hitler the cremation of so-called inferior races was excused as a necessary hygienic measure if Teutonic virility were to continue unimpaired. Since nations in the present anarchic world society tend to be repositories of their own morality, the ends-means formula has prevailed as an answer to the moral dilemma, for it is undeniably a concealed but essential truth that nations tend to create their own morality. In its extreme form, however, this development has found nations accepting as ethical whatever redounded to their own material advantage and judging whatever was detrimental to their purposes as being immoral and evil. Yet by the nature of man and politics, statesmen and nations never wholly escape the judgment of elementary ethical standards. The history of politics discloses that no peoples have divorced completely politics from ethics but have generally agreed that men were required to conform in their deeds to standards more objective than those of success.

One sign that ethics are accepted as relevant in most societies and cultures is the apparent compulsion felt by political actors to justify their deeds in moral terms. This tribute to a moral order has its consequences both in words and deeds. There is a striking dialectical movement of expediency and morality which has its impact on international politics. Moves in practical politics must be articulated in such a way as to pay tribute to moral principles. However limited and particular, acts of political expedience must seem to carry forward aims of justice and the common good. Thus political morality in these modest terms, forces the statesman who would justify expediency with ethics to choose his measures so that on some points at least the practical and moral march hand in hand. It is political wisdom to act successfully in accord with the interests of state. It is political and moral wisdom to choose the most moral of several alternatives through which both expedience and ethics may be served. The margin which separates cynicism from this form of wisdom is frequently narrow indeed but by it the statesman is saved from a fatuous "moralism" or the despair of unqualified expediency. It is the essence of moral judgment to transcend the limits of expediency and narrow self-interest in this one sense at least.

The development of a rational concept of international morality is illustrated best in the recent attempts to construct a concept of international morality possessing three dimensions or layers. The heart or core of this conception is the idea of the moral dignity of national interest. Whereas it is obvious that the first duty of a nation's foreign policy must be to safeguard the interests of its citizens and of past and future generations, it must follow that the moral values of that state are defended and promoted in this way. In practice a nation can indulge itself the private virtues of generosity and self-sacrifice only if its survival is not endangered thereby.[18] If in fact its external acts are restricted because of the threats to its security, the nation as a community of men of good will can as a minimum pursue moral ends and purposes at home and in this way contribute to international order and peace.

A second dimension of this conception of the norms and morality of international politics is the opposite side of the shield we have designated the national interest. It is the concept of reciprocal or mutual national interests. The practical importance of this phase of morality is inherent in the statement of Governor Adlai E. Stevenson of Illinois whose deep wisdom and realism have not been widely known. "The United States will find support among peoples in the free states to the degree that they believe we do not simply consult our own interests but give consideration to their interests as well—that we in truth have 'a decent respect for the opinions of mankind.' Other nations have a reciprocal obligation to give weight to our interests too. There is no doubt that our power gives us an advantage in this process, but neither is there room to doubt that if we wish allies who will go forward with us with courage and fortitude into the risks of the future, they must be willing and confident allies."[19]

The one thing which saves the idea of the national interest from itself is its essential reciprocity. To the extent that nations are in earnest not alone about their own self-interests but in their recognition of the application of similar criteria by others, the national interest as a guide escapes any temptation to conceal real designs for world aggrandizement. The English political philosopher Edmund Burke declared: "Nothing is so fatal to a nation as an extreme of self partiality, and the total want of consideration of what others will naturally hope or fear."[20] After a nation has determined its own objective interests in terms of its national security, it has an obligation to draw back as it were and appraise coolly and realistically the interests of its neighbors. In this way alone can nations decide if their interests are compatible or can be adjusted.

There is no other basis for true coexistence. It is as tempting as it is hazardous to treat other peoples as pawns in the struggle to preserve one's own national interest. There is a tendency to treat other nations as means instead of as ends embodied in their own national purposes. Yet in relations particularly with those societies in Asia and Africa which have most frequently been treated as instruments to be used and exploited by others, their claims upon international society to accord them means of national recognition and personal self-respect make such a tendency well-nigh fatal. It is essential that every nation pursue wisely its own best interests but the pathway for each nation must not be strewn with the remnants of the interests of others that were forgotten in its headlong drive to attain national security. Among nations with decent intentions there must be a reciprocal process of recognizing each other's vital interests and avoiding collisions and conflicts insofar as it is possible through the compromise of divergent interests.[21]

There are four reasons why the arch of international morality is properly conceived of as being the mutuality of national interests. The first of these we have discussed. As we have seen, mere national egotism without realistic attention to what other countries conceive their vital interests to be leads to the corruption of a nation's power and values. The second reason for the importance of this aspect of morality is inherent in the nature of international politics. Interests we know are capable of being compromised; principles can never be made the object of bargains. Yet if nations are to survive somehow they must find ways of compromising their differences while at the same time they succeed in protecting and safeguarding their interests. For as it is the essence of politics that individuals possess the capacity to compromise their differences, the art of diplomacy merely raises this process to the level of nations and founds it upon a structure of multiple national interests. Peace and order rest on the identification and accommodation of interests. Third, the unequivocal lesson of history is that conflicts which seem at the time to present to the parties a clear case of right and wrong, almost without exception have appeared to future historians, less blinded by passion and loyalty, as something infinitely more tragic than good men fighting bad ones. The real pattern of conflict and war is one of minor differences hardening into intractable political divisions, of men faced by terrible dilemmas and of nations eventually driven by the inner dialectic of events to wars which no one desired. The difference between a struggle between good and evil and actual struggles in world politics in which every party in some way is at fault but is unable to disengage itself from the tragic predicament of fearing others but never comprehending their counter-fears is the difference between the substance of "heroic" and "revisionist" or scientific history. In this predicament, each party has a sense of its own insecurity but never imagines that its own righteous efforts could have anything to do with the insecurity of others. After each military conflict, the minds of the early or "heroic" historians are locked in the combat expounding their own nation's cause. Their judgments are generally the kind that stem from self-righteousness. Subsequently, it remains for "revisionist" historians to rewrite the narrative in terms of the mutual fear of each side for the power of the other. In their histories of conflict the revisionist schools have frequently proved we have muddied the waters and darkened our minds about the true nature of a struggle when it has been interpreted in terms of certain accidental characteristics. In the present crisis between East and West, for example, historians may show that the ideological aspect of the struggle was accidental in comparison to the more profound and underlying political struggle. In this tragic predicament, the one source of relief from the struggle can come from the accommodation of conflicting political interests. The first step in this process is to discover what are the vital interests of the foe. The one escape from this human predicament is the patient quest of mutually compatible national interests if they are found to exist. And fourth and finally, a firm and steady endeavor to find out what are the interests of the other party to a crisis provides any nation with some basis for predicting its actions and in the same way of anticipating the faithfulness of its allies.

The third layer of international morality comprises such general moral principles as opposition to tyranny. Although politics are primarily power politics, human beings obstinately reject the view that state behavior is not in some ways a fit subject for moral judgment. Even one of the most brilliant of our contemporary analysts who has been in the vanguard of those who have contributed realist critiques of western political thought, has stated repeatedly that realism in statecraft was not enough. E. H. Carr, the well-known English author of *The Twenty Years' Crisis,* has exposed relentlessly the hollowness of utopianism in the inter-war years with its hazardous practice of identifying limited experiences and national policies with universal good. But he has also insisted that any mature outlook must contain elements of utopianism and realism, purpose and analysis, ethics and politics. "Consistent realism excluded four things which appear to be essential ingredients of all effective political thinking; a finite goal, an emotional appeal, a right of moral judgment, and a ground for action."[22] It is the task of the statesman to supply these deficiencies but no task is fraught with greater danger or perils. Whereas loyalty to the nation is morally tolerable only if it includes values which are wider than the nation, there is the baffling problem in means and ends of discovering what those values are and how they can be sustained by nations with limited power. The story of political realists who have discovered the primacy of power and national interest and then gone in search of moral principles by which to transcend them has too often been the melancholy account of an Odyssey in which the true goal of the journeyer is sacrificed for the early exhilaration of too simple, good-hearted moral positions. In practice most attempts to provide moral meaning for international affairs have been tainted with self-interest and hypocrisy. The realist turned moralist with the aim of providing a disinterested standard with concrete applications for the conduct of world affairs tends almost invariably to propose general principles such as the easy harmony of interests of a universal collective security system which are not principles at all but unconscious reflections of one party's national interests.

Yet most accounts of political action show quite plainly that realism is not enough and that there is a certain sphere in which moral principles must be operative. In any full and complete political system there must be room for both philosophy and action. There can be no more serious error than to confound these two. The realms of ideals and practice are not the same. However, it is equally false to imagine that they are two planes that never touch nor meet. For if the vertical dimension be conceived of as the line of ideals, it plainly intersects at certain points in history the horizontal dimension of political practice. In this sense, general moral principles though often inoperative and always subservient to national interest affect and influence international behavior. Yet in the impingement of these three layers of international morality and in their careful study would seem to reside the key to a better understanding of the scope and limits of the normative aspects of international morality.

II. The Methods of International Politics

The techniques and methods of inquiry in international politics are an outgrowth of the questions for which it seeks answers. In the phase of its development when diplomatic history was preeminent, the methods of international studies were indistinguishable from those of history in general. During the period when international law and organization overshadowed every other approach to the subject, the study of legal rules and institutions became the front line of research and inquiry. The one thing these two approaches held in common was a preoccupation with unique institutions and occurrences. The League of Nations was construed as a novel and unprecedented creation in much the same way that each event in diplomacy was construed by the historian as wholly distinct and unique. As we have seen this concern for the best way of studying what had happened only once and never before or since led to a spirit of cavalier indifference for what was similar and recurrent. The rich lessons to be gathered from that period in diplomatic history known as the era of the Concert of Europe were almost never related to the operations of the League of Nations. It was almost as if there had been a tacit agreement among scholars that the study of international politics was exhausted by an inquiry into the immediate experiences of the new League of Nations.

This predisposition to look only at what is unique in politics among nations has been superseded following World War II by a growing concern for the possibility of recurrence. It is a truism to say that events happen only once. But perhaps more important, those events are the manifestation of social forces which in turn are produced by the drives and tendencies inherent in human nature. It has become increasingly the interest of international politics to study with the aim of understanding instead of condemning or proscribing those forces which can be traced and identified in the conduct of groups as well as individuals. In these terms, priority has been given to developing concepts and methods appropriate to the study of politics as a struggle for power. Among individuals the struggle for power has been construed in the subjective terms of the individual's own conception of his quest for security which required him in practice to acquire influence and power. The individual seeks security which plunges him into a competition for influence and power with others whose object is the same as his own. In objective terms this results in a ubiquitous and unceasing struggle for power.

This same construct of the security-power dilemma which has been useful in accounting for rivalries among individuals, has been transferred to the international sphere. At that level the student of international politics is compelled to examine not primarily the motives of nations and statesmen but their capacity to pursue the objectives they have set themselves. Thus the study of national power has become a prime interest of contemporary international studies, and techniques and methods have been tailored to inquiries into this subject. An analysis of the geographic, demographic, industrial, and psychological bases of national power has replaced the study of laws and institutions. With politics and power at the center of their inquiry, students of international politics have been enabled to pose questions which experts on population, industrialization or national character might be expected to answer. By its concern for questions of national power, international politics has opened a wide range of possible inquiry for most social sciences.

However, in another important and fundamental way the study of international politics has turned from the cataloging of particular events to the examining of recurrences in international behavior. The foreign policies of nations have often been conceived of as merely the reflection of the philosophy of a party or of an individual leader or ruler. Yet there is considerable historic evidence and proof that for most nations foreign policy is a continuous and consistent adjustment to objective factors. The foreign policy of England conducted by the Socialists has carried on the main elements of the foreign policy that had been conducted by the Conservatives. Methods and techniques are ever subject to change but the basic objectives have remained constant. In fact, foreign policy in practice is the outgrowth of particular objective conditions which set limits to what any nation can do. There are clusters or aggregates of power and interests which when viewed by statesmen schooled in a common tradition of national policy tend to produce foreign policies that are relatively the same. It is an axiom of foreign policy that *plus ça change, plus c'est la même chose.*

The kind of questions which students of international politics are asking are best illustrated by those studies which have examined the particular national interests of major nation-states. It is not by accident that the most recent of the annual publications of the Brookings Institution directs attention to an inquiry into the national interests of the major world powers. Studies of this kind as well as original monographs by a notable procession of scholars from Charles A. Beard and Nicholas J. Spykman to Hans J. Morgenthau and George F. Kennan have radically altered the issues and problems and therefore the methods and techniques of international politics.

The Foundations of Methodology in International Politics

The scope and methods of international politics are the distillate of ways of examining issues and questions which scholars and professionals have alternately selected or ruled out through a process of inclusion and exclusion over several generations. In the early phases of international studies, and especially in the period falling generally between the two World Wars the foci of interest were diffuse and multitudinous in extent and character. A spirit of aimless humanitarianism motivated the scholar and made extraordinarily difficult the creation of a study that was in any sense new or different. Fragments of knowledge and isolated techniques from the humanities and natural sciences were blended indiscriminately with others that were taken from existing social sciences. But with the gradual limitations and refinement of its orbit of concern, inquiries into international problems began to apply a more rigorous methodology. It is instructive in this connection to report the history of attempts to establish a firmer and more limited conceptual framework. At approximately the midpoint of the inter-war period, Sir Alfred Zimmern was asserting: "the study of international relations extends from the natural sciences at one end to moral philosophy, or even further, at the other."[23] In those terms, in practice there was no area of knowledge or interest falling outside the competence of international studies. It should not be surprising, therefore, that no systematic approach toward defining a core or focus of interest was forthcoming during this period. The dissents of a few isolated scholars like Professors Spykman, Frederick Schuman, and Harold Lasswell were sounded, but generally the concept of international relations as an encyclopedic approach to all world problems prevailed, spurred on by the mission of rapidly inculcating international good will and understanding.

The first attempts at awakening understanding of the minimum prerequisites of a coherent and systematic methodology were the efforts of pioneers like Professor Spykman to define the scope and limits of international studies.[24] It was maintained that international relations was, from one point of view, an actual misnomer. In practice it was states and their representatives and citizens who carried on relations with individuals of other states. They and not necessarily the members of different nationalities were the chief participants. Insofar as this distinction was agreed to and accepted, it excluded as peripheral to the study of interstate relations the problems which arose merely in connection with interethnic associations. Thus the study began at this point to assume a political focus and to exclude certain areas from research by specialists in this field. "International" as a category is a purely formal concept and "relations" is so broad as to include any event or occurrence taking place within the whole range of international society. It was the intention of pioneers in the field to abstract from the total reality of this society, behavior which involved the struggle for power and the creation and maintenance of influence and leadership roles by particular states. Whereas in the study of politics in general, individuals take part as both the immediate and ultimate unit of behavior, the immediate unit in international politics is the state, which enjoys sovereign authority and power but in turn is subject to no higher authority or power; yet what is common to both environments is the struggle for power which goes on unceasingly, albeit within societies in which varying degrees of integration have been achieved. Therefore it is possible to ask the same questions about international politics that we would ask about politics in general notwithstanding the uniqueness of the respective orbits of social reality from which they are being abstracted.

These questions look toward general principles of politics providing uniformities for the study of international politics as conducted within or outside of particular international institutions. For it is apparent that the same questions which can be asked about politics among men striving for influence and control in the schools, the churches or the unions can likewise be asked about politics among nations insofar as what concerns us is the operation of an elemental bio-psychological phenomenon. The questions that are asked about the foreign policies of states must be general and not particular and must inquire after what is common to the behavior of all states instead of merely what is unique in the conduct of a single state. The political scientist who abstracts from international relations that aspect of behavior which involves the response of a nation in its conduct of foreign policy to a certain objective political situation involving both external and internal factors is thereby enabled to make comparisons when those factors are repeated. Indeed it is precisely in comparisons of this kind that the principles of international politics must be sought. If one situation evokes a particular foreign policy, the task of the student of international politics is to judge whether another situation differs fundamentally so that new policies and adjustments should be expected. Or if the similarities between the two situations allow for maintaining essentially the same policy then a basis can be established for appraising through many examples the importance of particular elements of uniqueness as against recurrence for shaping or anticipating a policy.

For example, we might inquire into what were the political factors responsible for early American foreign policy and what similarities and differences are present today?[25] What are the factors which account for the shift of Britain which in 1756 had aligned itself with Prussia against France and the Habsburgs to its position in 1939 when it was allied with France and Poland against Germany? To what extent does Washington's Farewell Address have meaning for American policymakers today and what are the similarities and differences with which the European situation confronted American foreign policy before both World Wars and in the aftermath of World War II? These are obviously issues to which the historian could hardly be asked or expected to turn his attention. For the chief property of history as a means of inquiry is its interest in the uniqueness of situations and events. But the political scientist by contrast can be expected to consider the similarities existing among different occurrences in the past and the present. Sometimes foreign policy is conducted by the state within an external environment which is relatively constant at a time when the factors of its internal situation are in flux. At other times it is the outside situation which changes and by measuring and comparing effects which result from the various combinations, the student may come forth with certain tentative propositions and judgments. They are judgments, however, which must rest on insight and perception of the nature of foreign policy and not fundamentally the statistical correspondence of situations and policies.

The Dilemma of Research in International Politics

It has oftentimes been said that the student of world politics knows through bitter experience what it means to starve in the midst of great plenty. We have seen that one aspect of the development of methodology has been to give first attention to political actions and functions within the totality of international society. Yet an estimate of the power of a nation at any moment requires estimates of the multiple elements which constitute in aggregate national power. There are population and industrial elements which among others determine the political influence a nation can exercise in relations with others. It is here that the dilemma for most contemporary researchers is presented in the most intractable terms. Most students of world politics are political scientists by trade. In departing from historians with their obsession for the unique, the political scientists as a rule are generalists in their field. Yet full knowledge of the elements of national power we have mentioned calls for specialists in population or industry and commerce. Yet few specialists have conceived their own spheres of inquiry in ways that would produce the hypotheses most essential for understanding the true nature of particular political situations.[26]

The student of world politics, himself a generalist, soon perceives his dependence on specialists from other fields. Yet few if any of them have reached conclusions or discovered implications which touch on the core of the generalist's inquiry. This predicament can be mitigated although not resolved by one of a number of possible alternatives.[27] First, it is possible that students of world politics should be encouraged to combine with their general understanding of the field some particular competence in a contributory field. To reverse this conception, another technique might be to invite recognized specialists to apply to the general field their data and hypotheses thus assisting those without preparation or knowledge of these important fields. Third, the collaboration of the generalists with the specialists in joint research is a final technique already employed effectively by the Brookings Institution. In practice any one of these resolutions of our dilemma is subject to difficulties which are substantial. No specialist can be expected to divide evenly his interests and energy between a special subject and the broad field of world politics. Thus specialists have been reluctant to embark on full-fledged appraisals of international politics. And generalists have shown the same reluctance when confronted with the need for interpreting developments in their newly-chosen field of specialization. Of the three techniques we have cited the practice of inviting specialists to consider questions of first import for the study of world politics has appeared most popular. At the same time, however, seminars and research projects undertaken under the auspices of institutes or universities have attempted to make up for the void which exists in fruitful interpretations of the influence of factors not purely political on the course of world politics. We may comment incidentally that the dilemma of the generalist whose best efforts presuppose the free activities of the specialist is by no means uncommon for it exists as well in public administration or any other branch of political science. It is to be expected that as older disciplines and fields have adjusted themselves to this problem, so will the study of international politics.

Materials for Studying International Politics

There was a time when research was primarily determined by available materials. Since at any given moment the government is predisposed to release to the public some documents rather than others, public policy has often determined the focus of scholarly inquiry. During much of the inter-war period this tendency resulted in excessive concern for legal and organizational problems. It meant that in practice the basic unsolved questions were generally not even formulated. In one sense this trend still continues insofar as opportunities for scholars to serve as participant-observers in some phase of government policy not infrequently determines the selection of their areas of research.[28] The risks from these two tendencies are that useful information-gathering takes the place of the search for general knowledge. If the student can retain his freedom of choice, however, it is obvious that this relationship can be profitable for all concerned.

Government handouts and bulletins are in fact a small part of the totality of materials for studying international politics. There are obviously a wide range of sources and papers from which general knowledge can be acquired. Diplomatic history is obviously a repository of the myriad of actions, events,

and situations which the generalist has yet to appraise and evaluate. The data
from history is abundant enough so that social scientists who insist on an adequate number of varying examples need not be disappointed. The process of
comparing and contrasting the data in search of similarities and differences
still remains for the student. Memoirs and autobiographies supply information that might otherwise not become available for some time. Letters and
newspaper articles are another conventional source. Treaties, state papers,
and background releases were at one time conceived of as being more central
to international studies than they are today.

In practice the trend has been away from depending primarily on these conventional data. Instead the new emphasis on realism that has superseded the
earlier note of reform has encouraged appeals to other social scientists whose
inquiries are considered to be relevant. Political analysis has become the foremost concern of the largest number of students in the field. In consequence
the study of conflict and adjustment of various foreign policies has taken top
priority. In this basic inquiry, the newer social sciences have not been backward
in offering their guidance. The study of alien cultures and especially their transformation by the imposing of a new social system has been the contribution
of present day anthropologists. Social psychologists and psychoanalysts have
joined forces to approach the problem of national character. Sociologists have
offered new insights which can be expected to gain increasing relevance. Other
social scientists have studied the data on which any sound estimate of stability
and instability in a society would have to be based. Nor have ideologies or domestic affairs been excluded in these studies. Political theories and sociologists
might be least indifferent to these problems. It is important to remember domestic factors were accountable in part at least, for the unresolved conflict between France and Britain between the Wars. The change in the two countries
from left to right at no time took place simultaneously and in practice the two
governments were in conflict. This problem called for an inquiry into domestic politics in order to understand international politics. Lord Curzon declared
several decades ago that foreign affairs were the most vital and domestic of
all the states' business. Today the sharp line which once separated the two has
been written off as impractical. There is a not inconsiderable amount of data
on the relation of domestic to international politics which can be exploited by
researchers who accept the notion that a nation's objective position sets limits

to its general foreign policy and then proceed to examine the effects in practice of domestic political conditions within these established limits.

III. New Perspectives in Inernational Politics

There are particular areas of research which seem especially urgent at this time. They include:

1. *The re-examination of general principles of foreign policy.*[29] The recurrent patterns of the foreign policies of nations which most diplomatists appear to take for granted have been scarcely examined by modern scholars. If these problems are to be explored, what is called for is, first, more general studies of the geographical, industrial, and physical position of a nation; of the peculiar historical circumstances in which these conditions have operated; of the actual adjustment of nations on the basis of their objective position to successive historical circumstances; and of the claims and declarations made by statesmen engaged in pursuing a certain historic foreign policy. It is the relationship of these four factors to one another and especially the first three to the fourth which ought to be studied systematically. The expectation of such studies would be that clear patterns of the national interest of countries would emerge as a result. In this way, the present confusion under which historians have operated, based on the silence of American statesmen like Wilson on the real political causes of World War I or World War II, would be dispelled. It has been fashionable to accept the notion that the study of foreign policy was exhausted when the declarations of statesmen had been scrutinized. By the juxtaposition of proclamations with objective political and historical factors this problem might be eased.

2. *The study of the inter-relationship of international organization with international politics.* The League and the United Nations have been accepted by some as ends in themselves. This would appear to place limits on research in the field for in these terms only structure and legal rules are of prime relevance. If instead of this emphasis, however, the viewpoint is more widely accepted that these new world institutions are merely new machinery for diplomacy then the study of a particular form of international political

process is opened up. What concerns the scholar in these terms is not the abstraction called the League but the political problems which result, say, from the unresolved conflict between the foreign policies of France and England within and outside that institution. The difference between the orthodox study of the League and Arnold Wolfer's *Britain and France between Two World Wars* is a measure of the contrast between the old and the new. The writings of William T. R. Fox and others in the journal *International Organization* are further examples of the new approach.

3. *The collaborative study of international phenomena* offers some prospect of resolving the dilemma which arises between generalists and specialists. In 1949 the Carnegie Corporation supported a collection of research projects on the inter-relations of specialized studies to international politics. For example, the relation of geographic factors to the formulation of foreign policy has been made the subject of a joint inquiry by political scientists and geographers at the University of Wisconsin and at the University of Michigan. It is obvious that somewhere between the pseudo-science of geopolitics, which has been roundly attacked, and the reckless abandon with which some contemporary students have ruled out the influence of geography altogether, lies the truth. The work going on at the Hoover Library in which world revolution is being studied by teams of social scientists is a further illustration of collaboration of this kind.

4. *The rules of international law may be studied in the light of underlying social forces which determine the likelihood of observance of the law.* The poverty of research and inquiry into international law is partly the result of an overemphasis on the normative aspect of international law. The one guide to the understanding of treaty-observance which has received widespread attention is the aphorism *"Pacta sunt servanda"* (Treaties ought to be observed). Yet what this has amounted to has been little more than a moral exhortation and has borne little relationship (in practice) to the actual conduct of states. What a handful of scholars like Professors Payson S. Wild and Hans Morgenthau have done is to suggest that the nature of the political situation is the paramount factor in treaty observance. International law is likely to be observed by states who have accommodated their conflicts or when their environment is characterized by a relatively stable balance of power. The new school of international law known as functionalism was launched be-

fore World War II as an advance on the positivist and natural law schools. Yet since many students of international law have turned to the study of international politics, this line of inquiry has not been fully explored.

5. *War and international politics are part of a common sphere of interest.* The most fruitful studies of national security and successful diplomacy have refused to draw a sharp line between war and the elements of military strength and contemporary international politics. The work being done at Princeton Harold and Margaret Sprout, Edward Meade Earle, and Alfred K. Vagts are examples of their point of view.

NOTES

Reprinted from *The Review of Politics* 14, no. 4 (October 1952): 433–67.

1. Waldemar Gurian, "The Study of International Relations," *The Review of Politics* 8, no. 3 (July 1946): 275–82.

2. Richard W. Leopold, "The Problem of American Intervention, 1917: An Historical Retrospect," *World Politics* 2, no. 3 (April 1950): 404–25.

3. William T. R. Fox, "Interwar International Relations Research: The American Experience," *World Politics* 2, no. 1 (October 1949): 67–79. The present writer is especially indebted to the author of this article.

4. Ibid.

5. Grayson Kirk, *The Study of International Relations* (New York: Council of Foreign Relations, 1947).

6. Examples of the old school of thought may be found in such volumes as Clyde Eagleton, *International Government* (New York: Ronald Press, 1948) and L. S. Woolf, *International Government* (New York: Brentano's, 1916).

The "political approach" to international government is developed most fully in the writings of Professors William T. R. Fox and Hans J. Morgenthau. Other selections include J. L. Brierly, *The Covenant and the Charter* (Cambridge: The University Press, 1947) and Herbert W. Briggs "Power Politics and International Organization," *American Journal of International Law* 39, no. 4 (October, 1945), 664–79.

7. Hans J. Morgenthau, *Politics Among Nations* (New York: Alfred A. Knopf, 1948); Frederick L. Schuman, *International Politics*, 4th ed. (New York: McGraw-Hill Book Company, Inc., 1948); Georg Schwarzenberger, *Power Politics*, 2nd rev. ed. (New York: Frederick A. Praeger, 1951).

8. John H. Herz, *Political Realism and Political Idealism: A Study in Theories and Realities* (Chicago: University of Chicago Press, 1951); C. K. Webster, *The Study of International Politics* (Cardiff: University of Wales Press Board, 1923).

9. George F. Kennan, *American Diplomacy, 1900–1950* (Chicago: University of Chicago Press, 1951).

10. Herz, *Political Realism and Political Idealism.*

11. Kennan, *American Diplomacy, 1900–1950,* 95–96.

12. Ibid., 96.

13. *Hansard Parliamentary Debates,* House of Commons, vol. 408, February 28, 1945, 1458–59.

14. Schwarzenberger, *Power Politics,* 5–6.

15. Ibid., 5.

16. Herbert Butterfield, "The Tragic Element in Modern International Conflict," *Review of Politics 12,* no. 2 (April 1950): 147–64; E. H. Carr, *Conditions of Peace* (New York: The Macmillan Company, 1944); Hans J. Morgenthau, *Scientific Man vs. Power Politics* (Chicago: University of Chicago Press, 1946); Reinhold Niebuhr, *Christianity and Power Politics* (New York: Charles Scribner's Sons, 1940); "Democracy as a Religion," *Christianity and Crisis 7,* no. 14 (August 4, 1947): 1–2.

17. See, for instance, Cordell Hull's comment on his return from Moscow Conference in 1943 as cited in the *New York Times,* November 19, 1943, 1.

18. Hans J. Morgenthau and Kenneth W. Thompson, *Principles and Problems of International Politics* (New York: Alfred A. Knopf, 1950), 33–41.

19. Adlai E. Stevenson, *Korea in Perspective* (Stamford, CT: The Overbrook Press, 1952), 16.

20. Edmund Burke, "Remarks on the Policy of the Allies with Respect to France" (1793), in *Works,* vol. 4 (Boston: Little, Brown, and Co., 1889), 447.

21. Butterfield, "The Tragic Element in Modern International Conflict."

22. E. H. Can, *The Twenty Years' Crisis, 1919–1939* (London: Macmillan and Co., 1949), 89.

23. Sir Alfred Zimmern, "Introductory Report to the Discussions in 1935," in *University Teaching of International Relations,* ed. Sir. Alfred Zimmern (Paris: International Institute of Intellectual Cooperation, League of Nations, 1939), 8.

24. Nicholas J. Spykman, "Methods of Approach to the Study of International Relations," in *Proceedings of the Fifth Conference of Teachers of International Law and Related Subjects Held at Washington, D.C., April 36–27, 1933* (Washington D.C.: Carnegie Endowment for International Peace, 1933), 60–69.

25. Morgenthau, *Politics Among Nations.*

26. Grayson Kirk, "Materials for the Study of International Relations," *World Politics 1,* no. 3 (April 1949): 426–30.

27. Ibid.

28. Frederick S. Dunn, "The Scope of International Relations," *World Politics* 1, no. 1 (October 1948): 142–46.

29. Statement of Objectives of the Center for the Study of American Foreign Policy, University of Chicago, Director, Hans J. Morgenthau.

CHAPTER 10

Courage or Perdition?

The Fourteen Fundamental Facts of the Nuclear Age

STEFAN T. POSSONY [FERREUS]

However distasteful it may be, nuclear weapons of the fission and fusion types have come to stay. Henceforth, they will be as much a part of human existence as rain and snow, morality and crime, the telephone and the airplane, pacifism and aggressiveness, freedom and tyranny, stupidity and wisdom. It is unlikely that this new invention can be undone except through the destruction of civilization itself. On the contrary, nucleonics sooner or later will provide the foundation of industrial civilization all over the globe. Given the anticipated increase in consumption of our energy resources, it appears that nuclear fuels, on a large scale, will have to be made available to industry within the life span of the present generation. Otherwise economic decline (and hence political catastrophe) must come about as the result of the gradual depletion of oil and coal deposits, the concurrent price rise of mineral fuels, the lack of a mineral energy basis in many countries, the rapidly rising demand for industrial goods, and the uninterrupted increase of population.

On a less cosmic scale, the continued progress of many individual industries is dependent, at least partially, upon the early utilization of nuclear techniques and materials. For example, the future of surface and possibly air transportation, of irrigation agriculture, and perhaps of the chemical and metallurgical industries, is interrelated with nuclear advances. Both energy needs and technological changes make it inevitable that large nuclear industries, including producers of fissile materials and atomic particles, will arise in presently industrialized countries. It is no less inevitable that such industries will grow in under-developed areas, because nuclear technology offers an unprecedented chance of cutting the time requirements for industrialization. Nucleonics are fast becoming a global necessity. Naturally, in a world where there are numerous installations using nuclear techniques, and where there are also many basic nuclear producers, there must be available manifold abilities to build nuclear weapons. *The inevitability of the nucleonic age and the emergence of nuclear industrial potentials is the first fundamental fact which we must grasp firmly.*

True, the mere existence of nuclear industries or even of atomic weapons does not by itself pose a security threat. This threat arises only when such weapons are in the hands of the politically immoral and uninhibited, and more particularly, in the hands of governments or political (and criminal) groups willing to employ such weapons for the blackmail or destruction of their opponents. It may be argued that, given governmental encouragement to the present tendency of society to decentralize, and given some efforts to reduce the vulnerability of factories and cities, the relative effectiveness of nuclear weapons could be reduced. It also may be argued that the employment of nuclear weapons could reduce war to a single battle of a few days' duration and that, while casualties in this battle would be very heavy, *total* casualties would be smaller than those resulting from a hypothetical protracted war fought without nuclear weapons. In comparison with wars of previous centuries, a nuclear war indeed need not be more destructive of human lives than, let us say, the Thirty Years' War (which, admittedly, would be scant solace). However, these arguments may be countered with equally, and perhaps more, cogent objections. In the end, the disputants should agree easily that wars in general, and nuclear wars in particular, are most unpleasant occurrences which all of us must make strong efforts to avoid. Hence the question arises: granting the inevitable existence of nuclear capabilities, are there feasible methods for avoiding a nuclear holocaust?

A nuclear *monopoly* in the hands of an aggressive dictator certainly would have spelled doom for much of mankind. If, by the end of the second world war, Stalin had possessed such a monopoly in the form of a significant weapons stockpile, he would have been able to establish a Soviet world dominion; in all likelihood, he would have proceeded to do so. Or, we may ask ourselves what might have happened if the Nazis had come into possession of an operational stockpile of atomic weapons prior to the Normandy invasion? Had not the United States achieved the first atomic stockpile in history, human society would have suffered the worst catastrophe in its history. Let us be grateful that this disaster was spared us.

If an aggressor were to use nuclear weapons in the future, he would do so in the expectancy of retaliation in kind. We probably are entitled to make some rationalistic assumptions with respect to "human nature," including the psychology of aggressors. If we assume then, that aggressors aim at the fruits of war but dare shoulder only the minimum of sacrifice, we should expect that in the face of a deadly retaliatory threat, aggressors might abstain from the employment of nuclear weapons. Yet this expectation cannot be firm because the aggressor may be able to neutralize, by military or political means, the capability or willingness of his opponents to retaliate; and secondly, because he may be a madman (in the clinical sense), and hence not be rationally mindful of the consequences of his acts—in fact, depopulation and the creation of ruin and chaos may be his primary objectives. Hence the concept that atomic attack is preventable through the threat of retaliation, while probably valid in general, cannot be relied upon in all and any circumstances.

There is a school of thought which denies that security against atomic destruction can be obtained at all through retaliatory threat. The fear is that retaliation would compound the evil. In different variants and mixtures, it is proposed that the supervised destruction of existing stockpiles and the establishment of an international control apparatus be undertaken in order to prevent the future production of nuclear weapons. Perpetual international control is the heart of this concept; its purpose is to make nuclear war impossible through nuclear disarmament. There have been numerous schemes setting forth "infallible" and "effective" control arrangements. Many supplementary and occasionally ingenious ideas have been proposed to provide for the closing of the loopholes which, invariably, appeared after a particular scheme had been analyzed closely.

The drawing of utopias has been the favorite pastime of our nuclear Morus, Campenellas, and Bellamies. It is amazing that such cerebrations have arrested the attention of political scientists and even of practicing statesmen (if we assume their attention was genuine). No less startling is the fact that discussions about such schemes usually ignore the practical difficulties which would arise even in the unlikely event of an international agreement undertaken in truly good faith.

Let us look at three of these practical difficulties.

1. Effective atomic control probably would entail the direct watching of no less than 100,000 industrial firms and factories the world over; hence at least 300,000 technically qualified inspectors would have to be assigned to the control of existing facilities. In reality, this world-wide requirement would be considerably larger and in addition to supervising industrial enterprises, it would be necessary to control many other economic activities, such as mining, trading, laboratory research, etc. I doubt that there are in the world enough technically—and linguistically—qualified persons to undertake such a task. (In the U.S. only 7,400 persons received M.A. and Ph.D. degrees in engineering and physical sciences during 1952.)

No elaborate statistics are necessary to show that commitment of such a corps of inspectors would swallow a large percentage of the world's scientists and technicians. While on control assignments, these men would be taken away from their primary professions. One can but picture the effect on future scientific progress. Yet if volunteers were not forthcoming in adequate numbers, personnel would have to be drafted, and this not just for a short emergency. The loyalty and the reliability of drafted inspectors probably would not rate very high. Since, actually, the world's entire technical economy must be supervised, literally every qualified citizen would have to become a part-time policeman. Even in this improbable case a modern state would possess enough resources and wits to outwit the honest inspectors, bribe the dishonest ones, blind the attention of the disaffected, and enlist the willing or forced cooperation of the ideologists and political careerists.

2. To avoid secret preparations in out-of-the-way places and uninhabited areas, approximately 30 million square miles would have to be supervised, with at least half of this area requiring frequent and close looks. This type of massive supervision can be done only through aerial reconnaissance. Assuming a range of aircraft of 1,000 miles and a photographic coverage per sortie of a two-mile strip, 15,000 aircraft sorties would be necessary for a single supervision or if a weekly check is desired, as it must, about 780,000 sorties per year. This estimate neglects additional sorties necessitated by bad weather and the need to survey sea areas, and it does not take into account the responsibility of following up suspected violations with detailed checks and precision photography obtainable only through large numbers of low-level flights (and con-

ceivably through airborne landings). With maintenance, repair, and loss, approximately 8,450 aircraft and about 2,000,000 men as well as very substantial photographic facilities would be required to do just the basic job. With all that investment and flying, it still would be possible—easily possible—to fool the air patrol: many infractions would be feasible in tunnels, underground installations, and even in innocent-looking city houses. Needless to say, such a global air patrol would deprive all states of their military security in non-nuclear weapons. Hence the patrol can be instituted only *after* states no longer are required to have military and industrial secrets. If so, would the air patrol not be superfluous?

Future technology, however, may modify the above requirements for control flights. With better aircraft, enlarged airbase systems and broader photographic coverage, the job may be done with fewer sorties. Substantial increases in commercial flying gradually may restrict the area which needs to be controlled. Still, the cost of the inspectors corps and the air patrol may be estimated at approximately 18 to 20 billion dollars yearly as compared to the current budget of the United Nations of less than 50 million dollars. Unquestionably, the United States would have to pay the lion's share of this budget. More significant perhaps, only the United States, the Soviet Union, and the United Kingdom would be able to make available adequate air facilities and personnel for the purpose. The air patrol would be an almost exclusive responsibility of the "super powers." Let us be content with the remark that such a state of affairs would present very great political hazards.

3. Nuclear weapons already are in existence. Before an agreement conceivably can be negotiated, there will be large weapons stockpiles in many countries. How on earth can it be assured that all these weapons would be destroyed and that sizeable numbers of "insurance weapons" would not be hidden? Yet if no reliable *and* practical method can be designed against this mortal danger of concealment, then the time for the establishment of *dependable* controls did pass years ago. While it may be a useful propaganda device to talk about control schemes (which I rather doubt since the spreading of illusions usually backfires), nuclear international control never again can be a safe security measure. *International control would be possible only as a sham and, if adopted, would constitute an extreme and unacceptable security hazard. This is the second fundamental fact which we must understand.*

For that matter, the point is entirely academic. So long as the Soviet government retains its present structure and political intent, and wants to remain safely in power as a dictatorship, it cannot, and will not, accept an international control agreement. This is so because it cannot allow thousands of foreign inspectors to investigate Russian industry and possibly ferret out major Soviet secrets. International control, moreover, would mean the end of the iron curtain and hence signify the end of this most essential prop of Soviet political survival.

Our concern must center on the threat of an atomic war within the next ten to twenty years. It is unlikely (though, naturally, not impossible) that during this period the Soviet government will have changed enough to make it any more amenable to mutual supervision. Hence even the best conceived control scheme will not help us with our problem of avoiding nuclear warfare in the immediate future. It may be granted, however, that should the Soviet government change substantially within this crucial period, a new look at the problem could become useful. For the time being, discussions of safe nuclear disarmament schemes are, at best, useless or naïve and, at worst, hypocritical or subversive. *Soviet talk about control is designed to disarm the United States, and enhance the nuclear posture of world communism. This is the third fact which we must always keep in mind.*

It also has been proposed to forego involved control schemes. Instead, a simple international agreement should be concluded, for example, in the form of a mutual promise never to use nuclear weapons. Proposals of this type are based on the assumption that it is, objectively, to the best interests of all to avoid nuclear war. Hence such a promise—it is alleged—would be undertaken in good faith by all states, at the risk of atomic perdition. To assume good faith in vital security matters is in flagrant contradiction to overwhelming historical evidence; as of the date of this writing, it cannot be shown plausibly that the advent of the new technology has invalidated the significance of historical precedent. To postulate that it would be against the interests of a potential aggressor *not* to use nuclear weapons, especially if other nations would have lived up to their word and would be unprepared for nuclear warfare, is hazardous to the point of advocating political suicide. The lack of proper nuclear capabilities in peaceful states would provide the aggressor with unparalleled opportunities for attack and with an historically unprecedented chance of all-inclusive victory. The atomic bomb is an attractive weapon for the Bolshevik. It places him within arms' length of fulfilling what was before an unattainable pipedream: The destruction of the United States and the accomplishment of world revolution, regardless of Russia's survival or demise. The nuclear bomb inevitably will become the aggressor's weapon *par excellence*. While the historical Alexanders, Napoleons and Hitlers were pitiable illusionists, *the atomically armed future aggressor may be the greatest military realist of all times, and hence end up as the first true world conqueror in history. This possibility is the fourth fact of the nuclear era.*

Agreements of any kind, and surely those dealing with key security matters, presuppose mutual trust. International agreements are, or should be, similar to those found in private life—they must not be entered into unless they are based on a calculable minimum of confidence. No sane businessman ever deals with a person whose credit rating is bad and who has a record of defaulting on his debts. If a "promissory" international nuclear agreement were concluded in the present situation, it would produce the strongest sense of insecurity and fear. For this reason alone, it probably would become inoperable and conceivably lead to war.

No nation in its right mind would risk its security through destroying its atomic stockpile in reliance upon a mere diplomatic agreement. With large nuclear industries in existence, such a paper agreement could be broken easily and rapidly. Let us not forget that governments change and that few governments consider themselves bound by the promises of their predecessors. To have any security at all therefore, nations would have to retain readily usable nuclear weapons in their arsenals. There is no other insurance against breach of promise. But, then, we would be back at the point where we started, namely at the existence of nuclear armaments. Naturally, it would be possible to conclude agreements limiting the number of nuclear weapons in the possession of each nation. Yet such agreements cannot be enforced in such a manner that violations would be made impossible; and presumably it would prove difficult to include in such agreements limitations on the number of *defensive* nuclear weapons.

No doubt, governments could pledge themselves not to use their nuclear weapons aggressively or offensively, and yet reserve the right to produce and maintain such weapons. It is conceivable that such an agreement would be kept. All that is necessary to make the agreement stick, is to produce a military situation in which the employment of nuclear weapons would be equally harmful to both sides, and in any event, extremely harmful to the first user. If there were such a situation—which cannot be defined properly or predicted, and which hardly would be of a stable and lasting nature—the agreement would be superfluous: the belligerents anyway would act according to their best interests. By contrast, if there were a military situation in which it would be advantageous for one belligerent to initiate the employment of nuclear weapons, even at the price of retaliation, then in all likelihood the agreement would be disregarded. The chances are that, within the next ten to twenty years, this latter rather than the former situation will prevail.

I will refrain from judging whether, at present, it would be advantageous for the United States to commit itself to the non-use of nuclear weapons. The fact is that the U.S. government has *not* made such a commitment (as little as it ever committed itself to forego the use of toxic gases). The effective abolition of nuclear weapons undoubtedly would reduce the dangers of a surprise attack against North America and also protect American cities. But this advantage would have to be paid for dearly and cannot be obtained without heavy risk.

The proscription of nuclear weapons would be meaningful *only* if the armed forces in their entirety were reorganized to wage non-nuclear war. In order to protect its security in the absence of nuclear weapons, the United States would have to acquire an entirely different military establishment. Any *surface* strategy replacing present air strategy would suffer from fatal geographical handicaps or, to phrase it differently, to compensate for Russia's advantages in a surface war, an extraordinary military effort of the United States would be necessary. For example, to balance Soviet ground strength, in such a manner that further Russian advances in Eurasia would not be invited, American land forces would have to be tripled and supporting air and naval forces be enlarged substantially; possibly the Strategic Air Command (non-nuclear) also would have to be doubled or tripled. The adoption of a non-nuclear air strategy would require even greater efforts. The maintenance of so considerably larger forces must demand a military budget on the order of 100 billion dollars or *more,* and could not be done without compulsory military service, perhaps of two to three years' duration. Despite such an exertion, the security of key areas in Europe and Asia could not be guaranteed.

I do not know whether the United States can "afford" such a military outlay. I do know that long lasting armaments of such a size would transform American society, and I doubt seriously that the United States soon would be inclined to arm on a 100-billion dollar scale during "peacetime." If this doubt were justified, then the abandonment of nuclear weapons could spell only the defeat, and ultimately the communist domination, of the United States. And yet, despite our nuclear forbearance, we could not be sure that the U.S. would be spared atomic attacks. Certainly, in the closing phases of war in which the USSR achieved air mastery, the Soviets would not refrain from using atomic weapons against American targets if the American nation otherwise would fail to surrender; or the soviets might use those bombs to further their objective of "liquidating" hostile "classes." For that matter, a parallel argument can be made for the Soviet Nation: Without nuclear weapons, the Soviets never can hope to defeat the United States. Hence, they will accept proscribing atomic weapons only *after* they have abandoned *first* their objective of world revolution.

Nuclear weapons are the key of modern military power, and hence the irreplaceable key to American security. This is the fifth fundamental fact of the nuclear problem. We are all free to deplore the situation but we are unable to change it unless we are willing to concede victory to the communists and to surrender without resistance as, indeed, has been proposed.

Such counsels of despair—if made in good faith—result from an improper analysis of the problem. Many of those who have been participating in the nuclear argument find it difficult to understand that, within the present world situation, the avoidance of nuclear catastrophe is a military and political task. *The nuclear problem is not susceptible to solutions by legal agreement, nor by any other trick aiming at the evanescence of nuclear weapons.* This is the *sixth fact* with which we must come to grips. It is true there is no guarantee, even if suitable military and political techniques were used skillfully, that there will be no nuclear devastation. Nor is there any guarantee that these techniques, in fact, will be used with dexterity and imagination. Since, however, there is no practical alternative solution, we must concentrate on the techniques which are available. If those who lose their time in chasing utopian butterflies could but devote some of their brain-power to the real problems before us, we might make some progress after all.

The military task, briefly, consists in maintaining armaments in such quantities and of such quality that the opponent of the United States will find it impossible to solve his military problem through the employment of nuclear weapons. More particularly, he must be prevented from knocking out the American retaliatory forces through surprise blows and delivering a substantial portion of his atomic stockpile on American targets. He also must be prevented from posing, as he does now, a *unilateral* nuclear threat to European and Asiatic countries. Once the various free nations have acquired quantities of nuclear explosives, the military problem becomes essentially a matter of delivery vehicles and defense systems, *viz.*, of overall technological superiority, as well as of constant readiness and a gradual reduction of the vulnerability of cities and people.

This military problem is of major dimensions and it will continue to grow. I need add only that the American people and the peoples of other free nations have not yet understood fully the scope of their military responsibilities. I do not believe that in order to solve its military security problems, the United States will have to be turned into an "armed camp" (a cliché which many abuse to argue against proper preparedness), but the United States no longer can afford to have military budgets which fall far short of satisfying minimum requirements. Present American and allied armaments and technological programs have many gaps which any military expert can identify without difficulty. Insufficient forces in being and inadequate quantities of modern weapons, as well as poor command, alliance, and decision-making structures which are not responsive to the requirements of rapid modern war, constitute an invitation to nuclear death, especially so *since in a modern war the first battle may decide the outcome of the entire conflict.* This is the *seventh fact* which we never should allow to be forgotten.

And we may immediately add the *eighth fact* that future wars hardly will be fought with weapons ordered and produced after the start of hostilities. Military and industrial mobilization after D-day is a concept which is not applicable to nuclear air war. *Hence, war potentials have lost much of their significance, while forces in being and weapons stockpiles have become of crucial importance.* This means that one of the main military assets of the United States, i.e., industrial superiority, no longer possesses its traditional significance. Current American military policies do not yet respond to this fundamental strategical change.

Politically, several different tasks have to be performed. There must be an effort to make all free nations understand that the dangers of atomic war cannot be obviated by paper promises, but only by painful security actions. There is further the task of inducing the free nations, including the United States, to acquire the ready military strengths they need. Third, there is the problem of convincing our allies and ourselves that we must sacrifice for our security and possibly accept economic hardship, in order to procure those weapon systems which are needed in a modern war rather than those which were needed half a generation ago. *Phony security is the excessive hazard in the present phase of the nuclear age. This ninth fact of the period often has been willfully and perilously overlooked.*

Such persuasions probably will not be feasible if they be done by words and dollars alone. Much more is needed. Let us mention the need, in many European countries, for a new concept of economy to bring about the transformation of old societies from paralytic structures, or at best slowly going concerns, into fast growing, open societies, in which discouragement and disaffection will give way to positive attitudes. It is at this point that nuclear technology, in its industrial applications, should be able to do wonders, not only because it will provide energy to areas where there are at present inadequate resources, but also because the establishment of new major industries must produce an economic upswing. The build-up of the nuclear and electrical industries could bring about a socio-economic mutation which would result in a vast improvement of living standards and an easing, relatively speaking, of the armaments burden. An economic rebirth on a new technological basis would demonstrate that the disintegration of the old society has been halted and that progress again has become possible. *Our tenth fundamental fact is that the industrial application of nuclear energy offers an excellent chance for the social strengthening of the free world.* Lest the impression arise that no basic reforms are required in the United States, be it painted out that there is an urgent need in this country to stimulate technological inventiveness and imagination and to bring about a more rapid exploitation of new inventions. To satisfy this need, undoubtedly, additional research funds may be required, but more important still would be the streamlining of overlylong and constricted bureaucratic "channels." *American technological and industrial time lags are too long. This is the eleventh fact to which we must pay attention.*

The political task, of course, should include efforts to persuade Soviet leadership that it is unwise for them to pursue their goal of world domination after, and in spite of, the onset of the nucleonic age: unwise because nuclear technology has all but destroyed the last vestige of the Marxian argument that due to the scarcity of resources, the abolition of private ownership is the prerequisite for material well-being of all members of society; and unwise, further, because the continued pursuit of the revolutionary goal, in disregard of the dangers of nuclear war and of the unpopularity of the Soviet government at home, may spell the doom of the communist regime (regardless of what would happen to the free world).

Western statesmen should not tire in explaining and emphasizing those two points. If, ultimately, the Soviet government were to accept those two propositions, a new era would have begun and unless a new aggressor were to arise, the danger of nuclear ruin *ipso facto* would have ended. Unfortunately, it is most probable that the Soviet government, at least in its present composition, will not accept the truth of those propositions and, partly for reasons of intellectual blindness, partly because of its inability to abandon its ideology which it needs to legitimize its rule, and partly because of the inertia of its power machine, will continue its relentless and hazardous drive toward world domination. Hence, the threat of atomic devastation is posed anew.

In the absence of adequate powers of persuasion, the threat of nuclear aggression against the free world can be eliminated only if the Soviet government is changed or replaced. An alternate, though less conclusive solution, would involve a substantial retraction of the Soviet power orbit. *Shall we consider the need to weaken, modify, or replace the Soviet government to be the twelfth basic fact of the nuclear age?*

An effective liberation policy appears as one of the few alternatives to continued life in the shadow of nuclear death, with its expensive and growing demands for constant military readiness. It is true that a policy of liberation in and by itself poses the threat of atomic conflict, the important difference being, however, that an initiative policy by the free world would make it impossible for the aggressor to rig the game entirely in his favor and to create situations which would be most favorable to his plans of attack. If the would-be aggressor were kept off balance and forced to busy himself with his own defenses rather than with offensive plans, the threat of atomic devastation might be diminished.

In the nuclear age, political and military *initiative* is an indispensible prerequisite of security, while loss of initiative poses insoluble problems. The term "initiative" is not used here as a circumlocution for preventive war. Hundreds of initiatives are possible without resort to military conflict. As an example of a successful American initiative, we may recall the decision to acquire the hydrogen bomb before the Soviet Union. However, the time may come when a dispassionate survey of the security problems of the free world would indicate that these problems cannot be solved except through the deliberate resort to force. We should hope that such a moment never will come. But we must remember that in order to secure our safety without an offensive strategy, our military posture would have to be strengthened considerably and that, conversely, if no such strengthening occurs, the fateful decision may become inevitable. It is easy to pronounce cliché opinions about this grave problem and to take pleasure in pointing out that "preventive war" is logical nonsense: War cannot be fought to prevent war. True; but war can, and occasionally must be fought to prevent disaster and perdition. *Only one thing is worse than nuclear war: Defeat in such a war. And this is the thirteenth fact to which I wish to call attention.*

Article I, Section 10, paragraph 3 of the Constitution of the United States anticipated the need of initiative and offensive security actions in case of "imminent danger as will not admit of delay"; if such dangers occur, the States may "engage in war . . . without the consent of Congress." So long as the United States clings to the concept that under no possible circumstances will it initiate war, not even while the opponent is preparing to strike, so long the initiative will remain in Soviet hands. In the seven generations of its existence, the United States has waged quite a number of wars and in every one of them—this possibly includes World War II—the United States faced up to the ineluctable decision and initiated hostilities on its own volition. There is absolutely no factual basis for the contention that democracy abhors war. The very nature of democracy demands that it accept its responsibilities and that, while it should not seek war lightly and do everything to avoid conflict, it must fight if and when there is no other choice but the destruction of the democratic system. Has it not become apparent now that the world would be a better place—and that many millions of innocent human beings still would be alive—if Hitler had been stopped between 1933 and 1936? The concept of peace *à outrance* has proved to be unmanageable, excessively costly, and utterly destructive.

No doubt, in the nuclear era, a war decision is of far graver import than a similar decision before 1945. Personally, I never would favor a war decision unless there is a clear, urgent, and immediate need to anticipate and forestall attack with no other solution being available, and unless there is no other way to avoid a clearly inevitable war at a later date and under significantly more unfavorable circumstances.

However, looking back at my own reactions of twenty years ago, I remember arguing, too, that war should be waged against Hitler only under conditions of extreme necessity. But was that policy so wise? Was it not based on the invalid assumption that the Nazi regime was unstable? Did this policy not provide Hitler with many trumps and allow him to out-arm his opponents? Maybe the ideals of pacifism are so lofty that the price which we had to pay—and which in the end possibly will have included a future World War III—was not too high. But again, was it such a good idea to refuse paying the relatively small price required to hold China during 1947 and 1949, seize North Korea in 1950, and liquidate Communist China after it actually had attacked United States forces? Far from embracing preventive war, the United States adopted a strategy of not fighting back and of deliberately averting its own victory. What did this new departure in militant peacefulness save for us in Southeast Asia? What will it have saved for us after Communist China and Russia will have developed modern industries and combined their military resources? Clearly, do we not have a policy of avoiding the smaller and easier wars to make the big and costly wars ever more inevitable? In any event, in proclaiming good intentions of peacefulness with respect to future wars we are forced to look hard at the *fourteenth fact of the atomic age which, perhaps, is the most ominous of all: That in an atomic conflict the force which plans to strike second never may be in a position to strike at all.*

In the discharge of its security duties toward itself, its allies, and toward the free world, the United States must seize the political initiative. Yet, this initiative cannot be seized so long as the opponent *knows* that the United States does not mean it seriously and will shrink away from the ultimate consequence. The United States also may have to seize the military initiative, but nothing effective can be done in either field so long as the opponent is allowed to count upon his double ability to determine the timing of the war and to strike the first blow. No sustained and successful American initiative is possible while the by far most important decision is left in Soviet hands.

Without vigorous initiative, there can be no liberation, nor can the Soviets be dissuaded from their clearly avowed aggressive intentions. Yet unless this

Soviet objective of world domination is eliminated, there is no real chance of avoiding war; and, naturally, unless the basic military initiatives are in free world hands, there will be no protection against devastation, loss of life, and defeat, nor preservation of free institutions and democracy. We may get away with a policy of the least effort, but only if our opponent is thoroughly frightened by what we can do to him after we received his first blows. It is in the nature of atomic war that he has no overwhelming reason to be excessively frightened.

To sum it all up: We have a policy of avoiding war, but we have achieved only this: the danger of war is becoming ever more unmanageable. To keep the military situation under control and to preserve our democratic institutions, we shall have to make a stand at *some* time. On the basis of the record of the years 1933 to 1954, we can say confidently that the sooner and the firmer the United States will make this stand, the easier the task will be and the greater the chance of forestalling atomic warfare.

The world is full of unprecedented dangers. We may argue about the means by which the dangers *could* be overcome, if such means were utilized. But we should realize that, in all probability, the dangers will persist. It is easy to predict the doom of our civilization and quite unrewarding to propose concrete—and costly and unpopular—military and political measures aiming to insure the survival of that civilization. I cannot help feeling, however, that this civilization is a spiritual force and, therefore, not susceptible to physical destruction. In any event, it cannot survive if the people who live under its blessings display a deplorable weakness of conviction and lack the ethos of courage. Nor can this civilization survive if its intellectual élites, fearful of risk, effort, and self-assertion, advise collective political suicide. This is a statement which can be supported with historical evidence and which I intend to be an objective proposition. I realize that the advocacy of suicide is not always intentional and that praiseworthy desires often are the midwives of deadly proposals.

I would like to add, and say it clearly, that I have nothing but contempt for those who are willing to surrender to communism in order to avoid nuclear war and thus to assure the physical survival and the enslavement of the maximum number. If such a spirit were typical of the free society, our civilization would be dead *now*. I do not believe that doom is near, let alone that it has come. But I am worried that the voices of cowardice are heard far more often than the voices of determination. I, too, want my family and my friends to survive and I do want to live to the end of my natural days. Everyone has the instinctive animal fear of death. But it hardly pays to survive for the blessings of a slave existence and it will be intolerable to purchase survival through the betrayal of value and conscience. Policies cannot be based just on the instinct of self-preservation. Do intellectuals and politicians have a lesser moral obligation than the simple private of whom they expect that he sacrifice himself when ordered into battle? Our entire society has been pushed into mortal conflict. In some way, most of us are now manning a battle station. Must we not be true to our duties?

The issue of the present world conflict is whether communism will be victorious or be destroyed. The hydrogen bomb has not changed this issue, not by one iota. If the desire for freedom were a variable dependent on the expected rate of casualties, we should not even attempt to fight. If, however, national and individual freedom is our highest political value, then we should do our best to keep casualties to a minimum—even in the country of our opponent—but we should not be deterred by the cost of the conflict; the cost of defeat and of loss of principle would be still higher.

We are living today twice as long as the generations who conquered freedom for us and established the foundations of good government. Our task is to preserve and improve freedom for ourselves and for our descendants, and to bring freedom to those who still are enslaved. The way to solve a serious problem is not to distort or ignore it, but to handle it; to take all precautions which prudence imposes, to accept the irreducible risks, to bear the required responsibilities and to follow the dictates of one's conscience. To cringe before the enemy, to bewail fate even before it is known, to become paralyzed from fear and pessimism, and to abandon oneself to the visions of apocalyptic horror is despicable. It is moral self-destruction to which atomic devastation would add little but physical confirmation and merited punishment.

NOTES

Reprinted from *The Review of Politics* 16, no. 4 (October 1954): 395–411.

Originally published under the pseudonym "Ferreus"—from the Latin meaning "hard as iron." Ed.

CHAPTER 11

Beyond National Interest

A Critical Evaluation of Reinhold Niebuhr's
Theory of International Politics

KENNETH W. THOMPSON

Until more or less recently, few students of international affairs have been pre-occupied with the theoretical aspects of their field. To the extent that theory is distinguished from history, law, and science, this is especially true. Histori-ans have sought to uncover the facts and recite them with the most fastidi-ous regard for the circumstances of time and place. Lawyers have tried to de-tect in the case law of international agreements and treaties the normative structure of international society. Political scientists have increasingly turned to new scientific methods and statistical techniques designed to measure pub-lic opinion and its influence on foreign policy. Few scholars have concerned themselves with the fundamental characteristics of international society or of good or bad foreign policy. In this intellectual environment any explicit, sys-tematic theory of international relations has had to await a threefold develop-ment. It has required a broader conception of the proper methods for study-ing international affairs, a clearer identification of basic concepts and "laws," and a more serious discussion of fundamental theoretical problems like the relation of theory to concrete problems.

More recently it has become increasingly obvious that the study of inter-national relations since 1946 has witnessed impressive attacks on all three of these problems. The intellectual resources of government and scholarship have at least in a limited way been mobilized to build a new framework or redis-cover the older structure of a theoretical approach to international politics. That extraordinary group who recently made up the Policy Planning Staff in the Department of State found that without the tools of theory, it was impossible to proceed in a rational manner. Insofar as their efforts were informed by a desire to separate consideration of the national interest from consideration of the probable domestic consequences of a particular course of action, they contributed in a most significant way to theory. It is obvious that the lectures by George F. Kennan contained in *American Diplomacy, 1900–1950* coupled with the more recent Stafford Little Lectures at Princeton serve this end. So do the books on foreign policy by Louis Halle, C. B. Marshall, and Dorothy Fosdick. In more systematic terms, scholars like E. H. Carr and Herbert Butterfield in England and Hans J. Morgenthau in the United States have added to our conception of theory. Undoubtedly it is not without significance that these authorities admittedly owe an important intellectual debt to the Protestant theologian, Reinhold Niebuhr, who as early as 1932 in *Moral Man and Immoral Society* elaborated a realistic theory of international politics. Not long ago Kennan in surveying the growth of interest among the small group of responsible theorists identified Niebuhr as the precursor of the so-called realists or, in Kennan's words, "the father of all of us." Morgenthau's first volume, *Scientific Man vs. Power Politics,* which remains in some ways more fundamental to his philosophy than all his subsequent writings, bears the imprint of Niebuhr's influence more than that of any other American scholar. Marshall, Halle, and Fosdick have not been hesitant in acknowledging their debt to Niebuhr.

Influence of this magnitude would indicate that Niebuhr's approach to the study of politics among nations might profitably be analyzed and systematically appraised. His writings which extend over nearly a quarter of a century and are contained in nearly a dozen published treatises and numerous major articles provide a rich background for discussion. In this connection the political essays which appear in the two journals he has edited, *Christianity and Crisis* and *Christianity and Society,* are often overlooked. The scholar who turns to the sources of Niebuhr's writings will discover that his contribution to international politics bears the closest relationship to the preconditions of growth for a legitimate theory of international relations. For as theory itself has required a broader conception of method, the identification of basic concepts and the illumination of resulting theoretical problems, Niebuhr's philosophy has been focused on the real issues foreshadowed in this enumeration of the threefold development of theory.

I. THE PROPER STUDY OF POLITICS

Most contemporary thought has assumed that the proper methods for the study of politics were those which have been so extraordinarily successful in the natural or physical world. It has been widely assumed that all that separated the physical and social sciences was an unfortunate cultural lag resulting from the use of archaic and imprecise methods by backward and unsophisticated social scientists. The techniques of social science "lagged far behind that of natural or laboratory sciences" and research scholars were advised "that concentrated efforts would have to be made if the old classical methodology of social science was to be broken down. In other words just as the natural sciences three hundred years ago were brought into a new era of realism, so the social sciences must be led to see that the understanding and control of human phenomena lies in the scientific analysis and appraisal of facts." Theory was held to be dependent on the use of the scientific method for "it is highly probable that the nature of theory development and testing will be substantially like that used in the natural and medical sciences which has involved the three closely related aspects of: (1) theory, (2) measurement techniques and (3) testing of the generalizations." Massive undertakings were envisaged in which social scientists would be produced in the same way that technicians in industrial establishments were trained and put to work. As late as 1949 it was being proclaimed that, "the greatest need is for men who can conceive problems in relation to scientific growth and to world development in which precise methods of analysis can be applied." To this date there is talk of training young men in the scientific techniques derived from twenty or more scientific disciplines essential for the conduct of any foreign policy. Science is looked upon as a kind of magic key not only to theory but to practice in the field of international politics.

Niebuhr's position on the role of the scientific method as the sole instrument in the growth of theory is almost unqualifiedly critical. In his view, scientific studies of human behavior are embarrassed by at least five illusions or fantasies. The first fantasy is the myth of a presuppositionless science. Objective social science today is given the wholly imaginary character of an approach characterized by the quest for autonomous, incontrovertible, and self-evident facts. In practice, responsible scholars have learned the impossibility of giving form or meaning to any social research in the absence of some kind of framework or rough outline for organizing their research. Ironically enough, modern social science itself is grounded in certain stubborn and inflexible assumptions which more often than not determine the focus of scientific inquiry and affect its conclusions. One of them is the idea of progress and of the perfectibility of man; this is the lodestar of contemporary social science. It is almost universally assumed that a better and more scientific world will provide tools for erecting general theories that will be more complete, precise, and scientific and thus permit man to solve his problems once and for all.

Another fantasy grows out of the concealment of all the conclusions which fail to conform to the facts. Modern culture despite its scientific progress has been caught in some obvious miscalculations. The brave new world of the twentieth century which rationalists of the eighteenth century predicted if men would only disavow their other-worldly illusions scarcely resembles utopia. The contradictions and errors inherent in a rationalist and scientific approach probably stem from the dual meaning of scientific. On the one hand, science as empiricism means humility before the facts; on the other hand, science identified with rationalism may mean the invoking of logical coherence as the test of truth. The two connotations may stand in contradiction because the test of rational coherence prompts men to deny obvious facts if they appear to violate the tenets of coherence.[1]

A third fantasy of present day social science involves the position of the social observer. In contrast with the physical scientist, the observer of the human scene is at the same time agent and observer. Whereas the natural scientist has only a stake in the discovery of truth, say, regarding cancer, the judgment of the student of society is beclouded by ideological taint, national loyalty, and social and economic status. He cannot be fully objective for his observations arise from his place in history and his responsibilities to a particular society and group. Not pure mind but the self with its interests and capacity for rationalization is the agent of the scientific method and no perfection of method can coerce these passions to fade away. Only when the observer is removed from his subject in time and place, as in certain historical studies, does this problem become less acute.

A fourth fantasy of the scientific approach results from modern conceptions of causation and prediction which ignore the complexity of causation and the intervention of contingent factors in history, including the human agent. Prediction which is the cherished goal of social scientists is possible in terms of rough probabilities. But Niebuhr maintains that: "In both nature and history each new thing is only one of an infinite number of possibilities which might have emerged at that particular juncture. It is for this reason that, though we can trace a series of causes in retrospect, we can never predict the future with accuracy."[2] There are recurrences and cycles in history but a strong leader, an economic catastrophe, or the juxtaposition of novel forces may channel history in unexpected ways. Moreover, in contrast to the scientific laboratory, nothing is exactly repeated in history. Analogies which infer that a policy pursued, say, in the Roman Empire prior to its decline and fall, will if followed in the present expose man to a similar fate are erroneously conceived in at least two basic respects. First, given the infinite variety of causal sequences to which every event is related, some other correlation of cause and effect based on another principle of interpretation might be equally plausible. Second, given the uncontrolled character of social inquiry and the interplay of multiple causes, judgments which are inevitably value judgments based on historical analogy can neither be proved nor refuted with the certainty of the physical sciences.

The fifth and perhaps the most persistent illusion is the conviction that science is "the profoundest, because it is the latest, fruit of culture."[3] Auguste Comte's conception of the history of culture as the movement from a religious to a metaphysical to a scientific age is partly true insofar as it correctly describes certain major historical tendencies. But as the value judgment of our culture endlessly prompted to assert that the latest attainments are the wisest, it is of doubtful validity. For modern culture, in its preoccupation with methods and details and its confidence that the human situation remains ambiguous only because of a residual ignorance which scientific discovery is certain to correct, has inevitably been shallow and barren in confronting the fundamental issues. In opposition to Comte, Niebuhr proposes that there must be a movement from philosophy to science and, from this point, the controlling aim of his approach becomes the recovery of the wisdom of philosophy and the humility and magnanimity of a transcendent religion. His writings on contemporary affairs find him delving beneath the surface of events to expose a general principle which he seeks to integrate into the framework of a general political and social philosophy. In this way, he departs from the scientific approach which avowedly eschews such analysis and generalization for the collection and classification of data within sharply defined limits.

For Niebuhr there is an alternative to the scientific method. It is political philosophy. The political philosopher observing the pattern of history is obliged to articulate the basis on which he interprets its meaning. At some point he must make explicit his theory of human nature. The practice of rooting political theory in political institutions and processes rather than probing deeper to the level of human nature belongs mainly to the last few decades. Niebuhr, by contrast, explicitly assumes that an understanding of political phenomena, whether international or domestic, is inseparable from a clear picture of human nature. The Gifford Lectures begun at the University of Edinburgh in the spring of 1939 as war-clouds hovered over Europe and completed in the autumn as the threat became a dreadful reality represent their author's most systematic attempt to demonstrate the need for and broad outlines of a realistic theory of human nature. The lectures begin: "Man has always been his most vexing problem. How shall he think of himself?"[4] Any affirmation he makes involves him in contradictions. If he stresses man's unique and rational qualities, then man's greed, lust for power, and brute nature betray him. If he holds that men everywhere are the product of nature and unable to rise above circumstances, he tells us nothing of man the creature who dreams of God and of making himself God and of man whose sympathy knows no bounds. If he believes man is essentially good and attributes all evil to concrete historical and social causes, he merely begs the question for these causes are revealed, on closer scrutiny, to be the consequences of the evil inherent in man. If he finds man bereft of all virtue, his capacity for reaching such a judgment refutes the terms of his judgment. Such baffling paradoxes of human self-knowledge point up the vexing problem of doing justice at one and the same time to the uniqueness of man and to his affinities with nature. Only a theory inspired by a knowledge of both qualities can be adequate. "The obvious fact is that man is a child of nature, subject to its vicissitudes, compelled by its necessities, driven by its impulses, and confined within the brevity of the years which nature permits its varied organic form, allowing them some, but not too much, latitude. The other less obvious fact is that man is a spirit who stands outside of nature, life, himself, his reason and the world."[5] Modern views of man which stress exclusively his dignity or his misery are fatuous and irrelevant chiefly because they fail to understand the dualism of man's nature.

The paradox of man's existence arises from the fact that he is suspended perilously between freedom and finiteness, spirit and nature. Through spirit he is enabled to survey the whole, but in so doing he is betrayed into imagining himself the whole. While enabled through freedom to use the forces and processes of nature creatively, he comes to ignore his own creatureliness. His ambiguous and contradictory position at the juncture of freedom and finiteness produces in him a condition of anxiety which is fundamental to understanding political behavior. Man is anxious because he is conscious of the imperialism of others while secretly aware of his own limitations. Yet as finite reason, he can never be sure of the limits of his possibilities and so endlessly seeks security in the pretense that he has overcome his finiteness and human limitations.

For our purposes, the most important observable expression of human anxiety is politically in the will-to-power. Man shares with animals their natural appetites and desires and the impulse for survival. Yet being both nature and spirit, his requirements are qualitatively heightened; they are raised irretrievably to the level of spirit where they become limitless and insatiable. "Man being more than a natural creature, is not interested merely in physical survival but in prestige and social approval. Having the intelligence to anticipate the perils in which he stands in nature and history, he invariably seeks to gain security against these perils by enhancing his power, individually and collectively."[6] To overcome social anxiety, man seeks power over his fellows endeavoring to subdue their wills to his lest they come to dominate him. The struggle for political power is merely an example of the rivalry which goes on at every level of human life.

However the human predicament has its roots primarily in what may be called the security-power dilemma. Weak men and nations assume that if they had more power they would be more secure. Yet: "The more power an individual and nation has, the more of its life impinges upon other life and the more wisdom is required to bring it into some decent harmony with other life."[7] In the political arena, groups are motivated much as individuals to seek dominion over one another. In 1944, Niebuhr answered the criticism that labor was jeopardizing the common interest by pressing its cause when he said:

"It is silly to talk of the danger of pressure groups. Labor has merely fashioned its own political power inside the Democratic party."[8] The various groups or corporate entities in society compete for power in the manner of the individuals who compose them. Their success is dependent on their unity and vitality for "in politics, as in warfare numbers without cohesion and organization, count for nothing."[9]

Power is the organization of factors and forces which are impotent without organization. Some group or coalition emerges as the holder of a preponderance or a balance of power. It assumes to itself the responsibility for government or the administration of the system wherein the power struggle continues. This group, in turn, is supplanted by another and the endless and inescapable conflict goes on. Effective limits on the struggle, especially among larger groups, are usually far more modest than is generally understood. "In the field of collective behavior the force of egoistic passion is so strong that the only harmonies possible are those which manage to neutralize this force through balance of power, through mutual defenses against its inordinate expression, and through techniques for harnessing its energy to social ends."[10] For Niebuhr the limits of human imagination, the easy subservience of reason to the passions, and the persistence of collective irrationalism and egoism make social conflict inevitable in human history, probably to its very end.

Moreover, the possibility of force or resort to coercion is present in all social conflict. "The threat of force, whether by the official and governmental representatives or by the parties to a dispute in a community is a potent instrument in all communal relations."[11] Coercion is inevitable and universal in even the most intimate community, the family. There it is expressed in the position of the father and his capacity for imposing his will upon his children. Political power represents a special form of coercion for it rests on the ability to use and manipulate other forms of social, economic, and religious power for the purpose of organizing and dominating the community.

Furthermore, Niebuhr notes the ferocity and intensity of the struggle among groups, when compared to the rivalry of individuals, stemming from the tendency of collectivities like the nation to express both the virtue and selfishness of their members. One consequence of modern mass society has been to thwart the attainment of personal security and the satisfaction of basic human aspirations, especially for particular groups. Frustrated individuals strive to fulfill themselves vicariously by projecting their ego to the level of the national ego. In mass society, collective attainments offer possibilities of self-aggrandizement which individual pretensions no longer serve. At the same time, appeals are made to the loyalty, self-sacrifice, and devotion of individuals in the group. In this way, social unity is built on the virtuous as well as the selfish side of man's nature; the twin elements of collective strength become self-sacrificial loyalty and frustrated aggressions. From this it follows that politics is the more contentious and ruthless because of the unselfish loyalty of the members of groups, which become laws unto themselves unrestrained by their obedient and worshipful members. Group pride is in fact the corruption of individual loyalty and group consciousness; contempt for another group is the pathetic form which respect for our own frequently takes. The tender emotions which bind the family together sometimes are expressed in indifference for the welfare of other families. In international society a nation made up of men of the greatest religious goodwill would be less than loving toward other nations for its virtue would be channeled into loyalty to itself thus increasing that nation's selfishness. The consequence for Niebuhr's political theory is his conclusion that "society . . . merely cumulates the egoism of individuals and transmutes their individual altruism into collective egoism so that the egoism of the group has a double force. For this reason no group acts from purely unselfish or even mutual intent and politics is therefore bound to be a contest of power."[12] Relations among such groups must always be essentially political before they are ethical and the study of political science becomes the study of the objective distribution of power.

II. Keys to a Theory of World Politics

It should be obvious from what has already been said that Niebuhr founds his theory of world politics on a general conception of human nature. His theory is essentially architectonic. Man in a condition of social anxiety seeks security in power only to find it escaping him. Nations as massive collections of individuals have recourse to much the same quest for prestige and influence heightened for them by the unabridged loyalties and contemporary frustrations of their members. In international society what nations claim they seek is some measure of attainment of national interest. Niebuhr is willing to concede that the concept of national interest is central to the study of world politics. He observes that: "Nations are, on the whole, not generous. A wise self-interest is usually the limit of their moral achievements. . . ."[13] The demands of self-interest and national self-protection inspire actions that appear to override all accepted moral impulses. For example, the decision to build the hydrogen bomb gave offense to many sincere people. However, Niebuhr more than once has cautioned humanitarian critics of American foreign policy against assuming that the limits of choice for a nation are broader than they are. Of the bomb he observed in 1950: "No nation will fail to take even the most hazardous adventure into the future, if the alternative of not taking the step means the risk of being subjugated."[14] "Every nation is guided by self-interest and does not support values which transcend its life, if the defense of these values imperils its existence. A statesman who sought to follow such a course would be accused of treason."[15] "No nation ever supports values which transcend its life if they are diametrically opposed to the preservation of its life."[16] Even in considering the Marshall Plan, Niebuhr declared: "As is always the case in international relations, what is called for is not an act of benevolence but of wise self-interest."[17]

This conception of the primacy of national interest broadly conceived has not been popularly acceptable or widely congenial in our liberal democratic age. Idealists and adherents of scientific humanism have maintained that concern for the safety, integrity, and preservation of the nation-state belonged to an older authoritarian age. Some observers have looked to international organization as one substitute for the national interest. Its more ebullient protagonists have implored others to abandon selfish national and parochial attachments for more universal loyalties. In contrast Niebuhr has conceived of international organization as essentially another framework within which historic and emergent national purposes might be pursued and adjusted. For him it has never symbolized the demise of national interests. Instead, action by an international organization has been associated with the vital stakes of one or more major powers. When the prospects of collective measures on the part of the League of Nations appeared brightest in 1935, Niebuhr suggested, "If British imperial interests were not at stake, the League would not act so energetically. . . ."[18] It should be obvious that this optimism was grounded in a miscalculation of British intentions rather than a misunderstanding of the ways of international organization reflecting the will of its most important members.

There is another popular approach to the displacement of the national interest deriving from the view that unresolved conflicts among nations would quickly be resolved once taken out of the hands of statesmen and assigned to men of culture. Niebuhr has associated this view with some of the work that has gone on at UNESCO. He has questioned the "belief that the difficulties which statesmen face in guiding their nations are due, not so much to their responsible relation to their several nations, as to their intellectual inferiority in comparison with cultural leaders. This misses the whole point in the encounter of nations with each other. Such an encounter is a power-political one, in which statesmen distinguish themselves from philosophers and scientists, not by their smaller degree of intelligence but by their higher degree of responsibility to their respective communities."[19] Any responsible leader must look first to his nation's security.

Sectarian Christianity and modernist religion in particular have sometimes promised release from the hard demands of the national interest through a religious renaissance whereby partial loyalties would be swallowed up in universal faith. In February 1941, Niebuhr founded his journal, *Christianity and Crisis,* with the primary goal of reexamining the Protestant and secular solutions to the complex problems of the political and economic order. But in contrast to those modern Christians who seek at almost every point to commend their faith as the source of the qualities and disciplines required to save the world from disaster, Niebuhr as Christian has remained self-critical, judicious, and reserved. For example, some Christian leaders have maintained in opposition to their secular critics that democracy is the product of the spiritual resources of religious faith. In their view, democracy is the direct outgrowth of Christian faith. However, this sweeping proposition is unacceptable to Niebuhr since, as a matter of history, both Christian and secular forces were involved in establishing the political institutions of democracy. Moreover, there are traditional non-democratic Christian cultures to the right of free societies which prove that the Christian faith does not inevitably yield democratic fruits. A fairer appraisal leads to the conclusion that free societies are a fortunate product of the confluence of Christian and secular forces. More specifically in this country,

Christianity and Judaism provide a view of man incompatible with his subordination to any political system, while secular and some forms of religious
thought combine to assure critical judgments of human ends and ambitions,
social forces and political powers, in order that the false idolatries of modern
tyrannies may be avoided. Christianity provides insights through which the
chances for democracy are improved, as with the Christian concept of human
dignity, making all efforts to fit man into any political program, even in the
name of social engineering, morally ambiguous or offensive. Moreover, individual freedom is encouraged by the assumption of a source of authority from
which the individual can defy the authorities of this world. ("We must obey
God rather than Man.") The Biblical insistence that the same radical freedom
which makes man creative also makes him potentially dangerous and destructive leads to the requirements of restraints or balance of power and the equilibrium of social forces upon which effective democracy in action generally
rests. Beyond this, however, there is another part of the story involving the
hazards of the relationship between Christianity and democracy and the positive contributions of secular thought. On the one hand, there are grave historical, psychological perils in associating ultimate religious truths with immediate and proximate causes. "Christians cannot deny that the religious theory
of divine right of kings has been a powerful force in traditional societies; nor
must they obscure the fact that even a true religion frequently generates false
identifications of some human interest with God's will."[20] On the other hand,
the ascribing of secular content to non-sacred objects and ends of society has
endowed a multitude of lesser activities with a practical moral respectability
and at the same time discouraged the premature sanctities in which both traditional societies and modern collectivism abound. It should be noted that an explicit secularism disavowing reverence for the ultimate may itself generate false
idolatries, such as the worship of efficiency or of the self-sufficient individual.
Compared with the noxious idolatries of modern secular totalitarianism, however, they are comparatively harmless, but they prove that an explicit denial of
the ultimate may be the basis for a secular religion with excessive pretensions
and sanctities of its own.

On the international scene, religion can be the means of inspiring patience,
humility, and forbearance among states, but the evidence of its transforming
qualities are more modest than is frequently claimed. We have recently heard

repeatedly from high places renewed requests for greater emphasis on spiritual values as contrasted with material or national interests. Spiritual values are considered abstractly as if they were something that could be added or subtracted from what a nation already had. Our problems, however, involve persistent questions like freedom and order or peace and power and it can be said that "we do not solve them simply by devotion to abstractly conceived spiritual values."[21] Moreover, these problems are nicely symbolized by the fact that the atomic weapons which give us an immediate security by deterring the aggressor, can easily become the means of civilization's material and moral destruction. "A Christian faith which declares that all of these horrible ambiguities would not exist if only we loved each other, is on exactly the same level as a secular idealism which insists that we could easily escape our predicament if only we organized a world government."[22] One Christian moralist recently observed that if Christians were only sufficiently unselfish to be willing to sacrifice "their" civilization as faith has prepared them to sacrifice "their" life we would quickly solve the problem of war. It is fair to ask how an individual responsible for the interests of his group is to justify the sacrifice of interests other than his own. Moreover, "in such terms, Christian unselfishness requires that we capitulate to tyranny because democracy happens to be 'ours' and tyranny is 'theirs.' Thus disloyalty and irresponsibility toward the treasures of an historic civilization become equated with Christian love."[23]

But modernist religion is as often irrelevant because it fosters a hard as well as a soft utopianism. A hard utopianism is best characterized by a crusading moralistic approach, wherein every moral scruple is subject to suppression because a nation assumes it is fighting for God and a Christian civilization against atheism. It is ironic that we should so endlessly appeal to the moral supremacy of our cause at the moment when communism as distinct from fascism was claiming to embody the absolute objective moral law. On reflection we can observe that communists are so evil primarily because they are idolators—not atheists—who in their fierce moral idealism are willing to sacrifice every decency and scruple to one wholly illusory value: the classless society. Democracies, by claiming too much for their moral cause whether by design or through ignorance of its partial and fragmentary character, run a somewhat similar risk. In describing the problems of postwar American foreign policy especially in maintaining allies, Niebuhr explains: "Our difficulty is significantly that we claim moral superiority over them too easily, not recognizing that each man and nation erects a pyramid of moral preferences on the basis of a minimum moral law."[24] Because of the pluralistic character of national values, this law is most universal when it states obligations in minimum and negative terms as "thou shalt not steal."

But the moral issue in international relations even with these restrictions remains the fundamental problem. If in international organization, men of culture and modern religion are unsuccessful in supplying the instruments by which national interest can be transcended, Niebuhr is nevertheless persuaded that men and states cannot follow their interest without claiming to do so in obedience to some general scheme of values. Two very grave moral and practical questions have continued to trouble him and have led him to make a series of distinctions regarding the national interest. First, he has asked whether a consistent emphasis upon the national interest is not as self-defeating in national, as it is in individual, life. Or put in other terms, does not a nation concerned too much with its own interests define those interests so narrowly and so immediately (as for instance in terms of military security) that the interests and securities, which depend upon common devotion to principles of justice and upon established mutualities in a community of nations, are sacrificed? Second, nations which insist on the one hand that they cannot act beyond their interest claim, as soon as they act, that they have acted not out of self-interest but in obedience to higher objectives like "civilization" or "justice." Applied to the conduct of contemporary American foreign relations, we claim more for the benevolence of our policies than they deserve and arouse the resentment of peoples already inclined to envy our power and wealth. Thus national interest is imperiled at one time by the hazard of moral cynicism and at another time by moral pretension and hypocrisy. In his earlier writings on the subject Niebuhr has dealt with the first of the questions and more recently with the second. In the evolution of his thinking, moreover, he has come to view them as parts of a single problem. The problem involves our continued ambivalence toward the moral issue, claiming at one moment that nations have no obligations beyond their interests and at the next moment that they are engaged in a high moral crusade without regard for interests.

Moral cynicism arises from the identification of the brutal facts with the normative aspects of international politics. Interest which is the lowest common denominator of political behavior is made the highest practical standard. It is, of course, obvious that the ultimate norms of religion are almost never the effective ethical standards of politics, which is generally marked by some form of coercion, force, or resistance.

Pacifists and perfectionists who undertake to translate the law of love of the Kingdom of God directly into the language of politics provide at best a protest and at worst a wholly unrealistic and harmful alternative to a more cynical approach. They try to make a success story out of the story of the Cross. There is one form of pacifism, pragmatic in character, which accepts the world as it is with interest set against interest and seeks through political imagination and intelligence to adjust, harmonize, and mitigate the conflict on the assumption that overt violence is a great social evil. For the most part, however, the purest standards of love and generosity are not directly relevant to the life of nations. But neither are they wholly irrelevant as final norms, for while love is impossible in that it is never fully realizable in history, it never loses its significance as an ultimate moral norm. It inspires and makes possible ethical conduct at a more proximate level and provides a standard against which social ethics may be evaluated and judged.

If the standard of love is to be made useful and relevant, however, it must be translated into relative and proximate terms more appropriate to the realities of politics. Justice for Niebuhr satisfies this demand as the most significant approximation of the ideal of love in politics. But justice involving the compromise of love with the darker elements of politics is also its contradiction. It should be explained that Niebuhr in his analysis of the international scene proceeds simultaneously at two levels. As we have seen, he constructs a rational theory of the behavior of states based on the primacy of their interests, and here he travels the same road as other contemporary realists. "Beyond national interest," however, he is concerned to establish a normative theory in order to avert what he has called the abyss of moral cynicism inherent in a merely rational theory. The decisive problem in connection with his theory arises precisely at this point. For in attempting to transcend the harsh realities that emerge from a realistic description of international politics, he is confronted with at least three crucial unsolved problems which must trouble and confuse any scholar who walks the lonely path of normative thought, especially as related to the anarchy of international relations.

First, he seeks to distinguish what is possible for governments from what is possible for nations. He maintains that while governments in their policies cannot transcend the national interest, the people by loyalties transcending the nation prevent the national interest from being conceived in too narrow and self-defeating terms. Most present-day realists would maintain that the continuum of national interest was more limited and precise than this statement seems to imply. They would say that the issue in practical statecraft was not between a narrow and broad interpretation but between an intelligent and rational as against an irrational view of the national interest. For example, once the stalemate had been reached in Korea, the issue was not whether American policy-makers should take a broad or narrow view but whether our interests in Korea, as contrasted with our interests elsewhere, measured against our antagonist's interests in holding the line conceived in terms of relative power called for a policy of armistice or stalemate, of withdrawal or of extension of the conflict. Popular loyalty to ends transcending the national interest, say to a military crusade against world communism heedless of the limits of our power, might have led to a policy directly at odds with the rational choice of those who served as the guardians of national security at the time. It is barely possible that in some crucial decisions for a democracy the chief obstacle to popular support of a rational foreign policy is exactly loyalty to principles transcending the national interest.

Second, Niebuhr conceives of justice in social and political ethics as involving "the harmony of the whole which does not destroy the vitality of the parts." The criterion of moral value becomes the freedom of each unique part to assert its vitality; equality and liberty are the informing and regulative principles of justice. In all communities, however, and in particular the international community, order sometimes demands the subordination of one member to another. Coercion and power introduce ambiguity into political morality, and equality and liberty are never simple possibilities. Self-interest is so powerful on the international scene that a nation cannot espouse a more universal value at the expense of its selfish interests. Hence Niebuhr's critics can legitimately ask what role is played by justice or equality or liberty if the highest morality possible for nations is, not a sacrifice of its interests to maintain other nations, but an effort to find the point of concurrence between its interests and those of others. If justice demands not conformity to some abstract formula but a tolerable harmony between competing forces, who are to be the contrivers of this harmony if not statesmen acting in response to their national interests? However, Niebuhr questions whether statesmen acting solely from self-interest are capable of discovering mutual interests unless they are motivated by a spirit of justice or a sense of obligation to a wider community. Against this it can be argued that between nations who share common moral values, as in NATO, a spirit of justice may be discovered, but peace between foes or rivals for power is probably little more than a forlorn hope if it awaits the development of a shared sense of justice. The discrimination of compatible national interests is a more modest, equally essential, if more cynical enterprise in which prudence and judgment are probably more significant than justice.[25] Soviet-American relations today symbolize this problem for while an uneasy armistice based on a negotiated territorial settlement the violation of which would constitute a "causus belli" can be conceived and imagined, a commonly accepted system of justice among the parties is inconceivable.

Third, Niebuhr who has been the father of the realist approach to international relations in this country has sought as do all men to reconcile realism with idealism as one aspect of a normative theory. In this effort, however, he has left to others the more precise formulation of the boundaries of political realism. Most students in the field recognize idealist approaches as those which look for conditions and solutions which are supposed to overcome and eliminate the selfish instincts of man. Realism, on the contrary, takes self-interest for granted and seeks in the improvement of society to work with men and political forces as it finds them. The test of a scientific theory is its capacity for bringing order and meaning to a mass of data which would otherwise remain unrelated. It is legitimate to ask whether the concepts of idealism or realism as formulated and applied by Niebuhr contribute more to this end than the definitions of other political scientists who conceive of politics, as distinct from economics or aesthetics, as the pursuit of interest defined in terms of power. It must be said that Niebuhr's formulation, while more satisfying from an ethical standpoint, leaves numerous questions. Realism for him is the disposition to take into account all factors in a social and political situation which offer resistance to established norms. The vital question concerns the meaning, application, and content of these norms. Is it not true that norms like equality become in the political arena objects of endless contention, rationalization, and self-deception? What, for instance, does the norm justice, which Niebuhr construes as requiring that each man be given his due, mean in practical terms? What are the standards by which to determine what "is due" labor and management, or the United States and Russia, in a concrete situation? Is it possible in politics, especially at the international level where the first standard of values is usually success, that the continuous transfusion of morals into politics which still remains politics or the struggle for power is the most we can ask? Can moral principles serve as standards of politics unless derived from political practice or filtered through circumstances of time and place? It must be said that Niebuhr's most serious political errors have arisen from a confusion of normative principles with the possibilities inherent in a given political context. For instance, he judged the New Deal against the background of its achievement of normative goals such as equality and justice, thus obscuring its character as a moderately progressive, pragmatic political movement. In 1945 he confused the abstract principles of British socialism with the realities of foreign policy when he proclaimed that Labor's victory "puts a stop to Churchill's abortive efforts to keep discredited monarchs on the throne in Greece and Italy.... It will most probably contribute to the invention of a *modus vivendi* between Russia and the Western world and thus reduce the peril of a third world war."[26] His failure to perceive the clash of historic Russian interests with Europe's interests led him to predict in the Winter 1944 issue of *Christianity and Society* that geographic propinquity and common sympathy for revolutionary ferment would encourage Russo-European relations more intimate in character than Europe's relations with the United States. It can be argued that these errors which Niebuhr has been the first to identify stem largely from an analysis which has subordinated interests to abstract norms.

III. Fundamental Problems of Theory and Practice

Edmund Burke, who is probably the greatest of English-speaking political philosophers, has bequeathed to the West a concept which Niebuhr appropriates in the most recent stage of his thinking. Theorists and more particularly scientists of society as we have seen have often yielded to the inclination of believing that the historical realm was analogous to the realm of nature and that the proper scientific or theoretical techniques would assure men mastery over their historical fate. Yet there is no more perplexing problem than that of the relation of political theory to the practice of statesmen despite the illusions most characteristically expressed in the influence of August Comte upon our social thought. Most of our scientific studies have been largely irrelevant to the practice of statecraft in a day when the watchword must be "sufficient unto the day is the evil thereof." The dimensions peculiar to history and politics have often been ignored and obscured. For Burke the problem of the relation of theory and practice is bound up in the concept of prudence. For him, prudence, not justice, is first in the rank of political virtues; she is the director, the standard, the regulator of them. Metaphysics cannot live without definition, but prudence is cautious how she defines.

Niebuhr, as he has moved in the direction of a pragmatic view of world politics, has dealt with increasing emphasis upon the limits of a rational as well as a normative theory in practice. He has been ever more impressed with the practical wisdom of a statesman like Churchill, who in his estimate of the present has found his way through the dogmatic predictions about history to the real unpredictabilities. While men can learn from the past they would do well not to make any past event into an analogy for unique present perplexities. Even the proximate moral norms of politics are seldom realized in practice and statesmen must settle more often than not for a series of infertile and uncertain compromises. Thus while normative theory can be made relevant in a remote regulative way, the opposite dimension from love, which is the dimension of interest and power, sets limits to the meaning of theory. Love expressed in abstract principles of justice in an absolute natural law is still unrealized in a relative natural law in which abstract principles are compromised by interest and power. Historical or civil law may embody the proximate principles of a more relative natural law, as for example with our Higher Law, but international affairs for the most part lies beyond mere legal enactments. In the irrational realm which remains, the struggle is so intense and perennial that the only possible peace is gained through armistice and the only order through a tentative balance among the various forces.

Niebuhr therefore returns to the sphere he early identified. His concern with theology and normative theory has in a way sometimes drawn him above and beyond national interest and left to his followers the systematic study of the "laws" of interest and politics. Yet if Niebuhr has failed to transcend the tragic paradoxes of politics, he has clarified and illuminated the problem as no other present-day political philosopher. If by accepting the brutal facts of the international scene, Niebuhr has limited the relevance of normative standards, he has invited for the people and their statesmen a kind of cosmic humility regarding the moral qualities of their action. Moral pretension which derives from policies of self-righteousness and generates conflicts and war is made the basis for Niebuhr's final conclusion that it is as necessary to moderate the moral pretensions of each contestant as to make moral distinctions regarding the national interest. Theory and practice in international politics are enveloped in the ambiguity which derives from the importance of rational and normative theory limited by its relevance for practice.

NOTES

Reprinted from *The Review of Politics* 17, no. 2 (April 1955): 167–88.

1. Reinhold Niebuhr, *Christian Realism and Political Problems* (New York: Charles Scribner's Sons, 1953), 4.

2. *Christianity and Society* 10, no. 2 (Spring 1945): 4.

3. Reinhold Niebuhr, *Faith and History: A Comparison of Christian and Modern Views of History* (New York: Charles Scribner's Sons, 1949), 53.

4. Reinhold Niebuhr, *The Nature and Destiny of Man*, vol. 1, *Human Nature* (New York: Charles Scribner's Sons, 1945), 1.

5. Ibid., 3.

6. Reinhold Niebuhr, *The Children of Light and the Children of Darkness* (New York: Charles Scribner's Sons, 1944), 20.

7. *Christianity and Society* 11, no. 3 (Spring 1945): 7–8.

8. *Christianity and Society* 10, no. 2 (Spring 1944): 7.

9. *Christianity and Society* 12, no. 1 (Winter 1946): 8.

10. Reinhold Niebuhr, *An Interpretation of Christian Ethics* (New York: Harper and Brothers, 1935), 140.

11. Niebuhr, *Nature and Destiny of Man*, vol. 2, *Human Destiny* (New York: Charles Scribner's Sons, 1945), 259.

12. Reinhold Niebuhr, "Human Nature and Social Change," *Christian Century* 50 (1953): 363.

13. *Christianity and Crisis* 9 (December 12, 1949): 162.

14. *Christianity and Crisis* 10, no. 2 (February 20, 1950): 10.

15. *Radical Religion* 4, no. 3 (Summer 1939): 7.

16. *Radical Religion* 4, no. 4 (Autumn 1939): 2.

17. *Christianity and Society* 12, no. 4 (Autumn 1947): 3.

18. *Radical Religion* 1, no. 1 (Autumn 1935): 7.

19. *Christianity and Crisis* 9, no. 17 (October 17, 1949): 132.

20. *Christianity and Crisis* 12, no. 3 (March 2, 1953): 20.

21. "The Cultural Crisis of Our Age," *Harvard Business Review* 32, no. 1 (January–February 1954): 34.

22. *Christianity and Crisis* 40, no. 1 (February 5, 1951): 3.

23. Ibid.

24. "Christianity and the Moral Law," *The Christian Century* 70, no. 48 (December 2, 1953): 1386.

25. The concept of distributive justice as developed by Niebuhr involving the rights and interests of rivals on opposite sides of a line or fence probably deals with our criticism even though he has not always made this application.

26. *Christianity and Society* 10, no. 4 (Autumn 1945).

CHAPTER 12

Reflections on the State of Political Science

HANS J. MORGENTHAU

I

In Plato's *Theaetetus* Socrates develops the character of the philosopher, the man of knowledge, in contrast to the atheoretical, practical man.[1] He endeavors to demonstrate the distinctive qualities of the philosopher by emphasizing his peculiar attitude towards the political sphere.

First, the philosopher has no political ambitions, and he does not care about what is going on in the political sphere. The philosophers

> have never, from their youth upwards, known their way to the Agora, or the dicastery, or the council, or any other political assembly; they neither see nor hear the laws or decrees, as they are called, of the State written or recited; the eagerness of political societies in the attainment of offices— clubs, and banquets, and revels, and singing-maidens—do not enter even into their dreams. Whether any event has turned out well or ill in the city, what disgrace may have descended to any one from his ancestors, male or female, are matters of which the philosopher no more knows than he can tell, as they say, how many pints are contained in the ocean.

Second, the philosopher is ignorant about political matters and incapable of acting effectively on the political plane. He "is wholly unacquainted with his next-door neighbor; he is ignorant, not only of what he is doing, but he hardly knows whether he is a man or an animal. . . . His awkwardness is fearful, and gives the impression of imbecility. When he is reviled, he has nothing personal to say in answer to the civilities of his adversaries, for he knows no scandals of anyone, and they do not interest him. . . ."

Third, the philosopher is morally uncommitted and indifferent to the values of politics.

When he hears a tyrant or king eulogized, he fancies that he is listening to the praises of some keeper of cattle—a swineherd, or shepherd, or perhaps a cowherd, who is congratulated on the quantity of milk which he squeezes from them; and he remarks that the creature whom they tend, and out of whom they squeeze the wealth, is of a less tractable and more insidious nature. Then again, he observes that the great man is of necessity as ill-mannered and uneducated as any shepherd—for he has no leisure, and he is surrounded by a wall, which is his mountain-pen. Hearing of enormous landed proprietors of ten thousand acres and more, our philosopher deems this to be a trifle, because he has been accustomed to think of the whole earth; and when they sing the praises of family, and say that some one is a gentleman because he can show seven generations of wealthy ancestors, he thinks that their sentiments only betray a dull and narrow vision in those who utter them and who are not educated enough to look at the whole, nor to consider that every man has had thousands and ten thousands of progenitors, and among them have been rich and poor, kings and slaves, Hellenes and barbarians, innumerable. And when people pride themselves on having a pedigree of twenty-five ancestors, which goes back to Heracles, the son of Amphitryon, he cannot understand their poverty of ideas. Why are they unable to calculate that Amphitryon had a twenty-fifth ancestor, who might have had a fiftieth, and so on? He amuses himself with the notion that they cannot count, and thinks that a little arithmetic would have got rid of their senseless vanity.

This political indifference and incapacity is the reflection of the philosopher's positive nature. The philosopher's

outer form . . . only is in the city. His mind, disdaining the littlenesses and nothingnesses of human things, is "flying all abroad" as Pindar says, measuring earth and heaven and the things which are under and on the earth and above the heaven, interrogating the whole nature of each and all in their entirety, but not condescending to anything which is within reach. . . . He is searching into the essence of man, and busy in enquiring what belongs to such a nature to do or suffer different from any other. . . .

This commitment to the search for the truth for its own sake and, concomitant with it, his divorce—morally and intellectually, in judgment and action—from the political sphere makes the man of theory a scandal in the eyes of the multitude. He "is laughed at for his sheepishness. . . . He seems to be a downright idiot." He "is derided by the vulgar, partly because he is thought to despise them, and also because he is ignorant of what is before him and always at a loss." Socrates tells "the jest which the clever witty Thracian handmaid is said to have made about Thales, when he fell into a well as he was looking up at the stars. She said, that he was so eager to know what was going on in heaven, that he could not see what was before his feet." And Socrates adds: "This is a jest which is equally applicable to all philosophers."
Yet the philosopher has his revenge.

But, O my friend, when he draws the other into upper air, and gets him out of his pleas and rejoinders into the contemplation of justice and injustice in their own nature and in their difference from one another and from all other things; or from the common-places about the happiness of a king or a rich man to the consideration of government, and of human happiness and misery in general—what they are, and how a man is to attain the one and avoid the other—when that narrow, keen, little legal mind is called to account about all this, he gives the philosopher his revenge; for dizzied by the height at which he is hanging, whence he looks down into space, which is a strange experience to him, he being dismayed, and lost, and stammering broken words, is laughed at, not by Thracian handmaidens or any other uneducated persons, for they have no eye for the situation but by every man who has not been brought up a slave.

We may well recognize in this juxtaposition of the philosopher with the practitioner the archetypes of a perennial conflict between the theoretical man who thinks for the sake of finding the truth, and the practical man who thinks for the sake of finding solutions to practical problems. Yet neither can we fail to recognize the limitations of the Platonic analysis, which is too neat, too "Greek" in its classical simplicity to satisfy us. While what Plato says is true, it is not the whole truth of the matter. There is, as we shall see, in the political thinker's place within the society about which he thinks an ambiguity—intellectual and moral—of which the ancients knew—and perhaps were bound to know—nothing. Yet with all its limitations Plato's statement conveys an insight into the nature of philosophy, theory, and science which, in turn, sheds an illuminating light upon the state of political science in America.

II

The impulse to which American political science owes its existence was overwhelmingly practical. It was nourished from two roots, one of which it has in common with all of modern political science, while the other is peculiar to itself.

Political science as an academic discipline everywhere in the western world owes its existence to the disintegration, after their last flowering in the early nineteenth century, of the great philosophic systems which had dominated western thought, and the concomitant development of the empirical investigation of the social world. All the social sciences are the fruit of the emancipation of the western mind from metaphysical systems which had made the social world primarily a subject for metaphysical speculation and ethical postulates. In certain fields, such as economics, that emancipation occurred early; in others, such as political science, it occurred relatively late (for reasons which, as we shall see, are inherent in the nature of political science).

This anti-speculative and empirical tendency of western thought, as it developed in the second half of the nineteenth century, could not but find a ready and, as it were, natural response in the propensities of the American mind. Yet while European political thought continued to combine an anti-metaphysical position with concern for theory, American political science was overwhelmed by the practical promises of the new discipline. The first departments of political science were established in America in the eighties of the last century, not for the purpose of theoretical understanding, let alone philosophic speculation, but primarily for the purpose of meeting the practical exigencies of the day.

It is illuminating in this context, and it is in a sense a moving experience, to read the address which was delivered on October 3, 1881, at the opening of the School of Political Science at the University of Michigan by its first dean, Charles Kendall Adams.[2] Of the perennial problems of politics, such as power, legitimacy, authority, freedom, forms of government, natural law, sovereignty, revolution, tyranny, majority rule, this address makes no mention. The only problems which concern it are the practical problems of the day, and the case it tries to make for political science in America rests exclusively upon the contribution the new discipline promises to make to the solution of the problems. Looking abroad, Dean Adams finds that the rapid recovery of France after 1871 was primarily due to the instruction in political science. "The close of their war was six years later than the close of ours; and yet long before we had gained our financial equilibrium, France was the most prosperous nation in Europe." In England, "political instruction . . . has been given by men, some of whom have been thought worthy of high places in Parliament, in the diplomatic service, and in the Cabinet. . . . Their pupils are all about them in Parliament and in the diplomatic service." In diplomacy and, more particularly, in economic reform the influence of university instruction has been persuasive. Dean Adams finds the same beneficial results in Germany. "Graduates of these schools (of political science) found their way into administration positions of influence in all parts of Germany. . . . Commissioner White . . . uses these words: 'In conversation with leading men in Southern Germany I have not found one who did not declare this and similar courses of instruction the main cause of the present efficiency in the German administration.'"

Having thus made a case for the advantages which political science has brought to the practice of European governments, Dean Adams must now dispose of the argument that American political institutions are superior to those of Europe and that, therefore, America has no need of political science. The argument is revealing in its exclusive emphasis upon the practical benefits to be expected.

Is it certain that our municipal governments are better than theirs? Are our systems of taxation more equitably adjusted than theirs? Do our public and private corporations have greater respect for the rights of the people than theirs? Can we maintain that our legislatures are more free from corruption and bribery than theirs? Was our financial management at the close of our war wiser than that of France at the close of hers? If these questions can be answered in the affirmative, and without the shadow of a doubt, I concede that an argument may be built upon them in favor of what may be called intuitive methods.

After passing in systematic review the operations of the three branches of government which are in need of improvement, Dean Adams turns to "several other fields of activity in which great influence is exerted." He singles out journalism and speech-making, which political science can help to improve. He sums up his argument in favor of political science by saying:

It is for the purpose of aiding in the several directions that have been hinted at, and in others that would be mentioned if there were time, that the School of Political Science in the University of Michigan has been established. It finds its justification where the other schools of the University find theirs: in the good of the people and the welfare of the State.

This exclusive concern with practical improvements is by no means an isolated instance. It dominates the virtually simultaneous establishment of a School of Political Science at Columbia University. The objective of that school was as practical as that of Michigan; yet while the latter's appeal was one of boundless vocationalism, the former's practical interests were narrowly confined to a particular profession, that of the civil servant. When President Barnard submitted the proposal for the establishment of the school to the trustees of Columbia University, he called it "Proposed School of Preparation for the Civil Service." Reflecting the philosophy of John W. Burgess, the driving spirit behind the proposal, we find the purpose of the school defined as "to prepare young men for public life whether in the Civil Service at home or abroad, or in the legislatures of the States or of the nation; and also to fit young men for the duties and responsibilities of public journalists."[3]

The first departments of political science in this country, then, did not grow organically from a general conception as to what was covered by the field of political science, nor did they respond to a strongly felt intellectual need. Rather they tried to satisfy practical demands, which other academic disciplines refused to meet. For instance, in that period the law schools would not deal with public law. It was felt that somebody ought to deal with it, and thus it was made part of political science. There was a demand for instruction in journalism, but there was no place for it to be taught; thus it was made part of political science. There was a local demand for guidance in certain aspects of municipal administration; and thus a course in that subject was made part of the curriculum of political science.

In other words, political science grew not by virtue of an intellectual principle germane to the field, but in response to pressures from the outside. What could not be defined in terms of a traditional academic discipline was defined as political science. This inorganic growth and haphazard character of political science is strikingly reflected in the curricula of the early departments of political science, such as those of Michigan, Columbia, and Harvard. In the address from which we have quoted, Dean Adams mentions the following subjects which were to form part of the curriculum of the School of Political Science: "General History," "The History of Political Institutions," "The Recent Political History of Europe," "The Political and Constitutional History of England," "The Political and Constitutional History of the United States"; several courses in Political Economy; under the general heading of Sanitary Science: "The Laws of Physiological Growth and Decay," "The Varieties and Adaptabilities of Foods," "The Best Methods of Supplying Pure Water and Air," "The Causes of Infectious Diseases," "The Proper Disposal of Decomposing Matter," "The Proper Functions of Boards of Health and Health Officers"; under the general heading of Social Science "The Prevalence of Crime and the Most Efficient Means of Diminishing and Preventing It," "The Best Methods of Treating our Criminals," "The Care of the Insane and the Management of Asylums," "The Proper Treatment of the Poor and the Proper Superintendence of Almshouses," "The Place and the Proper Equipment and Control of Hospitals"; courses in Forestry and Political Ethics; and finally "crowning the whole," "The Idea of the State," "The Nature of Individual, Social and Political Rights," "The History of Political Ideas," "The Government of Cities," "Theories and Methods of Taxation," "Comparative Constitutional Law," "Comparative Administrative Law," "Theories of International Law," "The History of Modern

Diplomacy." "Such," Dean Adams concludes, "in the briefest outline, is what it is the purpose of the school at present to teach. Additions to the corps and the courses of instruction will be added, from time to time, as the necessity is revealed."

While this program is but an extreme example of the practicality of early American Political Science, the list of courses which formed the curriculum of the School of Political Science of Columbia University from 1880–87 is typical of its eclecticism. According to Burgess, the "School of Political Science" was "the collective name which we give the graduate or university courses in history, philosophy, economy, public law, jurisprudence, diplomacy, and sociology."[4] These are the courses which were then taught: Physical and Political Geography, Ethnology, General Political and Constitutional History of Europe, Political and Constitutional History of England, Political and Constitutional History of the United States; Bibliography of the Political Sciences; History of Roman Law to the Present Day; Comparative Constitutional Law of the Principal European States and of the United States; Statistical Science, Methods and Results; Comparative Jurisprudence of the Principal European Systems of Civil Law, Comparative Constitutional Law of the Several Commonwealths of the American Union, History of Diplomacy, Comparative Administrative Law of the Principal States of Europe and of the United States; Comparative Administrative Law of the Several Commonwealths of the American Union; Private International Law; Social Sciences: Communistic and Socialistic Theories; Political Economy: History of Politico-Economic Institutions, Taxation and Finance; Philosophy: History of Political Theories from Plato to Hegel.[5]

Similarly, the courses differentiated in 1892–93 at Harvard under the heading of "Government" comprised: Constitutional Government; Elements of International Law (which included history of diplomacy); History and Institutes of Roman Law; Federal Government, Historical and Comparative; Leading Principles of Constitutional Law—Selected Cases American and English; History of Political Theories, with particular reference to the Origin of American Institutions; Government and Political Methods in the United States; and International Law as Administered by the Courts.[6]

In its further development political science as an academic discipline has undergone a process both of contraction and expansion. On the one hand, new schools and departments have absorbed much of the subject matter which was formerly taught in departments of political science because there was no other place in the university to teach them. On the other hand, however, new practical interests have continued to call for the inclusion of new subjects of instruction into the curriculum.

Thus today the curriculum of political science still bears the unmistakable marks of its haphazard origin and development. To pick out at random some courses from two departments of political science with which I am familiar, what have "Plato's Political Philosophy and Its Metaphysical Foundation" and "The Politics of Conservation" in common, or "General Principles of Organization and Administration" and "International Law," or "Conduct of American Foreign Relations" and "Introduction to Jurisprudence," or "Nationalism" and "Political Behavior and Public Policy," or "Russian Political and Economic Institutions" and "Public Personnel Administration"? The only common denominator which now ties these courses loosely together is a general and vague orientation towards the nature and activities of the state and toward activities which have in turn a direct bearing upon the state. Beyond that orientation toward a common subject matter, defined in the most general terms, contemporary political science has no unity of method, outlook, and purpose.

III

As concerns method, political science is split five ways, and four of these methodological positions have hardly anything in common. Their disparity is such that there is hardly even a possibility of fruitful discourse among the representatives of the different approaches beyond polemics which deny the very legitimacy of the other approaches. These approaches can be classified as philosophic theory, empirical theory, empirical science, description, and practical amelioration.

These five methodological approaches are not peculiar to political science. They have appeared in other social sciences—such as psychology, economics, and sociology—as well, yet with two significant differences. First of all, the other social sciences have traditionally shown a much greater awareness of the existence, nature, and separate functions of these approaches than has political science. Second, they have been able, at least at times, to rid themselves in good measure of the ameliorative and vocational approach which has by itself only a minimum of intellectual relevance. Political science, on the other hand, has never squarely faced the methodological problem in terms of the intrinsic character of these different approaches and the functions which they are able to perform for the understanding of the subject matter of political science. These five approaches have rather coexisted without clear distinction within the departments of political science, one to be emphasized over the others at different times and places according to the pressures of supply and demand. Here, too, the development has been haphazard and subject to accident rather than guided by certain fundamental requirements of theory.

Thus political science has not generally been able to make that distinction which is a precondition for the development of any true science: the distinction between what is worth knowing intellectually and what is useful for practice. It is this distinction which economics and sociology accomplished some decades ago when schools of business, home economics, retailing, social work and the like took over the practical concerns which at best develop practical uses for theoretical knowledge or else have but the most tenuous connection with it. Political science has taken a similar step in some instances by organizing the practical uses of political science for the amelioration of government activities in schools of administration and the like. But not only has this separation been exceptional rather than typical, it has also been made as a matter of convenience rather than in application of a generally accepted theoretical principle. In consequence, improvement of the processes of government is still generally considered not only a worthwhile activity to be engaged in by political scientists, but also a legitimate, and sometimes even the only legitimate, element of political science as an academic discipline, to be taught under any of the course headings composing the curriculum of political science.

It should be pointed out in passing that we are dealing here not with a specific subject matter, but with a particular method, a particular intellectual approach. This approach will naturally manifest itself most frequently and typically in those fields of political science which have a direct relevance to the operations of government, such as public administration, but it is by no means limited to them. The other fields of political science, such as international relations, American government, constitutional law, and parties, have at times been dominated by the practical approach seeking practical remedies for conditions regarded as being in need of amelioration.

Today, however, description is still the method most widely used in political science. Factual information arranged according to certain traditional classifications still dominates most of the textbooks in the field. While it is unnecessary to argue the case for the need for factual information, it ought to be no more necessary to argue that factual description is not science but a mere, however indispensable, preparation for the scientific understanding of the facts. It may, however, point toward a theoretical awakening that descriptive political science tends to dress up descriptive accounts of facts in theoretical garb and to use fancy classifications and terminologies in order to conceal the mere descriptive character of its substance. While the theoretical pretense of factual accounts shows an awareness of the need for theoretical understanding, that understanding itself requires more than the demonstrative use of an elaborate apparatus of classification and terminology.

With this last type of descriptive political science which overlays its descriptive substance with theoretical pretense, we are in the borderland where description and empirical science merge. Empirical science is today the most vigorous branch of political science which tends to attract many of the abler and more inventive students. Taking its cue from the natural sciences, or what it thinks the natural sciences are, it tries to develop rigorous methods of quantitative verification which are expected in good time to attain the same precision in the discovery of uniformities and in prediction to which the natural sciences owe their theoretical and practical success.

I have argued elsewhere against this analogy between the social and the natural sciences,[7] and this is not the place to resume the controversy. It must suffice here to state dogmatically that the object of the social sciences is man, not as a product of nature but as both the creature and the creator of history in and through which his individuality and freedom of choice manifest themselves. To make susceptibility to quantitative measurement the yardstick of the scientific character of the social sciences in general and of political science in particular is to deprive these sciences of that very orientation which is adequate to the understanding of their subject matter.

The inadequacy of the quantitative method to the subject matter of political science is demonstrated by the limitation of its success to the types of political behavior which by their very nature lend themselves to a certain measure of quantification, such as voting, and the barrenness of the attempts to apply the quantitative method to phenomena which are determined by historic individuality, rational or moral choice. As concerns these phenomena, the best quantification can achieve is to confirm and refine knowledge which theory has already discovered. It will not do to argue that this limitation is due to the "backwardness" of political science which could be overcome if only more and better people would spend more time and money for quantification. For that argument to be plausible the limitation is too persistent, and it becomes ever more spectacular as more and better people spend more time and money to make it a success.

Once quantification has left that narrow sphere where it can contribute to relevant knowledge, two roads are open to it. Either it can try to quantify phenomena which in their aspects relevant to political science are not susceptible to quantification, and by doing so obscure and distort what political science ought to know; thus much of quantitative political science has become a pretentious collection of trivialities. Or, dimly aware of this inadequacy, quantification may shun contact with the empirical phenomena of political life altogether and try to find out instead what the correct way of quantifying is. Basic to this methodological concern is the assumption that the failure of quantification to yield results in any way proportionate to the effort spent results from the lack of a correct quantitative method. Once that method is discovered and applied, quantification will yield the results in precise knowledge its adherents claim for it.

However, it is obvious that these methodological investigations, patently intended for the guidance of empirical research, have hardly exerted any influence upon the latter. This divorce of methodology from empirical investigation is not fortuitous. For it points not only to the inadequacy of the quantitative method for the understanding of much of the subject matter of political science, an inadequacy which must become particularly striking when quantification is confronted in its pure theoretical form with the actuality of political life. That divorce also illuminates a tendency, common to all methodological endeavors in the social sciences, to retreat ever more from contact with the empirical world into a realm of self-sufficient abstractions. This "new scholasticism," as it has been aptly called,[8] has been most fully developed in sociology; yet it has left its impact also upon political science. The new scholastic tends to think about how to think and to conceptualize about concepts, regressing ever further from empirical reality until he finds the logical consummation of his endeavors in mathematical symbols and other formal relations.

There is a revealing similarity, pointing to a common root in the disorders of our culture, between abstract modern political science and abstract modern art. Both retreat from empirical reality into a world of formal relations and abstract symbols, which on closer examination reveal themselves either to be trivial or else are unintelligible but to the initiated. Both share in the indifference to the accumulated achievements of mankind in their respective fields; Plato and Phidias, St. Thomas and Giotto, Spinoza and Rembrandt have no message for them. That divorcement from reality, contemporary and historic, deprives both of that wholesome discipline which prevents the mind from indulging its fancies without regard to some relevant objective standards. Thus one fashion, intellectual or artistic, follows the other, each oblivious of what has gone before, each relegated to limbo by its successors. Both abstract political science and abstract modern art tend to become esoteric, self-sufficient, and self-perpetuating cults, clustered around a "master," imitating his "style," and conversing in a lingo intelligible only to the members. Yet common sense, trying to penetrate the mysteries of the abstractions, cannot help wondering whether even the initiated understand each other and themselves. Perhaps, common sense continues wondering, some of the "masters" are just pulling the legs of their followers, who must pretend to understand in order to remain intellectually "up-to-date."

With this emphasis upon theoretical abstractions which have no relation to political reality, the methodology of political science joins a school which from the beginning to this day has occupied an honored but lonely place in the curriculum of political science: political theory. Political theory as an academic discipline has been traditionally the history of political philosophies in chronological succession, starting with Plato and ending, if time permits, with Laski. As an academic discipline, political theory has been hardly more than an account of what writers of the past, traditionally regarded as "great," have thought about the traditional problems of politics, with hardly a systematic attempt being made to correlate that historic knowledge to the other fields of political science and to the contemporary political world. "The danger," in the words of Ernest Barker, "of some subjects of speculation—I would cite in evidence literary criticism as well as political theory—is that they may be choked, as it were, by the history of their own past."[9] Thus political theory as an academic discipline has been intellectually sterile, and it is not by accident that some of the most important contributions to contemporary political theory have been made not by professional political scientists, but by theologians, philosophers, and sociologists.

Political theory has remained an indispensable part of the curriculum not because of the vital influence it has been able to exert upon our thinking, but rather because of a vague conviction that there was something venerable and respectable in this otherwise useless exercise. Thus the academic concern with political theory has tended to become an intellectually and practically meaningless ritual which one had to engage in, for reasons of tradition and prestige, before one could occupy oneself with the things that really mattered.

The awareness of this contrast between the prestige of political theory and its actual lack of relevance for the understanding of contemporary political problems has led theory closer to the contemporary political world. On the other hand, the awareness of the meagerness of the insights to be gained from strictly empirical investigations has made empirical political science search for a theoretical framework. Avoiding the limitations of the traditional approaches and fusing certain of their elements, contemporary political science is in the process of reviving a tradition to which most of the classics of political science owe their existence and influence. The intent of that tradition is theoretical: it wants to understand political reality in a theoretical manner, that is, by bringing to bear upon it propositions of both objective and general validity. These propositions claim to be objective in that their validity is not affected by the subjective limitations of the observer. They claim to be general in that their validity is not affected by the peculiar circumstances of time and place of the subject matter.

The subject matter of this theoretical concern is the contemporary political world. This branch of political science, which we call empirical theory, reflects in theoretical terms upon the contemporary political world. The political world, however, poses a formidable obstacle to such understanding. This obstacle is of a moral rather than an intellectual nature. Before we turn to the requirements of such an empirical theory and its central concept, we have to dispose of the moral problem with which political science must come to terms.

IV

The moral position of the political scientist in society is ambivalent; it can even be called paradoxical. For the political scientist is a product of the society which it is his mission to understand. He is also an active part, and frequently he seeks to be a leading part, of that society. To be faithful to his mission he would, then, have to overcome two limitations: the limitation of origin, which determines the perspective from which he looks at society, and the limitation of purpose, which makes him wish to remain a member in good standing of that society or even to play a leading role in it.

The mind of the political scientist is molded by the society which he observes. His outlook, his intellectual interests, and his mode of thinking are determined by the civilization, the national community, and all the particular religious, political, economic, and social groups of which he is a member. The "personal equation" of the political scientist both limits and directs his scholarly pursuits. The truth which a mind thus socially conditioned is able to grasp is likewise socially conditioned. The perspective of the observer determines what can be known and how it is to be understood. In consequence, the truth of political science is of necessity a partial truth.[10]

Upon a mind which by its very nature is unable to see more than part of the truth, society exerts its pressures, which confront the scholar with a choice between social advantage and the truth. The stronger the trend toward conformity within the society and the stronger the social ambitions within the individual scholar, the greater will be the temptation to sacrifice the moral commitment to the truth for social advantage. It follows that a respectable political science—respectable, that is, in terms of the society to be investigated—is in a sense a contradiction in terms. For a political science which is faithful to its moral commitment of telling the truth about the political world cannot help telling society things it does not want to hear. The truth of political science is the truth about power, its manifestations, its configurations, its limitations, its implications, its laws. Yet one of the main purposes of society is to conceal these truths from its members. That concealment, that elaborate and subtle and purposeful misunderstanding of the nature of political man and of political society, is one of the cornerstones upon which all societies are founded.[11]

A political science which is true to its moral commitment ought at the very least to be an unpopular undertaking. At its very best, it cannot help being a subversive and revolutionary force with regard to certain vested interests—intellectual, political, economic, social in general. For it must sit in continuous judgment upon political man and political society, measuring their truth, which is in good part a social convention, by its own. By doing so, it is not only an embarrassment to society intellectually, but it becomes also a political threat to the defenders or the opponents of the status quo or to both; for the social conventions about power, which political science cannot help subjecting to a critical—and often destructive—examination, are one of the main sources from which the claims to power, and hence power itself, derive.

It stands to reason that political science as a social institution could never hope even to approach this ideal of a completely disinterested commitment to the truth. For no social institution can completely transcend the limitations of its origin; nor can it endeavor to free itself completely from its commitments to the society of which it forms a part, without destroying itself in the attempt. Only rare individuals have achieved the Socratic distinction of unpopularity, social ostracism, and criminal penalties, which are the reward of constant dedication to the relevant truth in matters political. Yet while political science as a social institution cannot hope to approach the ideal, it must be aware of its existence; and the awareness of its moral commitment to the truth must mitigate the limitations of origin as well as the compromises between the moral commitment and social convenience and ambition, both of which no political scientist can fully escape. It is the measure of the degree to which political science in America meets the needs of society rather than its moral commitment to the truth that it is not only eminently respectable and popular, but—what is worse—that it is also widely regarded with indifference.

A political science which is mistreated and persecuted is likely to have earned that enmity because it has put its moral commitment to the truth above social convenience and ambition. It has penetrated beneath the ideological veil with which society conceals the true nature of political relations, disturbing the complacency of the powers-that-be and stirring up the conscience of society. A political science which is respected is likely to have earned that respect because it performs useful functions for society. It helps to cover political relations with the veil of ideologies which mollify the conscience of society; by justifying the existing power relations, it reassures the powers-that-be in their possession of power; it illuminates certain aspects of the existing power relations; and it contributes to the improvement of the technical operations of government. The relevance of this political science does not lie primarily in the discovery of the truth about politics but in its contribution to the stability of society.

A political science which is neither hated nor respected, but treated with indifference as an innocuous pastime, is likely to have retreated into a sphere that lies beyond the positive or negative interests of society. Concerning itself with issues in which nobody has a stake, this political science avoids the risk of social disapproval by even foregoing the chance of social approbation. The retreat into the trivial, the formal, the methodological, the purely theoretical, the remotely historical—in short the politically irrelevant—is the unmistakable sign of a "non-controversial" political science which has neither friends nor enemies because it has no relevance for the great political issues in which society has a stake. History and methodology, in particular, become the protective armor which shields political science from contact with the political reality of the contemporary world.

By being committed to a truth which is in this sense irrelevant, political science distorts the perspective under which the political world is seen. Certain eminent exceptions notwithstanding, it tends to pass in silence over such burning problems as the nature of power and of the truth about it, political ideologies, the political power of economic organizations, alternative foreign policies, the relations between government and public opinion, between tyranny and democracy, between objective truth and majority rule, as well as most of the other fundamental problems of contemporary democracy. By doing so, it makes it appear as though these problems either did not exist or were not important or were not susceptible to theoretical understanding. By its predominant concern with the irrelevant, it devalues by implication the really important problems of politics.

V

What, then, ought a political science to be like, which does justice both to its scientific pretense and to its subject matter? The answer to this question, insofar as it concerns the scientific pretense of political science, derives from three basic propositions: the importance of political philosophy for political science, the identity of political theory and political science, the ability of political science to communicate objective and general truth about matters political.

Political science, as all science, is both in the general conception of its scope and method and in its particular concepts and operations a—largely unavowed—reflection of philosophic propositions. Even the most anti-philosophic science of politics is founded upon a philosophic understanding of the nature of man and society, and of science itself. That understanding is philosophic in that its validity does not derive from its being capable of empirical verification (although it may be so verified), but rather from its logical consistency with certain general propositions which claim to present the true nature of reality. Political science can neither prove nor disprove the philosophic validity of these propositions, but assumes the fallacy of some and the validity of others. The choice of these philosophic assumptions cannot but limit the scope, outlook, method, and purpose of political science. Political science is of necessity based upon, and permeated by, a total world view—religious, poetic as well as philosophic in nature—the validity of which it must take for granted.

During most of the history of western political thought, the functions of political philosophy and political science were united in the same persons. The great political philosophers were also the great political scientists deriving concrete, empirically verifiable propositions from abstract philosophic ones. If the disintegration of the great political systems in the nineteenth century and the concomitant development of a separate political science to which we have referred above had led only to a division of labor between political philosophy and political science, no objection on principle would have been in order. However, the denial of the legitimacy and relevance of political philosophy for political science, prevalent in our day, is quite a different matter. For by denying that legitimacy and relevance, political science cuts itself off from the very roots to which it owes its life, which determine its growth, and which give it meaning. A political science which knows nothing but its own subject matter cannot even know that subject matter well. Contemporary political science, predominantly identified with a positivistic philosophy which is itself a denial of virtually all of the philosophic traditions of the West, has, as it were, mutilated itself by refusing itself access to the sources of insight available in the great philosophic systems of the past. Yet without that access it cannot even recognize, let alone understand, some of the perennial problems of politics which contemporary experience poses with almost unprecedented urgency.

Why is it that all men lust for power; why is it that even their noblest aspirations are tainted by that lust? Why is it that the political act, in its concern with man's power over man and the concomitant denial of the other man's freedom, carries within itself an element of immorality and puts upon the actor the stigma of guilt? Why is it, finally, that in politics good intentions do not necessarily produce good results and well-conceived plans frequently lead to failure in action, and why is it, conversely, that evil men have sometimes done great good in politics and improvident ones have frequently been successful? Here we are in the presence of the mystery, the sin, and the tragedy of politics. The problems which these questions raise are not scientific but philosophic in nature. Yet without the awareness of their legitimacy and relevance political science is precluded from even raising certain problems essential to the scientific understanding of politics.[12]

The same anti-philosophic position, prevalent in contemporary political science, is responsible for the common distinction between political theory and political science. Theory, being by definition useless for practical purposes, was assigned that honorific, but ineffectual, position to which we have referred before, and main emphasis was placed upon science whose immediate usefulness for society the natural sciences seemed to have demonstrated.

Perhaps no event has had a more disastrous effect upon the development of American political science than this dichotomy between political theory and political science. For it has made political theory sterile by cutting it off from contact with the contemporary issues of politics, and it has tended to deprive political science of intellectual content by severing its ties with the Western tradition of political thought, its concerns, its accumulation of wisdom and knowledge. When American political science became sporadically aware of that impoverishment suffered by its own hands, it resorted to the remedy of adding more courses in political theory to the curriculum, or making them compulsory, or requiring knowledge of political theory in examinations. However, the remedy has been of no avail; for it derives from that very dichotomy between political theory and political science, which is at the root of the disease itself.

Of that disease, the plight of comparative government as an academic discipline provides a striking example. The comparison of different political institutions and systems requires logically a *tertium comparationis,* that is, a proposition which provides a standard for comparison. That standard, in order to be meaningful, cannot be merely empirical, but must have a theoretical significance, pointing to propositions of general validity. Comparative government, in order to be an academic discipline at all, then, requires a theory of politics which makes meaningful comparisons possible. In the absence of such a theory, it is not fortuitous that comparative government is hardly more than the description of, or at best, a series of theories about, individual political institutions and systems without comparison.

The very distinction between political theory and political science is untenable. Science is theoretical, or it is nothing. Historically and logically, a scientific theory is a system of empirically verifiable, general truths, sought for their own sake. This definition sets theory apart from practical knowledge, common-sense knowledge, and philosophy. Practical knowledge is interested only in truths which lend themselves to immediate practical application; common-sense knowledge is particular, fragmentary, and unsystematic; philosophic knowledge may be, but is not of necessity, empirically verifiable. What else, then, is scientific knowledge if not theory? It follows that political science cannot be made more theoretical by increased emphasis upon the separate field of political theory, but only by infusing all branches of political science susceptible of theoretical understanding with the spirit of theory.

The same philosophic position which has made political science disparage philosophy and separate itself from theory has also made it deny the existence and intelligibility of objective, general truths in matters political. That denial manifests itself in different ways on different levels of discourse. On the level of the general theory of democracy, it leads to the conclusion that the decision of the majority is the ultimate datum beyond which neither analysis nor evaluation can go. On the level of the analysis of political processes and decisions, it reduces political science to the explanation of the ways by which pressure groups operate and the decisions of government are reached. A political science thus conceived limits itself to the descriptive analysis of a complex of particular historic facts. Its denial of the existence and intelligibility of a truth about matters political that exists regardless of time and place implies a denial of the possibility of political theory both in its analytical and normative sense. What a political science of the past has discovered to be true, then, is true only in view of the peculiar and ephemeral historic circumstances of the time, carrying no lesson for us or any other period of history, or else is a mere reflection of the subjective preferences of the observer. The political science of the past is thus reduced, insofar as it seeks empirical analysis, to the description of an ephemeral historic situation and, as normative theory, becomes undistinguishable from political ideology. This being so, contemporary political science is caught in the same relativism and is no more able to transcend the limitations of time and place than were its predecessors.

We cannot here enter into a detailed discussion of this fundamental problem; two observations must suffice. Political science, as any science, presupposes the existence and accessibility of objective, general truth. If nothing that is true regardless of time and place could be said about matters political, political science itself would be impossible. Yet the whole history of political thought is a living monument to that possibility. The relevance for ourselves of insights which political scientists of the past, reflecting upon matters political under the most diverse historic circumstances, considered to be true points toward the existence of a store of objective, general truths which are as accessible to us as they were to our predecessors. If it were otherwise, how could we not only understand, but also appreciate, the political insights of a Jeremiah, a Kautilya, a Plato, a Bodin, or a Hobbes?

VI

The content of political science is not to be determined *a priori* and in the abstract. A theory is a tool for understanding. Its purpose is to bring order and meaning to a mass of phenomena which without it would remain disconnected and unintelligible. There is a strong tendency in contemporary political science to force theory into a Procrustes bed by judging it by its conformity with certain preestablished methodological criteria rather than by its intrinsic contribution to knowledge and understanding. The result is an academic formalism which in its concern with methodological requirements tends to lose sight of the goal of knowledge and understanding which method must serve. One is reminded of the answer which Galileo is reported to have received when he invited some of his critics to look through a telescope at an astronomical phenomenon the existence of which they had denied; they said that there was no need for them to use this empirical instrument since according to Aristotle such a phenomenon could not exist. One is also reminded of the tendencies of the French literature of the seventeenth, the German literature of the eighteenth, and the French art of the nineteenth centuries to make the compliance with certain formal requirements the ultimate standard of literary and artistic value. And one takes heart from the impotence of such attempts to prevent for long the human mind from seeking and finding what is important in science, literature, and art.

The validity of a theory, then, does not depend upon its conformity with *a priori* assumptions, methodological or otherwise. It is subject to a purely pragmatic test. Does this theory broaden our knowledge and deepen our understanding of what is worth knowing? If it does it is good, regardless of its *a priori* assumptions; if it does not, it is worthless, again regardless of its *a priori* assumptions.

The content of theory, then, must be determined by the intellectual interest of the observer. What is it we want to know about politics? What concerns us most about it? What questions do we want a theory of politics to answer? The replies to these three questions determine the content of political science and the replies may well differ not only from one period of history to another, but from one contemporaneous group of observers to another.

Hypothetically one can imagine as many theories of politics as there are legitimate intellectual perspectives from which to approach the political scene. But in a particular culture and a particular period of history, there is likely to be one perspective which for theoretical and practical reasons takes precedence over the others. At one time theoretical interest was focused upon the constitutional arrangements within which political relations take place; in view of the theoretical and practical problems to be solved, this was then a legitimate interest. At another time in the history of political science, theoretical interest was centered upon political institutions and their operations; in view of what was worth knowing and doing at that time, this theoretical interest was again legitimate. Thus political science is like a spotlight which, while trying to illuminate the whole political world, focuses in one period of history upon one aspect of politics and changes its focus in accordance with new theoretical and practical concerns.[13]

In our period of history, the justice and stability of political life is threatened, and our understanding of the political world is challenged, by the rise of totalitarianism on the domestic and international scene. The novel political phenomenon of totalitarianism puts in doubt certain assumptions about the nature of man and of society which we took for granted. It raises issues about institutions which we thought had been settled once and for all. It disrupts and overwhelms legal processes on which we had come to look as self-sufficient instruments of control. In one word, what has emerged from under the surface of legal and institutional arrangements as the distinctive, unifying element of politics is the struggle for power, elemental, undisguised, and all-pervading.[14] As recently as a decade ago, it was still held by conservatives, liberals, and Marxists alike either that the struggle for power was at worst a raucous pastime, safely regulated by law and channeled by institutions, or that it had been replaced in its dominant influence by economic competition, or that the ultimate triumph of liberal democracy or the classless society, which were expected to be close at hand, would make an end to it altogether. These assumptions and expectations have been refuted by the experience of our age. It is to the challenge of this refutation that political science must respond, as political practice must meet the challenge of that experience.

Yet while political science must thus come to terms with the problem of power, it must adapt its emphasis to the ever-changing circumstances of the times. When the times tend to depreciate the element of power, it must stress its importance. When the times incline toward a monistic conception of power in the general scheme of things, it must show its limitations. When the times conceive of power primarily in military terms, it must call attention to the variety of factors which go into the power equation and, more particularly, to the subtle psychological relation, of which the web of power is fashioned. When the reality of power is being lost sight of over its moral and legal limitations, it must point to that reality. When law and morality are judged as nothing, it must assign them their rightful place.

It may be pointed out in passing that all great contributions to political science, from Plato and Aristotle to *The Federalist* and Calhoun, have been responses to such challenges arising from political reality. They have not been self-sufficient theoretical developments pursuing theoretical concerns for their own sake. Rather, they were confronted with a set of political experiences and problems which defied understanding with the theoretical tools at hand. Thus they had to face a new political experience, unencumbered by an intellectual tradition which might have been adequate to preceding experiences but which failed to illuminate the experience of the contemporary world. Thus they were compelled to separate in the intellectual tradition at their disposal that which is historically conditioned from that which is true regardless of time and place, and to pose again the perennial problems of politics, and to reformulate the perennial truths of politics, in the light of the contemporary experience. This has been the task of political science throughout its history and this is the task of political science today.[15] There is, then, in political science what might be called a "higher practicality," which responds to practical needs not by devising practical remedies, but by broadening and deepening the understanding of the problems from which the practical needs arose.

By making power its central concept, a theory of politics does not presume that none but power relations control political action. What it must presume is the need for a central concept which allows the observer to distinguish the field of politics from other social spheres, to orient himself in the maze of empirical phenomena which make up the field of politics, and to establish a measure of rational order within it. A central concept, such as power, then provides a kind of rational outline of politics, a map of the political scene. Such a map does not provide a complete description of the political landscape as it is in a particular period of history. It rather provides the timeless features of its geography distinct from their ever-changing historic setting. Such a map, then, will tell us what are the rational possibilities for travel from one spot on the map to another, and which road is most likely to be taken by certain travelers under certain conditions. Thus it imparts a measure of rational order to the observing mind and, by doing so, establishes one of the conditions for successful action.

A theory of politics, by the very fact of painting a rational picture of the political scene, points to the contrast between what the political scene actually is and what it tends to be, but can never completely become. The difference between the empirical reality of politics and a theory of politics is like the difference between a photograph and a painted portrait. The photograph shows everything that can be seen by the naked eye. The painted portrait does not show everything that can be seen by the naked eye, but it shows one thing that the naked eye cannot see: the human essence of the person portrayed. Thus a theory of politics must seek to depict the rational essence of its subject matter.

By doing so, a theory of politics cannot help implying that the rational elements of politics are superior in value to the contingent ones and that they are so in two respects. They are so in view of the theoretical understanding which the theory seeks; for its very possibility and the extent to which it is possible depends upon the rationality of its subject matter. A theory of politics must value that rational nature of its subject matter also for practical reasons. It must assume that a rational policy is of necessity a good policy; for only such a policy minimizes risks and maximizes benefits and, hence, complies both with the moral precept of prudence and the political requirement of success. A theory of politics must want the photographic picture of the political scene to resemble as much as possible its painted portrait.

Hence, a theory of politics presents not only a guide to understanding, but also an ideal for action. It presents a map of the political scene not only in order to understand what that scene is like, but also in order to show the shortest and safest road to a given objective. The use of theory, then, is not limited to rational explanation and anticipation. A theory of politics also contains a normative element.

VII

A curriculum of political science which would try to put such a theoretical understanding of politics into practice for the purposes of teaching would have to eliminate all the subjects which do not serve this theoretical understanding. It would also have to add subjects which at present are not included, but which are essential to such understanding.

The process of elimination must move on two fronts. First, it must affect the subjects which have been traditionally included in the field but which have no organic connection with its subject matter or with the perspective from which contemporary political science ought to view it. In this category belong, for instance, all the legal subjects with which political science concerns itself because the law schools at one time did not. However, this practical consideration is unfounded today when law schools offer courses in jurisprudence, administrative, constitutional, and international law. Political science is not interested in any legal subject *per se,* yet it has indeed a vital interest in the interrelations between law and politics. It must look at law not as a self-contained system of rules of conduct, but rather as both the creation and the creator of political forces.

On the other hand, there has been a strong tendency in political science to add to the curriculum subjects which happen to be of practical importance at a particular moment, regardless of their theoretical relevance. However, what is worth knowing for practical reasons is not necessarily worth knowing on theoretical grounds. A certain innovation in municipal administration or international organization may attract at one time wide attention by virtue of the practical results it promises, or the political developments in a certain area of the world may become a matter of topical interest for public opinion. It still remains to be shown on theoretical grounds that such topics ought to be included as independent subjects in the curriculum of political science. On a limited scale this problem raises again the issue of liberal vs. vocational education.

The additions to the curriculum of political science, too, must be of two different kinds. On the one hand, the curriculum must take into account the fact that its central concept is a general social phenomenon which manifests itself most typically in the political sphere, but is not limited to it. The phenomenon of power and the social configurations to which it gives rise play an important, yet largely neglected, part in all social life. A configuration, such as the balance of power, is a general social phenomenon to be found on all levels of social interaction. The theoretical understanding of specifically political phenomena and configurations requires the understanding of the extent to which these political phenomena and configurations are merely the specific instances of general social phenomena and configurations and to which they grow out of their specific political environment. One of the cornerstones of the curriculum of political science, then, ought to be political sociology, which deals with the phenomenon of power and the social configurations to which it gives rise in general, with special reference, of course, to those in the political sphere.[16]

On the other hand, the contemporary political scene is characterized by the interaction between the political and economic spheres. This interaction runs counter to the liberal assumption and requirement of actual separation, which is reflected in the academic separation of the two fields. This interaction reverts to a situation which existed before political science was established as an academic discipline and which was reflected by the academic fusion of the two fields in the form of political economy. The curriculum of political science must take theoretical notice of the actual development of private governments in the form of giant corporations and labor unions. These organizations exercise power within their own organizational limits, in their relations to each other, and in their relations to the state. The state, in turn, exercises power over them. These power relations constitute a new field for theoretical understanding.

Yet what political science needs above all changes in the curriculum—even though it needs them too—is the restoration of the intellectual and moral commitment to the truth about matters political for its own sake. That restoration becomes the more urgent in the measure in which the general social and the particular academic environment tends to discourage it. Society in general and that particular society of which he is a professional member pull and push the political scientist towards being useful here and now and playing it safe forever. If the political scientist cannot resist these pushes and pulls by repairing to the vision of the searcher for the political truth, which Plato brought to the world, and of the professor of the political truth, which the prophets exemplified, what will become of him as a scholar, and what will become of a society which has deprived itself of the ability to measure the conflicting claims of interested parties against the truth, however dimly seen?

A society which has thus closed its eyes to the truth about itself has cut its tie with what connects it with the mainsprings of civilization. For without at least the assumption that objective, general truth in matters political exists and can be known, order and justice and truth itself become the mere byproduct of ever-changing power relations. In such a society the political scientist has still an important part to play: he becomes the ideologue who gives the appearance of truth and justice to power and the claim for it.

Political science, as we have tried to show before, can indeed not help performing such an ideological function. Yet it is the measure of the awareness and fulfillment of its mission as a science of politics that it is conscious of the existence of an objective, general truth behind ideological rationalizations and justifications and that it seeks the comprehension of that truth. In order to fulfill that mission the political scientist must live within the political world without being of it. He must watch it with intense interest and sympathy, yet the gaze of his mind and the impulse of his will must transcend it. He must understand it as well and better than does the politician, and yet his ambition has nothing in common with the latter's. His primary moral commitment is not to society but to the truth and, hence, to society only in so far as it lives up to the truth. Only so can he at least approach the ideal of political justice, he only among those concerned with political matters; for in the words of Goethe: "The actor is always unjust; nobody has justice but the observer."

At such impracticality in action and ambivalence in moral commitment, the handmaids of all ages, the born servants of society, can only laugh. Of them, however clever and witty they may be, history reports nothing but laughter. Yet what they laugh at is the moral and intellectual outlook from which stems our heritage of political knowledge and wisdom.

NOTES

Reprinted from *The Review of Politics* 17, no. 4 (October 1955): 431–60.

1. Part of this paper was originally prepared for a conference held at Northwestern University in June, 1954.

2. Charles Kendall Adams, *The Relations of Political Science to National Prosperity* (Ann Arbor, 1881).

3. R. Gordon Hoxie et al., *A History of the Faculty of Political Science Columbia University* (New York: Columbia University Press, 1955), 13.

4. "The Study of the Political Sciences in Columbia College," *International Review* 12 (1882): 348.

5. Hoxie et al., *A History of the Faculty of Political Science*, 305–6.

6. Anna Haddow, *Political Science in American Colleges and Universities, 1636–1900* (New York: D. Appleton-Century Company, 1939), 175.

7. Hans J. Morgenthau, *Scientific Man vs. Power Politics* (Chicago: University of Chicago Press, 1946).

8. Barrington Moore, Jr., "The New Scholasticism and the Study of Politics," *World Politics* 6 (1953): 122–38.

9. Ernest Baker, *The Study of Political Science and Its Relation to Cognate Studies* (Cambridge: The University Press, 1929), 25–26.

10. Cf. below, pp. 269 ff, the comment on the changing perspectives of political science. The views, expressed here necessarily in an aphoristic form, develop further what was said in *Scientific Man vs. Power Politics*, 166, 167.

11. For an elaboration of this theme, see *Scientific Man vs. Power Politics*, 155 ff; *Politics Among Nations*, 2nd ed. (New York: Alfred A. Knopf, 1954), 80 ff.

12. Cf. on this general problem the discussion on values in the social sciences in *America* 92, (October 9 and 30, 1954).

13. Cf. my "Area Studies and the Study of International Relations," *International Social Science Bulletin* 4 (1952): 654–55.

14. Cf. W. A. Robson, *The University Teaching of Social Sciences: Political Science* (Paris: Unesco, 1954), 17, 63.

15. Cf. Alfred Cobban's important article, "The Decline of Political Theory," *Political Science Quarterly* 68 (1953): 321–32.

16. Cf. the important, but largely neglected monograph by Frederick Watkins, *The State as a Concept of Political Science* (New York and London: Harper and Brothers, 1934), esp. 81 ff.

CHAPTER 13

History and Diplomacy as Viewed by a Diplomatist

George F. Kennan

While our subject is the very broad one of "History and Diplomacy," I thought I would narrow it somewhat and attempt merely to describe something of the aspect in which diplomatic history presents itself to a diplomatist who has turned late in life to the study and writing of history.[1] In doing so, I hope that I have not taken too great a liberty with the subject our hosts had in mind.

I must first offer the usual disclaimer about generalizations—in this instance, of course, with regard to that race of being which goes by the name of diplomatist. There are all shapes and sizes of people, today, within the increasingly generous and hazy delimitations of this profession. I naturally cannot pretend to speak for all of them. But I believe that what I am about to say would meet with understanding on the part of most of those who have had their noses rubbed for long in the classic and central diplomatic function, which is the wearisome duty of negotiating and mediating between governments with conflicting interests—and that this would be true not only of those who are our contemporaries but also of a long succession of diplomatic representatives stretching back into history at least as far as the Venetians. Prior to that, I gather, very few people were ever saddled with the necessity of practicing this thankless, disillusioning, and physically exhausting profession as a permanent and regular livelihood.

Diplomatic history is, of course, only one phase of political history generally. It is a part of the study of man in his behavior as a political animal; and it concerns itself with what occurs at that particular point of friction where the activity of one sovereign political authority rubs and grates on that of another.

It is, of course, the element of *sovereignty* on both sides that gives to the contact at this point that peculiar delicacy, that charged, explosive quality, that final unpredictability by which it is distinguished. All other human contacts, it seems, take place within the limits of some recognized framework of obligation, supported by some sort of physical sanction. There is always, at least in theory, some rule or some higher authority to which appeal may be taken. But the sovereign national state, this child of the modern age, notwithstanding the mantle of nebulous moral obligation in which it likes to wrap itself, still recognizes in the crucial moments of its own destiny no law but that of its own egoism—no higher focus of obligation, no overriding ethical code. I am often accused of approving this state of affairs because I insist on the recognition of its reality. Actually, I think, no one could be more sadly conscious than is the professional diplomatist of the primitiveness, the anarchism, the intrinsic absurdity of the modern concept of sovereignty. Could anything be more absurd than a world divided into several dozens of large secular societies, each devoted to the cultivation of the myth of its own overriding importance and virtue, of the sacrosanctity of its own unlimited independence? A thousand times right are the enthusiasts of world government in their protest against the philosophic childishness of this concept, however many times wrong they may be in their ideas as to how it might be corrected. But the diplomatist, as people frequently forget, is the servant of this system of national states; it is precisely to the working of this imperfect mechanism that his efforts are dedicated. He is professionally condemned to tinker with its ill-designed parts like a mechanic with a badly built and decrepit car, aware that his function is not to question the design or to grumble over the decrepitude, but to keep the confounded contraption running, some way or other.

When, therefore, the diplomatist thinks about diplomatic history, his thoughts turn in the first instance to the nature and personality of the sovereign state. He knows this in part, of course, from the example of the governments with which he has been obliged to deal as a foreign representative. But he knows it better still from his intimacy with his own government. The personality of his own government presses itself upon him over the course of the years with a great vividness, with a sort of inexorable and commanding finality. It is the primary, overriding, inalterable reality of his professional world. And he is often moved to reflect on the extraordinary nature of this governmental personality: on its imperious authoritarianism toward its servants; its indomitable self-righteousness; its smugness and self-centeredness; its infuriating air of optimism and unconcern; its preposterous claim to infallibility; its frequent impoliteness; its stubborn and impudent silences; its insistence on the right not to answer letters; its bland assumption that because it has not made up its mind, reality should be expected to stand still until it does. And when the diplomatist, saturated as he is with the consciousness of this personality, then chances to pick up a book about diplomatic history, or to thumb through old dispatches in some dusty Foreign Office archives, he soon observes, not without a touch of exquisite intellectual pleasure, that it is not only his own government and not only governments in his own age that are this way; but that governments have been this way for a long time in the past, throughout, in fact, the entire range of history of the national state.

Realizing this, the diplomatist is moved, first, to marvel that a number of institutional personalities so difficult, so impossible by every normal criterion of social behavior, so outrageous in all respects, should have been able to live side by side in the same world and to deal with each other as long as they have, without even a larger number of conflicts and catastrophes. But secondly, he would have to be very uncurious indeed if he failed to inquire what it is, in the experience of being sovereign, that makes governments behave the way they do. And in this way he soon finds himself led unerringly to the classical problems of political science: to the inquiry as to how men tend to behave in the exercise of governmental power, and why they behave just this way.

Now I cannot attempt to generalize about the political philosophy of the devotees of my former profession. There is probably not much more agreement among them than there is among the rest of us on these questions that have divided the contemplative portion of mankind since the days of Plato and Aristotle.

But the diplomatic representative is made aware at every point of one curious feature of the sovereign government: and that is the duality of its motivation as between national interest and party interest. I have often found in my friends among the enthusiasts for universal international organization what seems to be a somewhat naïve view of the nature of the governmental voice in world affairs. These people assume that when a government speaks its word or casts its vote in an international forum, what one hears is the genuine expression of the aspirations of the people for whom it speaks. Now that may conceivably be the case and sometimes is; but it is not necessarily so; and it is rarely entirely so—for the following reason. It is clear that every government represents only the momentary product of the never-ending competition for political power within the respective national framework. In the most direct sense, therefore, it speaks only for a portion of the nation: for one political faction or coalition of factions. There is always another portion of the nation that is in opposition to it and either challenges its right to speak for the nation as a whole or accepts it only grudgingly and unhappily. This is true, in one version or another, whether the country's political life operates on the principle of parliamentary representation or whether it is based on some form of authoritarianism.

Yet it would be wrong to jump to the other extreme and to assume that the voices of governments, as heard on the international forums, reflect exclusively domestic-partisan interests. The interests of every political regime will be found to be bound up with, and in a certain area identical with, the interests and fortunes of the nation as a whole.

What emerges, therefore, from the hopper of the political process in each country and proceeds to speak for the country in international affairs is always to some degree a corrupted voice—in part the expression of national interests or aspirations, as seen by those momentarily entrusted with their definition and manifestation, but also partly the expression of the desire of one group of men to retain the power they already enjoy and to defend their position against their competitors within the national framework. And the diplomatist sees that there is very often a conflict between these two elements of motivation, and that the men who write his instructions and define the governmental position he must represent are torn, in conscience and interest, between the one and the other. He sees that in the great dramatic moments of history—especially when danger presents itself in the purely physical and external form, as when war threatens or already exists—the domestic political competition is, by common consent, thrust somewhat into the background, and statesmen even find it possible to think almost exclusively, for a time, in terms of the interests of the nation as a whole.

But he also sees that in the long dull intervals between these dramatic moments, in those prosaic reaches of everyday life where the element of danger is more remote and more subtle and often not entirely external—in these times the primacy of domestic policy comes into its own and the voices that resound on the forums of international intercourse are more apt to be the voices of internal factions, intent on their competition with other factions within the given country, saying and doing on the international plane those things which, in their judgment, are most likely to promote their political prospects at home.

And this is a great pity; because it is precisely in these long, dull periods of peace that the most decisive things really happen. It is in these times that the predicaments and dilemmas are created, from which the wars and catastrophes then flow. Yet people are rarely aware of this at the moment. And by the time circumstances have developed to a point of drama and danger and simplification at which people realize that solemn issues, overriding the interests of this generation alone and beshaming the ambitions of any single political faction, are at stake, it is usually far too late for any remedy. And then all the idealism, all the capacity for sacrifice, all the comradeship and nobility of spirit are poured out—alas—into the negative undertaking of war—an undertaking which people like to picture to themselves at the moment as conducive to some glorious end; and one which may indeed, in certain circumstances, be preferable to its immediate alternatives; but one which represents in reality a physical and emotional debauch from which every people emerges in some respects poorer and unhappier, its strength and substance in some degree wasted, its youth brutalized, its social fabric weakened, its future mortgaged by the wastage of so much young blood, the exhaustion of so many hopes and energies, and the inevitable abuse practiced on the habits of its life. Into this sad and depressing exercise—the product of man's failures rather than his successes—are invariably poured his highest capacities, the ultimate of what he can muster in the way of unselfishness, heroism, and devotion. But in the long period between wars, when there is opportunity not only to avoid further debauches of this nature but also to do things that might promote the beauty and health of human existence and bring men closer to a situation where they could contemplate the future of the race with feelings other than horror and dismay—during these times, selfishness and short-sightedness again ride supreme; the primacy of foreign policy is forgotten; and the microphone for international discussion is returned to those who are interested in it only incidentally as a means of improving their competitive fortunes at home.

In this way international affairs become once more a fumbling encounter among the distracted and the semi-blind—an absent-minded Donnybrook among participants each of whom is preoccupied with his own parochial problems and has something less than half an eye for this ulterior involvement.

I must confess that the professional diplomatist is often possessed by a congenital aversion to the phenomenon of domestic-political competition. He sees it, everywhere, as a seething cauldron in which there rises to the surface, by the law of averages, a certain mutation of the human species. And while this mutation differs somewhat in every country, depending on the nature and tradition of government, the diplomatist takes a dim view of it everywhere. Too often, it appears to him as the distillation of all that in human nature which is most extroverted, most thick-skinned, most pushing, most preoccupied with the present, least given to a sense of historical proportion, least inclined to be animated by any deeper and more subtle philosophy of human affairs, and—by that same token—least inclined to look deeply into the realities of international life, to comprehend the relativity of all national virtues, and to grasp the need for tolerance, forbearance, dignity, generosity, and integrity in the dealings between states. There are, of course, always the great and wonderful exceptions; we have them today—we have had them in the past. Without their efforts, God knows where we should now be. But by and large the diplomatist, sensitive as he is to the immense demands that modern scientific advance has placed on man's ability to adjust international differences, looks with misgiving to the domestic-political personality in its confrontation with the problems of international life. He has little confidence in its vision or disinterestedness, little tolerance for its egotism, its ambition, its thirst for popularity, its taste for the phrase and the cliché. The diplomatist inclines, I fear, to the view that only those men are truly adequate to the responsibilities of statesmanship who do not seek them but come to them reluctantly, from a sense of duty, and with great distaste.

Let me be quite plain. It is not the humdrum ranges of the domestic-political process to which these feelings relate. Most diplomatists understand very well, I think, the legitimacy and indispensability of the political profession—the inalterable necessity of reconciling a thousand stubborn and conflicting interests at the grass roots. They recognize the immense qualities of common sense, patience, and insight that go into this process. It is not the modest workhorses of politics to whom the diplomatic skepticism relates; on the contrary, the diplomatist feels a certain affinity to them; for their task resembles, in its thanklessness and strenuousness, his own. His suspicion and dislike are reserved for the more pompous and ruthless and successful of the political fraternity: for the bombast, the demagogue, the jingo, the poseur, the man touched with the intoxication of power, the man for whom the issues at stake in his country's relations with the outside world are means to a personal end. And too often it seems, to one looking at it from an embassy in a foreign capital, that such are the natures bound by the law of averages to be propelled most often to the surface in the uninhibited workings of political competition.

Out of such reflections are born, I think, the weary skepticism that characterizes the more experienced ranges of the diplomatic profession in their approach to diplomatic history. The professional sees the relations between governments as largely the product of the follies and ambitions and brutalities of that minority of the human race which is always attracted by the possibility of exercising power over the remainder of it in whatever political framework the age provides. He sees the task of diplomacy as essentially a menial one, consisting of hovering around the fringes of a process one is powerless to control, tidying up the messes other people have made, attempting to keep small disasters from turning into big ones, moderating the passions of governments and of opinionated individuals, and attempting to transmit to one's own government the unwelcome image of the outside world—but always, mark you, only in discreet, moderate doses, bearing in mind the lowliness of the diplomatic estate in the general governmental order—bearing in mind that the truth about external reality will never be wholly compatible with the internal ideological fictions which the national state engenders and by which it lives.

The diplomatist believes deeply in the importance and necessity of his menial function. He harbors the desperate, instinctive conviction that if he were not there to perform it, things would be much worse. And he cherishes this conviction with double intensity, because he is so lonely in it. He knows that he has little possibility of ever making his usefulness widely comprehensible to the people he serves. He knows that he could win much greater approval and popularity, at any given moment, by a liberal measure of charlatanism: by abusing the responsibilities he bears, by exploiting the ignorance and prejudice of others, by inflaming rather than assuaging the passions of men and then making himself the mouthpiece of those passions. But this, happily, is rarely—almost never—his nature. It goes against the grain of the inner discipline that his profession exerts.

As one who is no longer a member of the diplomatic fraternity, I may perhaps be permitted to say that in its obscure and tireless activity and in the modest, almost despairing view that most of its devotees take of their efforts and achievements, there is a surprising measure of real idealism, and sometimes even of nobility. But do not look to the diplomatist for any verbal acknowledgement of this idealism, for any belief in human perfectibility, for any optimistic philosophy of public affairs. The professional diplomatist is, after all, only a species of physician. He has, like all physicians, a shabby and irritating group of patients: violent, headstrong, frivolous, unreasonable. He will go on treating them as long as he is permitted to, saving them from such of their follies as he can, patching up the damages done by those follies from which he could not save them. He will do this because it is his professional nature to do it, and because he probably loves these shabby patients in his heart even while he despairs of them. But do not ask him to enthuse about them, to idealize them, or to expect them to change. Whether he approaches them from the vantage point of a diplomatic chancery abroad or from the standpoint of a late and poorly baptized historian, the difficulty is the same. He has seen them too much. He knows them too well.

Notes

Reprinted from *The Review of Politics* 18, no. 2 (April 1956): 170–77.

1. This paper was presented to the meeting of the American Historical Association in Washington, D.C., December 29, 1955.

CHAPTER 14

The Role of the Learned Man in Government

PAUL H. NITZE

In the context of government, what do we mean by the phrase "a learned man"?[1] I take it we can mean a variety of things. On the one hand, we can have in mind the specialist, the expert, the man with an intensive and specialized background in a particular field of knowledge. On the other hand, we can have in mind the man with general wisdom, with that feeling for the past and the future which enriches a sense for the present, and with that appreciation for wider loyalties which deepens patriotism to one's country and finds bonds between it and Western culture and links with the universal aspirations of mankind.

And when we refer to such a learned man—whether the expert or the man of generalized wisdom—in government, we can think of him in various roles. We can think of him as an advisor. We can think of him as a responsible official politically accountable for his actions. We can think of him in one or the other branch of government, in the judiciary, in the legislature, or in the executive. And if he is in the executive branch we can think of him as a diplomat, a soldier, a civil servant with general administrative duties or as an elected or politically appointed official with full political accountability.

Now what are the issues which arise with respect to the learned man in government? I propose to discuss two of them. The first question is that of the desirability of having learned men in government. In what circumstances can they play a useful role? In what circumstances are they inadequate or misplaced?

The second and directly related question is that of the special privileges or exemptions which it is advisable or inadvisable to give to the learned man to get the most out of what he has to contribute and to protect him from direct political assault. These are issues which are not often objectively debated. Generally the issue gets itself posed in excessively simple terms as a polemic for or against egg-heads. In academic circles and in most of the responsible press, the usual position is that all men good and true should fight against the anti-intellectual currents of our time and protect the man of learning from the vulgar pressures of public opinion and the corrupting influences of politics. I propose that there is more to the issue than that.

Let us deal first with the question of the expert. There can be no doubt that in a business as complex as that of government in today's world the expert is indispensable. No one would think of conducting government today without the service of expert specialists in everything from accounting, agronomy, astronomy, and ballistics through the alphabet to experts in the making of wood pulp and in the care and feeding of zebras.

During the war I was for a time in charge of the overseas development and procurement of strategic materials for the war production effort. We had a team of some thousand geologists, mining engineers; experts in the growing of rubber, of sisal, and of chinchona bark; and specialists in the procurement of what were called casings but were really sheep guts, dried Mexican prairie bones to be used in the manufacture of glue, pig bristles for paint brushes, and even dried cuttlefish bones for the grinding of precision lenses. The political ideas or policy orientation of such experts, when functioning in the government solely as experts, is of secondary importance. Their role is to give specialized advice on technical matters of fact. Their primary function does not include providing the answer to important "should" propositions—to propositions of political policy.

It happens that almost all mining engineers are not only Republicans but tend to be on the conservative side of Republican politics. I rather suspect that this comes about because, in so speculative a business as that of finding and developing underground mineral resources, there is a very real need for careful and conservative patterns of action. In any case, almost all the mining engineers engaged in strategic materials work during the war were Republicans. Our immediate boss during those years was Vice President Henry Wallace who was then far over on the left wing of the Democratic party. He was somewhat worried about the politically conservative views of his mining engineers and they were somewhat concerned by what they considered to be their boss's radical political position. But the technical work went on with no real friction. Both sides agreed that there was a war to be won and that expert technical work could help win it.

Subsequently, in the 1949–1950 period, a more serious issue arose over the testing of a thermonuclear weapon. Dr. Oppenheimer was Chairman of the General Advisory Committee to the Atomic Energy Commission and also served from time to time as a consultant to the State Department. When the question arose as to whether or not to proceed with a test of a thermonuclear weapon, it was our view in the State Department that Dr. Robert Oppenheimer was to be considered an expert on scientific matters, not an expert on political or military matters. We sought and used his advice on judgments of scientific fact. We had no scruple whatsoever in ignoring his views on general policy. We saw no reason why he should not have views on political matters. Every expert, in addition to being an expert in his particular field, is as entitled to political views as any other citizen. But, as we saw it, specialized knowledge in one field does not lead to a presumption of superior wisdom in all other fields. Furthermore, the responsibility for the political decisions involved in proceeding or not proceeding with a thermonuclear test was that of the President, advised by his Secretaries of State and Defense, and not the responsibility of Oppenheimer or any committee of atomic scientists. Acheson disagreed with Dr. Oppenheimer's political judgments and recommended a course of action to the President contrary to the one recommended by the scientists. It never occurred to us, however, to be annoyed by Dr. Oppenheimer's political views or to think that he should be penalized for them. In our view his responsibilities did not include political judgments of the kind involved in that particular decision. Inasmuch as we did not propose to be guided by his political views we felt we could avail ourselves of his undoubted scientific expertise while ignoring those of his recommendations which seemed to be based on political rather than scientific considerations.

The point about the expert is that the politically important decisions should be, and generally are, taken with the technical advice of experts, where technical matters are significant factors, but on the authority and final judgment of men with political responsibility. And success in carrying political responsibility usually calls for general wisdom more than it calls for specialized knowledge. Specialized knowledge and general wisdom are not necessarily in conflict. They are, however, not the same thing; and are not always to be found together in the same man.

Our analysis has now brought us around to a consideration of the role of the man of general wisdom in government and his relationship to political responsibility.

First, let me say a few words in comment on the distinctive contribution which the learned man of general wisdom can bring to government. In the introductory paragraph to this paper I suggested three aspects of that contribution. The first aspect is suggested by the word "general," a willingness and an ability to concern himself with the full range of implications and considerations which bear on a decision.

A second quality of the learned man is that of being able to relate the past and the future to the present—the ability, on the one hand, to tap the wisdom of the past and give it continuity into the present, and, on the other hand, to sense the possibilities and the needs of the future as they emerge from the developing present. Perhaps this quality is more directly associable with outstanding leadership, the leadership of a Churchill or a Lincoln, than with learning as such. I prefer to think, however, that it is not unconnected with humanistic learning, particularly with care for and understanding of history.

A third quality associated with the learned man of general wisdom is that appreciation for wider loyalties which deepens patriotism to one's country and finds bonds between it and Western culture and links with the universal aspirations of mankind. I am reminded of a marginal note in one of the books in John Adams' library in which he asks himself the following question: "In truth what is comprehended in the spirit of patriotism?" He answers: "Piety or the love and fear of God; general benevolence to mankind; a particular attachment to our own country; a zeal to promote its happiness by reforming its morals, increasing its knowledge, promoting its agriculture, commerce and manufactures, improving its constitution, and securing its liberties; and all this without the prejudices of individuals or parties or factions, without fear, favor or affection." Not only do men exist in our government who have precisely the zeal that John Adams described but they are reasonably numerous. They constitute the hard core of that selfless band of civil servants without whom the great and constructive projects carried forward by our government since the war could not have been executed. They have, when not suppressed by more narrowly chauvinistic elements, given to our policy a breadth and a humanity the effects of which have even yet not been entirely lost.

But, if so many good things can be said about the learned man, the man of general wisdom, in government, why is there an issue? Why can't one take the simple course of saying all power to the egg-heads, down with the anti-intellectuals? Why should we have certain reservations?

I think the answer is to be found in two related circumstances. The first is that the learned man, or at least the man whose orientation is primarily analytical or academic, finds it difficult to act resolutely within the limits prescribed by the real situation with which, in the realm of government, he is always faced, and finding it difficult he tends to have a distaste for full political responsibility. The second circumstance is that, not desiring to accept full political responsibility, he nevertheless strives for a free and controlling hand in the guidance of those matters on which his interest focuses. The result is a tendency toward separating responsibility from power, and power from responsibility.

Let us expand somewhat upon these thoughts. I take it that the analytic and academic approach to policy problems is apt to exhibit two tendencies: the first is a tendency toward abstraction and generalization; the second is a tendency to emphasize historical analogies. These tendencies have their virtues but also have shortcomings which are the obverse of those virtues.

I recall Acheson's instructions to us in the days when George Kennan, and then I, were directing the Policy Planning job in the State Department. Acheson said he wanted from us continuous and forthright advice as to the courses of United States governmental action in international affairs which in our judgment would best serve the interests of the United States without regard to the domestic acceptability of those courses of action or the feasibility of securing Congressional support for them. He said that Truman, with his, Acheson's advice and that of others whose judgment he respected, would take the responsibility for adjusting, modifying, and compromising the suggested courses of action to bring them into accord with the realities of the domestic political scene. But he and Truman did not want that job done twice. They did not want a recommended course of action to be watered down because of domestic political considerations at several different levels. They wanted to have a clear idea themselves as to what compromises were being made and for what reasons. The staff work which we undertook was therefore abstracted from the reality of the political scene by the elimination of one important category of real consideration—domestic political factors. Even within the remaining field the use of simplifying generalizations and abstractions was necessary in order to compress the vast complex of relevant data into a manageable analytic framework. Generalization is necessary and useful. Without it staff work cannot be done. But its product is essentially staff work. The final decision must be taken by someone prepared to take all the real factors into consideration and to breathe completeness and life back into otherwise arid analytic generalizations.

Similar considerations apply to the tendency of academically oriented advisors to hark back to the analogies of history. Historical analogies have great utility in illuminating complex situations and in helping one to sort out the significant from the merely striking. But action based too closely on historical analogies is apt to be sterile and unimaginative.

The other day I came across a passage in Maurice Paléologue's memoirs in which he quotes a comment Delcassé, the French Foreign Minister, made to him in 1904. Paléologue had just read him a passage from a Polish student of Russian history who drew an analogy between recurrent Russian behavior and that of an avalanche. Delcassé snapped back at him:

> Why do you make me read such stuff? . . . You know I don't consider history of any practical use. . . . All historians are false guides because they are out of touch with reality, or rather, because they see it *a posteriori*, in retrospect, after events have happened and it is no longer possible to change their course. . . . It is just the opposite for the statesman: he sees events *on their way*, with all the risks, openings, possibilities and opportunities for skillful handling which they offer. . . . Can you see me consulting a history book in a crisis? Not I! At such moments what counts most is flair, a cool head, courage, resolution and nimble wits. . . . Beware of history, my dear Paléologue!

Paléologue, however, concluded his report of Delcassé's reaction with the following comments: "All the same, Waliszewski's ominous prediction seemed to have got home; twice did he mutter in gloomy tones: *Beware of the avalanche! . . . Beware of the avalanche!* Then with an irritable frown, he turned to the business of the day."[2]

I can remember occasions on which Acheson was similarly dubious as to the help which more academically or analytically minded men could give him in enabling him better to handle the very real and concrete problems and opportunities which faced him. It is reported that today Dulles says that he would welcome assistance from those who have more knowledge of and experience with the foreign policy problems which the world now faces than he has, but he asks where are there such people.

We are faced then with a possible gulf between the learned expert and the man carrying political responsibility. George Kennan has given expression to the effect which this gulf can have upon the point of view of a trained diplomat. In a paper[3] presented before the American Historical Association in December 1955, he compares the trained diplomat to a mechanic condemned to tinker with a badly designed car or to a physician with a shabby and irritating group of patients. He will go on treating them as long as he is permitted to, saving them from such of their follies as he can, patching up the damages done by those follies from which he cannot save them.

Kennan further comments that the professional sees the relations between governments as largely the product of the follies and ambitions and brutalities of that minority of the human race which is always attracted by the possibility of exercising power over the remainder of it, in whatever political framework the age provides. He sees the task of the trained diplomat as essentially that of hovering around the fringes of a process he is powerless to control and of which he deeply disapproves. The picture that he paints of the professional is that of a hopeless man dedicated to a menial task.

Contrast this with the picture given by Acheson in a letter discussing the reasons why young men might be encouraged to choose a career in government service.

And yet I would be eager to see them [young, and, also, old men of quality] steered toward a career, perhaps a life, of public service, as some of their ancestors were. Why? Not because I see the gleam of a halo forming about their heads, . . . but because there is no better or fuller life for a man of spirit. The old Greek conception of happiness is relevant here: 'The exercise of vital powers along lines of excellence, in a life affording them scope.'

This is the Geiger-counter which tells us where to dig. It explains also why to everyone who has ever experienced it the return from public life to private life leaves one feeling flat and empty. Contented, interested, busy— yes. But exhilarated—no. For one has left a life affording scope for the exercise of vital powers along lines of excellence. Not the only one, I am sure. Undoubtedly Einstein, Michelangelo, Savonarola, Shakespeare, and others could give testimony on other lives. But outside of aesthetics and teaching—religion belongs to both—the requirement of 'scope' is hard to come by in this age, outside of public life. . . . It gives a feeling of zest, a sense that the only limitation upon the exercise of all one's vital powers is one's capacity. . . .

Today, more than ever before, the prize of the general is not a bigger tent, but command. The managers of industry and finance have the bigger tents; but command rests with government. Command, or, if one prefers, supreme leadership, demands and gives scope for the exercise of every vital power a man has in the direction of excellence.

How, then, does one present to the youth a life of public service? Not, I am sure, as an evangelist appealing to the young squires to turn their backs on the world and dedicate themselves to a secular order for ministering to the peasants. . . . Rather, I think, one educates them to know the world in which they live, to understand that government will go on whether they take part in it or not, that command is too important to be entrusted to the ignorant, even though they may be well-meaning and dedicated, and to an understanding of the good life, of happiness as the Greeks saw it, of the joy of exercising vital powers in a life affording them scope, of the limitless scope of governmental responsibilities. In addition, they might learn, as an authority on the process of revolution has pointed out, that 'Brave men are not uncommon in any system, but there is a tendency in most systems to make courage and a disciplined openness of mind to the significant facts mutually exclusive. This is the immediate cause of the downfall of every ruling class that ever falls.'"[4]

Here we have two points of view. The one looks upon the politically responsible process as being largely reserved to the follies of the ambitious and the brutal. The other looks upon the politically responsible process as being the arena in which human excellence can have scope for its full development.

In part these contrasting views reflect differences in the character of the two men. They, also, derive from differences in temperament, sensibility, and outlook. What to one is an opportunity for the display of courage and excellence, oppresses the other as being tainted with ambition and brutality. A task which one welcomes as offering a personal opportunity, the other looks upon as a duty which he must perform despite his distaste for it.

But over and beyond these indications of a difference in character is a difference in the situation in which they found themselves, the roles which they were called upon to fill in government. One was Secretary of State under a President whose complete confidence he enjoyed. He was, thus, able to play a full political role with the essential elements of command. The other functioned as a staff officer called upon for specialized knowledge and advice in a limited though vital field—the power of decision being reserved to others.

The relationship between the specialist and the responsible wielders of political authority in government is always somewhat awkward. The specialist is asked to keep his eyes focused on fact, to avert them from partisanship, special interest, and immediate political pressures. The wielder of political authority must somehow deal with, compromise, and manage just these interests and pressures and do so from a position of party responsibility. Various techniques must therefore be worked out to enable each group to relate itself to the others.

In the judicial branch of the government we feel the need for men of general wisdom who will take into consideration the wider implications of their decisions but who are insulated from the full heat of the immediate political turmoil. We protect our judges from arbitrary political pressure by giving them long or life tenure, removable only by impeachment proceedings. But we expect from them a corresponding restraint in their political conduct. We expect them to forego partisanship, to refrain from making political speeches, to keep above political intrigue. Even in his private life we expect the judge to be a segregated man.

Among our military men the tradition has been to keep the military out of politics and politics out of the military. The Joint Chiefs of Staff attempt to advise the President and his civilian advisor from the purely military point of view. In a democratic society it is of the utmost importance that domestic politics and military considerations be kept in as distinct compartments as possible.

But consider the case of General MacArthur. Here we have a man of the highest competence in his particular field who had perhaps an even lower opinion of the political leadership under which he was carrying out his military responsibilities than that expressed by George Kennan. General MacArthur frowned upon any communication or contact between his subordinate officers and the executive branch of the government in Washington. He himself refused to go near Washington while Roosevelt or Truman remained in office. He carried to an extreme the thesis that the great specialist and expert is entitled, when serving his government, to a complete exemption from domestic political responsibility and even from contact with those who happen to be carrying the burden of executive leadership.

Many of the scientists would like to carve out a similar area where they can carry out what they consider to be in the national interest in the realm of science without political interference. George Kennan would exempt, as far as may be possible, the field of diplomacy from direct political interference and turn it over to the substantial control of the trained diplomatic experts.

At one time it was proposed by a very able group of physical and social scientists that a headquarters for the conduct of the cold war be set up in Washington. It would be unpublicized, manned by experts, and would issue instructions to the Secretary of State, the Secretary of Defense, our economic agencies, the Voice of America, and even to the military. It would thus give expert coordination and direction to our struggle with the communists free from the handicap of political accountability. It seemed to me at the time that this was the ultimate *reducito ad absurdum* of the tendency of our experts to attempt to create walled-off and exempted centers of specialized power and authority separated from political responsibility and accountability. It seemed to me a project to be fought with all the energies at one's command. What survived of this project was the Psychological Strategy Board which subsequently became the Operations Coordination Board. But both of these boards as finally established were firmly subordinated to politically accountable direction in the person of the Under Secretary of State.

It is conceivable, had the right experts been chosen and given fuller powers than they were given, that they could have done a better job than has in fact been done. But who is to assure that the right and not the wrong experts are chosen? And are those who have to produce the necessary resources, to provide the military man power, and who have to bear the ultimate risks, to have no voice in the policies decided upon? In a democratic society how does one assure that there is consent for the policies adopted unless the responsible officials are politically accountable?

The Kennans, the MacArthurs, and the Oppenheimers may well be more competent in their chosen fields than are those who are politically accountable. The point is that one group of men is politically accountable—the other not.

Furthermore, a special effort is required for the expert to abandon concentration upon his chosen field and broaden his interests and temper his judgments to that humanity which is necessary to deal successfully with politics in a democracy.

Dr. Robert Elliot Fitch deals with one aspect of this as it bears upon the scientist:

> The scientist is prone to fall into three errors with reference to public affairs. He may, like the mediaeval anchorite, withdraw from society by living in the cell which is his laboratory. Or, emerging from his cell, with its austere discipline and chaste aspirations, he will be profoundly shocked to see the way his truth and power are prostituted to ends with which he cannot become reconciled. He will then do like all pietists before him: propose simple solutions to complex problems, see all issues naïvely and out of context, and make absolute moral judgments where the need is for shrewd compromise.
>
> The third possibility is that, being vain even as other men are vain, he will accept the inducements that are offered to him from every hand, will bestow an indiscriminate blessing upon whatever enterprise will ensure him the prestige and perquisite which he feels are his due.
>
> There are ways that do not lead to such dead ends for the scientist, but they are difficult ways. One is the way of a Conant or a Killian: deliberately to enter into the experiences and to assume the responsibilities and the disciplines that have to do with the art of human relations. The product of

this dual discipline, in the scientist-statesman, can be one of our most valuable public servants in times like this.

For those who do not have a genius for the double task, there is another choice. This is simply to put their truth and their power in the service of a democracy instead of in the service of a tyranny. In a free society the scientist will play his role as citizen like anyone else. The new priest like the old priest will have to learn that, no matter how potent the mana that he commands, no matter how great his power and his truth, he is not vested with any peculiar authority to decide on its uses. In a democracy, that authority resides in all persons alike.[5]

A question, however, can be asked about the last sentence of this quotation from Dr. Fitch's views. It is not clear that in a democracy effective authority resides in all persons alike.

The other day an astute observer commented on the viewpoint of Nehru. Someone had said that Nehru is sympathetic to American democracy. This observer suggested that a distinction should be made between Nehru's view of American political institutions, its economic system, and its cultural democracy. He suggested that Nehru approved our democratic political institutions, that he believed we just did not understand economic democracy which, in his opinion, required far more social orientation and governmental direction, but that he positively disapproved of what he understood to be our democratic culture. As he understands American culture, it comes up from below and amounts to a vulgarization of all values. Nehru is obviously wrong about American culture. The learned and the wise do have a special role in developing, in preserving and in propagating our cultural values. But they do it not through the coercive power of the state. They do it by the accountable process of persuasion and consent.

Similarly our political leaders have a special share in political authority. But theirs is an accountable authority, not an arbitrary authority.

I have dealt at length with the role of the specialist, the learned man separated from, or exempted from, political authority and accountability. But learning and wisdom are not the monopoly of those so exempted. The hope of the democratic system depends upon the opposite proposition—the proposition that men of general wisdom will in fact be selected to carry political responsibility and accountability.

It undoubtedly has been true that in the great days of American political development we have had men of learning and of general wisdom in the politically important offices. During the days of Washington, of Benjamin Franklin, of Adams, of Jefferson, of Madison, I can hardly imagine that the issue could have arisen as to the relation between the man of political responsibility and the man of wisdom. They obviously went hand in hand.

In the post–Civil War era they quite clearly did not go hand in hand. *The Education of Henry Adams* and Henry Adams' *Democracy* give one an insight into the frustration felt by a learned man, anxious to play a role in government but unable to stomach the compromises that the politics of the day made mandatory.

I am reminded of the testimony of Albert Speer, the Nazi Minister of War Production, when we interrogated him at the end of the war in Europe. Speer, who had been an architect before the war, had demonstrated a phenomenal versatility and power of mind in developing and maintaining German war production despite the force of allied bombing and the stupidities of Hitler's interference. I have rarely met a more powerful intellect. We could not resist asking him how it had come about that he had worked with Hitler's gang and had let himself be associated with the inhumanities and the stupidities of which they were guilty. He said it was difficult for an outsider to put himself in the place of a man torn by loyalty to his country and a political climate in which survival and power and the possibility of making some order out of chaos could only be achieved by associating oneself with people and with action of which one disapproved.

The other option, the option of opposition or of non-involvement, the option of Adenauer during the Nazi days, of Henry Adams, or of Plato, is more congenial but it also can have its frustrations and its tragedy.

It cannot be the good fortune of all mankind to live in Athens under the leadership of a Pericles, in Florence under the Medici, in the United States under a Washington or a Lincoln. Nor is it the usual fate of mankind to live under a Cleon, a Nero, a Stalin, or a Hitler and thus have an unambiguous case for withdrawal from government or opposition to it. The usual case is a mixed one in which the task of the learned man, the man of general wisdom and with a taste for politics, is to manage, to deal with, to nudge the existing situation toward the best that is within the realm of the politically possible, to find such scope as he can for his courage, his fortitude, and his willingness to view facts with an open mind. When given half a chance the combination of courage and an open mind can do wonders. This suggests a final quotation from Delcassé: "Take my word for it, *cher ami,* courage is the cleverest thing in the world."[6]

NOTES

Reprinted from *The Review of Politics* 20, no. 3 (July 1958): 275–88.

1. This article was originally delivered as a speech to the Catholic Commission on Intellectual and Cultural Affairs, Washington, D.C., April 26, 1958.

2. Maurice Paléologue, *Three Critical Years: 1904–05–06* (New York, 1957), 59.

3. Printed in *The Review of Politics* 18, no. 2 (April 1956): 170–77. [Chapter 13 in this volume. Ed.]

4. This letter was quoted by James Reston in the *New York Times,* February 2, 1958.

5. Robert Elliot Fitch, "The Scientist as Priest and Savior," *The Christian Century* 75 (March 26, 1958): 370.

6. Paléologue, *Three Critical Years: 1904–05–06,* 137.

Chapter 15

The Ethical Dimensions of Diplomacy

Kenneth W. Thompson

Ancient traditions have stressed the intervention of the gods and contemporary moralists picture God as being on their side in international conflicts. Pharisaism, Manichaeism, and the morality of progress are other distortions of political ethics. The first step in a more profound understanding of the ethical dimension of diplomacy is a clear-eyed view of the good and evil in human nature informed by philosophy and history. However, differences exist among political realists and international lawyers who have examined human nature in these terms. Some emphasize the relevance of ethics for international politics while others question it. Democratic foreign policy poses special problems for those who discuss international morality. Such issues are resolved at least partly within the tradition of practical morality, which the article considers in conclusion.

William Graham Summer wrote: "The amount of superstition is not much changed, but it now attaches to politics, not to religion." In ancient societies, men called on the gods to rid their world of evil, conflict, and suffering. If war persisted, they asked the gods to reward their side with victory. What men in their frailty could not accomplish, the gods in their mercy would provide. They would protect the weak and reward virtue. If men could not defend justice in the social order, the gods would assure that justice was done. From ancient tribal deities to the gods who presided over the knights of the round table, their task ultimately was to smooth out the troubled path along which heroic men had to walk.

An opposing view of morality is rooted in classical traditions and certain historic versions of the Judeo-Christian faith. Moralists, nationalists, and religiously oriented people are tempted to make a success story out of their faith. Yet no one, and least of all authentic religious leaders, can guarantee prosperity and success, even though spokesmen of some early religious movements in the colonies and thirteen states sought to demonstrate that outer signs of well-being pointed in the direction of inner virtue. Attacking this viewpoint, Reinhold Niebuhr wrote of two men, one who tithed from his youth and gained great wealth. That man explained his success as deriving from a lifelong observance of religious practices. The other man, Adam Denger, who employed the young Niebuhr in his grocery store in Lincoln, Illinois, generously extended credit to miners who had lost their jobs. However, the miners left Lincoln without paying their debts and their benefactor suffered bankruptcy. In her biography of Niebuhr, June Bingham writes: "Mr. Denger kept believing that God would protect him if he did what was right. But God let Adam Denger go bankrupt and his young assistant grew up to preach against sentimentality and reliance on special providence."[1] Niebuhr chose as his text the biblical passage: "For He makes his sun to rise on the evil and the good alike and sends rain on the just and the unjust." According to Niebuhr, it is a corruption of religion to hold out the promise that the good man or the virtuous nation will always triumph or that evil empires will be destroyed. Religious people too often are found lobbying in the courts of the Almighty proclaiming their goodness and offering their piety as proof that they deserve special favors. A more profound understanding of man and God would emphasize the tragic element in history. The unending process in diplomacy of balancing the forces of harmony and disharmony is at war with the notion that those who are good and virtuous are destined through some form of divine intervention to inherit prosperity and success.

A more contemporary version of the intrusion of false and superstitious notions about ethics and diplomacy is what Louis J. Halle has called "Pharisaism." He asserts that the posturing of those who claim to be more virtuous than their fellowmen is not true morality. In the parable of the pharisee and the publican (Luke 18:10–14), those who make ostentatious display of their morality, striking moralistic poses and pointing to the iniquity of others, are condemned for their false morality. Politicians and diplomats who are overwhelmingly concerned with the morality of others ought as a rule to be mistrusted. By their attitudes, they would have others believe they have achieved so complete a level of morality they are qualified to judge others. They depend not on the gods for their morality but on their own supposed moral perfection.

Another version of morality is that of Manichaeism which portrays the world in radical terms of absolute good and evil or right and wrong. Americans are predisposed to a form of Manichaeism by early childhood distinctions between good guys and bad guys or cops and robbers. The false logic of Manichaeism lies at the heart of every crusading ideology and of civilization's long record, ever since the wars of religion, of unspeakable brutalities of one people against another. In the end, Manichaeism becomes a negative morality based on punishment and retribution. According to the mythology of Manichaeism, a particular group or class is seen as a Satanic evil. For the Germans the Jews, for the Allies the Germans and Japanese, for the bourgeoisie the communists and for the communists the bourgeoisie are the one evil force in the world. Once that evil has been rooted out and eradicated, peace and harmony will prevail. Not by accident, Khomeini depicts the United States as the Great Satan in what is but the most recent form of Manichaeism. Those who belong to groups who for others personify evil may in the name of morality be chastised or destroyed in order that justice be done.

A final version of morality identifies the good with the changing and the novel and evil with past practices. Since the end of the Napoleonic Wars, ever larger groups of Western leaders have denounced diplomacy and international politics as an unhappy stage in the progress of mankind that was bound to disappear once the particular historical circumstances that gave rise to it had been transformed. European diplomacy was an archaism that history would eliminate when reason and morality prevailed. For some writers, a particular social evil caused the corruption of international society: colonies for Jeremy Bentham, trade barriers for Cobden and Proudhon, capitalism for Marx, and the absence of self-determination and self-government for liberals. For others, foreign relations themselves were the evil. It was Richard Cobden who declared: "At some future election, we may probably see the test 'no foreign politics' applied to those who offer to become the representatives of free constituencies."[2]

Following World War I, the Nye Committee in 1934–36 on behalf of the United States Senate investigated the role of certain financial and industrial interests suspected of having been responsible for the entry of the United States into that war. Not the requirements of the national interest but certain self-seeking groups who profited from the war had plotted the nation's involvement. A small band of manufacturers of war materiel and international bankers had lured us into war. According to the devil theory of war, a handful of munition makers were responsible. If the nation could rid itself of their conspiratorial and nefarious influence, peace would prevail.

In a similar vein, others saw in European diplomacy and power politics the cause of all conflict. In 1943, Secretary of State Cordell Hull on returning from the Moscow Conference, which prepared the way for the creation of the United Nations, proclaimed that the new international organization would lead to the end of power politics which had ravaged European society. Earlier President Woodrow Wilson, prematurely as history was to record, prophesied that the common interests of mankind were replacing national interests. In 1946, British Minister of State Philip Noel-Baker rose in the House of Commons to say that his government was "determined to use the institutions of the United Nations to kill power politics, in order that, by the methods of democracy, the will of the people shall prevail."[3]

The underlying premise of all these views is the conviction that a certain group or a particular social and international order are the evil forces which alone explain the immorality of diplomacy and politics. Along the pathway to a moral international order these evil forces will disappear. Once they are rooted out, an ethical international system will emerge and conflict will come to an end.

I. HUMAN NATURE AND DIPLOMACY

Opposed to the essentially utopian views of the several versions of morality and diplomacy discussed above is a fundamentally different conception of human nature and diplomacy. According to this perspective, human nature has not changed since the days of classical antiquity. Man is good and evil; his virtues and vices persist no less in a technologically advanced than a primitive society. Politics and diplomacy bring out the harshest side of man's nature though sometimes also the best. In ancient Greece, Thucydides whom Hobbes described as "the most Politick Historiographer that ever lived" wrote in the Melian dialogue of the clash between morality and power. Melos had remained neutral during the war between Sparta and Athens but the Athenians, during a long truce, confronted Melos with an expeditionary force and called on it to join the Athenian alliance or be exterminated. When the Melians resisted, Thucydides records the ensuing dialogue. The Athenians explain that justice depends upon the power to compel; the strong do what they have the power to do and the weak accept what they must. Even the gods will not help because they behave toward one another and toward men as the Athenians plan to behave toward Melos. The Athenians conclude: "It is a general and necessary law of nature to rule wherever one can. This is not a law we made ourselves, nor were we the first to act on it when it was made. We found it already in existence, and we shall leave it to exist forever among those who come after us." Melos resists and is destroyed.

Frederick the Great in his *Origin of the Bismarck Policy* or *The Hohenzollern Doctrine and Maxims,* written for his successor to the throne, summarizes his opinions on religion, morals, politics, and diplomacy by saying: "We monarchs take what we can, when we can, and we are never in the wrong, except when compelled to give up what we had taken."[4] Of religion, Frederick wrote: "Religion is absolutely necessary in a State government. . . . [But] there is nothing which tyrannizes over the mind and heart so much as religion, because it agrees neither with our passions, nor with the high political views which a monarch should entertain. . . . When he is about to conclude a treaty with some foreign power, if he only remembers that he is a Christian, all is lost: he will always suffer himself to be duped or imposed upon."[5] Frederick defended the right of religious sects to pray and seek salvation as they wished but found they were destined never to agree. Of justice, Frederick declared: "We owe justice to our subjects as they owe us respect . . . but it is necessary to take care that we are not brought under subjection by justice itself."[6] For Frederick: "Justice is the image of God. Who can therefore attain to so high a perfection."[7] "Behold all the countries in the world, and examine if justice is administered exactly in the same manner."[8] What troubled Frederick most was that if the trends he observed continued, one-tenth of his kingdom's subjects in the next century would be engaged in the administration of justice with "that sure and steady way of proceeding which lawyers have . . . [and] that clever manner of preserving their advantages under the appearances of the strictest equity and justice."[9]

On statesmanship and diplomacy, Frederick reduced all moral and political practice to three principles and practices: "The first is to maintain your power, and, according to circumstances, to increase and extend it. The second is to form alliances only for your own advantage and the third is to command fear and respect even in the most disastrous times."[10] Harsh as his maxims seem, Frederick formulated them into a doctrine of reason of state. He warned against displaying pretensions with vanity but insisted that every ruler must have "two or three eloquent men" and leave justification for his actions to them. Only when Prussia has become more powerful will she be able to assume an air of "constancy and good faith, which, at most, is fit only for the greatest powers and for petty sovereigns."[11] Of diplomats, Frederick sought "those who have the gift of expressing themselves in ambiguous terms and susceptible of a double meaning."[12] He went on to say it would not be improper for a sovereign to have political locksmiths to pick locks or open doors nor physicians to dispose of troublesome people who might be in the way. With regard to embassies, Frederick preferred envoys rather than ambassadors for it was difficult to find men of wealth and noble birth and "by adopting this system, you will save enormous sums of money every year, and, nevertheless, your affairs will be transacted all the same."[13] Yet there were cases in which embassies must be on a scale of magnificence, as when rulers sought a political or matrimonial alliance. But such instances were exceptional. Above all, neighbors must believe "that you are a dangerous monarch, who knows no other principle than that which leads to glory."[14]

It is tempting in the modern age to dismiss the insights of Thucydides and Frederick the Great and writers like Hobbes who spoke of a state of nature involving a "war of every man against every man" or the acute analysis of politics by Machiavelli in which might makes right. Yet diplomacy in the last two decades of the twentieth century goes on under the shadow of war. It is worthwhile recalling the political thought of the Founding Fathers. Because of man's nature and the need to remedy "the defect of better motives," the Founders turned to constitutionalism as providing a system of checks and balances. They wrote of the interplay of opposite and rival interests as a means of equilibrium and constitutional order. Because they understood the human traits of which earlier men had written, they displayed a mistrust of political power, not only that of other states but within their borders. As John Adams put it:

> Power always thinks it has a great soul and vast views beyond the comprehension of the weak and that it is doing God's service when it is violating all His laws. Our passions, ambitions, love and resentment, etc., possess so much metaphysical subtlety and so much overpowering eloquence that they insinuate themselves into the understanding and the conscience and convert both to their party.

Adams was not alone in his concern about power. His intellectual adversary during much of the period, Jefferson, could write in 1798: "Confidence in the men of our choice . . . is . . . the parent of despotism: free government is founded in jealousy and not in confidence; it is jealousy and not confidence which prescribes limited constitutions to bind down those whom we are obliged to trust with power. . . . In questions of power then let no more be heard of confidence in man, but bind him down from mischief by the claims of the Constitution." The exercise of power and the imposing of the will of an individual or group on others was "of all known causes the greatest promoter of corruption." However the Enlightenment may have shaped the thought of early Americans, their views of power reflected a sturdy realization of the hazards and reality of power. Their view of human nature was not far removed from Pascal who explained: "Man is neither angel nor brute, and the unfortunate thing is that he who would act the angel acts the brute." Whatever one's conclusions about ethics and diplomacy ultimately may be, it is important to recognize the limitations which the more sordid and selfish aspects of human nature place on the conduct of diplomacy, including diplomacy in the nuclear age.

II. The Nature of Diplomacy and Morality

The most cynical of all views of diplomacy is that attributed, whether rightly or not, to Sir Henry Wotton who allegedly identified "an ambassador as an honest man who is sent to lie abroad for the good of his country." The three elements which such a definition embraces are: a concept of the role of lying in diplomacy, an implication that privately the ambassador is an honest man but publicly he is something else, and an acceptance of the inevitability of the "official lie." The conventional response of moralists is to dismiss any reference to deceit in diplomacy yet moralists run the risk of moving to an opposite extreme. As Sir Harold Nicolson wrote: "The worst kind of diplomatists are missionaries, fanatics and lawyers; the best kind are the reasonable and humane skeptics. Thus it is not religion which has been the main formative influence in diplomatic theory; it is common sense."[15] Truth-telling in diplomacy is limited by the fact that diplomacy is not a system of moral philosophy. It is the application, as Sir Ernest Satow wrote, of intelligence and tact "to the conduct of official relations between independent states."[16] Honesty in diplomacy, said an experienced diplomat, doesn't mean telling everything you know.

It is self-evident that differences exist between eighteenth- or nineteenth- and twentieth-century diplomacy. The former involved relationships between monarchs and rulers who belonged to an aristocratic elite. Twentieth-century diplomats are envoys of the people. Broadly speaking, the former were professionals while the latter are amateurs in statecraft. Yet with all the differences, diplomacy everywhere brings into play common characteristics. In describing what was needed of the twentieth-century diplomat, Nicolson called for "a man of experience, integrity and intelligence, a man, above all who is not swayed by emotion or prejudice, who is profoundly modest in all his dealings, who is guided only by a sense of public duty, and who understands the perils of cleverness and the virtues of reason, moderation, discretion and tact." Having said all this, Nicolson coyly added: "Mere clerks are not expected to exhibit all these difficult tasks at once."[17]

The crux of the matter is that foreign policy is conducted by sovereign governments. As a function of governmental responsibility, foreign policy must serve the purposes of governments generally; "its primary purpose must be to preserve the union" (Lincoln), informed by the national interest and the dictates of national security. On this point, two well-known American authorities on diplomacy differ in emphasis while agreeing in their conclusions.

The champion of political realism, Hans J. Morgenthau, repeatedly argued that the conduct of foreign policy is not devoid of moral significance. Political actors come under moral judgment and witness to the values of their societies. However, the contemporary environment of international politics is marked both by moral improvement and retrogression. There have been advances in man's respect for human life since the fifteenth and sixteenth centuries when, for example, the Republic of Venice carried on its rolls an official poisoner whose employment depended on his success in disposing of the leaders of rival states. Compare this with the sweeping moral indignation Winston S. Churchill expressed when Stalin at Teheran proposed, half mockingly but not wholly in jest, that killing 50,000 officers would put an end to the threat of German aggression. Or contrast it with the public reaction in the United States to disclosures concerning possible plans for political assassinations by the CIA. Yet the contemporary international scene witnesses to the decline of international morality, indicating that moral restraints are weakening if not disappearing, as in distinctions in wartime between combatants and noncombatants. According to the Hague Conventions of 1899 and 1907, only soldiers ready to fight were considered combatants and objects of war, but by World War II this distinction had effectively been obliterated in the saturation bombings and harsh treatment of prisoners of war by both sides. The international environment was marked by a decline in international morality brought about in part by the technology of warfare and in part by a diminution of standards concerning the sanctity of human life.

Thus in war as in peace the world has seen moral improvement in some spheres but a decline in others resulting from the fact that universal moral principles which are omnipresent are filtered through circumstances of time and place and through national concepts and cultural practices determining their application. In peace, there remains an enormous gap between, say, American respect for the elemental principle of respect for human life (our refusal to take human life except in extraordinary circumstances—capital punishment, abortion, euthanasia, and other carefully defined and delimited exceptions) and practices in other civilizations which have been far more extravagant in imperiling human life for political and ideological purposes (Stalin and the Kulaks, Hitler and the Jews, and the punishment of thieves in Saudi Arabia by cutting off their hands). The relations of universal principles to time and circumstances and to the necessities and norms of different nations and civilizations have been controlling. Particular moral imperatives are obeyed by particular nations at particular times and not by others, and this is the overarching characteristic of today's international environment.

George F. Kennan, brilliant American diplomatist and writer, goes further than Morgenthau in writing:

> The governing of human beings is not a moral exercise. It is a practical function made necessary, regrettably, by the need for order in social relationships and for a collective discipline to control the behavior of that large majority of mankind who are too weak and selfish to control their own behavior.

Ambassador Kennan declares further that "government, particularly democratic government, is an agent and not a principal." No more than any other agent (for example, the corporation or the church, especially since the Protestant Reformation) can it substitute itself for the conscience of the principal. In a particularly strongly worded statement applying this thought to the American government as agent of the American people, Kennan asserts:

> The government could undertake to express and to implement the moral impulses of so great a mass of people only if there were a high degree of consensus among them on such questions as: what is good and what is bad? And to what extent is it the duty of American society to make moral judgments on behalf of others and to improve them from the standpoint of those judgments? Such consensus would be difficult to achieve even if we were dealing with a highly homogeneous population, with firm and unanimously-accepted concepts of an ethical nature as well as of the duties and powers of the state. In the case of a polyglot assemblage of people such as our own, it would be quite impossible. If our government should set out to pursue moral purposes in foreign policy, on what would it base itself? Whose outlooks, philosophy, religious concepts would it choose to express? Imbedded in our population are hundreds of different traditions, beliefs, assumptions and reactions in this field. Are we to assume that it, the government, knows what is right and wrong, has imparted this knowledge to the people at large, and obtained their mandate to proceed to bring about the triumph of what is right, on a worldwide scale?

Opposed to the views of the two diplomatic writers is a large and respected body of thought resulting from international law writings. The former American Judge on the International Court of Justice, Philip Jessup, singles out five criteria as essential to an ethical and therefore a successful foreign policy: "sincerity, loyalty, legality, humanitarianism" and what he has called "proper objectives." By sincerity he means the same as honesty or an absence of deceit, vital as he sees it, especially in peacetime. A government suffers from the label that it is not to be trusted. Jessup acknowledges there may be imperatives which lead to deceit of a government's own citizenry but these must find justification if at all under "proper objectives." Louis J. Halle who belongs to the first group of diplomatic writers offers a dissenting commentary on Jessup's opinion, saying:

> From 1955 to 1960 . . . the United States regularly sent its U-2 spy planes over the Soviet Union at high altitudes to locate military installations and report on military activities. Presumably, such planes would have been able to detect any preparations for a surprise attack on the United States in time to give warning. . . . A Soviet system of espionage operating inside the United States was alert to detect any preparations for a surprise attack on the Soviet Union. This mutual espionage contributed to the preservation of the peace, because the observations of the spies on either side, showing that the other was not preparing a surprise attack, enabled each to remain calm and restrained. If such observations had not been available, each side might have been the victim of panic-making rumors that would have impelled it to feel that its survival depended on striking before the other was able to realize some rumored intention of doing so itself.

Halle goes on:

> However, in 1960 when an American U-2, illegally violating another country's air space, was shot down in the middle of the Soviet Union, many idealists in the West were shocked to learn that such espionage by the United States had been going on, for they regarded it as both immoral and incompatible with the advancement of the cause of peace. . . .

Peace is more secure today, and the prospects of arms control are better, to the extent that the Soviet Union and the United States, through their espionage (in which satellites have replaced spy planes), can each be sure of what armaments the other possesses.[18]

There are significant differences between diplomatic analysts and international lawyers, therefore, on truth-telling. The former are more inclined to say that while there is a universal moral code of truth-telling, there are differing social contexts in which it is applied. In personal and national affairs, men operate within an integrated society where lying is seldom necessary. Mayor Daley's creed for Chicago politics was that a politician's last resource is his word and that lying is not good politics ("if you must lie, it is better not to say anything"). International affairs differ and the difference is one between conditions of civilization and conditions of nature, where because of the half-anarchic character of international society "one man is to another as a wolf." However, for the second group of writers, the international lawyers, truth-telling is an aspect of sincerity plus loyalty plus legality. Law's basic norm—Pacta sunt servanda—is a part not only of our own moral creed but of the Koran and most religious teachings. Pragmatism and morality came together in the Hague and the Geneva conventions on the treatment of civilians and prisoners evolving from the pragmatic test of reciprocity.

III. MORALITY, DEMOCRACY, AND THE INTERNATIONAL SYSTEM

A nation, particularly a democratic nation and most particularly the United States, tends to view its actions as taking place within a moral framework. On one hand, it sees itself as subject to certain moral limitations and judgments; on the other, it looks to national goals and historic traditions as the explanation and moral justification for its course of action. Seldom if ever is foreign policy defended by arguing solely for the maintenance or increase of national power or of national survival. Americans and most other people speak rather of standing for moral purposes beyond the state: democracy or communism, freedom or equality, order or justice, and historical inevitability. Whatever cynics may say, foreign policy tends to be articulated in moral terms, even in most authoritarian regimes, whether those terms be social justice, economic equality, the overthrow of colonialism, national liberation, or putting an end to an unjust status quo.

To know that men and nations espouse goals and values that transcend national defense or survival is a first step or approach but not a solution to the moral problem. In fact, it is more a claim than an approach; it may bespeak what George F. Kennan and Hans J. Morgenthau have called moralism as distinguished from morality. Moralism is the tendency to make one moral value supreme and to apply it indiscriminately without regard to time and place; morality by comparison is the endless quest for what is right amidst the complexity of competing and sometimes conflicting, sometimes compatible moral ends. Paul Freund of the Harvard Law School based his 1976 Thomas Jefferson Memorial Lecture of the National Endowment for the Humanities on Lord Acton's aphorism "when you perceive a truth, look for a balancing truth." According to Freund, we suffer in Western civilization from the decline of the ancient art of moral reasoning, the essence of which is weighing and balancing not only good and evil but competing "goods."

Freedom and order, liberty and justice, economic growth and social equality, national interest and the well-being of mankind are each in themselves worthy moral ends. How much simpler moral choice would be if the leader could select one value as his guiding principle and look upon the rest as secondary or instrumental. In every human community, however, the choice between right and wrong is endlessly fraught with complexity and grounded in deep moral pathos. There is an inescapably tragic character to moral choice. Within the family, men all too often may be driven to choose between family interests and professional responsibilities. Loyalty to spouse and children may conflict with caring for the needs of aging parents. Within the nation, freedom of speech and assembly may clash with the requirements of security and order. The Supreme Court has declared that freedom of speech does not involve the right to cry fire in a crowded theatre. The right to a fair trial may collide with the right to know and the freedom of the press. Freedom of scientific inquiry apparently does not justify the right of a graduate student to produce a nuclear bomb in his kitchen. Even within the most developed democracy every political and constitutional principle coexists and is related to every other principle, and each is at most a partial expression of morality; for as Reinhold Niebuhr wrote:

Democracy cannot exist if there is no recognition of the fragmentary character of all systems of values which are allowed to exist within its frame.

On the international scene, the recognition of "the fragmentary character of all systems of values" is more difficult. Nations, and especially the superpowers, see themselves as the repositories of values and ideas that are good for all mankind. National self-determination which postulated the right of every nationality group to organize itself within a nation-state has been supplanted by crusading nationalism with its unique and exclusive mission for the world. Whereas the nation-state was the endpoint of political development for eighteenth- and nineteenth-century nationalism, it is the beginning of communism and democracy. If the aim is to extend the benefits of systems of values and beliefs to peoples everywhere, it is difficult if not impossible to accept their fragmentary character. It is this reality which characterizes the international system today.

IV. PRACTICAL MORALITY AND DIPLOMACY

The prevailing approach to the ethical dimension of diplomacy is one which has placed stress on morality pure and simple. Oftentimes defenders of this approach have been driven to take positions their critics describe as moralism and legalism. Those who question whether morality exists for diplomacy ask whether there exist more proximate moral positions that can be discussed under the heading practical morality.

One such approach is that of workability as opposed to the proclamation of abstract moral principles. The objective of foreign policy should be the reduction of human suffering and promotion of social welfare and not the unqualified triumph of abstract principles. Moral appeals to the generality of mankind often constitute not morality but Pharisaism.

Workability is also the test of certain diplomatic historians, notable among them the cold war historian, Norman Graebner of the University of Virginia. History suggests that whenever the United States has introduced towering humanitarian objectives as the main guide to policy it has added to rather than diminished human suffering and subsequently abandoned unworkable policies.

In the 1950's, Secretary Dulles's liberation foreign policy offered by the Republicans as a more dynamic alternative to the postwar policy of containment inspired Hungarian freedom fighters to revolt only to discover that American national interest and the facts of geography and power precluded American intervention.

The question is whether proclaiming moral principles may sometimes not do more harm than good. Workability leads diplomatists to measure possible consequences. The issue is not settled by saying the United States must give the world a vision of hope. The question raised by practical morality is where will that vision lead and will the overall effects be better or worse than what has gone before.

If the first issue is workability, the second is the nature of the international society. The diplomatic school sees the world of American foreign policy as subject to many of the same rules and constraints known at the founding of the republic. To the question posed by the historian Carl Becker at the end of World War II, *How New Will the Better World Be,* they answer it is neither wholly new nor necessarily better. Why? Because of the nature of man, of international politics and the persistence of the nation-state system. In discussions at Virginia, Hans Morgenthau stated:

> The purpose of foreign policy is not to bring enlightenment or happiness to the rest of the world but to take care of the life, liberty and happiness of the American people.

International lawyers are more inclined to argue the existence of a new and better world, the birth of an embryonic world community. The Charter of the United Nations and the Declaration and some nineteen Covenants of Human Rights are said to embody core principles of human rights and fundamental freedoms foreshadowed in the American Declaration of Independence. Judge Philip C. Jessup quoted Secretary of State Elihu Root writing in 1906 to the American ambassador in St. Petersburg regarding a protest concerning the persecution of Jews in Russia:

> I think it may do some good, though I do not feel sure of it. I do not know how it will be received. It may merely give offense. I am sure that to go

further would do harm. I am sure also that to publish here the fact that such a dispatch has been sent would do harm, and serious harm to the unfortunate people whom we desire to help. Any possible good effect must be looked for in absolutely confidential communication to the Russian Government. The publication that any communication has been made would inevitably tend to prevent the Russian government from acting, to increase the anti-Jewish feelings and to make further massacres more probable.

But then Jessup added that the situation today may differ "since human rights have become the subject on international agreements."[19]

Each of the great political traditions has its own conception of human values in society and the good life. For the Christian belief in God and serving one's fellowman is uppermost. For the disciple of classical political thought, the search for virtue in society is the highest calling. For modern political thinkers, the establishment of the best social and constitutional arrangements within existing societies is the foremost objective. The Christian and the classical traditions depend on certain objective values and standards within society and the political process. The values of the two older traditions are ultimately transcendent while those of modern political thought are immanent. Contemporary exceptions include those political theories for which the earlier traditions have residual importance, such as those of the Founding Fathers of the American constitutional and political system.

The prospects of all three political traditions have been diminished by certain forces at work within the present-day nation-state. Christian thought from its beginnings assumed that man necessarily and inevitably lived in two worlds, the city of man and the city of God. The former was the temporary realm of contingencies, imperfection, and sin; the latter was the enduring realm of certainty, perfection, and the good. The one was realizable here and now, the other in eternity. The social and political order was structured to reflect, partially at least, the reality of the two worlds. The Christian vision provided for both a horizontal and vertical dimension in human life, with men reaching out to one another in the social order and seeking to know God in the spiritual order. Government was the custodian of the social and political order and citizens were enjoined to give to Caesar what was Caesar's. The

Church was the custodian of the spiritual order and believers were enjoined to serve God with what was God's.

The rise of the modern nation-state and the breakdown of the Corpus Christianum diminished, if it did not destroy, the vision of the two cities. The authority of the one universal church was undermined by the Reformation and the Renaissance. The religion of the prince within emerging political societies determined the religion of the people. Religion and patriotism tended to reinforce one another whereas earlier they had constituted checks and balances on one another. If the universal Catholic church was in part responsible for the union of the two because of its tendency to equate and make itself coextensive with the city of God, the embryonic nation-state was also responsible by becoming the repository of individual and group morality in order to assure political cohesion. Whereas the Church had taught believers the commandment "Thou shalt not kill," princes and rulers taught "Thou shalt kill to preserve the nation-state."

Moreover, other forces were at work weakening the hold of the Christian tradition. The Christian tradition in its historical formulation presupposed a world of sheep and shepherds. The modern era has witnessed the growth of ever more complex societies in which the individual to whom Christianity ministered was further and further removed from primary human relations with his fellowmen. The great society supplanted the good Samaritan. Furthermore, Christianity itself became more and more fragmented. In America a destructive Civil War found Northern and Southern soldiers praying to the same God and justifying their acts from the same Scriptures. During the conflict President Abraham Lincoln wrote that "each party claims to act in accordance with the will of God. Both *may* be, and one *must* be wrong. God can not be *for*, and *against* the same thing at the same time." In recent days Martin Luther King and Jerry Falwell invoked the same Scriptures to defend actions affecting millions of people in diametrically opposite ways. Maintaining a universal Christian tradition is complicated by the rise of sovereign nation-states. Who would deny that the nation provides its citizenry with concepts of political philosophy, standards of political morality, and goals of political action?

If the Christian tradition has been challenged by the circumstances surrounding the modern nation-state, the classical tradition has also been threatened. Modernity has brought about a shift from discussions of the good man and the good state to discourses on political power and political tactics. Classical political philosophy was not unaware of the realities of good and evil in human nature. The Platonic dialogues are filled with examples of cynical and selfish men overriding reason and virtue in their political attitudes and conduct. Yet for the philosopher, contemplating the overall human drama, reason was superior to the irrational and virtue was the standard by which cynicism and selfishness were judged. Man approached his true and best nature in participating in the social and political order. He realized himself as a social and political animal. Classicists also maintained that human fulfillment was attainable within the polity, a small-sized political community marked by face-to-face political discourse. By contrast, few citizens in large nation-states have little if any contact with rulers.

The history of modern times throws a shadow over the classicists' argument for reason and virtue. Wise students of political history such as Reinhold Niebuhr, Herbert Butterfield, and Hans J. Morgenthau have traced the influence of the irrational in politics. The German people, whose culture matched any in Europe, followed a fanatical leader, Hitler, who stirred popular emotions with slogans depicting the Germans as racially superior. Legislative assemblies, intended for prudent deliberation, become the scene of chauvinist and bellicose debate. National self-determination, which had promised satisfaction and peace to the world's people, was Hitler's rallying cry for the annexation of the Sudetenland. Reason proved defective in anticipating the consequences of thousands of apparently reasonable acts. Unintended and unforeseen consequences of reasonable historical acts outweigh the expected or intended results. The Protestant Reformation rested on the right of each individual to read and interpret the Bible, but by strengthening nationalism caused a weakening of individualism. The French Revolution, which promised liberty, equality, and fraternity, led to the submergence of liberty and equality in the Napoleonic Empire.

If Christian and classical thought are criticized for too much opposition to modernity and too great a faith in historical political values, modern political thought links modernity with progress. Whereas the older traditions stand partly in opposition to present trends, modern political theory tends to sanctify them. It glorifies the state and, more particularly, certain branches of government which it favors one after the other as the cycle turns. Transposed to the international scene, modern thought manifests an exaggerated confidence in institutions as instruments for transforming international politics. The rise and fall of popular enthusiasm for each of these institutions in turn has thrown into question the judgment of modern thought. It has also led some contemporary thinkers to reopen the question of the relevance of Christian and classical thought to present-day problems.

Not only has the rise of the nation-state profoundly affected the relation of the great political traditions to politics but so have the changing patterns of international politics and diplomacy. Historically, the Christian and classical political traditions assumed a consensus on values within the Christian and classical worlds. Four developments have altered the political world within which any of the historic traditions must operate. First, a worldwide system of political ideologies and conflicting religious faiths has replaced the Christian Europe of which historians like Christopher Dawson wrote in tracing the formation of Western Christendom. Universal Christendom has lost out to a pluralistic international system of competing nation-states and cultures. Second, the political faiths which inspired men took on the characteristics of the terrestrial world rather than the adornments of the heavenly city. To the extent the latter existed at all it was as this-worldly utopias. Carl Becker wrote about the heavenly city of the eighteenth-century philosophers; Marx and Lenin elaborated a creed that identified the end of history with the Marxist classless society. Salvation was achievable here and now and its standards were not outside but within history. The direct application to international problems of the Christian tradition was undermined by the breakdown of a consensus on values and the disappearance of faith in effective objective moral principles outside history.

Two other developments coincided with and reinforced the above-mentioned changes. They profoundly affected the relevance of the classical tradition. One of these was a consequence of the vast increase in the size of viable political units. The movement from city-states to nation-states culminated in the postwar emergence of the superpowers. That good men would create good regimes became a more difficult proposition to sustain. Good and bad men alike seized power in large collective states claiming that only they were capable of solving the momentous social problems of great masses of people. Events that good men had prophesied were rationally impossible, such as global depressions, world wars, and totalitarianism, followed one another in rapid succession. Mass populations responded to programs defenders argued served all the people. If Americans had any doubt concerning the far-reaching effects of this third development, they had only to compare the deliberative processes of leaders addressing the New England town meeting with Mussolini or Hitler haranguing the German and Italian people with the claim, "forty million Italians (Germans) can't be wrong." In short, the concept of popular sovereignty replaced that of personal virtue.

A fourth development was the radical transformation of political communication. Classical political thought had maintained that personal and collective morality were indivisible. In the modern era not only totalitarian rulers but democratic leaders determined what was moral and the right interests of states. While certain moral principles applicable to individuals survived in the eighteenth-century idea of raison d'etat, contemporary rulers maintained that whatever their personal moral standards on war or slavery, criteria of national unity and preserving the state took precedence. Thus both Christian and classical thought lost their force in the face of far-reaching historical changes.

Modern political thought appeared to offer an alternative to the decline of the ancient traditions. Especially liberalism held out the promise to the great mass of the people of human improvement through universal public education. Today's pressing problems would yield to the workings of free enlightened society. Individuals, ever more transformed by reason and science, would throw off aggressive human traits and archaic political ideas and institutions that had led throughout history to conflict and war. Individual man pursuing his selfish interests would be guided nationally and internationally as if by a hidden hand to act for the common good. Nationally, the process would operate in free-market economies guaranteed to serve the general welfare. ("What is good for General Motors is good for America," a cabinet member in the Eisenhower administration proclaimed.) Internationally, national self-determination promised a peaceful world. Its architects little dreamed that Hitler would invoke a Wilsonian principle to justify his expansionist policies. Then national and international economic stagnation in the 1930s led millions of people to turn to new and more dynamic collectivist solutions. Scientific efficiency also made possible the holocaust.

Not only did the four developments sound the death knell for the meaningfulness and coherence of the three great political traditions; another factor sped the disintegration of the international political order. The values which had introduced a limited degree of stability within single political communities proved ineffective on the international stage. The standards that had assured relative peace within nations proved ineffectual or largely irrelevant in international affairs. What was disallowed or dealt with as an exception to the normal processes of national societies was accepted as inevitable in international society. While civil war represented the breakdown of the political order within nations, war was accepted as the continuation of diplomacy by other means in relations among nation-states.

The problem, as Reinhold Niebuhr discussed it in a succession of treatises on foreign policy, was that in international politics no single moral principle existed for ordering all other moral principles. In international politics, rough-and-ready norms such as "damage limitation" became the overarching principles rather than such benign standards as the quest for the good society or for communities aimed at human self-fulfillment. In the end modern political thought which had promised a new and better world became an even more tragic victim to the bludgeonings of history than Christian or classical thought.

For all these reasons the culmination of history on the international stage has witnessed not the heavenly city but the nuclear age. The end of warfare which liberal political thinkers had predicted yielded to the specter of warfare as universal human destruction. Yet hope has had a rebirth alongside impending disaster. Ironically, human advancement and progress have led not to the refutation of ancient political truths but to their rediscovery. Prudence has once more become the master virtue in international politics at a moment in time when its absence becomes a threat to human existence. But political prudence was an idea that Aristotle set forth as a guide for political practice as distinct from political contemplation. From Aristotle and Augustine through Edmund Burke to Niebuhr and John Courtney Murray, prudence as an operative political principle was not the rigid formulation or precise definition of what was right or wrong but a method of practical reason in the search for righteousness and justice under a given set of circumstances. Practical morality involves the reconciliation of what is morally desirable and politically possible.

It offers few absolutes but many practical possibilities. Prudence, then, is the cardinal precept in the ancient tradition of moral reasoning which some contemporaries would revive. It recognizes with Holmes the need for moral man in an immoral world to find his way through "a maze of conflicting moral principles" no one of which reigns supreme. It undertakes to transform abstract reason into political reason. In a word, it aims to rediscover the ethical dimensions of diplomacy as philosophers and statesmen have searched for and discovered them throughout the ages.

NOTES

Reprinted from *The Review of Politics* 46, no. 3 (July 1984): 367–87.

1. June Bingham, *Courage to Change: An Introduction to the Life and Thought of Reinhold Niebuhr* (New York: Charles Scribner's Sons, 1961), 62.

2. Quoted in A. C. F. Beales, *A Short History of English Liberalism*, 195.

3. *House of Commons Debates*, 5th ser., vol. 419 (1946), 1262.

4. Frederick the Great, *Origin of the Bismarck Policy*, European Pamphlets, vol. 12 (Boston: Crosby, Damrell, 100 Washington Street, 1870), 6.

5. Ibid., 12.

6. Ibid., 21.

7. Ibid., 22.

8. Ibid.

9. Ibid., 23.

10. Ibid., 43.

11. Ibid., 48.

12. Ibid., 48–49.

13. Ibid., 50.

14. Ibid., 51.

15. Sir Harold Nicolson, *Diplomacy* (London: Oxford University Press, 1939), 50.

16. Quoted in ibid., 45–46.

17. Ibid., 76.

18. Quotations from Morgenthau, Kennan, Halle and Jessup are taken from unpublished papers written for a conference on "Morality and Foreign Policy" held in Charlottesville, Virginia, in June 1977, and jointly sponsored by the Department of State and the University of Virginia.

19. Ibid.

CHAPTER 16

Realism, Neorealism, and American Liberalism

KEITH L. SHIMKO

Neorealism has recently been portrayed as an attempt to systematize the insights of classical realism in order to put them on a more solid theoretical foundation. This essay rejects this common characterization of the emergence of neorealism by arguing that neorealism constitutes a fundamentally different conceptualization of international politics than that provided by classical realists. Neorealism is best understood as an alternative to classical realism shaped by enduring liberal traditions in the United States, which is where neorealism emerged and thrives.

One of the most widely accepted observations about the American political experience is the dominance of liberalism as the framework of American political discourse. There appears to be little quarrel with Louis Hartz's conclusion that the only political tradition of consequence in the United States is liberalism; politics in America is distinguished by the lack of any genuinely radical or conservative political movements which contend for power. As Hartz observed, "the ironic flaw in American liberalism lies in the fact that we have never had a real conservative tradition."[1] Indeed, conservatives have often debated among themselves whether a genuine conservatism is possible in America (the free-market "conservatism" which is found in the United States is actually a version of classical liberalism, of course, not philosophical conservatism).[2] The reasons for the political hegemony of liberalism are the subject of lively debate, but divergent explanations for the dominance of liberalism should not be allowed to obscure the basic consensus that what passes for political conflict in America occurs largely within the confines of liberalism.

The impact of the liberal tradition on American thinking about international affairs is a somewhat more contentious issue. The most common analysis emphasizes the resulting naïveté, legalism, and moralism which supposedly plagued American foreign policy, at least until the onset of World War II. In the postwar period, so the story goes, hard-nosed realism replaced wooly idealism as the prevailing intellectual perspective in the United States. Woodrow Wilson was out; Hans Morgenthau was in. As neatly as this story unfolds, the plot remains unsatisfying. The unresolved question should be obvious: how did realism, which has (or had) important roots in conservative political philosophy, take hold in a nation whose entire political tradition was liberalism?

The thesis of this essay is that "classical" realism never did establish firm roots among American students of international affairs. After the war realism triumphed largely by default; liberal idealism and its attendant utopianism were discredited and radical perspectives did not receive serious attention until the Vietnam War and the rise of cold war revisionism. Classical realism, whose primary exponents were often European emigrees such as Hans Morgenthau, Nicholas Spykman, George Liska, and Henry Kissinger, did not mesh well with the innate liberalism of most American intellectuals. As Robert Cox points out, it was "European-formed thinkers like Reinhold Niebuhr and Hans Morgenthau who introduced a more pessimistic and power-oriented view of mankind into the American milieu conditioned by eighteenth-century optimism and the nineteenth century belief in progress."[3] There were some native Americans who espoused versions of classical realism, the most prominent being George Kennan and Reinhold Niebuhr, but their intellectual orientation was more European than American. Despite Cox's claim that these thinkers "introduced" this conservative realism into American thought, one wonders how successful the introduction was. There is little doubt that the rhetoric of realism was adopted by both supporters and critics of American policy—that is, an emphasis on power, the balance of power, struggle, etc—but it is more doubtful that the philosophical roots ran deep enough to take firm hold. The difficulty of transplanting realism to the United States is to be found in the main conflict between classical realism and American liberalism—

the former's pessimistic view of man, which is at odds with the basic optimism of liberalism.[4]

This is where neorealism enters the picture. Neorealism's great accomplishment is that it preserves much of the structure of classical realist analysis while abandoning some its more objectionable (read "unliberal") foundations. Behind all the claims of neorealism's methodological and epistemological superiority, all of which may or may not be true, lies a more basic explanation for the rise and popularity of neorealism among American scholars. We cannot fully understand the popularity of neorealism in the United States without examining it and classical realism in the context of the American liberal tradition. Theoretical perspectives, particularly in the social sciences, thrive not merely because of their scientific superiority, but also because they are consonant with a society's prevailing values and beliefs.

I. Classical Realism in the United States

A good place to begin this discussion is to examine how most people think of realism today in the context of general debates over international relations theory, because as one does so it becomes clear that there are some problems. Two of the most recent and widely used surveys of the field are K. J. Holsti's *The Dividing Discipline* and Kauppi and Viotti's *International Relations Theory.*[5] Holsti identifies three contending paradigms—the classical tradition, theories of global society, and neo-Marxist approaches. Kauppi and Viotti also present three schools of thought—realism, pluralism, and globalism. It is clear from reading these overviews that the different categorizations are basically the same (i.e., realism is the classical paradigm, pluralism is theories of global society, and globalism is the same as neo-Marxist approaches). The analysis and citations in both volumes also makes it clear that the authors see the classical paradigm (Holsti) or realism (Kauppi and Viotti) as the dominant framework for understanding international relations in the United States. Even the most cursory examination of the literature suggests that this judgment is correct.

The problems emerge when different labels are employed and when we look at the specific issue of international conflict. In *Why War?*, for example, Nelson and Olin lay out three philosophical approaches to understanding war—conservatism, liberalism, and radicalism.[6] This tripartite categorization is analogous to those provided by Holsti and Kauppi and Viotti, which we can tell from the fact that all the authors cited in these works as realists are also included in Spencer and Olin's discussion of conservative approaches. That is, Holsti's classical paradigm and Kauppi and Viotti's realism are the same as Nelson and Olin's conservatism. As a result, one is led to conclude that if realism is the dominant approach of American students of international relations, then conservatism must be the prevailing intellectual orientation and political philosophy toward understanding international conflict. This is a more difficult issue because the logical answer would seem to be yes, but this would conflict with what I believe to the correct assumption of liberal dominance. This raises a number of key issues concerning the relationship between realism, conservatism, and liberalism in America which guide the present essay. How, one wonders, does realism thrive in a liberal milieu when some of its key assumptions are at variance with liberal beliefs?

II. CLASSICAL REALISM, LIBERALISM, AND CONSERVATISM

It is always dangerous to attempt to summarize the key aspects of rich and varied traditions in a short space; centuries of political thought are not easily reduced to a few sentences. At the risk of being overly simplistic, however, we can say the debate between liberals and conservatives revolves in large part around disagreements concerning the nature of man and his social institutions—the human condition. They offer differing assessments of the human condition because they present divergent portraits of man. Liberalism is ultimately dependent upon an optimistic assessment of man and his potential. As David Sidorsky explains:

> When liberalism is considered as a secular faith, its central vision is a conception of man, of society, and of history. In simplest terms, it is, first, a conception of man as desiring freedom and capable of exercising rational free choice. Second, it is a perspective on social institutions as open to rational reconstruction. . . . It is, third, a view of history as progressively per-

fectible through the continuous application of human reason to social institutions.[7]

The liberal mindset entails a view of man as a creature of reason, capable of overcoming the more obnoxious features of his natural and social environment by applying his ever-expanding body of knowledge. Social problems such as war are the result of inadequate information and/or faulty, but reformable, institutional structures. More modest versions of liberalism downplay the notion of perfectibility, emphasizing instead more limited, though inevitable, progress: liberalism, according to Kukathas, is merely "meliorist, affirming the corrigibility and improvability of all social institutions and social arrangements."[8]

A conservative orientation, on the other hand, rests upon a pessimistic analysis of man stressing his limits and shortcomings. In some ways the conservative view of man is more complex, and several strains of thought can be found in conservative analyses. Some, such as Burke, stress that people are creatures of habit, tradition, and custom who desire stability and order above other values. Other facets of conservatism, however, stress more negative features of human nature. In its more religious manifestations, some conservatives stress notions of original sin and man's fall from grace with God. Man's inherent spiritual and moral inadequacies, according to this view, stand in the way of the progress anticipated by liberals. More secular variants of conservatism tend to portray man as an animal of lust, passion, self-interest, egoism, and emotion. It is not that man is purely evil, lustful or irrational; it is simply that these elements of human nature are integral components of man's social relations: the "irrational" facets of human nature inevitably influence man's behavior and are reflected in his necessarily imperfect social institutions.[9]

Classical realists by and large accepted the conservative view of human nature, and these assumptions about human nature were central elements of the classical realist perspective on international relations (in saying this I mean mainly that they adopted the more negative, secular view of man as inevitably being motivated, in part, by emotion, lust for power, and greed). Certainly some emphasized human nature more than others, but as Michael Joseph Smith observes in his recent analysis of realist thought, "Realists assume an ineracible tendency to evil, a universal animus dominandi among all men and women. . . . This treatment of human nature, reaching back to Thucydides, informs every facet of realist analysis."[10] Still, some discussions of realist thought proceed without any mention of such assumptions. The survey by Viotti and Kauppi, for example, attempts to lay out the "major actors and assumptions" of realism, but one searches in vain for any mention of human nature whatsoever.[11] John Vasquez maintains that there are three fundamental assumptions of realism:

1. Nation-states or their decision-makers are the most important actors for understanding international relations.
2. There is a sharp distinction between domestic politics and international politics.
3. International relations is a struggle for power and peace. Understanding how and why that struggle occurs and suggesting ways for regulating it is the purpose of the discipline.[12]

Again, no discussion of human nature. Robert Keohane has singled out three assumptions which supposedly form the "hard core" of a realist research program: (1) the state-centric assumption, (2) the rationality assumption, and (3) the power assumption.[13] Keohane does recognize Morgenthau's assumptions about human nature, but for some reason they are judged insufficiently important to warrant inclusion in the "hard core" of the realist paradigm.[14] Joseph Grieco also lists the assumptions of realism without reference to any view of human nature.[15] From most accounts of realist thought, one would have little indication that realists had anything at all to say about the matter.

All of this seems very odd, since it was the classical realists' assumptions about the nature of man which led to their argument that politics inevitably involved a struggle for power. Nonetheless, the realist view of human nature, which Smith argues influenced every facet of realist analysis, is routinely relegated to some theoretical never-never land, swept under the rug, or treated as if it were a tangential and disposable element of realism. Over the past few decades we have witnessed a slow and steady transformation of realism which reached its logical conclusion in Waltzian neorealism. The alterations of realism have made it more compatible, or less incompatible, with political liberalism.

III. CLASSICAL REALISM AND HUMAN NATURE

A complete survey of realists is neither possible nor necessary. Suffice it to say that it is impossible to read the works of such prominent realists as Kissinger, Niebuhr, Kennan, and, most importantly, Morgenthau without coming to the realization that their entire outlook on international politics rested on an unflattering view of man. As David Mayers observes in his biography of Kennan, "Reinhold Niebuhr, Hans Morgenthau, and Henry Kissinger have in their distinctive ways shared with Kennan [an] orientation toward foreign politics that emphasizes a pessimistic notion of human nature."[16] Assumptions about human nature were not merely afterthoughts, excess intellectual baggage, or flowery rhetorical flourishes; they were the cornerstone of the classical realist analysis of political conflict.

This emphasis was not unique to postwar realists: as Smith points out, one can find commentary about the importance of human nature in realist thought as far back as Thucydides' observation that in war "human nature, always ready to offend even where law exists, showed itself proudly in its true colors, as something incapable of controlling passion, insubordinate to the idea of justice, the enemy of anything superior to itself."[17] Not surprisingly, Niebuhr's Christian realism grew out of his assumptions concerning man's inherent flaws, though his views had a more secular tone than earlier theologians such as St. Augustine. For Niebuhr, the tragedy of the human condition was rooted in man's egoism and will to power. In his influential *Moral Man and Immoral Society* Niebuhr argued that "the easy subservience of reason to prejudice and passion, and the consequent persistence of irrational egoism, particularly in group behavior, make social conflict an inevitability in human history, probably to its very end."[18] According to Niebuhr, "man is ignorant and involved in the limitations of a finite mind; but he pretends not to be limited. . . . All of his intellectual and cultural pursuits, therefore, become infected with the sin of pride. Man's pride and will-to-power disturb the harmony of creation."[19] Richard Fox explains the importance of Niebuhr's ideas:

> The real significance of *Moral Man* lay not in its call for proletarian fortitude or even its justification of violence as an ethical resource. . . . Its chief importance lay in Niebuhr's biting repudiation . . . of the historic liberal

Protestant quest for the Kingdom of God. He dismissed with utter derision the hope that animated thousands of liberal and radical Christians . . . the hope that human history would eventually see the inauguration of a community of love.[20]

Fox concludes that, despite Niebuhr's liberal and even radical politics during the 1930s, he was "alien to the Anglo-Saxon Protestant tradition that gave rise to [the] transformative dream." By questioning whether egotistical man could transcend his nature and eradicate war and violence, Niebuhr was rejecting what Fox identifies as "the central heritage of American social thought, both Protestant and secular."[21] That is, in accepting the inevitability of conflict and violence stemming from man's inherent flaws, Niebuhr was repudiating key elements of the liberal social and political creed. As Cox observes, Niebuhr's "revival of a pessimistic Augustinian view of human nature challenged the optimistic Lockean view native to American culture."[22]

Kennan's analysis of international politics was less philosophical than Niebuhr's and less explicitly theoretical than Morgenthau's, but his conservative approach to understanding the human condition was, if anything, even more pronounced. Considering the rise and nature of fascism in Europe and totalitarianism in the Soviet Union, Kennan tried to disabuse his compatriots of their comforting belief that they were somehow different than the Germans and Soviets:

> I wish I could believe that the human impulses which give rise to the nightmares of totalitarianism were ones which Providence had allocated only to other peoples and to which the American people had graciously been left immune. Unfortunately, I know that that is not true . . . the fact of the matter is that there is a little bit of totalitarian buried somewhere, way down deep, in each and every one of us.[23]

Kennan warned of "the incorrigible vanity and tragedy and futility of all human endeavor" and the "built-in tragic nature of the individual human predicament which men ha[ve] always had to face!"[24] During a visit to Switzerland several years after the end of World War II Kennan wondered whether men could really sustain such a civilized and pristine society: "Man is still an animal, whose physical nature depends on combat; and whether he can ever find self-expression and peace in these gleaming well-ordered stables, where the discipline of good social behavior is demanded of him as in no other place, seems doubtful."[25] Kennan was skeptical because "the individual cannot do anything about the beast in himself."[26] Kennan's writings are infused with the traditional conservative fear that civilization is a fragile enterprise and that slightly beneath the veneer of order and civility lay a festering violence waiting for release. Mayers is a prophet of the obvious when observing that Kennan's view of man "has never really commended itself to the jaunty American outlook, based on optimism, materialistic success, and the legend of the rugged individual who triumphs over all odds."[27]

Kennan and Niebuhr, however, did not devote their attention specifically to articulating and constructing a theory of international relations. Niebuhr focused on theological issues and polemics about current affairs while Kennan was more concerned with the practical conduct of American diplomacy. In the area of international relations they are best viewed as thoughtful critics and commentators, not theorists. When one thinks of explicit attempts to devise a theory of international relations along classical realist lines, there is really only one name which comes to mind, Hans Morgenthau.

Even though Morgenthau argued that students of international relations should focus their attention on the behavior of states (hence the frequent and proper identification of a "state-centric" assumption in Morgenthau's realism), he consistently emphasized that behavior of states and the resulting dynamics of international relations could not be understood without reference to fundamental aspects of human nature. Morgenthau's two most important works in this respect were *Scientific Man vs. Power Politics,* which was a heated polemic against liberal and rationalist approaches to politics, and, of course, *Politics Among Nations,* which applied Morgenthau's general orientation toward politics to the specific problems of international relations.[28]

Examining *Politics Among Nations* one quickly discovers that two of the key elements of realism which most seem to focus on—the state as the most important international actor and rationality in state behavior—do not really jump out. Though present, these issues seemed relatively muted in comparison to Morgenthau's emphasis on power, struggle, and human nature, and it was clear that his view of the role of power in politics could not be divorced from his assumptions about the forces which drove men. That is, Morgenthau's view of human nature was the center of his theory of international politics; everything else was extrapolated from it. He spoke of "human nature, in which the laws of politics have their roots" and argued that "the world . . . is the result of forces inherent in human nature."[29]

Just as one cannot escape the conclusion that Morgenthau's view of man was the foundation of his theory, it is also hard to deny that his assumptions about human nature were conservative. It is no coincidence that Morgenthau opened *Scientific Man vs. Power Politics* by quoting Edmund Burke: ". . . and politics ought to be adjusted, not to human reason, but to human nature; of which reason is but a part, and by no means the greatest part."[30] Morgenthau's reference to Burke was favorable. Following some of the themes stressed by Niebuhr, Morgenthau claimed that "the selfishness of man has limits; his will to power has none . . . his lust for power would be satisfied only if the last man became the object of his domination."[31] He warned of "the immorality inherent in all human action."[32] According to Morgenthau:

> It is the ubiquity of the desire for power which . . . constitutes the ubiquity of evil in all human action. Here is the element of corruption and sin which injects itself into the best of intentions at least a drop of evil and thus spoils it. On a grand scale, the transformation of churches into political organizations, of revolutions into dictatorships, of love of country into imperialism, are cases in point.[33]

This unquenchable lust for power which Morgenthau viewed as essential to our understanding of politics in general was, of course, a necessary component of any attempt to comprehend the conflictual and violent aspects of international politics. The reason "international politics, like all politics, is struggle for power" is that men, acting alone or in concert, inevitably seek to dominate others.[34] All of this must have been disconcerting to scholars raised in a liberal society. Justin Rosenberg notes wryly that "Morgenthau, it will be recalled, had some rather unflattering and unsophisticated views of human nature, and an embarrassing habit of parading them as the philosophical basis of Realism."[35]

IV. First-Image Realism Versus Third-Image Realism

Morgenthau's emphasis on human nature as the cornerstone of his approach to understanding political conflict led Waltz in *Man, the State, and War* to classify him as a "first-image" theorist of war.[36] Morgenthau located the causes of war in characteristics of individuals. The essentially conservative content of Morgenthau's image of man meant that he was, in Waltz's terminology, a "pessimistic" first-image theorist in the same league as St. Augustine, Niebuhr, and Spinoza. Foreshadowing his future intellectual development, Waltz was highly critical of first-image explanations such as that presented by Morgenthau, preferring "third-image" theories which found the causes for war in deficiencies of the international system. In his insightful discussion of the confusion which often surrounds discussions of realism, Kjell Goldman highlights the fundamental difference between classical realism of the Morgenthauian variety and so-called neorealism—the relative "explanatory power" of anarchy and human nature.[37] Neorealism, which is more appropriately labeled structural or systemic realism, seeks to explain international conflict and war in terms of the imperatives imposed on states by an inherently insecure, anarchical environment. It is the dynamics of the system which compel states to behave in certain ways if they wish to survive, and survival is assumed to be the minimum objective of all states. Neorealism provides a situational or environmental explanation of state behavior. States seek to maintain or expand their influence because they are forced to do so by the logic of the system, not because they are disposed to do so. As Goldman notes, this type of explanation "is radically different from [explaining behavior] in terms of man's nature."[38]

Although anarchy was an important fact of international life in Morgenthau's analysis, he did not stress the explanatory power of anarchy. Anarchy was relevant in the sense that it failed to provide constraints in the form of a higher authority to restrict man's baser desires, which are reflected in state behavior, to dominate others. Anarchy does not cause, and does not lead to, the struggle for power in Morgenthau's analysis. Anarchy in the classical realist scheme is a permissive force, not a causal force. Neorealists such as Waltz provide a "top-down" explanation for state behavior; Morgenthau provided a "bottom-up" explanation, which meant that he committed the cardinal Waltz-ian heresy of "reductionism." In Morgenthau's view, the desire of states to maintain and expand their control over others was not an anarchy-induced im-perative, but rather a collective reflection of man's lust for power and domina-tion. Morgenthau talked about the process of man "transferring his ego-tism and power impulses to the nation."[39] Anarchy was important because it allowed these impulses to have free reign; in international politics, Morgenthau explained, "there is no centralized authority beyond the mechanics of the balance of power which could impose actual limits upon the manifestations of [the state's] collective desire for domination."[40] Anarchy was significant be-cause it failed to impose constraints, not because it imposed behavior.

Thus, classical realism and neorealism part company when it comes to the basic question of international relations theory: Why do states behave as they do? As is usually the case in disagreements in the social sciences, the basic point of contention is the divergent assumptions about what motivates the behavior of the actors whose conduct is being analyzed. In a model which stresses the explanatory power of anarchy, the primary motive for state competition is the fear of domination by others; in one which emphasizes human nature, the central motive is the desire to dominate others. An anarchy model explains the international struggle for power as the tragic result of systemic inadequacies; a human nature model portrays the struggle as the inevitable reflection and ex-tension of man's inadequacies. Neorealism is not merely an attempt to make classical realism more rigorous, as some would have us believe; it is, instead, a fundamental reconceptualization of international political dynamics. The basic motivational dynamic has been altered.

One may object to this distinction by arguing that the fear of domination on the part of some presupposes the existence of some actor(s) who is (are) genuinely pursuing domination. Logically, however, the fear of something does not assume the existence of that which is feared. Fears can be based on misperceptions, misconceptions and overreactions derived from the worst-case thinking promoted by anarchy. The neorealist formulation of the secu-rity dilemma and the prisoners dilemma embodied in game theory do not as-sume that some of the actors are out to exploit others; they are agnostic on this issue. The only thing that need be assumed is the possibility of being exploited, not the desire to exploit.

Even if the distinction is accepted as analytically valid, it may be dismissed as practically and theoretically insignificant in the sense that the result is the same—international struggle, self-help, and insecurity. That is, these two assumptions about what motivates states may appear equally pessimistic. But this argument cannot be sustained either. One need only look at this on a personal level. Most of us would rather be surrounded by people who fear us than people who want to dominate us. If someone's conflict with me is motivated by their fears and uncertainties, I may be able to do something that could alleviate the fears. But if someone desires to control me, submission would be the only way to quench this desire. Recall that in Morgenthau's view, the desire of states to dominate one another sprang from inherent and unalterable features of human nature. The fear of the neorealists is imposed on states by the situation in which they find themselves. Fear is the product of circumstance and situation, not a fundamental feature of human existence. The result might be struggle nonetheless, but what produces the struggle is different and the character of the struggle is likely to be different and less amenable to resolution. The move away from first-image realism did not, of course, originate with Kenneth Waltz. Early formulations of the security dilemma, which emphasized the explanatory significance of international anarchy, were provided by Arnold Wolfers and, particularly, John Herz.[41] But it was not until Waltz that the third image blossomed into a full-fledged theory of international relations. The security dilemma of Herz and Wolfers was primarily a heuristic construct designed to highlight a basic element of international politics; there were no real pretensions to theory as with Waltz.

What might account for this transformation of realism? Why has Waltz's third-image realism triumphed over Morgenthauian first-image realism? The "official" explanation is that neorealism represents an attempt to refine classical realism and place it on a more "scientific" footing. Classical realism was supposedly too fuzzy and intuitive for those schooled in the methodologies of modern political science. Steve Smith, for example, attributes the emergence of neorealism to a behavioralist distaste for the unempirical and testable elements of classical realism, particularly its assumptions about the nature of man: "Morgenthau's account of international relations relied on unobservable laws of human nature, all of which was unacceptable to positivists, whose definition of theory started with a desire to explain what was observable."[42]

According to Robert Keohane, neorealism was the product of efforts to "systematize" the insights of classical realism into a more rigorous theory of international politics. Joseph Nye shares Keohane's analysis of neorealism: "the significance of Waltz's work is not in elaborating a new line of theory, but in the systematization of realism."[43] Adopting Lakatosian terminology and standards, Keohane treats neorealism as a "progressive problem shift" within the realist paradigm, which entails a preservation of the theory's "hardcore."[44] Apparently, Keohane thinks it possible to retain the core assumptions of realism while rejecting the pessimistic view of human nature, or any view of human nature for that matter.

Casting a more skeptical eye on the shift from first to third image realism, Richard Ashley describes developments in less cozy terms:

> For the neorealist rescue of realist power politics, [the] structuralist move was decisive . . . neorealists seemed to cut through the subjectivist veils and dark metaphysics of classical realist thought. Dispensing with the normatively laden metaphysics of fallen man, they seemed to root realist power politics, including concepts of power and national interest, securely in the scientifically defensible terrain of objective necessity.[45]

As the tone of Ashley's account suggests, the "official" version of neorealism's origins, as embodied in Keohane's analysis, presents a wonderfully reassuring and possibly naïve picture of how and why theoretical notions emerge and evolve. Implicit in such an account is a view of social science as being divorced from broader contextual forces such as interests, values, and cultural predispositions: social theorizing is seen as a purely "scientific" enterprise rather than a social process. Such a view is, at best, problematic.

V. Neorealism and American Realism

The switch from first- to third-image realism may, in fact, lead to a superior theory of international politics. It may be a "progressive problem shift," though I would deny that "hardcore" assumptions have been preserved. There were and are problems with the classical realist formulation that needed to be tackled. I do not want to argue that the conflict with liberalism was the only reason why American scholars thought it necessary to revise and refine realism. Nor do I wish to argue that neorealism was developed consciously and specifically to make realism more compatible with liberalism: Waltz and others did not set out to liberalize realism. Basic values and philosophical perspectives exert a much more indirect and subtle impact. It is surely no coincidence, however, that the elimination of assumptions about human nature also produces a version of realism bereft of its conservative philosophical roots. The result is, in Rosenberg's words, a "more palatable" form of realism based on a rational choice model which falls well within the liberal paradigm.[46] Though neorealism is occasionally criticized for the apparently pessimistic implications of its analysis of international conflict, which is something it supposedly shares with classical realism, upon closer examination one detects a residual, though subdued, optimism, or at least a possible basis for optimism. The extent to which this optimism is stressed or suppressed varies, but it is there if one wants it to be.

Such claims might seem odd in view of the common perception of neorealism as a conservative response to the interdependence and transnationalism literature which gained wide currency in the mid 1970s. While there is no doubt that the assumptions and analyses of neorealists tend to be more pessimistic than those found in these perspectives, the neorealists did not fully return to the theoretical and philosophical pessimism of Morgenthau, Kennan, and Niebuhr. The analysis of neorealism, however, is complicated by the fact that the label is applied to scholars with sometimes very different perspectives. Robert Keohane, for example, is considered a neorealist by Ashley and Cox (and maybe even by himself), but Joseph Grieco argues that Keohane's deviations from realism and neorealism are so great that he should not be considered a realist at all. Grieco classifies Keohane as a neoliberal or "liberal institutionalist." Since people are free to use whatever labels they wish, the waters occasionally become muddied.

To my mind, neorealism represents an attempt to devise a theory of international relations on systemic or structural grounds—international anarchy and the distribution of power. Neorealists reject attempts to explain the central phenomena of international relations by referring to features and characteristics of states and/or individuals. Neorealists treat states as self-interested, rational, unitary entities whose tendencies toward conflict and/or cooperation are primarily a function of systemic forces—anarchy, power distributions, and the presence or absence of factors which inhibit or exacerbate the conflictual consequences of anarchy.

The main differences between Grieco and Waltz on the one hand and Keohane on the other revolve around exactly what "self-interested" means as well as the extent to which regimes and institutions can counteract the adverse consequences of anarchy. Grieco and Waltz see rational, self-interested states as status maximizers (or, at a minimum, status conscious)—they are concerned about relative, not absolute, gains and benefits. Confronted with opportunities to cooperate, states will ask: will we benefit *more than* others. This is different from the view of Keohane who portrays states as utility maximizers, what he calls "rational egoists." Here Keohane is following the lead of Axelrod's influential work on the evolution of cooperation (it is also interesting to compare this to Niebuhr's claims about the persistence of "irrational egoism").[47] Faced with cooperative options, utility maximizers will simply consider whether they will gain; it is not necessary that they gain more than others. Interpreting self-interest as status maximization is more pessimistic than assuming utility maximization in the sense that the requirements for cooperation are stricter: two actors can simultaneously increase their utility, but they cannot simultaneously improve their status vis-à-vis each other.[48] As a result, Grieco and Waltz are much less optimistic about the ability of regimes and international institutions to promote cooperation than is Keohane.

There is no question that this is an extremely significant difference among scholars often lumped to together as neorealists. Whether states are primarily concerned with status or absolute utility is a matter of great theoretical and practical importance. Nonetheless, this should not be allowed to obscure the basic similarity which unites various neorealists and distinguishes them from the classical realists—the systemic or structural emphasis. In each case, international anarchy is the critical explanatory variable. States must be concerned with status because of the fear imposed by the potential threats arising in an anarchic environment. Cooperation among utility maximizers is inhibited by anarchy and the consequent concerns about cheating but promoted when the uncertainties and fears of anarchy can be ameliorated. Whereas, according to Smith, "the realist picture of the world *begins* with a pessimistic view of human nature," neither version of neorealism begins with such a view. In Grieco's own words, "[neo]realists do not argue that anarchy *causes* states to be rational egoists but, instead, to be what I shall term 'defensive positionalists.'"[49] Grieco sums up the key similarity (which I think is most important) and the key difference (which he thinks is most important): there is disagreement among neorealists about what exactly anarchy causes, but there is agreement that anarchy causes it.

In neorealist analyses the behavior of states is not, as was the case for Morgenthau, Kennan, and Niebuhr, a magnification or reflection of features of human nature. Gilpin is correct in observing that "political realism itself, as Richard Rosecrance once aptly put it, is best viewed as an attitude regarding the human condition . . . [which] is founded on pessimism regarding moral progress and human possibilities."[50] But does neorealism fit the bill? What is there in neorealism about moral progress or human possibilities? Neorealism is ultimately not a view of the human condition. Without an explicit view of man, it cannot have any view of the "human condition," good or bad. It is philosophically antiseptic.

It is this purging of the conservative, pessimistic view of the human condition which is critical. Once this is gone, the underlying reason for the philosophical and theoretical pessimism of the classical realists is eliminated. This opens the door for possible optimism, at least on a theoretical level. The first source of potential optimism is found in the distinction between fear and desire as motivations for state behavior. The point is quite simple: the desire to dominate emphasized in classical realism cannot be overcome because it supposedly reflects basic features of man's nature; the fear of the neorealists can be overcome because it results from the insecurities of anarchy. One may disagree with this line of argument by claiming that the practical problems associated with transcending anarchy and/or ameliorating its consequences are staggering. But this is not the same as claiming that conflict results from unalterable features of human nature. Practical pessimism is not the same as theoretical and philosophical pessimism; classical realists were the latter, neorealists the former (in differing degrees). Putting a slightly different emphasis on the same point, one can locate a glimmer of optimism in neorealist analysis because no reason is provided to assume that international anarchy is an immutable characteristic of international politics. Though Waltz and others tend not to dwell on the possibilities of transcending anarchy or speculate about alternatives, they also do not explain why international anarchy is an inevitable element of the human condition. As a result, there is no necessary, theoretical reason why the conflicts generated by the insecurities of anarchy cannot ultimately be overcome by transcending anarchy. Classical realists, however, traced the roots of international conflict to something which by definition is unchanging—human nature. While neorealism does not necessarily lead to an optimistic outlook, it does not preclude one either; classical realism, on the other hand, cannot lead to an optimistic outlook.

A final source of optimism may be found in the differing implications of classical realism and neorealism in terms of whether or not there exists a harmony of interests between national actors. When actors are motivated by a fear of each other, there is no inevitable, objective conflict of interest; overcoming these fears would provide both with security. When actors are motivated by a desire to dominate each other, there is an inevitable conflict of interest; logically, all sides' desires cannot be met simultaneously. Thus, classical realism argues that there is an inevitable conflict of interests between social actors such as nation states; neorealism does not.

One may highlight some of these issues by posing the following question: If anarchy were transcended tomorrow in a manner that provided security for all, would conflict and violent conflict persist? That is, if nations no longer feared that others would attack or exploit them, would they cease wanting to exercise control over others? And would the conflicts emerging from the attempts to exert control disappear? Given the classical realist emphasis on the importance of what Gilpin, following Dahrendorf, calls "conflict groups" and the desire for control and domination emphasized by Morgenthau, Niebuhr, and Kennan, one would still expect conflict and occasional violence. In the neorealist formulation, the source of conflict and violence (i.e., the uncertainties and insecurities resulting from anarchy) would be gone: if one is secure, there is no reason to control and dominate others according to neorealism. If two actors feel secure, what would be the source of conflict between them in neorealism? One is hard pressed to identify any source of recurring conflict. These are very different approaches to understanding conflict, with the neorealist, systemic orientation being clearly more optimistic than the classical realist formulation.

When viewed from this perspective, we can see that the emergence and popularity of neorealism as a significantly modified version of, or alternative to, classical realism has gone a long way toward reconciling a realist approach to international politics with the enduring liberal tradition in America. I do not want to argue that neorealists embrace liberalism and all that implies. The point is simply that the version of realism which dominates American thinking about international relations does not derive from the conservative philosophical premises that provided the foundation for much classical realist thought. The circle has been squared in a sense. Those who found Morgenthau's insistence on human nature "embarrassing" (to use Rosenberg's phrasing) need no longer be embarrassed. American students of international relations can be realists without shedding their liberal predispositions.

Notes

Reprinted from *The Review of Politics* 54, no. 2 (Spring 1992): 281–301.

The author would like to thank Stanley Michalak, Patricia Morris, Harvey Starr, Michael Stohl, and Cynthia Weber for useful comments and suggestions on earlier drafts of this article.

    1. Louis Hartz, *The Liberal Tradition in America: An Interpretation of American Political Thought Since the Revolution* (New York: Harcourt, Brace and Company, 1955), 57.

    2. George Nash, *The Conservative Intellectual Movement in American Since 1945* (New York: Basic Books, 1976), 186–253.

    3. Robert W. Cox, "Social Forces, States, and World Orders," in *Neorealism and Its Critics*, ed. Robert O. Keohane (New York: Columbia University Press, 1986), 240–41.

    4. Readers may want to examine Stanley Hoffmann's seminal essay, "An American Social Science: International Relations," *Daedalus* 106, no. 3 (Summer 1977): 41–60. Hoffmann's argument differs from the one offered here in two respects: first, he does not emphasize the difficulties of adopting realism in the United States in terms of its conservative assumptions; and second, Hoffmann did not and really could not have specifically addressed issues dealing with neorealism (Waltz's *Theory of International Politics* did not appear until 1979).

    5. K. J. Holsti, *The Dividing Discipline: Hegemony and Diversity in International Theory* (Boston: Allen and Unwin, 1984); Paul R. Viotti and Mark V. Kauppi, eds., *International Relations Theory: Realism, Pluralism, and Globalism* (New York: Macmillan, 1987).

    6. Keith L. Nelson and Spencer C. Olin, *Why War? Ideology, Theory, and History* (Berkeley: University of California Press, 1979).

7. David Sidorsky, ed., *The Liberal Tradition in European Thought* (New York: Capricorn Books, 1970), 2.

8. Chandran Kukathas, "Conservatism, Liberalism, and Ideology," *Critical Review: A Journal of Books and Ideas* 1, no. 3 (Summer 1987): 37; see also John Gray, *Liberalism* (Minneapolis: University of Minnesota Press, 1986).

9. See Robert L. Schuettinger, ed., *The Conservative Tradition in European Thought* (New York G. P. Putnam's Sons, 1970), 11–34.

10. Michael Joseph Smith, *Realist Thought from Weber to Kissinger* (Baton Rouge: Louisiana State University Press, 1986), p. 219.

11. Kauppi and Viotti, *International Relations Theory*, 6–7, 32–67.

12. John Vasquez, *The Power of Power Politics* (Rutgers, NJ: Rutgers University Press, 1983), 18.

13. Robert O. Keohane, "Theory of World Politics: Structural Realism and Beyond," in Keohane, *Neorealism and Its Critics*, 164–65.

14. Not all accounts are deficient in this respect. See, for example, James Dougherty and Robert Pfaltzgraff, *Contending Theories of International Relations* (New York: Harper and Row, 1981), 84–86.

15. Joseph Grieco, *Cooperation among Nations: Europe, America, and Non-Tariff Barriers to Trade* (Ithaca: Cornell University Press, 1990), 3–4.

16. David Mayers, *George Kennon and the Dilemmas of US Foreign Policy* (New York: Oxford University Press, 1988), 7.

17. Smith, *Realist Thought*, 103.

18. Reinhold Niebuhr, *Moral Man and Immoral Society: A Study in Ethics and Politics* (New York: Charles Scribners' Sons, 1934), xx.

19. Quoted in Smith, *Realist Thought*, 103.

20. Richard W. Fox, *Reinhold Niebuhr: A Biography* (New York: Harper and Row, 1987), 140.

21. Ibid., 140.

22. M. Cox, "Social Forces, States, and World Orders," 249.

23. George F. Kennan, *Memoirs 1925–1950* (Boston: Little, Brown and Company, 1967), 319.

24. George F. Kennan, *Sketches from a Life* (New York: Pantheon, 1989), 47, 225.

25. Ibid., 176.

26. In John W. Coffey, *Political Realism in American Thought* (Lewisburg, PA: Bucknell University Press, 1977), 32–33.

27. Mayers, *George Kennan*, p. 328.

28. Hans Morgenthau, *Scientific Man vs. Power Politics* (Chicago: University of Chicago Press, 1946); Hans Morgenthau, *Politics Among Nations: The Struggle for Power and Peace* (New York: Alfred Knopf, 1967).

29. Morgenthau, *Politics Among Nations*, 4, 3.

30. Morgenthau, *Scientific Man*, ii.

31. Ibid., 193.

32. Ibid., 188.

33. Ibid., 194–95.

34. Morgenthau, *Politics Among Nations*, 25.

35. Justin Rosenberg, "What's the Matter with Realism?" *Review of International Studies* 16, no. 4 (October 1990): 292.

36. Kenneth Waltz, *Man, the State, and War* (New York: Columbia University Press, 1959), 21–27.

37. Kjell Goldman, "The Concept of 'Realism' as a Source of Confusion," *Cooperation and Conflict* 23 (1988): 7–9.

38. Ibid., 8.

39. Morgenthau, *Scientific Man*, 198.

40. Ibid., 197.

41. See John Herz, "Idealist Internationalism and the Security Dilemma," *World Politics* 2, no. 2 (January 1950): 157–80; Arnold Wolfers, *Discord and Collaboration* (Baltimore: Johns Hopkins University Press, 1962).

42. Steve Smith, "Paradigm Dominance in International Relations: The Development of International Relations as a Social Science," *Millennium: Journal of International Studies* 16, no. 2 (June 1987): 205.

43. Joseph Nye, "Neorealism and Neoliberalism," *World Politics* 40, no. 2 (January 1988): 241.

44. Keohane, "Theory of World Politics," 160–63.

45. Richard K. Ashley, "The Poverty of Neorealism," in Keohane, *Neorealism and Its Critics*, 263.

46. Rosenberg, "What's the Matter with Realism?" 292.

47. See Robert Axelrod, *The Evolution of Cooperation* (New York: Basic Books, 1984).

48. For more on this issue see Duncan Snidal, "International Cooperation among Relative Gains Maximizers," *International Studies Quarterly* 35, no. 4 (December 1991): 387–402.

49. Grieco, *Cooperation among Nations*, 36.

50. Robert Gilpin, "The Richness of the Tradition of Political Realism," in Keohane, *Neorealism and Its Critics*, 304.